Japanese Firms in Europe

Studies in Global Competition

A series of books edited by John Cantwell

Further volumes in preparation

Volume 1

Japanese Firms in Europe
Edited by Frédérique Sachwald

Volume 2

Technological Innovation, Multinational Corporations and New
International Competitiveness: The Case of Intermediate Countries
Edited by José Molero

Japanese Firms in Europe

Edited by

Frédérique Sachwald

Institut Français des Relations Internationales
Paris

harwood academic publishers

Australia • China • France • Germany • India • Japan
Luxembourg • Malaysia • The Netherlands • Russia • Singapore
Switzerland • Thailand • United Kingdom • United States

Copyright © 1995 by Harwood Academic Publishers GmbH.

Originally published as *Les entreprises japonaises en Europe* © Masson, Éditeur, Paris, 1993.

3 Boulevard Royal
L-2449 Luxembourg

British Library Cataloguing in Publication Data

Japanese Firms in Europe. – (Studies in
Global Competition; Vol. 1)
  I. Sachwald, Frédérique   II. Series
  338.8895204

  ISBN 3-7186-5626-4

Contents

Introduction to the Series

This book series collects together high-quality research monographs written from various perspectives. The study of global competition is increasingly at the centre of an "academic crossroads" at which different research programs and methods of investigation are now meeting. In particular, global competition has become a focus of attention for researchers working in five areas: international business, business strategy, technological change, geographical or locational analysis, and European integration. Most of these researchers have backgrounds in economics, geography or business strategy. The series will include books undertaken from these backgrounds on the global economy as a whole, corporate reorganization, national and corporate competitiveness, and the role of the city-regions.

Contributors

RENÉ BELDERBOS is a researcher at the Tinbergen Institute of Erasmus University in Rotterdam. He has worked extensively on Japanese direct investment abroad and has stayed in Japan several times to conduct his research.

SOPHIE GARNIER is a doctoral student, working on the management of Japanese companies abroad.

FRANÇOISE NICOLAS is a research fellow at IFRI (Institut Français des Relations Internationales) in Paris and an associate lecturer at the University of Marne-La Vallée.

MARINA PAPANASTASSIOU is a research fellow in the Department of Economics, University of Reading. She received her doctorate for a thesis on 'Creation and development of technology by MNEs' subsidiaries in Europe: the cases of UK, Greece, Belgium and Portugal'. Her current research covers many aspects of R&D and technology transfer in MNEs, including issues of human resource management and organisation, and she has published many articles in these areas. She is co-author of *The technological competitiveness of Japanese Multinationals: The European Dimension.* (University of Michigan Press).

ROBERT PEARCE is Reader in International Business, in the Department of Economics, University of Reading. His current research interests are in the global technological operations of MNEs (including decentralised R&D), and their relation to the strategic evolution of these companies. He is also researching the implications of these developments for national competitiveness. His most recent publications are *The Growth and Evolution of Multinational Enterprise*(Edward Elgar) and *Globalising Research and Development* (Macmillan).

FRÉDÉRIQUE SACHWALD is senior research fellow at IFRI (Institute Français des Relations Internationales) in Paris. Her main research area is the role of firms in international economics. She has worked extensively on cooperative agreements between firms, both from a theoretical and an empirical point of view. Her previous book in English is *European Integration and Competitiveness, Acquisitions and Alliances in Industry* (1994).

Acknowledgements

This book is the outcome of a research project which has been supported by a grant from the Foundation Franco-Japanaise Sasokawa.

The authors have benefited from the comments of various researchers and experts: John Cantwell, Pierre Jacquet, Steve Thomsen and Hideki Yamawaki (for chapters 1, 2, 7 and 8); Martin Carrce, Michel Delapierre, Jeroen Potjes and Joop Stam (for chapter 3); Marie-Claude Bélis-Bergouignan, Béatrice de Castelnau, Vincent Mangematin and Christian Mory (for chapter 4); Jean-Pierre Durand (for chapter 6).

A number of institutions have also been helpful by providing various data: the Bank of Japan in Paris. DATAR (*Délégation à l'Aménagement du Territoíre et à l'Action Régionale*), JETRO in Paris (Japanese External Trade Organization), the Japanese Ministry of Finance and the SESSI (*Service des Statistiques Industrielles, French Ministry of Industry*).

The views expressed in the book are those of the authors, who take full responsibility for the analyses presented here.

NA

1 - 3

bK Title:

Introduction

THE JAPANESE CHALLENGE

Within two decades, the Japanese presence abroad has gained importance. It first came through bright successes on export markets. During
the 1980s, the internationalization of the Japanese economy entered
a new phase with the rapid increase of direct investment flows abroad.
Moreover, during that period, investments were reoriented towards
industrialised countries and away from Asia and Latin America.[1]
Japanese investments to the United States have rapidly increased from
1984 to 1990, while Japanese investments to Europe have increased
from 1986.

  Japanese investments have aroused hostile reactions on both sides
of the Atlantic. They have been interpreted as yet another sign of the
Japanese might and as a threat to host economies. In Europe, the
wave of Japanese investments has given rise to similar concerns as
those resulting from the previous wave of investments by American
companies during the 1960s. From this perspective, the Japanese
challenge had replaced the American challenge.[2] As with American
firms 20 years earlier, Japanese companies have been considered
mighty and exotic competitors coming to fight on European firms'
own turf. But is this the correct way to define the Japanese threat?
European firms have managed to learn from their American competitors and can also gain some benefit from the Japanese presence on

---

[1] That tendency has been reversed at the beginning of the 1990s.
[2] To use the expression coined by J-J. Servan Schreiber in his book (*Le défi Américain*,
  Denoël, 1967).

1

the continent. This debate requires a detailed analysis of Japanese firms' competitive advantage. Indeed, the Japanese challenge has to be evaluated according to both Japanese firms' performances abroad and to the reproductibility of their competitive advantage by competitors. Japanese firms' competitiveness will be enhanced by their ability to transplant their production system abroad and diminished in that foreign competitors will be able to adapt this system.

This book analyzes in detail Japanese direct investments in Europe, their importance, their determinants and their consequences both for host countries and for the evolution of the world competitive game in a number of sectors. It examines quantitative data, but also analyses Japanese firms' strategies and behaviour in Europe in order to assess their degree of specificity.

STRUCTURE OF THE BOOK

In order to understand the evolution of Japanese direct investment abroad, it is necessary to elaborate on the general context of the world economy since the 1980s and in particular on the phenomenon of globalisation. Chapter 1 underlines the fact that Japanese FDI is part of this general phenomenon by exploring the evolution of the different flows of FDI. It shows in particular that all industrial countries have increased their investments abroad, even if the evolution has not been as dramatic as that of Japan. Japanese investments in Europe have grown particularly rapidly during the 1980s, but the United States remains the first center of interest of Japanese firms abroad while Asia constitutes a very dynamic and attractive pole of economic activity.

Chapter 2 examines the determinants of Japanese firms' decisions to invest abroad. It first focuses on the theoretical aspect, with two objectives. The first one is to underline the fact that both the motivations of foreign direct investments have evolved through time. In this perspective the "Japanese" theory of FDI corresponded well to the economic environment and to Japanese firms' strategies in the 1960s, but much less so to the investment boom of the 1980s. The second objective of this chapter is to propose a general framework of analysis of firms' decisions with respect to FDI, which is then used to examine the Japanese firms' investments in Europe.

Three sectoral studies illustrate and detail the general approach of these first two chapters. The electronics and automobile industries have been considered as obvious case studies since they represent a very important part of Japanese firms' investments in Europe. Moreover, these investments have focused much attention given the Japanese firms' impressive competitive advantages. The chemical industry has been chosen as the third case study because it exhibits quite different characteristics and because Japanese firms' investments correspond to a different set of motivations.

Two chapters deal with the question of the management of foreign units by Japanese companies. Japanese firms have become multinationals more recently than their American or European counterparts and they have had to adapt to this major evolution. Chapter 6 examines two aspects of management: the relationships with suppliers and human resources management. Chapter 7 assesses the international organization of R&D activities by Japanese firms.

Chapter 8 deals with the consequences of Japanese investments for European host countries. It analyzes the different potential effects on employment, on the balance of payments and on technology transfers in particular and then considers the case of Japanese investments in Europe, and more particularly in France.

The general conclusion summarizes the main results in order to assess the significance of the Japanese presence for the European productive system.

1

The Expansion of Foreign Direct Investment

Françoise Nicolas

Foreign direct investment (FDI) is an increasingly important form of economic interaction and probably the major means of international economic integration today. This is illustrated by the much faster growth of such international involvement, compared to that of both world trade and output. Unlike trade flows which have markedly slowed down over the last two decades, FDI flows have grown dramatically over the same period of time. During the last decade, FDI has grown more than twice as fast as world exports and almost three times faster than world output. As a result, FDI has become as important an engine of economic growth and international competitiveness as trade and this is why a good understanding of its global patterns is so important. Global direct investment is expected to have reached $217.2 billion in 1990, bringing the cumulative outflow of direct investment since 1970 to an estimated $2 trillion (UNCTC, 1992).

The present chapter analyzes the evolution of Japanese direct investment abroad, in particular in the EC. In order to gain a sense of perspective about Japanese FDI in Europe, the first section describes the global environment and the general trends in FDI. The second section focuses on the form and nature of the expansion of Japanese involvement abroad while the final section zeros in on Japanese activities in Europe and compares it to US involvement there. The main point is to identify and highlight possible peculiarities in Japanese behavior.

1.1   GENERAL TRENDS IN FOREIGN DIRECT INVESTMENTS

1.1.1   FDI as a Means of Globalization

The expansion of foreign direct investment is part of the so-called process of globalization. As argued by Julius (1990) among others, the recent explosion in FDI, together with the gradual internationalization of financial markets and the rise in capital movements, is the second stage of an ongoing process, which first involved the expansion of international trade flows and will eventually give rise at a later stage to a complete globalization of the economy, where firms operate on the basis of a worldwide rather than a multicountry strategy (Ostry, 1990).

The globalization of production (in the form of FDI) appears to be tightly linked to the process of financial globalization. This hypothesis is confirmed by the observation that mergers and acquisitions have become much more frequent than traditional forms of FDI, i.e. the creation of new production units (or greenfield investments), since the beginning of the 1980s.[1] Over the last decade, external growth operations have been clearly favored by the internationalization of capital markets. As most direct investments abroad are financed through borrowing in the host country, a number of large mergers and acquisitions in the US (Péchiney/American Can, Rhône-Poulenc/Rorer, Saint-Gobain/Norton, etc.) were only made possible by the extraordinary "depth" of the American financial market. The advance of global finance made the expansion of FDI easier. In other words, increased financial capital mobility may be seen as one of the prerequisites for the internationalization of production. (Bourguinat, 1990). Be that as it may, the explosion of FDI since the early 1970s, and in particular since 1980, has been quite dramatic (Table 1).

The parallel increases in the flow of direct investments abroad and in exports are clear proof of the intensification of the so-called globalization process. These two phenomena do not fully do justice to the globalization process though, as other new forms of investment abroad, such as cooperative agreements for instance, have also expanded quite rapidly.

The explosion of FDI seems to have come to a standstill recently, as the rate of growth suddenly dropped from 23% to 4.5% in 1990

---

[1] M&A activity accounted for 80% of total FDI in the US in 1989 for instance (JETRO, 1992a; Sachwald, 1993).

Table 1: Foreign Direct Investments, Exports, and Output (world totals in billion dollars)

	Foreign Direct Investments (Flows)	Merchandise Exports	Gross Domestic Product
1970	12.2	288.1	3123.7
1980	47.4	1901.2	12132.8
1985	63.1	1807.8	13347.6
1986	92.6	1990.4	14550.6
1987	136.4	2347.9	15138.9
1988	162.8	2686.2	17018.3
1989	207.7	2891.7	19981.2
1990	217.2	3450.6	23250.8
1991	180.0	3999.6	21500.2
Average Annual Rate of Growth			
1970–80	14.5	20.8	16.6
1981–85	4.2	-0.2	2.1
1985–90	24.6	12.2	9.5
1991	−22.0	2.3	3.1

Sources: JETRO (1991a, 1992a), IMF *International Financial Statistics*; CHELEM, UNCTAD (1993).

and turned negative in 1991 and 1992. This slowdown is obviously due to the sluggishness of economic activity worldwide. The overall trend may, however, reach a plateau soon as the optimal level of foreign involvement (from the investor's point of view) may have been achieved, at least in some countries. In other words, the share of foreign production in overall production cannot be increased any further in some cases.

1.1.2   The leading role of services

The rapid increase in the flows of direct investment abroad over the last decades has been accompanied by a shift in their sectoral distribution. FDI in non-manufacturing activities, particularly in services,

Table 2:   Sectoral Distribution of FDI Flows from the Five Major Investors (1981–84 and 1985–89; in national currency and in percentage)

Country	1981–84	1985–89	1981–84	1985–89
	Average annual flows		percentage	
United States				
Services	5981	10289	52	57
Non services	5435	7804	48	43
Total	11416	18093	100	100
France				
Services	8031	29213	41	49
Non services	11468	30790	59	51
Total	19498	60004	100	100
Japan				
Services	5280	26723	61	73
Non services	3448	9770	39	27
Total	8727	36493	100	100
Great Britain				
Services	1396	5699	35	38
Non services	2650	9360	65	62
Total	4046	15059	100	100
Germany				
Services	8415	6160	55	64
Non services	6865	3455	45	36
Total	15280	9615	100	100

Source: UNCTC, World Investment Report (1991)

has been increasing at a much faster rate than in manufacturing. While investments in the primary products sector, especially in the mining sector, were prevalent in the 1960s, FDIs are nowadays heavily concentrated in the service sector, which accounts for more than 55% of annual FDI flows worldwide and for about 50% of the world stock of FDI in 1990, compared to 25% at the beginning of the 1970s and less than 20% in the early 1950s.[2]

---

[2] (UNCTC, 1991) and (Greenaway and Balasubramanyam, 1992).

This pattern has become even stronger over the last ten years; Table 2 clearly shows both the primacy of the services sector and an increase in the share of FDI in this sector during the 1980s, whatever the investing country.[3] This rise is particularly striking in the case of Japanese investments, even though the relative share of services was initially higher for Japan than for all the other countries. This observation is at odds with the view that Japanese producers mainly invest abroad in order to produce abroad. Purely productive activities are obviously not their only focus of interest.

It is not actually surprizing that services should account for such a large share of FDI since services are usually non-tradable internationally, thus requiring direct contact between the buyer and the seller. In addition, economic activity is increasingly oriented towards the service industry, as a result both of technological advances and of liberalization and deregulation processes.[4]

However a number of qualifications are warranted. First of all, services constitute a highly heterogenous category of economic activities so that highly aggregated figures may reflect completely different phenomena. As a result, inter-country comparisons are necessarily fraught with difficulties. Moreover, the importance of services (as opposed to manufacturing activities) may be overestimated for a number of reasons. First of all, in some countries investments in services, particularly in banking, are mere conduits for manufacturing investments elsewhere. Similarly, important financial services are very often at the disposal of manufacturing firms. Even though direct investment in the non-manufacturing sector is more akin to portfolio capital than to FDI,[5] these two types of investment are closely related. Investments in the financial sector for instance may ease eventual investments in the productive sector. Such investment may clearly be designed to support the operations of manufacturing firms. The same also holds true for investment in distribution. It seems that the establishment of distribution networks is a first step; it is usually highly correlated with the development of exports and may eventuallly be followed by the establishment of productive facilities.[6] In other words,

---

[3] The United Kingdom is an exception; the large investments by oil companies create a bias towards the primary sector and the relative importance of the service sector is small as compared to other G5 countries.

[4] A number of service industries, such as banking, insurance and communications are gradually open to international competition.

[5] See the Appendix for a definition of FDI.

[6] See Yamawaki (1991) for empirical evidence on this issue.

investment in non-manufacturing activities may be a deliberate strategy designed to strengthen the productive and marketing efficiency of manufacturing firms. In addition, FDI in services may be an important facet of the long-run globalization strategy on the part of the investing firms.[7]

1.1.3   Who Invests?

Until the 1970s the phenomenon of FDI was from an empirical point of view dominated by US outward direct investment, so much so that some authors came to characterize multinational corporations as a peculiarly American institution rather than as a global phenomenon.[8] Furthermore, as long as US subsidiaries abroad comprised the major part of world FDI, theorizing about the nature of FDI and its consequences for economic efficiency and welfare focused almost exclusively on the single pattern of one way FDI by one home country, the US, in various host countries.[9] During the 1970s a dramatic change took place and the US emerged rather suddenly as a leading host country, edging out Canada in this role by the end of the decade. Other industrial countries, such as the United Kingdom, Germany, Japan, and to a lesser extent France, started engaging actively into FDI. Between 1970 and 1975, the foreign production of all these countries rose from 1.6 to 2 times their exports. By the early 1980s FDI had ceased to be an exclusively American phenomenon.

The global explosion in FDI was characterized by an interesting feature which has come to be known as cross-FDI, meaning that FDI stopped being a one-way flow. In other words, countries started serving as home and host countries simultaneously. Two-way flows signal that American companies no longer have a monopoly on competitive advantages required for international expansion. This phenomenon has been accompanied by another, usually referred to as intra-industry FDI.[10] This is defined as cross-border FDI by multinationals of similar industry group in each other's home countries.

The most dramatic change observed since the early 1970s is the emergence of Japan as a major international investor. In 1985,

---

[7] On this point see Greenaway and Balasubramanyam (1992).

[8] See Erdilek (1985).

[9] See Chapter 2.

[10] This phenomenon parallels the expansion of intra-industry trade.

Table 3a: Flows of Direct Investment Abroad from the 5 Major Investors, Average Annual Flows over the Period (1961–88, in million $ 1980)

Investor	1961–65	1966–70	1971–75	1976–80	1981–85	1986–88
United States	9330	12973	16690	21281	9547	18803
Japan	237	461	2205	2400	4785	19656
Germany	563	995	2197	3721	3508	7892
France	865	746	1540	2341	1935	5166
Great Britain	3502	4238	7564	9580	7445	15819

Source: Julius (1990).

Table 3b: Outflows of FDI from the 5 Major Investing Countries, 1989–92 (billions of $ and percentage)

Investor	1989–90	1991–92	1986–90	1992	1986–90	1992
	Billions of dollars		Share in total (%)		Growth rate (%)	
United States	55	65	13	24	16	24
Japan	92	47	19	11	32	−48
Germany	46	38	9	11	27	−19
France	54	41	10	11	45	−29
Great Britain	53	33	17	10	2	−17

Source: UNCTAD (1993).

the proportion of production undertaken by Japanese firms overseas was, however, only 3% of total Japanese production, compared to 16.2% for the US and 19.3% for the Federal Republic of Germany for instance. (Saucier, 1989). The real explosion in Japanese involvement abroad took place over the period 1985-90, as can be seen in Table 3a. The trend has been slowing down since then as a result of domestic economic turbulence, as shown in Table 3b (see below for further details).

The gradual decline of the United States and the rise of Japan as a major direct investor over the last decade appears even more clearly in Table 4 which shows the shares of the major investors in the world stock of FDI. Japan's share rose from less than 7% in the early 1980s to about 15% in the second half of the decade.

Table 4: Distribution of the World Stock of FDI (Shares of the Major Investing Countries; 1960–90)

	1938		1960		1980		1985		1992	
	bn $	%	bn $	%	bn $	%	bn$	%	bn $	%
Total world stock	26.3	100	67.7	100	551.0	100	714.0	100	1949	100
United States	7.3	28	31.9	47	220.3	40	250.7	35	474	24
Japan	0.8	3	0.5	1	36.5	7	83.6	12	251	13
Great Britain	10.5	40	12.4	18	81.4	15	104.7	15	259	13
Germany	0.3	1	0.8	1	43.1	8	60.0	8	186	9
France	2.5	9	4.1	6	20.8	4	21.6	3	151	8

Source: Greenaway and Balasubramanyam (1992), du Grandrut (1990) and UNCTC (1993).

Even though the overall level of FDI has increased over the last twenty years or so, these flows are still highly concentrated geographically and most of these investments are due to five or six leading investing countries. Altogether, the G5 countries (USA, France, UK, Germany and Japan) remain the major investors but their respective role has varied over the period.

Table 5:   FDI Flows from the 5 Major Investing Countries, 1985–90

Investor	1985	1987	1989	1990	1991	1992	1981–1985	1986–1990	1992
			(billion dollars)					(share in %)	
France	2	9	19	35	24	17	6	10	11
Germany	5	9	18	28	21	17	9	9	11
Japan	6	20	44	48	31	16	11	19	11
Great Britain	12	31	35	18	18	15	19	17	10
United States	13	26	26	29	29	36	23	13	24
Total G5	38	95	142	158	123	101	68	68	67
Developed countries	52	133	203	225	178	145	98	97	97
LDCs	1	2	10	9	5	5	2	3	3
Total	53	135	213	234	183	150	100	100	100

Source: UNCTAD (1993).

During the last decade, the share of the G5 countries in the overall investment flows has proved fairly stable (around 70%) but the distribution among the different countries has varied quite significantly since 1985. The United Kingdom, the United States and Japan were the largest home countries for FDI outflows throughout the 1980s. Japan ranked third at the beginning of the period; outflows from Japan gradually surpassed those from both the United States and the United Kingdom. During the period 1986–90, Japan was the largest source country of investment flows, accounting for about 20% of total worldwide outflows of direct investment abroad. France and Germany have also gained importance throughout the decade, but to a far lesser extent than Japan.

1.1.4   And where?

In the most recent periods, developed countries have been the major recipients of FDI, but their share of the world total stock of FDI has varied quite substantially over time, fluctuating from 35% in the 1930s to 70% in the early 1970s.[11] During the last couple of decades, FDI has been primarily a developed countries' phenomenon and the five major home countries (with the notable exception of Japan) are also among the largest host countries, with an average share of 68% of world flows during the 1980s.

Table 6:   Average Annual FDI Flows by Region of Destination

Host region	1970 –79	1980 –85	1986 –90	1991 –92	1970 –79	1980 –85	1986 –90	1991 –92
	Billions of dollars				Share of all inflows			
Developed countries	17	37	124	97	76	75	83	71
Developing countries	5	13	26	40	24	25	17	29
Latin America	3	6	9	16	13	12	6	12
Asia	1	5	14	22	7	10	9	15
Africa	1	1	3	2	3	3	2	2

Source : UNCTC (1992, 1993).

[11] See du Granrut (1990).

One salient feature of the last decade is the sharp, although irregular, decline in the share of FDI flows into the developing countries. This trend seems to have come to an end in the early 1990s, as FDI flows resumed towards both Latin America and Asia.

At the beginning of the 1980s, FDI flows to less developed countries slowed down significantly, dropping from $28.2 billions in 1981 to $11.5 billions in 1985. Towards the end of the decade, FDI flows resumed towards the developing world to reach $32 billion in 1990. On average, the less developed countries received altogether $25 billion a year between 1986 and 1990. FDI in this region is, however, unevenly distributed. Among developing countries, the 10 largest host countries continue to receive approximately two thirds of all inflows. The flows are mainly directed to dynamic Southeast Asian economies, the so-called Newly Industrializing Countries as well as Indonesia, Malaysia, and Thailand; East and South East Asia's share was 51% of all inflows to the developing world in 1991. Latin America is another important host-region, with 38% of FDI inflows, mainly concentrated in Mexico and Brazil, while Africa was systematically avoided (with a share of 7% or $2.2 billion — a decrease of 50% from 1989).[12]

By 1992, the levels of FDI in Central and Eastern Europe, as well as in the Commonwealth of Independent States, were still extremely modest by international standards. Yet investments in those regions could expand quite significantly in the near future depending to a large extent on the success of the reforms implemented in the various countries.

In 1990, the major individual recipients of FDI flows were the United States, the United Kingdom and Spain. The inflow of direct investment into the EC expanded quite dramatically from 1985 to 1990, raising Europe's share of the world's direct investment inflows from 39.3% in 1989 to 52.8% in 1990, thus making Europe the first recipient region in the world before the United States. The prospect of an emerging single market certainly has something to do with such a development, together with the fact that the US market may get close to saturation. The opening of Central and Eastern Europe as a result of the demise of communism is another factor enhancing the attractiveness of the EC, as the member-countries of the Community may serve as beachheads from where to supply the rest of the continent.

---

[12] FDI flows to Africa are approximately equivalent to the inflows to Portugal during that year. These figures are based on the IMF *Balance of Payments Statistics*.

The members of the so-called triad (the US, the EC and Japan) are on the whole both the largest home and the largest host countries. FDI flows are thus very highly concentrated within the Triad, giving rise to a clear trilateral structure of mutual investment (JETRO, 1992a). Japan is the only exception among the G5. It has been and continues to be an insignificant host to inward FDI, and this is why Japanese direct investment in both the US and Europe is so often seen as an unfair practice. The major reason why foreign involvement is so low in Japan is that very restrictive regulations were imposed on foreign investors until the early 1980s. The volume of US and European FDI flows to Japan is still very modest (Table 7), even though it has been rising substantially over the last several years, especially in the case of European flows (+10.1–fold). The share of direct investments by the members of the triad directed to other members of the triad, excluding intra-EEC investments, rose on average to more than 50% in the 1980s and fell back to 47% at the very end of the decade. Japan is clearly the country which invests most within the triad; recently the share of its overall FDI directed to other countries of the triad shot up to 70%.

Table 7:   Destination of FDI Flows from the US, Japan and the EC (in million $)

Cumulative Flows	1979–81	1982–84	1985–87	1988–90	1988–90/1979–81
Japan to the US	3620	6031	20171	65791	+18.2
Japan to the EC	1101	1982	7876	26566	+24.1
United States to Japan	1306	1106	2623	3180	+2.4
United States to the EC	23313	11653	23844	35848	+1.5
EC to Japan	152	155	226	1533	+10.1
EC to the US	25681	30515	70687	84433	+3.3
Sub-total	55173	51442	125427	217351	+3.9
Japan to the World	10177	14177	40451	126364	+12.4
US to the World	52174	19249	62886	84704	+1.6
EC to the World	79553	59124	129308	251769	+3.2
Intra-EC FDI	8193	7830	23961	66542	+8.1
Sub-total	141904	92490	232645	462837	+3.3
Share of the triad	38.9	55.6	53.9	47.0	

Source: JETRO (1992a), Table 3.

The high intra-Triad concentration also appears in the geographical distribution of the world stock of FDI: intra-triad FDI accounted for 39% of the total stock of FDI in the world in 1988 (compared to less than 30% in the early 1980s).[13]

Another interesting conclusion to be derived from the above table is that Japan clearly appeared to be the fastest growing source of FDI in the 1980s (it increased 18-fold in the US and 24-fold in the EC). This phenomenon is examined more closely in the following section.

1.2   SKYROCKETING JAPANESE DIRECT INVESTMENT ABROAD

1.2.1   General trends

The dramatic increase in Japanese direct investments abroad is certainly the most striking feature of past decades. Japanese direct investments abroad have been rising almost steadily since the mid-1970s but the rate at which Japanese investors purchased controlling interests in productive facilities or in services abroad was much more rapid during the second half of the 1980s. In current prices, the annual average rate of growth, which was around 19% for the period 1974–79, rose to almost 34% in the 1980s. Annual flows of FDI from Japan which averaged around $3.6 billion a year during the 1970s shot up to $22 billion a year during the 1980s.

Moreover, the nature of Japanese direct investment abroad has changed tremendously. Japanese investment developed initially in two forms: one involved vertical integration backward into natural-resource extraction and processing in developing countries, in particular in Latin America; the other form was horizontal investment in simple manufacturing activities in nearby Asian countries. Significant investment in industrial countries began in the mid to late-1970s, first in the US and eventually in Europe, as Japanese producers became engaged in geographical diversification and production globalization (Caves and Drake, 1990).

A number of factors (domestic as well as external) may explain the recent boom. Those most commonly mentioned are the current account surplus, the appreciation of the Yen, the soaring land and stock prices in Japan (the so-called bubble effect),[14] the financial

---

[13] UNCTC (1991).

[14] This is refered to as the bubble effect because the stock price boom in Japan

deregulation and integration process, the persistence of trade frictions with the EEC, etc. In actual fact, all of these factors contribute to create an environment which is propitious to the expansion of FDI but they do not account for the choice of FDI as opposed to portfolio investment for instance. It is worth remembering at this stage that in the case of the US in particular, the explosion of FDI followed a wave of portfolio investment. More fundamentally, the path of overseas investment can be seen as functionally related to the path of industrial restructuring at home (Ozawa, 1989).[15] As a result, the expansion of Japanese investments occurred in three successive waves, one from 1969 to 1973, with the relocation of productive activities in Asia, one from 1978 to 1984, as a result of the oil shock and the increase in energy prices, and finally from 1986 to 1990, as part of globalization strategies.[16]

The last period of remarkable expansion may have come to an end as Japan's FDI has been demonstrating a trend of decline in 1991 and 1992 after hitting the highest record in the first quarter of 1990 (JETRO, 1992b). The decline is, however, likely to be temporary, since overseas production remains less than 8% of the total output of Japanese corporations, well below that of US and German corporations, with 25 and 17% respectively. Shorter-term considerations, in particular the protracted economic slump in Japan, may be dominating now but the longer-term trend should be upward.

1.2.2 Geographical distribution

Asia was once the first recipient of Japanese FDI, but this is no longer the case, even though recent trends suggest that Japanese FDI in this region is on the increase again. Japanese FDI flows to the NICs in South East Asia, and more generally to all developing countries, have fallen in importance since the early 1980s.

---

was deemed to be due to highly speculative factors. As with an appreciation of the Yen, a boom in Japanese stock prices raises the foreign currency value of the liquid assets held by Japanese investors, thus giving them a financial edge over their foreign competitors. By the same token, because of the historic plunge in stock prices in 1991 and 1992, Japanese companies are facing huge difficulties raising cheap capital to finance their FDI. See (Emmott, 1992).

[15] See Chapter 2.

[16] Other authors offer alternative views on the evolution of Japanese direct investment abroad; according to Komiya (1990) quoted in Sazanami (1991) the third upsurge in Japanese DI started in 1981.

Table 8:   Expansion Phases of Japanese Direct Investment Abroad ($ million)

Sector	1st phase (1969–73) Aggregate	Share	2nd phase (1978–84) Aggregate	Share	3rd phase (1986–89) Aggregate	Share
Total	8259	100	49220	100	170246	100
Region						
North America	1870	22.6	16070	32.6	82028	48.2
Latin America	1390	16.8	9262	18.8	21219	12.5
Asia	2000	24.2	11699	23.8	21002	12.3
Middle East	448	5.4	1448	2.9	431	0.3
Europe	1784	21.6	5997	12.2	33969	20.0
Africa	193	2.3	2284	4.6	1905	1.1
Oceania	572	6.9	2462	5.0	9691	5.7
Sector						
Manufacturing	2678	32.4	14911	30.0	41727	24.5
Non-Manufacturing	4929	59.7	33073	67.2	126180	74.1
– of which mining	2077	25.1	5845	11.9	3455	2.0
services*	1575	19.0	13533	27.5	58894	34.6

Source: Monthly Report of Financial Statistics (in JETRO (1991)).

* Services include basically commerce and finance and insurance.

From this time on, Japanese firms started reshuffling their investments towards the industrial world. As a result, the geographical distribution of Japanese direct investment abroad is increasingly directed toward major developed countries. This change in the pattern of FDI flows corresponds to a shift in Japanese firms' strategy from vertical integration to geographical diversification. (Froot, 1991). As a number of Asian countries gradually industrialize, the observed trend is likely to be reversed, with Asia again receiving an increasing share of direct investments from Japan. The latest data on Japanese FDI flows apparently confirm this hypothesis; Asia's share has slightly increased in 1991 and 1992.[17]

Since the mid-1970s or so, the US has remained the major recipient of Japanese FDI, even though Japanese involvement in Europe has

---

[17] Surveys conducted in 1991 and 1992 by the Exim bank also confirm this trend, see Tejima (1992).

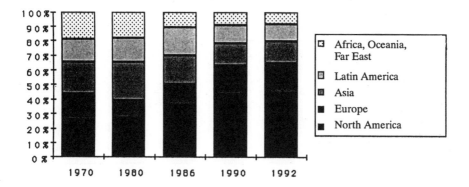

Source : MoF

Figure 1: Distribution of Japanese FDI Stock by Region of Destination (cumulative flows)

intensified quite dramatically over the last several years. The importance of Japanese involvement in Europe (about 19.5% on the basis of the cumulative flows since 1951) is quite low compared to the level of involvement in North America, and in particular in the US, with respectively 43.9 and 42.5% of the total. Japanese total involvement in Europe is, however, now exceeding Japanese involvement in Asia, with only 15.2%.

Although the US hosts a higher proportion of Japanese FDI than the EC, the rate of expansion of those investments in Europe has been much higher (24-fold increase) than in the US (18-fold increase) over the last couple of years (Table 7).[18] The attractiveness of Europe can be explained by a number of factors. Protectionism certainly played an important role, even though some authors feel that the importance of this factor tends to be overestimated (Thomsen and Nicolaides, 1991). Trade restrictions imposed on Japanese exports, such as so-called voluntary restraint arrangements (VRAs), undoubtedly encourage an increase in European production. The VRA imposed on Japanese Video Cassette Recorders for instance encouraged

---

[18] It is worth noting that the level of Japanese investment in the EC was initially very low.

Table 9:   Japanese Direct Investment Flows since 1989, Geographical Distribution (in million $)

Region	1989	1990	1991	1992	1951–92
North America	33902	27192	18823	14572	169580
EC	13707	13298	8781	6641	73373
Asia	8238	7054	5936	6425	59880
Latin America	5238	3628	3337	2726	46547
Africa & Oceania	5289	4717	4026	2644	30595
Middle East	66	27	90	709	4231

Source: MoF

Japanese companies to move production facilities to Europe to get around the quantitative restrictions on their sales through imports. What the available information can demonstrate is that Japanese companies have made considerable investments in European VCR production facilities and that these investments have displaced VCR exports from Japan. (Tyson, 1993).[19] Other factors were also at play. The establishment of productive facilities in Europe is part of a broader strategy of globalization; in addition it probably aims at taking advantage of the "single market" effect.[20]

The different host regions were hit more or less severely by the recent decline in Japanese direct investment abroad. Investment flows dropped by about 30% in 1991 and again by more than 20% in 1992 both in the US and in Europe, while Asia appears to have escaped relatively lightly so far with a mere 15.8% decline for 1991 (Table 9) and a slight increase (8.1%) in 1992.

The share of Asia in the flows of Japanese FDI has increased from 12.2% in 1989 to 18.8% in 1992, simultaneously the US share dropped from 48.2% to 40.5% while the European share stayed almost constant at around 22% (JETRO, 1992b). Due to the current economic slowdown, Japanese investors have to be extremely cautious and selective in their choices. The potential for expansion of demand in local markets is certainly an extremely attractive feature of the Asian market. In addition, the region is probably part of an integrated

---

[19] See Chapter 3.

[20] See Chapter 2 on the determinants of FDI.

production network designed to supply both local demand and industrialized markets, as well as Japan itself. Japanese MNCs locate their subsidiaries in the regions that provide the most attractive conditions for their global strategies. Japan's investments in Asia would, however, have to be much more intensive in order to catch up with those in other parts of the world.

1.2.3   Sectoral Distribution

The intentions of Japanese investors are revealed in the breakdown of FDI flows by industry. A striking feature of Japanese investment abroad is its heavy concentration in the services sector. At the aggregate level, Japanese investments in non-manufacturing activities account for more than 70% of total Japanese FDI.

The predominance of the non-manufacturing sector has been a constant in the pattern of Japanese direct investment abroad (except in Asia) although the distribution of the various areas of activities has varied quite substantially. Until the early 1980s, Japanese direct investment was heavily biased towards mining and primary products which accounted for more than 26% of the total in 1970. The share of these activities has gradually shrunk to less than 6% in 1992. Nowadays, the bulk of Japanese non-manufacturing direct investment is in banking and insurance (28%), real estate (22%), trading and services (16% each).[21]

The fall in Japanese direct investment abroad in 1991 and again in 1992 was apparently more strongly felt in the non-manufacturing (−29%) than in the manufacturing sector (−20%). In the manufacturing sector, there was a shift from textiles and wood, pulp and paper products (which accounted for about 21% of Japanese FDI at the end of 1970) towards iron, steel and non ferrous metal products, and eventually towards electric and electronic machinery (24% in 1992 compared to 8% in 1970) as well as transport equipment (14% in 1992 compared to 9% in 1970). (Yoshitomi, 1991; Sazanami, 1991). The relative importance of the various sectors differs quite significantly across the different host-regions, as shown in Table 11. Overall, Japanese investments in Europe are comparable to investments in North America: Almost 75% of all Japanese investments in Europe are in the non-manufacturing sector. In the US, non-manufacturing

---

[21] See Table 11.

Table 10: Japanese Direct Investment Abroad, Sectoral Distribution (1951-92) (in million US $)

	1951–70	1951–86	1951–92
Manufacturing	929	28206	103981
Food products	51	1218	5234
Textiles	189	2147	5043
Wood, pulp & paper	213	1178	3711
Chemicals	48	4337	14558
Iron & steel,			
Non-ferrous metals	138	5518	12040
General machinery	68	2597	10320
Electric equipment	73	4734	24473
Transportation equipment	87	4202	14065
Other manufacturing	61	2277	14537
Agriculture & forestry	55	796	1773
Fishery	26	494	900
Mining	804	12425	18812
Construction	36	1047	3353
Commerce	382	14538	40268
Banking & finance	319	18099	74869
Other sectors	628	26886	135690
Total flows	3577	105970	386530

Source: Japanese Ministry of Finance.

activities account for about 70% of total Japanese FDI.[22] In both regions, investments in real estate and financial corporations have led the way, even if the emphasis may vary from one location to the other. In North America the largest share of non-productive Japanese investments are in real estate (34%), while in the EC, banking and finance rank first in the non-manufacturing sector (with 53%).

In the manufacturing sector, the largest chunk of investments, in value terms, is in the electrical sector, both in the US and in Europe (ranging from 26 to 32% of overall manufacturing investment). In

---

[22] The share of non-manufacturing activities is much smaller, around 57% for Europe and 45% for the US, if data on the number of subsidiaries as collected by the MITI are taken into consideration. The difference observed between the two sets of data is probably due to the higher capital requirement in non-manufacturing as compared to manufacturing activities.

Table 11: Japanese Direct Investment Abroad by Industry and Region (cumulative flows 1951–92; number of cases in 1992)

Region Industry	North America Cases	North America Value	Europe Cases	Europe Value	Asia Cases	Asia Value	Total Cases	Total Value
Manufacture								
Subtotal	5559	50367	2422	17331	11250	24691	21187	103981
Foodstuffs	704	2587	122	597	853	1396	1983	5234
Textiles	232	1058	362	1130	1553	2312	2387	5043
Lumber & pulp	207	2508	30	124	526	611	941	3711
Chemicals	558	5923	256	2006	1258	4282	2285	14558
Iron & steel	446	5027	400	734	1147	3310	2268	12040
General Machinery	840	4723	373	2858	1156	2117	2565	10320
Electrical	1050	12707	369	5257	1973	5587	3582	24473
Transportation Equipment	440	6312	125	3003	502	2061	1201	14065
Others	1082	9524	385	1623	2282	3016	3975	14537
Non-Manufacture								
Subtotal	19196	117595	5990	55974	9105	34115	46321	275666
Agriculture & forestries	254	510	21	34	485	372	1376	1773
Fisheries	105	189	24	33	339	285	849	900
Mining	420	2484	102	1811	313	7980	1460	18812
Construction	342	1556	51	285	596	1001	1194	3353
Commercial	7817	21074	3040	9296	3430	5259	15867	40268
Financial & insurance	584	22661	905	28598	573	5711	2748	74869
Service industry	3273	27801	928	5039	1603	6731	6926	46610
Transportation	340	769	140	365	384	1530	4839	21652
Real estate	5104	38326	545	9457	850	3608	7916	59895
Others	957	2225	234	1056	532	1639	3146	7533
Branches	437	1133	253	2354	663	1038	1495	6289
Real estate Acquisitions	2005	485	180	38	162	37	2538	595
Total	27197	169580	8845	75697	21180	59880	71541	386530

Source: Japanese Ministry of Finance

Europe, machinery (including electrical machinery) comes first, with 47% of total manufacturing investment, followed by transportation equipment (17%), and chemicals (11%). In the US, the next most important sector behind electrical machinery is transportation equipment and chemicals (12% of the manufacturing FDI each).

The situation of Japanese investments in Asia is quite different with a much stronger emphasis on the manufacturing sector. More than 40% of Japanese investments in Asia (in value terms) are in the productive sector.[23] The emphasis switched from textiles in the 1951–76 period to electric appliances, chemicals and iron and steel products in the current period. In the non-manufacturing sector, mining is still the most important sector for Japanese investors, but the service industry and the financial and insurance sectors also loom large.

The contrast between Japanese investments in Asia on the one hand and in the US and Europe on the other, can be explained rather easily. The high concentration of Japanese direct investment into machinery, electrical products and transport equipment in both Europe and North America is due to the existence of a market for high value-added sophisticated products (consumer electronics, office equipment, automobiles). Moreover, persistent trade frictions with various EC countries forced Japanese firms to start local production. By contrast, Japanese FDI in Asian developing countries was initially motivated mainly by a desire to take advantage of the relatively low wage labor they provided and much of this manufacturing investment was low value-added and export oriented. (Sazanami, 1992). The textile industry is certainly the best example in this respect. Japanese investments in Asia can be said to be more of the factor-based type while investments in the US and in the EC are rather market-based. Japanese manufacturing affiliates located in the US and the EC sell mainly to the local market (be it the host country or the whole region), whereas a substantial share (around 16%) of the sales by Japanese affiliates in Asia are exported back to Japan (Table 12).[24]

In the US and the EC the banking and trading sectors are, however, much easier to penetrate than the technology-intensive manufacturing industries (which are highly protected most of the time). As time goes by, and as Asian economies gradually industrialize, Japanese FDI in Asia should become more comparable that in

---

[23] The manufacturing sector is even more dominant on the basis of MITI data.

[24] For more detailed figures see Chapters 3 and 8.

Table 12: Patterns of Sales of Japanese Manufacturing Affiliates Abroad

Location of affiliates	Total sales (bns Yen)	1986 Region (%) Local	Japan	Third country	Total sales (bns Yen)	1991 Region (%) Local	Japan	Third country
(A)								
Europe	1655	95.9	1.2	2.9	4910	95.5	1.2	3.3
Asia	3203	67.5	15.8	16.7	7187	69.6	11.8	18.6
N. America	4309	95.9	3.3	0.8	12078	93.5	3.3	3.2
(B)								
Europe	1655	70.3	1.2	28.5	4910	57.6	1.2	41.2
Asia	3203	54.7	15.8	29.5	7187	59.6	11.8	28.6
N. America	4309	92.8	3.3	3.9	12078	90.1	3.3	6.6

Note: In (A), local sales refer to sales to the total region; In B, local sales refer to sales to the country where the affiliate is located.

Source: MITI, Kaigai Jingyo Katsudo Kihon Chosa, 3rd and 4th.

both Europe and the US, but it will be a long time before the structure of investments in Asia is comparable to that of the US and the EC.

1.2.4 The Means of Japanese FDI

The changes in the type of investments made by the Japanese have been accompanied by changes in the means of FDI. However the situation is quite contrasted across host countries. Whereas in the 1970s the typical FDI transaction in the US was a greenfield investment; today an increasing share of FDI transactions are through acquisitions which have been particularly popular since 1985. During the period 1979–86, Japanese FDI through acquisitions accounted for a mere 23% of all transactions, compared to over 50% for other investors, while investments in new plants or plant expansion accounted for 48%, compared to 30% for other investors. From 1986 onwards, acquisitions became more frequent and the fraction of Japanese FDI spent on acquisitions rose to 31% in 1987, while the share of new plants and plant expansions plummeted to 25% (Froot, 1991). In 1989, a good 55% of Japan's direct investment in the US was through acquisitions while new plants and plant expansions accounted for around 10% each

(JETRO, 1992a). By contrast, greenfield investment is still the most common form of Japanese involvement in Europe: 100% Japanese investment account for about 50% and joint ventures with local firms for 25%, while acquisitions merely account for a little more than 20% (JETRO, 1992b).[25]

Yamawaki (1992)[26] also observes that even though Japanese firms tend on the whole to prefer greenfield investments to acquisition and capital participation, the two latter forms are more likely to be used as a method of entry in the US than in Europe. The situation is however contrasted across sectors; acquisition and capital participation are quite popular in the US in the chemical and food industries, while the same holds true for Japanese FDI in Europe in the transportation equipment.[27] In addition, entry through acquisition and capital participation is more frequently associated with diversifying entry in the US than in Europe.

Also, and more importantly, diversification activity is higher in the US than in Europe: 15% of the Japanese subsidiaries located in the US produce goods that are different from their parents' principal products, while 8% are in a comparable position in Europe. These results are preliminary and further investigation is warranted before definite conclusions can be reached. All that can be said so far is that the historical difference in the development of these two areas to host Japanese multinationals has played an important role; it is thus not necessarily the case that the pattern observed for Japanese FDI in the US in the 1970s will be reproduced by Japanese FDI in Europe in the 1980s and 1990s.

1.3   JAPANESE INVESTORS IN EUROPE

1.3.1   General trends

Japanese direct investment in Europe is both the most recent and the fastest rising form of Japanese involvement abroad. The surge

---

[25] See Table 19, section 3.5.

[26] The study uses a data set constructed from the individual subsidiary level data collected in Toyo Keizai, Kaigai shinshutsu kigyo soran: 1991 (Directorate of Japanese Multinational Corporations: 1991). See the Appendix for further details about the content of this data base. The paper examines whether there exists a strategic link between Japanese FDI activity in the US and in Europe and whether Japanese activity is similar or dissimilar between these two areas.

[27] See Chapter 4.

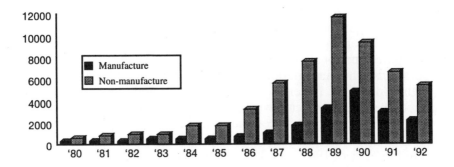

Source: MoF (1992)

Figure 2:   Japanese Direct Investment in Europe

in Japanese FDI started in 1986. The growth has been more rapid in the manufacturing sector (the flows since 1989 account for 48% of the total flows) than in the non-manufacturing sector (with 30% of the total flows since 1989). Among the different sectors, the electrical sector has been expanding most rapidly (58% of the total flows have taken place in the last two years).

As mentioned above, after ten years of remarkable expansion, the growth of Japanese direct investment in Europe began falling off in 1990. This decline was felt most heavily in the non-manufacturing sector; while investments in the manufacturing sector continued to rise in 1990 and started dropping in 1991. It is still too early to know whether this trend will go on in the next few years; the slowdown is a priori a cyclical phenomenon.

Despite the acceleration of the Japanese advance into Europe in the 1980s, the initial starting point was so low that the Japanese presence in Europe is still quite small as a share of total Japanese direct investment abroad, since Europe accounts for less than 20%, running well behind North America, with more than 40%, but ahead of Asia, with 15.2% (1991 figures). The share of Europe in total manufacturing direct investment by Japanese firms is even smaller, about 16%, while North America hosts 49% and Asia 23% of the total. (Table 11).

The Japanese presence is also quite small if compared with other foreign presences, and in particular with US investment in Europe and intra-EC direct investments (Thomsen, Woolcock, 1993). Despite the surge of foreign direct investment in Europe, most of the industrial mergers and acquisitions which have taken place in the EC since 1985 were intra-EC operations. In 1991, 41% of these M&A were purely national operations, 37% were cross-border European operations, while international operations accounted for a mere 22% (Sachwald, 1993). In terms of cumulative annual flows, 50% of the direct investments which have occurred in the EC from 1985 to 1990 were intra-EC operations, compared to 32% for US investments and 18% for Japanese operators (Table 7).

On the basis of 1989 cumulative data, total US direct investment in Europe amounted to $177 billions (four times larger than Japanese direct investment with $44972 millions). Focusing on manufacturing direct investment, the discrepancy is even more striking as the US has invested more than 5 times more than the Japanese in Europe. The data on cumulative flows are certainly not the best measure of foreign involvement in a country; however, additional data on employment levels, on production levels, etc. tell basically the same story.[28]

1.3.2   Geographical Distribution

Be it on the basis of recent annual flows or of cumulative flows, total Japanese direct investments in the EC are highly concentrated in five countries, namely Great Britain, Luxembourg, the Netherlands, Germany and France. Great Britain is, however, well ahead of the others, with more than 40% of the total.

The ranking is slightly modified if we focus on the manufacturing sector. In this sub-sector, Spain appears as the fifth European host-country, while Luxembourg becomes negligible. The ranking for manufacturing investment is again modified in terms of the number of productive units rather than the amount of cumulative flows. Great Britain still remains the focal point of Japanese investment, followed by France, Germany, Spain, Italy and the Netherlands. The discrepancy between the results is most probably due to the difference in the average size of Japanese firms operating in the various countries, this is likely to be related to the sectoral specialization of the different host-countries. Employment data (from the MITI) tell a slightly different story. Great Britain is still number one among the European

---

[28] See for instance Micossi & Viesti (1991).

Table 13: Geographical Distribution of Japanese Manufacturing Investments in the EC 1991

	Number of productive units (JETRO data)	Japanese Direct Investments (1951–91, million $)		Employment (MITI data)
		Total	Manufacturing	
Great Britain	195	26186	5184	64397
Netherlands	44	14776	3223	4345
Germany	111	5802	1725	23417
France	128	4973	1576	20737
Spain	67	2245	1336	18228
Belgium	39	1941	609	9986
Italy	47	1222	472	4620
Ireland	30	716	206	
Portugal	14	192	119	11615
Luxembourg	3	5873	105	

Source: JETRO (1992b), MoF and MITI.

host countries, but Germany comes second, followed by France, Spain and Belgium.[29]

Interestingly enough, US direct investment in Europe is also mainly directed to Great Britain, Germany, France and the Netherlands (the latter country hosting mostly non-manufacturing investments); Italy also appears as a major location for US manufacturing affiliates, however, while Spain still remains marginal.[30]

1.3.3   Sectoral Distribution

As already mentioned above, Japanese investment in Europe is quite heavily biased towards non-manufacturing activities, which account for 78% of the total. By contrast, US investment in Europe is almost evenly split between manufacturing and non-manufacturing activities, with 44% and 56% respectively.

---

[29] Employment data should be interpreted with extreme caution. As noted in Thomsen and Nicolaides (1991) the Spanish employment figures are inflated by the fact that Japanese producers have had to acquire overmanned firms.
[30] See Survey of Current Business (Aug. 1992).

Table 14: Total Production of Japanese Manufacturing Affiliates in Europe (by sector, as of March 1991, in million Yens)

Total	Foodstuffs	Textiles	Chemicals	Iron & steel	Non ferrous metals	General machinery	Electrical equipment	Transport equipment	Precision machinery	Other
1349865	9949	5621	45603	16585	14440	208106	599638	113396	16795	319732
(100)	(0.7)	(0.4)	(3.4)	(1.2)	(1.1)	(15.4)	(41.5)	(8.4)	(1.3)	(23.7)

Note: Shares are indicated between brackets.

Source: MITI.

The major part of Japanese manufacturing direct investment in Europe is in electronics and transport machinery; these two broad sectors account for almost 50% of total manufacturing investment. More importantly, the share of these sectors has been increasing recently. Electrical and electronic equipment account for 32% of Japanese manufacturing investment. Figures on production by Japanese affiliates in Europe tell a similar story, as can be seen in Table 14 based on a survey conducted by the MITI.

While both Japanese and US investment in the European manufacturing sector is primarily directed to high value added fabricating and processing industries, a finer analysis reveals that the sectoral pattern of Japanese manufacturing FDI is different from US investment in Europe, which is mainly concentrated in non-electrical machinery and in chemicals, with 21% and 22% of total US investment respectively. The latter sector is far less important for Japanese investments (around 11%).[31] Food products also loom large in US investments in the EC (about 10%) while its share is quite small for Japanese investors (less than 4%).[32]

In the non-manufacturing sector, banking, finance, insurance and real estate dominate both Japanese and US investments in Europe (with 66 and 55% of total investments respectively).

Japanese and US firms in Europe behave otherwise basically in the same way, in the patterns of sales as can be seen from Table 16. Almost 70% of their sales is directed to the very country where the affiliate is located. In addition, if the whole region is taken into account rather than the country of location, the share of local sales rises to 96% in the case of Japanese affiliates in Europe and to 92% for US-owned affiliates. 29% of the sales by Japanese affiliates in the EC are thus directed to European countries other than the country of location, compared to 23% for US affiliates. This is a clear indication that the size of the European market is the main factor that lured both Japanese and US investors. The objective of Japanese FDI is hence clearly market-seeking, just like its US counterpart. The behavior of both Japanese and US affiliates is quite different in Asia where a larger share of the sales (between 16 and 23%) is exported back to the home country.

---

[31] This is confirmed by JETRO data based on regular surveys of individual firms.

[32] See Dunning (1992) for a comparative analysis of Japanese and US manufacturing investment in Europe.

Table 15: Distribution of Japanese and US Direct Investment Stake in the EC Manufacturing Industry

	Japan (March 1992)*		US (December 1991)	
	$ million	%	$ million	%
Food products	546	3.7	9060	10.6
Chemicals & allied products	1618	11.1	18845	22.0
Metals	572	3.9	3941	4.6
Textiles & clothing	979	6.7		
Wood related products	56	0.4		
Electrical & electronic equipment	4748	32.6	5539	6.5
Non-electrical machinery	2332	15.9	17878	20.9
Transportation	2442	16.7	9796	11.4
Other products	1286	8.8	20606	24.0
TOTAL MANUFACTURING	14579	100.0	85664	100.0
Wholesale trade & commerce	7863	15.9	16243	15.7
Banking, finance, insurance & real estate	33051	66.8	56686	55.0
Other services	4137	8.3	7258	7.0
Other industry	4401	8.8	22858	22.2
TOTAL OTHER INDUSTRIES	49452	100.0	103045	100.0
TOTAL ALL INDUSTRY	64031		188710	

Source: Japan – Ministry of Finance
            US – US Department of Commerce (1992)

*Represents cumulative foreign direct investment April 1951 to March 1992

Table 16: Pattern of Sales of Japanese and US Manufacturing Affiliates in the EC (1989)

	Local sales	Sales to home country	Sales to third countries within EC	Other
US affiliates	69.0	4.6	23.1	3.3
Japanese affiliates	66.5	1.7	29.6	2.2

Sources: US – US Direct Investment Abroad, US Department of Commerce (1991)
Japan – MITI

1.3.4   Sectoral and geographical distribution combined

A relatively clear picture emerges from the tables on Japanese affiliates in Europe classified by country and industry. Table 17a is based on cumulative flows, Table 17b gives the number of firms by country and sector, Table 17c gives the distribution of sales by Japanese affiliates established in the EC by country and location and by sector of activities while Table 17d gives the number of employees by country and sector. Whatever the reference, the classification is basically unchanged.

Non-manufacturing investments dominate Japanese involvement in Europe, even though the situation is quite contrasted across countries. The European economies can be classified into three broad categories. In the first category, which includes the European countries with large and active financial centers (the UK, the Netherlands and Luxembourg) the share of manufacturing investments is smaller than average (around 20% for the UK and the Netherlands and less than 2% in the case of Luxembourg). The second category includes countries such as France, Germany, Belgium, and Italy; in these economies the share of manufacturing investment ranges from 30 to 38% of total Japanese involvement. Finally, Spain, Portugal and Greece build up a category of their own, where manufacturing investment accounts for about 60% of the total, and even more in the case of Greece. In the latter economies, Japanese investors obviously try to take advantage of low-wage labor needed in labor-intensive manufacturing activities. This is confirmed by the larger than average size of the manufacturing firms located in these countries (about 450 workers, compared to 200 in the UK, France and Germany).

Focusing on the manufacturing sector, we observe that electric equipment is the leading sector in a number of countries, such as the United Kingdom and the Netherlands, with more than 40% of total manufacturing investment. It is also quite large in Germany where it is comparable to the chemical sector (around 30%). This sector is however not as important in the Netherlands when assessed on the basis of the number of productive units, the level of sales or employment. Transportation equipment is the second most important sector in the UK, while general machinery comes next on the line in both Germany and in the Netherlands. General machinery is dominant in France and food products are the second most important sector of involvement by Japanese investors in this country; this is obviously due to their active participation in a number of wineries in the Bordeaux area.

Table 17a: Japanese Direct Investment in Europe by Industry and Country (Cumulative Flows 1951–1991 — Unit: million US $)

COUNTRY / SECTOR	UK	France	Germany	N'lands	Belgium	L'bourg	Ireland	Spain	Italy	Portugal	Greece	TOTAL
MANUFACTURING	5.184	1.576	1.725	3.223	609	105	206	1.336	472	119	99	14.654
Food products	135	293	17	75	13	–	0	3	8	2	–	546
Textiles	222	157	54	237	2	–	104	59	101	39	4	979
Wood, pulp & paper	–	0	54	2	–	–	–	0	0	0	–	56
Chemicals	168	152	546	390	148	–	0	173	24	1	16	1.618
Iron & steel,												
Non-ferrous metals	94	127	1	189	25	–	6	103	4	23	76	572
General machinery	713	412	360	425	163	84	27	84	63	1	–	2.332
Electric equipment	2.120	219	541	1.436	27	4	43	259	96	3	–	4.748
Transportation equipment	1.338	73	25	272	43	–	–	591	85	15	0	2.442
Other manufacturing	395	142	128	197	187	17	25	64	92	36	3	1.286
AGRICULTURE & FORESTRY	0	7	1	5	–	3	0	0	–	–	–	16
FISHERY	1	–	–	–	–	–	2	1	0	–	–	4
MINING	867	57	–	–	–	–	17	1	–	–	–	942
CONSTRUCTION	35	9	28	46	1	–	–	5	0	0	–	124
COMMERCE	2.094	802	2.073	1.903	418	3	7	189	342	30	2	7.863
BANKING, FINANCES & SECURITIES	11.264	392	955	6.083	638	5.551	28	48	79	10	–	25.048
SERVICE	920	695	189	1.336	35	45	442	215	46	–	–	3.923
TRANSPORTATION	83	5	20	45	14	43	–	3	1	–	–	214
REAL ESTATE	4.291	1.025	312	2.080	41	22	11	114	97	10	–	8.003
OTHER SECTOR	707	17	58	49	11	101	1	–	5	0	–	949
TOTAL FLOWS	28.186	4.973	5.805	14.776	1.941	5.873	716	2.245	1.222	192	102	64.031

Source: Ministry of Finance

Table 17b: Japanese Manufacturing Enterprises in Europe Classified by Country and Industry (721 firms as of the end of January, 1992)

	Total	UK	France	Germany	N'lands	Belgium	L'bourg	Ireland	Spain	Italy	Denmark	Portugal	Greece
TOTAL	721	195	128	111	44	39	3	30	67	47	3	14	3
Food & related products	32	4	21	3	2	1			1	1			
Textile mill products	14	5	2					2	1	1		2	
Apparel & other finished products	18	4	5	1					1	7			
Furniture & fixtures	5	1	2	1					1				
Pulp, paper & paper products	5			1		1			1			1	
Chemicals & allied products	118	27	20	13	11	12	1	4	11	8		2	1
Medicines	18		3	5	1	1		3	4	1			
Rubber products	14	2	4	2	1			1	1	1		1	
Stone, clay & glass products	18	3	3	3	1	4		1	2	1			
Iron & steel	6	1		1	1	1			1				1
Non-ferrous metals & products	7	2	3					1	1				
Fabricated metal products	28	7	3	3	2	1		2	3	1		1	
General machinery & equipment	89	18	16	21	7	3		2	7	8	1		

Table 17b: *Continued*

	Total	UK	France	Germany	N'lands	Belgium	L'bourg	Ireland	Spain	Italy	D'mark	Portugal	Greece
TOTAL	721	195	128	111	44	39	3	30	67	47	3	14	3
Electronic equipment, electrical machinery, equipment & supplies	115	41	23	21	3	6	1	3	9	8			
Electronic parts & components	73	23	8	18	5	3		10	2	2		1	
Transport equipment	20	6	2		1	1			5	3		2	
Parts & components of transport equipment	49	19	5	4	3	2			10	2		2	
Precision machinery & equipment	33	8		10	2		1	1	1				
Others	59	24	4	4	4	3			5	4	2	2	1
Design centers R& D facilities	203(54)	73(19)	30(9)	39(14)	6(1)	10(3)	0(0)	2(1)	23(0)	8(2)	1(1)	0	0

Note: The number of Design Center & Facilities are separately counted and are not included in the total in this table. Any design centers and/or R&D facilities established as an organization of Japanese-manufacturing enterprises in Europe (design centers and/or R&D facilities formed within a Japanese-manufacturing enterprise in Europe shall be counted as one (1) center and/or facility irrespective of their actual number of offices), and any independent design and/or R&D firms are included in the number of Design Centers & R&D Facilities. Figures in parentheses indicate the number of independent design and/or R&D firms out of the total of Design Centers & R&D Facilities.

Table 17c: Sales by Country of Location and by Sector of Activities

	Total m'fact'ing	Foodstuffs	Textiles	Lumber & pulp	Chemicals	Iron & steel	Non-ferous metals	General machinery	Electrical equipment	Transport equipment	Precision machinery	Other
UK	1.473 351	2.577	9.964	0	24.014	342	2.013	227.617	902.697	226.161	14.383	63.583
France	793.026	11.190	0	0	17.523	0	2.286	188.170	363.140	108.558	14.798	87.361
Germany	805.444	0	795	0	119.848	16.585	0	222.139	333.534	925	11.603	100.015
Italy	274.779	0	18.056	0	9.383	0	0	148.493	41.560	45.838	0	11.449
Netherlands	465.304	0	714	0	52.898	0	0	332.969	20.432	35.920	0	22.371
Belgium	299.441	0	0	0	35.733	0	0	17.679	38.050	82.619	0	125.360
Switzerland	69.497	0	0	0	30.582	749	0	886	32	30.111	6.848	289
Spain	515.628	1.952	0	445	12.912	0	789	4.799	127.568	363.724	0	3.439
Other	213.284	0	6.316	39	15.994	0	14.161	3.599	53.362	90.745	0	29.068
Total Europe	4.909 754	15.719	35.845	484	318.887	17.676	19.249	1.146351	1.880375	984.601	47.632	442.935

Source: MITI

Table 17d: Number of Employees (by country and by sector)

	Total m'fact'ing	Foodstuffs	Textiles	Lumber & pulp	Chemicals	Iron & steel	Non-ferous metals	General machinery	Electrical equipement	Transport equipment	Precision machinery	Other
UK	64.397	27	553	0	1.482	13	162	9.642	37.435	9.496	898	4.689
France	20.737	328	15	0	294	0	103	3.322	6.047	3.352	487	6.168
Germany	23.417	0	5	0	4.217	13	0	5.575	7.230	47	734	5.596
Italy	4.620	0	551	0	339	0	0	1.738	1.069	369	0	554
Netherlands	4.345	0	8	0	2.036	0	0	859	222	211	0	1.009
Belgium	9.986	0	3	0	899	0	0	187	1.026	876	0	6.995
Switzerland	1.203	0	0	0	852	5	0	13	4	311	34	11
Spain	18.228	413	0	22	520	0	57	323	4.045	12.250	0	240
Other	11.615	0	277	89	286	0	1.382	212	1.809	5.305	0	2.065
Total Europe	158.548	768	1.412	111	10.898	31	1.704	21.971	58.977	32.217	2.153	27.327

Source: MITI

Another striking feature of this sectoral distribution of Japanese direct investment by country is the leading role of the textile sector in Ireland, Italy and Portugal. The high degree of agregation does not allow to derive any definite conclusion; it seems, however, that investments in Italy are more heavily concentrated in clothing while investments in Ireland and Portugal concern textile mill products. Such a pattern of specialization has again obviously something to do with the existence of low-wage labor in both Portugal and Ireland.

The number of design centers and R&D facilities has increased twofold from the end of January 1990 to the end of January 1991, rising from 73 to 144 centers (of which 51 are located in the UK). In the course of 1991 and 1992, it rose again to reach 232 as of the end of January 1993. Among those, some 165 facilities were set up along with productive bases while the remaining 67 were dedicated exclusively to design and R&D. The most obvious advance was observed in Great Britain, France, Germany and Spain.[33] The 1992 JETRO survey also found that more than 75% of the firms investigated recognised the necessity of doing R&D in local markets where they were operating (JETRO, 1992b).[34] It is thus expected that the European operation of Japanese manufacturers will be increasingly localizing their R&D activities.[35]

1.3.5 Means of Investment

More than half of the Japanese subsidiaries operating in the EC are wholly-owned subsidiaries. In this respect, Japanese investors' behavior apparently evolved over time. According to the JETRO, most of the firms which started operations before 1980 were created either by joint venture or through acquisition, with wholly-owned subsidiaries accounting for a mere 38% of the total, whereas those enterprises which started operations in the 1980s are mostly wholly-owned (JETRO, 1992b).

The means of investment differ widely across countries. Wholly-owned subsidiaries show a high percentage in Belgium, (60%), the Netherlands (61%), the United Kingdom (65%) and Germany (50%).

---

[33] Over the last two years, the increase has been almost threefold in France (11 to 30), the United Kingdom (24 to 86) and Germany (14 to 44) (JETRO, 1992b).

[34] This trend is confirmed by the survey conducted by the JETRO in October and November 1992.

[35] See Chapter 7.

Table 18:   Number of Japanese Manufacturing Enterprises for Each Type of Presence by Country and Area of Location (end of January 1992)

	TOTAL	100% Japanese	Joint venture with local firms	Capital parti'tion	Merger & acquisition	Other measures
TOTAL	394	188 (47.7)	97 (24.6)	21 (5.3)	81 (20.6)	7(1.8)
UK	125	81 (64.8)	19 (15.2)	2 (1.6)	19 (15.2)	4 (3.2)
France	55	19 (34.5)	20 (36.4)	2 (3.6)	13 (23.6)	1 (1.8)
Germany	64	32 (50.0)	12 (18.8)	6 (9.4)	14 (21.9)	− (−)
Netherlands	26	16 (61.5)	3 (11.5)	1 (3.8)	6 (23.1)	− (−)
Belgium	20	12 (60.0)	4 (20.0)	− (−)	4 (20.0)	− (−)
Spain	39	2 (5.1)	19 (48.7)	5 (12.8)	12 (30.8)	1 (2.6)
Italy	16	2 (12.5)	12 (75.1)	− (−)	2 (12.5)	− (−)

Source: JETRO (1992).

In France, by contrast, a substantial share of investments (40%) still takes place through joint ventures with local firms or through capital participation.[36] The share of wholly-owned subsidiaries is however on the rise (it went up from 26% in 1990 to 35% in 1992) (JETRO, 1992); finally mergers and acquisitions account for a little less than 25% in France. The same ranking also holds for Spain, where joint ventures and capital participation account for 62% of Japanese direct investments, while wholly-owned firms are a minority, with 5%.

Such contrasted behaviors obviously relate to local regulations towards FDI. Some countries such as Great Britain have been favorable to the establishment of wholly-owned foreign subsidiaries for a long time, while others such as France and Spain were initially quite reluctant. It is not easy to relate the means of investment and the sector of investment; the only thing that can be said is that joint-ventures tend to be more frequent in the sectors where Japanese producers do not have a competitive edge over their European competitors (as the chemical sector for instance). By contrast, wholly-owned subsidiaries are more frequently found in sectors where

---

[36] These two forms of involvement, however, accounted for more than 45% of Japanese operations in 1990.

Japanese investors are particularly competitive (as in the electronic sector for instance). Finally, in sectors in which there was a surplus capacity, Japanese firms have entered the European market by acquiring existing producers, rather than by setting up new greenfield ventures.[37]

1.4 CONCLUDING REMARKS

A number of lessons can be drawn from the statistical analysis. First of all, the explosion of Japanese direct investments abroad over the last decade, and in particular in the EC since 1986, is part of a general trend. The surge of Japanese FDI is one among many signs of the growing internationalization of economic activities worldwide. American and European FDI have also been quite intensive during the period under consideration.

Moreover, even though the rise in Japanese FDI has been most dramatic in the EC over the last decade, the share of this region in the Japanese producers' portfolio is still much smaller than that of the US; as a result, the movement is very likely to go on in the coming years, yet probably at a much lower pace. In addition, Japanese direct investments in the EC are still much smaller than both American and intra-European investments.

Japanese FDI also tends to be highly concentrated in a limited number of sectors, with a strong emphasis on non-manufacturing activities. In the manufacturing sector, the concentration is also quite strong and the electric and electronic industries clearly lead the way. Sizable differences can be observed from country to country, so that a finer sectoral analysis is clearly warranted.

The intensification of Japanese direct investment abroad is the result of a catch-up phenomenon since Japanese firms were, and still are, far less internationalized than their major competitors from the G7. The Japanese economy is gradually becoming "normalized" but cross-FDI flows between this country and the rest of the Triad are still far from fully balanced.

Finally, the surge of Japanese FDI cannot be explained by cyclical factors and macroeconomic considerations. Neither the Japanese current account surplus nor the exceptionally high value of Japanese assets (due to the speculative bubble in Japan) can account for the rise

---

[37] See Dunning (1992).

in FDI. These are enhancing factors but the genuine driving forces are to be found elsewhere. The actual reasons for such a move are of a microeconomic kind and this is why the following chapters focus on the motivations and strategies of Japanese firms.

REFERENCES

Bourguinat, Henri, "Investissement direct étranger et globalisation financière", *Revue d'économie financière*, hiver 1990.

Caves, Richard, E., Drake, Tracey, A., "Changing Determinants of Japan's Foreign Investment in the United States", *Mimeo*, Harvard Institute of Economic Research, Cambridge, May, 1990.

CE/CNUST, (Groupe conjoint sur les sociétés transnationales), *Les sociétés transnationales japonaises en Europe, Structures, Stratégies et nouvelles tendances*, Nations Unies, New York, 1991.

Commissariat général du Plan, *Investir en France, un espace attractif, Rapport du groupe "localisation des investissements transnationaux"*, la Documentation Française, Paris, 1992.

Dourille-Feer, Evelyne, "L'Europe sur l'échiquier productif du Japon, le cas des industries électronique et automobile", *Economie prospective internationale*, no. 49, 1er trimestre, 1992.

Dunning, John, H., Cantwell, John, A., "Japanese manufacturing direct investment in the EEC Post 1992 some alternative scenarios", *Mimeo*, 1989.

Dunning, John H., "Japanese and US Manufacturing Investment in Europe: Some Comparisons and Contrasts", *Mimeo*, INSEAD, Euro-Asia Centre Fontainebleau, June 26-27 1992.

Emmott, Bill, *Japan's Global Reach*, Century, London, 1992.

Erdilek, Asim (ed.), *Multinational as Mutual Invaders: Intra-Industry Direct Foreign Investment*, New York, 1985.

Froot, Kenneth, A., *Japanese foreign direct investment*, NBER, Working Papers, no. 3737, Cambridge, June, 1991.

Granrut, Charles du., "Les investissements directs internationaux : ampleur et conséquences", *Futuribles*, décembre 1990.

Greenaway, David, Balasubramanyam, V.N., "Economic Integration and Foreign Direct Investment : Japanese Investment in the EC", *Journal of Common Market Studies*, Volume XXX, no 2, June 1992.

HEC Eurasia Institute, *Europe Japon — Surmonter les déséquilibres*, Chambre de Commerce et d'Industrie de Paris, 1991.

Houde, Marie-France, "L'investissement direct international", *l'Observateur de l'OCDE*, no. 176, juin-juillet 1992.

JETRO (Japanese External Trade Organization), *White Paper on Foreign Direct Investment 1992, The Role of Direct Investment in Filling the Gap between Capital Demand and Supply*, Summary, 1992a.

JETRO (Japanese External Trade Organization), *8th Survey of European Operations of Japanese Companies in the Manufacturing Sector*, 1992b.

JETRO (Japanese External Trade Organization), *White Paper on Foreign Direct Investment 1991, Direct Investment Promoting Restructuring of Economies Worldwide*, Summary, 1991.

Julius, DeAnne, *Global Companies and Public Policy, The Growing Challenge of Foreign Direct Investment*, The Royal Institute of International Affairs, Londres, 1990.

Liouville, Jacques, "Localisation des entreprises japonaises dans la CEE", *Analyse de la SEDEIS*, no. 82, juillet 1991.

Lipsey, Robert, E., *Foreign Direct Investment in the US: Changes over three Decades*, NBER, Working Paper, no. 4124, Cambridge, July, 1992.

Micossi, Stefano, Viesti, Gianfranco, "Japanese direct manufacturing investment in Europe" in Winters, Alan, L., Venables, Anthony, J. *European integration: trade and industry*, Cambridge University Press, September, 1990.

MITI (Ministry of International Trade and Industry), *21st Overseas Business Activities of Japanese Companies* (in Japanese), Tokyo, 1992.

Mosbacher, Robert, A., *US Direct Investment Abroad, Operations of US Parent Companies and their Foreign Affiliates*, Preliminary 1988 Estimates, US Department of Commerce, Bureau of Economic Analysis, July, 1990.

Ostry, Sylvia, *Governments & Corporations in a Shrinking World. Trade & Innovation Policies in the United States, Europe & Japan*, Council on Foreign Relations Press, New York, 1990.

Ozawa, Terutomo, "Europe 1992 and Japanese Multinationals : Transplanting a Subcontracting System in the Expend Market", *Mimeo*, Roundtable on Multinational Firms and European Integration, University of Geneva, Switzerland, May 12–13, 1989.

Sachwald , Frédérique (ed.), *L'Europe et la globalisation. Acquisitions et accords dans l'industrie européenne*, Masson, Paris, 1993.

Satake, Takanori, "Trends in Japanese Foreign Direct Investment in Fy 1989", in *Exim Review*, Volume 11, Number 1, July, 1991.

Saucier, Ph., "New Conditions for Competition between Japanese and European Firms in the Post 1992 unified Market", *Mimeo*, Roundtable on Multinational Firms and European Integration, University of Geneva, May 12–13 1989.

Sazanami, Yoko, "Globalization" strategy of Japanese manufacturing firms and its impact on trade flows between Europe. Asia and North America", *Mimeo*, March, 1992.

Sazanami, Yoko, "Determinants of Japanese Foreign Direct Investment. Locational Attractiveness of European Countries to Japanese Multinationals", Mimeo, French Economic Society Meeting, September 24–25, Paris, 1991.

Scharrer, Hans-Eckart, Krägenau, Henry, "Die Finanzierung deutscher Direktinvestitionen im Ausland", *Wirtschaftsdienst*, no. 1, 1990.

Takeuchi, Sawako, "Japanese Direct Investment in France: Changing Political Climate", *Mimeo*, The Royal Institute International Affairs, 1990.

Tejima, Shigeki, "Japanese Foreign Direct Investment in the 1980s and its Prospects for the 1990s", in *Exim Review*, Volume 11, no. 2, 1992.

Thomsen, Stephen, Nicolaides, Phedon, *The evolution of Japanese direct investment in Europe*, Harvester Wheatsheaf, New York, 1991.

Thomsen, Stephen, Woolcock, Stephen, *Direct Investment and European Integration. Competition among Firms and Goverments*, RIIA Pinter Publishers, London, 1993.

Tyson, Laura d'Andrea, *Who's bashing whom. Trade Conflict in High Technology Industries*, Institute for International Economics, Washington, 1993.

UNCTAD (United Nations Conference on Trade and Development — Programme on Transnational Corporations), *World Investment Report 1993 — Transnational Corporations and Integrated International Production*, United nations, New York, 1993.

UNCTC (United Nations Centre on Transnational Corporations), *The Determinants of Foreign Direct Investment, A Survey of the Evidence*, United Nations, New York, 1992.

UNCTC (United Nations Centre on Transnational Corporations),*World Investment Report 1991; The Triad in Foreign Direct Investment*, United Nations, New York, 1991.

Winters, Alan, L., Venables, Anthony, J., *European integration: trade and industry*, Cambridge University press, September, 1990.

Yamawaki, Hideki, "Japanese Multinationals in US and European Manufacturing Industries: Entry, Strategy and Patterns", *Mimeo*, Catholic University of Louvain, June 1992.

Yamawaki, Hideki, "Location decisions of Japanese Multinational Firms in European Manufacturing Industries", *Mimeo*, Department of Economics Catholic University of Louvain, July 1991.

Yamawaki, Hideki, "Exports and Foreign Distributional Activities : Evidence on Japanese Firms in the United States", *Review of Economics and Statistics*, volume 73, no. 2, 1991.

Yoshitomi, Masaru, *Japanese Direct Investment in Europe, Motives, Impact and Policy Implications*, The Royal Institute of International Affairs and Sumitomo-Life Research Institute, Avebury, England, 1991.

2

The Decisions of Japanese Firms
to Produce in Europe

Frédérique Sachwald

The objective of this chapter is to explore the determinants of location in Europe by Japanese firms. Three elements should be examined : the strong increase in Japanese investment in Europe since the 1980s,[1] the choice of location within Europe and the choice of an organizational mode to produce in Europe.

The first part of this chapter deals with the theoretical framework recalling the different relevant theories on the determinants of multi-nationalization and explain perspective. The second and third sections analyze empirical results on the motivations of Japanese firms to set up production units in Europe. The final part discusses the role of the sectoral competitive game in firms' decisions to internationalize.

2.1   A THEORETICAL FRAMEWORK

The theoretical hypotheses which have been put forward in order to explain the occurence of foreign production have been influenced by two sets of factors. Firstly, authors have been able to observe various types of foreign investment at different periods. Secondly, authors have adopted different perspectives and have worked on

---

[1] This has been the case in all sectors (see Chapter 1). This chapter only deals with manufacturing.

slightly different questions. In particular, there is a clear difference between those who analyze investment flows along the same lines as trade flows and who insist on the role of national factor endowments and those who consider the point of view of the firm taking the decision to produce abroad.[2]

This section explains the choice of the analytical framework which is used here to examine the determinants of Japanese direct investments in Europe (in sections 2.2 to 2.4). It shows that the so called *Japanese model* of foreign direct investment has been a historically limited phenomenon, as the product cycle model, which could have been called the *American model* but also that the analysis of the firm's decision determinants should be complemented with an account the sectoral context, with both its technical and national features.

2.1.1   *Does the Japanese Model Exist?*

Quite generally, the theoretical assumptions have been influenced by the type of FDI which existed or seemed particularly relevant at different periods in time. As a result, the theoretical anlyses of FDI and multinationals have evolved, with some delays, with the degree of internationalization of the world economy and with the spreading of multinationals as a way to organise production. The case of Japanese direct investment is particularly interesting in this respect. Indeed, in the 1970s, Japanese authors proposed a specific explanation of Japanese direct investment, based on observations of the 1950s and 1960s. They have contrasted Japanese direct investment in Asia with American investment in developed countries and have considered that the product cycle explanation for direct investment was irrelevant to Japanese investment. Actually, both the product cycle explanation and the "Japanese" explanation now appear as specific explanations for specific and historically limited types of FDI.

The theory of the product cycle, which was proposed by Raymond Vernon in the 1960s, establishes a relationship between the innovativeness and the technological sophistication of a country on the one hand, and its exports and propensity to develop production units abroad on the other hand. A new product is first manufactured in the country of innovation where the market is sophisticated enough and where

---

[2] On the importance of the point of view for theoretical analyses of foreign direct investment, see (Mucchielli, 1985; Cantwell, 1991; Dunning, 1993).

demand is sufficiently abundant from the start.[3] In the original version of the theory that market was the United States, which was then the most technologically advanced country, the richest economy and by far the largest foreign direct investor. In 1960, the stock of direct investment originating from the United States represented about 50% of the total world stock.[4] According to R. Vernon, firstly exports and then foreign direct investment result from the maturing of the product. As a new product matures, its technology becomes standardized and more available. Imitators appear on the domestic market and price competition becomes more relevant. Lower costs thus offer an incentive to delocalise production abroad, which is possible when the technology has become relatively standardized. Typically in this model, foreign production would first take place in relatively advanced countries such as in Europe, and would eventually reach less developed countries. The product cycle model of direct investment thus establishes relationships between the age of a product, the diffusion of the relevant technology, the type of competition faced by firms and the location of production. It relates the national characteristics of both the home and host countries with firms' incentives to delocalize production.

The product cycle explanation of foreign production works well for American direct investment after the Second world war, but has been unable to explain a number of more recent developments, in particular the diversification of the countries involved in FDI and the sectors concerned. One set of considerations relate to the notion of the product cycle itself, which is not entirely valid for a number of products. In particular, once the maturity phase is reached there can be a number of additional innovations to *rejuvenate* a product.[5] Moreover, the product cycle does not deal with the question of the production process as such. Innovation in this area can constitute a very efficient competitive weapon and offer a source of *de-maturity*. Both types of disturbances have for example altered the product cycle of the automobile.[6] A second development has also lowered the relevance of the product cycle model ; the diversification of the sources of foreign direct investment and of the sources of sophisticated tech-

---

[3] (Vernon, 1966) explains that he is mainly concerned with innovations in consumer goods, and more particularly in those which aim at saving time.

[4] For estimates, see (Dunning, 1983; Jacquemot, 1990).

[5] And maintain production in the most technologically advanced countries.

[6] On this question, see (Volpato, 1983; Sachwald, 1989, 1993).

nology. The European countries and Japan have become important sources of direct investment and have achieved comparable levels in terms of technological achievements. Thus, the product cycle theory can not propose a satisfactory explanation for the multiplication of multinational companies and for the extend of rapid diffusion of products (new, rejuvenated..) around the globe.[7]

The "Japanese model" is the expression used here to summarise the analyses of K. Kojima and T. Ozawa, which have been very much influenced by the first important wave of Japanese foreign direct investment in the 1960s.[8] T. Ozawa (1979) thus observes the development of Japanese foreign direct investment from the 1960s on and examines the "relevance of Western theories" in order to explain it.[9] He concludes that Japanese direct investment requires a different type of explanation. During the 1960s, Asia was the most important zone of Japanese foreign investment; for example, from 1969 to 1973, it represented 24.2% of the total, while flows to North America represented 22.6%.[10] This type of investment was thus quite different from that of American multinational companies which settled units of production in industrial countries in order to keep reaping benefits from innovations.

The objective of the Japanese model is to explain direct investment within the framework of comparative advantage, that is to say by considering the factor endowments of the home and host countries. Foreign direct investment does not only transfer capital, but a larger package of resources, including technological and managerial assets which are specific resources of the country of origin. In such a perspective, direct investment from a technologically advanced country can enhance the efficiency of a less developed country for the production of labor intensive goods. The objective of the investor is to increase the return on its assets since labor is more abundant and thus cheaper in the less developed country.

---

[7] R. Vernon (1979) has recognised the inadequacy of the model in the 1970s.

[8] The main characteristics of the model are described below and it is referred to as the "Japanese model", even if several authors have made specific contributions ; see in particular (Ozawa, 1979). Moreover, only the main explanation is dealt with. (Ozawa, 1979) for example also mentioned that Japanese investment can be motivated by the search for natural resources which are . . .

[9] T. Ozawa (1979) mostly includes in the Western theories the industrial organization approach (S. Hymer, C. Kindelberger, R. Caves) and the product cycle approach.

[10] For a general statistical description of Japanese direct investment, see Chapter 1.

The Japanese model shows that this type of investment creates trade by increasing the comparative advantage of the less developed country in the production of labor intensive goods. It is essentially why foreign direct investment "Japanese style" (Ozawa 1979) has been opposed to the typical American foreign investment which substituted foreign production to trade.[11] But the "trade creating" Japanese investment did not last. The structure of Japanese investment has evolved rapidly to become more comparable to that of the other industrialized countries, which means that both the sectoral and geographical distributions do not match the model anymore. Japan now largely invests in services and in technologically sophisticated sectors. Since the 1960s, its foreign investment flows have also tended to increase more rapidly in industrialized countries, even though Asian countries retain a substantial part of them.[12] Moreover, a number of the Japanese production units abroad notoriously result in trade destruction. It is in particular the case for those units which have been set as an answer to protectionist pressures and which are trade substituting.[13]

T. Ozawa (1979) summarizes his model as an "industry-cycle approach".[14] He opposes it to the product cycle approach, but common features do exist. In both models, firms relocate more or less mature industries abroad in order to keep exploiting some competitive advantage, while overcoming the increase in domestic costs (Cantwell, 1991). Moreover, in both cases, foreign production operates technology transfers, from the United States to Europe in the case of the product cycle and from Japan to less developed Asian countries in the case of the Japanese model.

Neither the product cycle model nor the Japanese model of foreign direct investment are entirely valid when taken out of the historical context in which they were formulated. However they both include interesting elements to analyze Japanese direct investment in Europe. These elements are related to the existence of competitive advantages of Japanese firms and to the formation of these advantages within the national context.

---

[11] Japanese FDI had other specific characteristics such as the fact that small companies were quite active, sometimes with government support.

[12] See Chapter 1.

[13] The role of protectionist pressures is dealt with below.

[14] T. Ozawa (1989) has further explored this idea and linked the evolution of the Japanese direct investment pattern with industrial development.

2.1.2   The Firm's Decision and the Sectoral Context

It is possible to establish a distinction between the motivations of firms to produce abroad and the precise determinants of each of their decisions. Motivations can be classified into two main categories: the search for resources (natural resources, technology or other strategic assets) and the search for markets.[15] These motivations result from the firm's strategy; for example the fact that a firm has decided to penetrate a certain foreign market. Then the direct determinants of the investment result from the assets of the firm and from the obstacles which it may encounter in trying to implement its strategy. To develop the above example, the firm can experience difficulties in penetrating the foreign market through exports and thus consider direct investment instead. Actually, the distinction between the motivations and the determinants is not always easy to establish as the empirical studies show.[16] This chapter analyzes the factors which can determine the decision to invest abroad in general, and then considers the sectoral context which enables us to understand the strategic motives of firms.

The eclectic paradigm of foreign production provides an appropriate framework to analyze the determinants of the decision to produce abroad. The purpose of the eclectic paradigm is *"to point to a methodology and to a generic set of variables which contain the ingredients for any specific explanation of particular types of foreign value-added activity"* (Dunning, 1991). According to the paradigm, the occurence of international production depends on the configuration of three sets of determinants: the competitive advantages of the firm, the location advantages of the country and internalization advantages of the transaction. Firstly, the firm which invests abroad in order to access a foreign market must possess a *competitive advantage*,[17] in particular over foreign firms in order to be able to sustain competition in an environment which is relatively unfavorable. The foreign countries, by the very fact that they are foreign and relatively unknown, present a number of barriers to entry. Competitive advantages can be of various origins: product, technology or other types of competence. In the case of multinationals, a specific competitive advantage can derive from

---

[15] For another classification, see (Dunning, 1993).

[16] And this holds for the surveys which are used later in this chapter.

[17] The term competitive advantage seems more appropriate than ownership advantage which is also used and which insists rather on the fact that the firm owns a number of assets (tangible or intangible).

their organisational capabilities, at the international level in particular. Secondly, the firm must be willing to produce in a given country, which entails that the country presents a *location advantage* of some sort for the firm. That advantage can be due to natural resources, low labor costs or highly qualified labor in specific sectors; it can also result from national regulations, and in particular protectionist measures. Finally, there must be an *internalization advantage*, which means that the transfer of the relevant assets to the foreign country should be more efficient within the firm than by resorting to markets. Generally, the firm perceives the internalization of foreign production as a source of profitability because of market imperfections and transaction costs for some intermediary asset.[18] A company will become multinational if it cannot export its product and cannot exploit satisfactorily its specific competitive advantage through market mechanisms. Different authors have especially discussed internalization advantages in the case of intermediary goods and services such as raw materials or knowledge.[19]

This brief presentation of the eclectic paradigm shows that it is indeed compatible with a number of more specific explanations for the occurrence of multinational production.[20] However, it focuses on the firm's decision, and not on the motives for this decision, which sectoral and macroeconomic analyses have emphasized. This chapter emphasizess two extensions of the paradigm which seem particularly relevant to the analysis of contemporary multinational firms. Firstly, cooperative agreements and various forms of partial internalization have to be explicitly included in the scope of analysis — even if they do not always imply foreign direct investment flows. Secondly, it seems important to insist on the sources of firms' competitive advantages and in this respect, a sectoral perspective is necessary.

Joint ventures and various types of cooperative agreements, which may or may not entail capital participation, have become very numerous since the 1970s, and now play an important part in the competitive

---

[18] Transaction costs are the costs of using markets. They result from the need to search for and compute costly information, the fact that the value of some assets can be related to specific transactions (these assets are much less valuable in other uses) and to opportunist behaviors from economic agents. See for example (Williamson, 1985).

[19] See for example (Caves, 1982; Stuckey, 1983; Hennart, 1991b). (Kogut, Zander 1992) have argued in favour of an evolutionary perspective, in which firms are particularly efficient at creating and transfering tacit knowledge.

[20] Like those presented above for example. For more detailed expositions and explanations of the paradigm, see (Dunning, 1988, 1991, 1993).

game of several sectors. This is the case, for example in electronic sectors, in the automobile and automobile component industries, in aerospace as well as in pharmaceuticals.[21] They can fullfil various objectives, and they have been widely used as a means to penetrate foreign markets, and even to produce abroad. Hence it is important to incorporate inter-firm agreements and networks into the analysis. This can be done by extending the examination of the internalization decision to cooperative agreements — which can be considered as partial internalization.

Transaction cost analysis proposes a relevant framework to explain the choice of the type of arrangement for a transaction, given the characteristics of the asset or product to exchange and the characteristics of the market (or absence of market). One fundamental contention of transaction cost analysis is actually that these two sets of characteristics are interdependent. In certain cases, in order to combine the services of assets held by two or more firms, neither transaction on a market, nor complete internalization through the acquisition of one of the partners for example is the most efficient way to procede. This is the case in particular for a whole set of intangible assets, such as know-how for example. Jean-François Hennart (1991b) underlines the fact that transaction cost theory of the multinational can account for partial internalization and thus for the "hybrid institutional forms used in international business".

Empirical studies have shown the interest of transaction cost analysis to explain the hybrid institutional forms of transactions for both national and international operations.[22] However, the transaction cost perspective is relevant only once some transaction, like the use of some new asset for example, has been decided upon (Sachwald 1990,1992). In fact the decision process is comparable to that of foreign production: one can distinguish between the motivation and the determinants of the choice of a specific transaction mode. The motivation results from the confrontation of the firm's strategy and resources, hence the importance of the sectoral analysis. The determinants of the choice of a mode of transaction then depend on the opportunities and obstacles that the firm encounters and the need to resort to partial internalization develops. In particular, when a firm

---

[21] See (Contractor, Lorange, 1988; Mowery, 1988; Mytelka, 1991; Sachwald, 1994). These studies also deal with other industries than those quoted in the text above.

[22] See in particular (Monteverde, Teece, 1982; Globerman, Schwindt, 1986; Sachwald, 1990, 1993; Hennart, 1991a).

learns about a particular national environment, it may progressively reconsider its need for a local partner. There are a number of examples of cooperative entries on foreign markets by Japanese firms which have ended in total control, in total internalization.[23]

The eclectic paradigm assumes the need for ownership advantages as a determinant of internationalization, but does not claim to analyse the source of this advantage. The same remark applies to the location advantage. As a result, the paradigm should be all the more powerful once it is set within a sectoral analysis. By taking such a perspective, one can propose a more integrated interpretation of international production. As for the analysis of competitiveness, there are relationships between firms' strategies, which result from the confrontation of objectives and resources, the sectoral competitive game and national characteristics.[24] The objective of the sectoral perspective is to underline the fact that the competitive game can generate pressures to multinationalization (Cantwell 1991).

A sectoral perspective, by identifying the source of ownership advantages and the relationships between firms within an industry, can also explain the interactions between different decisions to produce abroad. This is particularly important in the case of Japanese firms given their specific organization of production.[25] The general idea is that if in the country of origin a firm has a close relationship with a supplier, which may be a component of its ownership advantage, it will need to keep that supplier abroad. And in certain conditions that may mean that the supplier also ventures to produce abroad. In such a case, the observation that numerous companies set production units in a given country or region over a short period of time should not be interpreted along the market power line,[26] but take into account organizational constraints. A sectoral perspective can also account for the fact that a firm may invest abroad without a clear competitive advantage over the local competitors; the motivation is then mostly resource oriented.

---

[23] See the sectoral chapters and section 2.3 below.

[24] On this point for the analysis of competitiveness, see in particular (Porter 1990; Sachwald 1994).

[25] See below (section 2.2 and 2.3), and also in other chapters from this volume.

[26] The market power interpretation considers that the decision to produce abroad is motivated by the objective of maintaining or enhancing market power. See in particular (Hymer 1976; Knickerbocker 1973) and also (Vernon 1966).

2.2   JAPANESE FIRMS' DECISIONS TO LOCATE ABROAD

This section relies on various types of empirical results and more particularly on surveys regarding Japanese firms' motivations to develop production in Europe in order to examine the relevance of the analytical framework discussed above. Three types of survey have been used: five of the periodical surveys on Japanese manufacturing in Europe by the Japan External Trade Organization (JETRO), the survey conducted by J. Dunning in 1986 and the survey conducted by Neil Hood in 1990.

The survey conducted by Dunning (1986) has been conceived to assess the role of the determinants which are identified by the eclectic paradigm (ownership advantages, location advantages and internalization advantages). Surveys from the JETRO (1983, 1988, 1990, 1991, 1992) focus on location factors, and, to some extent, on the internalization question. The survey by N. Hood (1992) focuses on the process of the location decision itself. These surveys did not use the same sample or methodology and their results are not directly comparable.[27] Moreover, as it is generally the case and as the discussion below shows, the interpretation of firms' answers to questionnaires should be cautious.[28]

Dunning classifies the reasons for firms to invest abroad according to the categories of the eclectic paradigm. The objective here is not to propose another list, but rather to rank the actual motivations used in the surveys. However, it seems important to underline that the different forms of protectionism, including tariff and non-tariff barriers, are considered as a source of location advantages for the country or region which implements them. Dunning lists the avoidance of government intervention such as quotas and tariffs under the internalization advantages heading,[29] while artificial barriers to trade and investment incentives are listed as location specific variables. Barriers to trade are certainly market imperfections, but they constitute an incentive for location in the country which enforces them rather than an incentive to internalize or choose a specific type of transaction. Protectionist measures induce barrier jumping production units, but

---

[27] The main characteristics of the surveys and some results are explained in the appendix to this chapter. For a comparison between the surveys by JETRO and other sources, see the general appendix.

[28] In the case of surveys on Japanese investment in Europe, (Thomsen, Nicolaides 1991) also mentions this problem.

[29] (Dunning, 1986) Chapter 3, page 35.

the type of control over these units is not determined by the measures themselves.[30]

The decision of suppliers to produce abroad in order to follow their clients has been mentioned above as a characteristic of the recent Japanese wave of direct investment. How should these new production units be analyzed according to the determinants proposed by the eclectic paradigm? The supplier possesses competitive advantages, part of which rests on its relationship with its client.[31] Given the set of physical, organizational and information constraints, the close relationships between the two firms may be endangered by the installation of the client abroad, in which case the supplier is induced to follow and also locate abroad.The location factor is linked to the fact that the client decides to produce abroad. Finally, the internalization factor can largely be analyzed as in other cases. Indeed, the supplier needs to produce close to its client, which does not mean that it will necessarily choose a specific mode of internalization. It can set a greenfield production unit, but can also organize a joint venture.

2.2.1   The Motivations to Produce in Europe

General results

Dunning (1986) has asked 24 Japanese manufacturing affiliates in the UK to assess their competitive advantages vis-à-vis their uninational competitors. The three items which appear as the most decisive according to this survey[32] are: product quality and reliability (1), process technology (2) and keeping the delivery dates (3). It should be noticed that some of the items proposed to firms in the survey are interdependent, and possibly redundant. For example, the two items which arrive in 4th position are "management philosophy" (which can be related to process technology or work organization which also both score high as ownership advantages) and favored access to R&D. Dunning (1986) concludes that it is the package of these advantages which "most marks off Japanese affiliates from their UK competitors" (p. 38). Indeed, the production system and

---

[30] See below and the sectoral chapters.

[31] Details and examples are provided in Chapters 3, 4 and 5.

[32] See the Appendix for the method and results.

the organization of the production units and of the relationships with suppliers have been identified as the strongest competitive advantage of Japanese companies by detailed studies.

Dunning (1986) deals with the location advantages in two steps. He firstly shows that investment in the UK was largely aimed at supplying European markets (and first the UK), even though the firms had not established an integrated network in Europe at the beginning of the 1980s. As a second step, Dunning asked his sample of firms to assess the importance of the location advantages of the UK vis-à-vis Japan and vis-à-vis other European countries.[33] The two most important factors for choosing to locate in the UK (as opposed to Japan) were the existence of import duties or controls (1) and transport cost of finished products to customers (2). It should be noticed that the importance of protectionist variables depends on the sectors to which firms belong (this question is dealt with below in more details). The survey shows that Japanese affiliates considered that UK production costs were unfavorable as compared with Japan. They also have a poor view of British "component supplies".

The JETRO does not refer to any specific theoretical framework in order to conduct its periodical surveys on Japanese manufacturing units in Europe. Moreover, the surveys consider both motivations and determinants of the decision to produce in Europe (to use the distinction made above in section 1). Finally, the format of the surveys and the questions asked to firms vary from one survey to the other. This presentation of the results from different surveys deals with the questions which are relevant to the decision of location and tries to organize the items which appear in the surveys according to the categories of the eclectic paradigm.

In the 1983 survey, the question of the motives and purposes of incorporation in Europe proposes a set of possible answers out of which each firm is invited to select 3 at most. They are ordered in large categories: factor cost saving investment, export substitution investment,[34] investments to avoid trade friction, investments to acquire information, and others.[35]

---

[33] This second point is discussed below.

[34] The JETRO mentions that export substitution is equivalent to the willingness to develop new markets, which tends to show that the development of these new markets cannot be done through exports.

[35] See the Appendix for a complete list of the items within the broad categories used in Table 1.

Table 1: Motives and Purposes of Incorporation in Europe According to the 1983 JETRO Survey

	Type of motive												
	Cost saving			Export substitution			Trade frictions			Acquisition of infor'tion			Others	Number of firms*
Order°	1	2	3	1	2	3	1	2	3	1	2	3	–	
Answers	8	19	14	62	21	2	8	20	10	2	13	30	24	105
In % of the total answers	3	8	6	27	9	1	3	8	4	1	5	13	10	–

° Firms were asked to order their responses according to their importance; the columns 1, 2 and 3 correspond to this ordering. For example the figure in each column "1" is the number of answers which designate this type of factor as the most determinant.

* Number of firms which answered this question of the survey. The questionnaire had been sent to the 157 Japanese affiliates which the JETRO had identified (defined as those with at least 5% Japanese capital participation).

Source: (JETRO 1983)

Table 1 shows that the most important set of motivations for Japanese firms to start production in Europe is the substitution to exports (also called the development of markets). This category is actually quite diverse and is difficult to interpret within the theoretical framework. Indeed, some of the items which it contains are not correctly formulated in this respect. One item refers to the development of local markets and another to the development of markets in other European countries, a third one to recommendations from the company's importer in Europe (see the appendix to the chapter). Moreover one item from this category refers to import duties while there is another large category dealing with trade frictions, so that it is impossible to have a clear idea of the role of protectionist measures and pressures on Japanese production units in Europe. According to Table 1 protectionist pressures come fourth in the ranking of motives for investing in Europe, the second category being production factors and the third the acquisition of information. It should be noted that this ranking changes when only the first one or two motives (columns 1 and 2) are taken into account. In particular, protectionist pressures appear as relatively more important.

Table 2: Motivations for Starting Production in Europe, According to the 1988 JETRO Survey.

| | Motivations° | | | | | | | | | |
	1	2	3	4	5	6	7	8	9	10
Total	82	54	50	23	23	21	21	19	9	22
As a % of answers*	26	15	14	6	6	6	6	5	2	6

° The list of motives is as follows: 1. Development of a new market 2. Meet the diversified needs of consumers 3. Avoid trade friction 4. Build up overseas market information capabilities 5. Maintain the orders from sales subsidiaries or the parent company 6. Avoid the risk of exchange rate fluctuations 7. Reducing production cost 8. Preferential tax treatment 9. Acquisition of cheap raw materials 10. Other.

* The total number of answers is 359 due to the possibility of multiple (up to 3) choices.

Source: (JETRO 1988)

The 1988 JETRO survey asked 282 firms[36] what their motivations had been for starting to produce in Europe. Again firms could choose up to 3 answers in a list of motives. Table 2 summarizes the answers to this question.

The most important category is the development of new markets. However, as with the 1983 survey, it is possible that these markets are to some extent simply substitutes for exports. The second most important motivation is the objective to meet the diversified consumer needs. This type of motivation was already important in the previous survey; it belonged to the acquisition of information category. A number of analyses have shown that firms now need to produce in foreign markets to be able to be follow closely and understand consumer needs. This evolution is largely due to the combined effects of product differenciation and rapid innovation. The third most important motivation is the desire to avoid trade frictions. Trade frictions may have become more important as motivations to sct up production units in Europe. They come third in the 1988 survey instead of fourth in 1983.[37] However, as noted above, the trade friction motives

[36] The questionnaire had been sent to 282 Japanese affiliates with at least 10% Japanese participation in the capital.

[37] Even if the two motivations relating to cost reductions (no. 2 and 4) are added for the 1988 survey.

are not clearly identified since they appear at least in two items (1 and 3 in the 1988 survey).

The 1990 JETRO survey on Japanese manufacturing enterprises in Europe proposed as many as 18 different motives to firms. One item mentions the increase in economic activity resulting from the EC's integration. This accounts for a possible "Single market effect" which may not have been perceived in 1987 when the previous survey (JETRO 1988)[38] was conducted. An other item mentions the prospective developments due to the European Economic Space and the liberalization of East European markets. An important new motivation also appears: direct investment in Europe as part of a glob-alization strategy. With respect to the analytical framework discussed above, this motivation is vague and cannot be classified according to the theoretical framework presented above. This constitutes a serious problem since this motivation gets the highest score in the 1990 survey. Moreover, a number of other items can be considered as constituents or consequences of a globalization strategy (consumer needs, European R&D...).

Table 3 gives the results of this survey by grouping together the motivations which appear very similar in the JETRO survey — the appendix to this chapter gives the complete list of these motivations and explains the relationship between them and the categories ap-pearing in Table 3. The total number of valid answers was 755 from 270 firms, while the questionnaire had been sent to 529 firms (plural answers were allowed).

The second most important category pertains to protectionist mea-sures of some sort. The fact that this type of motivation ranks higher than in previous surveys may be due to the process of the single market, which has elicited worries about a possible "Fortress Europe". The third category is the desire to supply the European markets from local production. As mentioned with the previous surveys, this category can hardly be used to analyze the motivations for producing in Europe. The fourth category refers to the need to be close to the market so as to satisfy differentiated needs (it is thus related to globalization strategies).The other categories are much less important. In this respect, one can notice that production costs have a diminishing influence.

The 1992 JETRO survey, does not include the globalization moti-vation anymore, and the objective of shifting from exports to local

---

[38] This paper does not review all the JETRO surveys.

Table 3:   Motives of Advance into Europe according to the 1990 JETRO Survey

| | Motivations° | | | | | | | | | | |
	1	2	3	4	5	6	7	8	9	10	11
Total 90	178	136	130	100	41	41	36	27	26	12	28
As a % of answers*	23	18	17	13	5	5	5	4	3	2	4

° The list of motives is as follows: 1. As a step towards a globalization strategy 2. To avoid trade restrictions and anti-dumping regulations, which are perceived as rising with EC's integration 3. To shift from exports to local production to meet increased demand (in particular due to European integration) 4. To meet consumer needs, including the use of European designs 5. To supply Japanese firms in Europe 6. Investment incentives 7. To reduce production costs 8. To avoid exchange rate fluctuations risks 9. To carry out R&D in Europe 10. To benefit from the presence of the parent company in Europe 11. Other.

* The total number of answers is 755 due to the possibility of multiple (up to 3) choices.

Source: (JETRO 1990)

Table 4:   Motives of Advance into Europe according to the 1992 JETRO Survey

	1	2	3	4	5	6	7	8	9	10
Total 92	331	251	166	63	55	47	41	38	26	79
As a % of answers*	30	23	15	6	5	4	4	3	2	7

° The list of motives is as follows: 1. To shift from exports to local production to meet increased demand (in particular due to European integration and East European markets) 2. To avoid trade restrictions and anti-dumping regulations, which are perceived as rising with EC's integration 3. To meet consumer needs, including the use of European designs 4. To supply affiliates of Japanese firms in Europe 5. Investment incentives 6. To carry out R&D in Europe 7. To reduce production costs 8. To benefit from the presence of the parent company in Europe 9.To avoid exchange rate fluctuations risks 10. Other.

* The total number of answers is 1097 due to the possibility of multiple (up to 3) choices.

Source: (JETRO 1992)

production appears as the first motivation. Table 4 summarizes the results of the survey by grouping the answers proposed in the survey into 10 categories. The appendix to this chapter lists all the answers proposed by the survey and the 10 groupings which appear in Table 4.

Table 4 shows that the avoidance of trade frictions of various sorts remains a strong motivation for Japanese firms. Thus, as in previous surveys, it appears that access to European markets which are considered particularly attractive, constitutes the foremost motivation for Japanese investment. The willingness to answer the needs of the European consumers by producing locally is also confirmed as an important motivation. A larger number of affiliates mention the supply of Japanese firms in Europe as a determinant of their own decision (from 45 to 63, Tables 3 and 4); the share of this factors grows thus from 5 to 6% total. The role of investment incentives remains stable (5% of the total number of answers). The desire to carry out R&D in Europe becomes more important; it represents 4% of the answers, as opposed to 2% in 1990; moreover, in 1992, this motivation has become more important than costs. Since the beginning of the 1980s, the cost motivation has become less and less important as has the avoidance of exchange rate fluctuations.

2.2.2   Sectoral Differences

Dunning (1986) has divided his sample of firms into two groups in order to identify firms from the electronic sectors.[39] Motivations to set up production units in Europe differ significantly between the two groups.

In the electronic industries, the UK has been considered primarily as a point of entry to European markets, which is not the case for the other industrial sectors where the first objective was to supply the UK. The most striking difference is in the factors influencing choice of location in Europe. For the electronic industries, protectionism appears strongly as the first motivation. Indeed, the two motivations scoring the highest in the survey are non-tariff barriers (first) and import duties and controls (second). The third motivation relates to exchange rates. For other industries, the most important motivation was transport costs. Then came import duties and control as well as exchange rates (with the same score). Dealing with these sectoral

---

[39] See the Appendix on the presentation of the survey.

Table 5: Sectoral Distribution[1] of the Motivations for Starting Production in Europe, according to the 1988 JETRO Survey

| | Motivations[°] | | | | | | | | | | Number |
	1	2	3	4	5	6	7	8	9	10	of answers
Chemicals &											
pharmaceuticals	9	4	1	2	0	2	3	6	4	4	35
Metal products	5	4	2	1	0	4	1	2	0	1	21
General machinery	10	8	7	3	0	2	2	0	1	1	33
Electronics &											
electrical equipment	20	14	25	6	12	5	6	5	0	4	98
Transport machinery	8	4	5	0	4	3	2	0	1	4	31
Precision machinery	4	3	5	2	3	2·	0	0	0	1	20
Total by type	82	54	50	23	23	21	21	19	9	22	324
As a % of											
total answers*	25	17	15	7	7	6	6	6	3	6	–

[1] Only the sectors with more than 10 Japanese affiliates in Europe have been retained in this table.

[°] The list of motives is as follows: 1. Development of a new market 2. Meet the diversified needs of consumers 3. Avoid trade friction 4. Build up overseas market information capabilities 5. Maintain the orders from sales subsidiaries or the parent company 6. Avoid the risk of exchange rate fluctuations 7. Reducing production cost 8. Preferential tax treatment 9. Acquisition of cheap raw materials 10. Other.

* The total number of answers is 324 due to the possibility of multiple (up to 3) choices.

Source: (JETRO 1988)

differences, one should recall that when this survey was conducted (end of 1983 to mid-1984), there was no major Japanese investment in the British automobile industry.

Table 5 presents the sectoral distribution of results from the 1988 JETRO survey with respect to the motivations for starting to produce in Europe. It shows that the most important motivations vary across sectors. As opposed to other sectors for which the development of a new market is the first motivation, the electronics and electrical equipment sector exhibit a specific behavior. For them, the most important motivation is to avoid trade frictions with the development of a new market coming in second position. This is a very important result given

Table 6: Sectoral Distribution[1] of the Motivations for Starting Production in Europe, according to the 1992 JETRO Survey, in % of the Total Number of Answers

	No of firms[3]	Motivations[2]									
		1	2	3	4	5	6	7	8	9	10
Electronics and electrical equip.[4]	134	27	32	14	6	6	2	2	4	2	4
Chemicals & pharmaceuticals	58	38	13	10	7	9	4	6	2	4	7
Transport machinery[4]	49	28	22	13	10	5	10	5	4	5	6
General machinery	31	29	33	13	3	1	2	2	3	1	11
Metal products	24	46	18	6	8	3	1	1	1	8	6
Precision machinery	13	42	10	27	2	0	0	5	0	5	7

[1] Only the sectors with more than 10 Japanese affiliates in Europe have been retained in this table.

[2] The list of motives is as follows: 1. To shift from exports to local production to meet increased demand (in particular due to European integration and East European markets) 2. To avoid trade restrictions and anti-dumping regulations, which are perceived as rising with EC's integration 3. To meet consumer needs, including the use of European designs 4. To supply affiliates of Japanese firms in Europe 5. Investment incentives 6. To carry out R&D in Europe 7. Reducing production cost 8. Avoid exchange rate fluctuations risks 9. To benefit from the presence of the parent company in Europe 10. Other.

[3] Number of firms which have answered to the question. The total number of answers is higher due to the possibility of multiple (up to 3) choices.

[4] Including parts and components.

Source: (JETRO 1992b)

the importance of the electronic sector with respect to Japanese investments in Europe. The desire to avoid trade frictions comes as the second motivation in the transport equipment sector and third for general machinery.

The second most important motivation which was identified on the total sample (Table 2), to meet the diversified needs of consumers, comes second only for the machinery sectors. It comes third for chemicals, electronics and transport machinery. Cost considerations are important only for the chemical sector.

Table 6 gives the sectoral distribution for the 1992 survey by using the same groupings as Table 4 above in order to clarify the types of motives (see the appendix for details).

Table 6 shows that the distinction between the motives for investment according to industries persists. The demand factor is the first
one for the majority of industries; it is reinforced by the expectations
of further integration within Europe. However, protectionist pressures
constitute the first motivation for electronics and electrical industries
as well as for general machinery. They also come second in the case
of transport machinery, chemicals and metal products. The need to be
close to the European customer is the second motivation in the case of
precision machinery, but appears in third position for most the other
sectors.

If calculations are made for assembly industries on the one hand
and component industries on the other, results are clearly different.[40]
Protectionism is the first motivation for assembly industries, while it
comes second for parts and components sectors (behind the expansion
of demand). Moreover, for the latter, the supply of Japanese firms in
Europe represent 12% of the answers (as opposed to 2% for assembly
industries). The development of Japanese foreign production units
has thus led to an evolution of the motivations; since the end of the
1980s, a number of new production units have been motivated by the
operation of Japanese firms in Europe. This is more particularly the
case for suppliers which delocalize part of their production in order to
stay close to their clients.

2.2.3　*The Choice of a Particular European Country*

In his survey, Dunning (1986) asked the firms to assess the relative
advantage of the UK over other European countries to decide upon
location.[41] The UK scores especially well for environmental factors,
and within this category, particularly for language and cultural factors;
on the contrary, technological and educational infrastructures score
badly. The next best score is that of government policies affecting
FDI. More precisely, the UK is considered as having largely better
policies vis-à-vis foreign direct investment than the other European
countries. The UK scores well on the relative cost of labor, but quite
badly on industrial relations and productivity. Finally, it benefits from
an aggregation effect; a number of companies set up production in the

---

[40] The calculations are not reported here, they are made from Table III-1 in (JETRO
1992).

[41] This is done through a system of notation going from −5 to +5.

Table 7: Reasons[1] Determining the Choice of a Country within Europe, According to the 1991 JETRO Survey

Country	1	2	3	4	5	6	7	8	9	10	11	12	13	Total
UK	38	21	38	23	24	50	18	35	27	16	9	4	24	327
France	6	10	11	4	4	2	3	8	3	2	0	6	20	79
Germany	23	26	17	9	18	7	6	19	0	7	11	5	11	159
Netherlands	9	1	16	2	6	13	1	5	0	4	1	2	2	62
Belgium	4	1	9	0	5	7	1	7	1	3	2	1	6	47
Ireland	1	0	2	1	0	12	0	9	3	12	0	0	5	45
Spain	6	13	7	8	1	2	2	7	11	8	0	3	8	76
Italy	1	7	2	3	1	1	0	2	2	2	1	2	5	29
Portugal	0	0	2	0	0	1	0	2	7	4	0	1	3	20
Total[2]	93	80	109	51	62	99	31	99	56	62	24	27	87	880

Area

	1	2	3	4	5	6	7	8	9	10	11	12	13	Total
Major 3 countries	67	57	66	36	46	59	27	62	30	25	20	15	55	565
South Europe[3]	7	20	13	11	2	5	2	11	21	15	1	7	17	132
North Europe[4]	2	1	3	1	1	13	0	10	4	13	0	0	6	54

[1] The list of reasons is as follows: 1. Infrastructure 2. Large domestic market 3. Favorable geographical conditions for distribution 4. Supporting industries for supply of components 5. Good traffic networks 6. English speaking people can be employed as managers 7. Presence of other Japanese manufacturers in the projected site of business 8. Good relative quality of labor 9. Low cost of labor 10. Pro-Japanese sentiment 11. Sending children to Japanese schools matters little 12. Raw materials can be found easily at favorable cost 13. Other

[2] Total number of answers by 308 companies from all Europe, i.e including the countries where less thant 10 firms have answered (Greece, Norway...).

[3] Italy, Spain, Greece, Portugal

[4] Finland, Norway, Sweden, Denmark, Ireland

Source: (JETRO 1991)

country in order to be next to other Japanese firms which have already invested there.

JETRO surveys deal with this question of the choice of a particular European country differently. They ask firms to choose two or more of the 13 possible reasons for selecting specific European countries. Table 7 presents a summary of these results for 1991; it does not reproduce the results for the European countries for which less than 10 firms answered.

The reason which is the most frequently mentioned is the good geographical conditions for physical distribution, which seems to indicate that production is aimed at the European markets in general. The possibility of employing English-speaking managers and the quality of labor come second. Infrastructures, which are covered by items 1 and 5, are also considered very important, and even more so in the case of the 3 major countries of investment. Generally, the factors which are considered as the most important in a given country reflect the location advantages of that country. For example, low labor costs constitute the first reason to invest in Southern Europe. These rankings vary according to the type of industry. For example, the geographical distribution factor is very important for components and chemicals, but for processing and assembly industries, the first factor is the large size of the domestic market.

Neil Hood (1992) has conducted a series of interviews with senior executives at 22 Japanese manufacturing plants throughout the UK in order to trace the location decision processes. The interviews were conducted during the second half of 1990. Hood concludes that the decision process lasts for up to 5 years and is divided into three phases.The initial impulse has generally been given by the European sales office, which had to overcome the resistance of the Japanese production engineers. According to the survey the protectionist pressures were the best argument in this respect.

The discussion phase involves lengthy information collecting work. The question of the market size is crucial. In this respect, it should be noted that 18 of the firms surveyed were in the electronic sectors.[42] The presence of Japanese affiliates in the country is also important because it reduces the uncertainties about the environment. The study revealed that some countries, such as the Netherlands and Ireland, are included in the preliminary data collection phase because of the visibility which they have acquired through marketing efforts.

The decision phase typically lasts for 1 or 2 years and is conducted by a project team of between 3 and 10 people. Most of the firms in the sample had already developed a preference for the UK by the beginning of this phase; but the feasibility team has to confirm this preference. The dominant issues which have been identified confirm the results of other studies: English language, labor supply

---

[42] For which market size is more important, see above.

and costs, supportive attitude by the Government. The difference with the other surveys examined above is the absence of factors related to infrastructures and transport conditions possibly because these had been considered in the previous phase.

The final stage of the process involves the micro-level examination of the selected regions, which is not considered here. Let us just say that at this stage, the most important considerations relate to the actual, daily working of the production unit and to the facilities available to the personnel in the neighborhood.

2.3   THE CHOICE OF THE TYPE OF TRANSACTION

As recalled above (section 2.1.2), firms can choose several modes of organization in order to produce abroad. There are four main modes of entry by which a firm can set up a production unit in a foreign country. The most obvious solution is to invest in a greenfield unit, that is to say, to create a new unit of production (by internal growth and not by acquisition). The second solution is to buy a firm in the foreign country. The third solution is the joint venture. The joint venture can either create a new unit or result from the reorganization of the control of an existing one. Partners of the foreign firm in joint ventures are often local firms, but two or several firms may also team up in order to set up a production unit abroad. Finally, a foreign company can resort to various sorts of cooperative agreements, which may include some sort of capital participation.

The type of investment chosen in order to produce in a foreign country depends on two broad categories of factors: transaction cost considerations, as explained in section 1 and the availability of partners when they are necessary (cooperation or acquisition). The transaction cost approach analyzes the trade-off between the need to control operations and the fact that local partners can facilitate the access to additional resources. In general, multinational firms tend to prefer full control over their foreign subsidiaries. It is often the case because their ownership advantage includes intangible assets and knowledge which is difficult to trade, or even through adequate contracts.

Japanese subsidiaries in industrial countries are mostly under Japanese control. Table 8 shows that both in Europe and in the United States, Japanese firms own more than 50% of the capital of their foreign subsidiaries in more than 90% of the cases. Joint ventures and

Table 8: Types of Investment by Japanese Firms in Different Regions, in % of the Number of Firms

Japanese part in the capital	United States	EC	Europe	NIES	ASEAN
Less than 25%	3.2	1.2	1.7	1.7	5.4
(25%, 50%)	5.6	8.2	8.8	13.7	46.8
(50%, 100%)	11.4	13.2	13.3	22.2	26.9
100%	79.8	77.4	76.6	51.6	21.0

Source: (MITI 1992)

partial control are much more substantial in NIES, and even more so in ASEAN countries, where host countries frequently insist on a partial domestic control and various transfers from the multinational company. The relatively higher importance of joint ventures for Japanese production units abroad is confirmed by the survey of the EXIM bank of Japan (Tejima 1992).

JETRO classifies the Japanese production units in Europe into 4 categories: wholly owned, M&A, joint ventures with local interests and capital participation. Wholly owned subsidiaries and M&A imply control over the firm and these two categories represent nearly 70% of the European subsidiaries (JETRO 1991, 1992). Joint ventures with local interests represent 24.6% of the European Japanese units. This figure is comparable with the data from the MITI where the Japanese participation is between 25 and 100% (Table 8).

According to Dunning (1986), there are two main reasons for Japanese firms to prefer an equity investment rather than a licensing agreement[43] to produce in the UK: the difficulty of guaranteeing quality control (1) and the need to maintain full product, process and market flexibility (2). This set of reasons for internalization is reinforced by the fact that other related variables also score high in that survey. It is the case in particular of the "company policy to prefer 100% equity ownership". It is also the case for the need to control distribution outlets. Indeed, one of the traditional reasons for this control is to check the quality of the services delivered by the distribution network.

---

[43] Dunning (1986) labels as "licensing arrangement" all forms of non-equity participation.

Japanese firms have traditionally not been keen on acquisitions abroad. This attitute could be because mergers and acquisitions are quite rare in Japan itself. However, with respect to foreign operations, the fact that Japanese firms aimed at transfering their specific production system and organization has constituted a strong hindrance. Indeed when a firm acquires another, it has to transform the practices of the acquired units of production, which may prove much more difficult than building greenfield units and hiring fresh manpower especially since the acquired units may be poor performers. These problems are quite general with respect to acquisitions and in the case of foreign operations, and they are compounded with cultural problems. The acquisition of Firestone by Bridgestone offers a good illustration of these problems. At the beginning of the 1980s, Bridgestone had hesitated to acquire the American tyre company which had experienced difficulties because it feared these traditional problems. But Bridgestone nevertheless bought Firestone in 1988... and has had a lot of problems in trying to reform the firm's practices (Emmott 1992).

The attitude of Japanese companies with respect to acquisitions has been evolving and they are now more favorable to this solution (HEC 1990). They may have been influenced by the fact that these operations are frequent in the countries in which they have settled. Overall, this development is quite logical as they acquire more experience in managing international operations and in adapting to different national environments. Returning to the above example, it seems that Bridgestone's lack of confidence in its capability to impose its managing practices and its production system has slowed down the process of decision.

J-F. Hennart (1991a) has investigated the reasons for the propensity of Japanese firms to enter the United States with wholly owned units as opposed to joint ventures.[44] His results *"suggest that the degree of ownership taken by Japanese manufacturing investors in their American subsidiaries is driven by the same general factors that determine the choices made by their European counterparts"*. In particular, transaction cost analysis seems to be relevant. The influence of four sets of factors is particularly well supported by the econometric test. The first two sets relate to the complementary assets and information which the

---

[44] He defines joint ventures as being the cases where the Japanese parent company owns between 5 and 95% of the capital of the American subsidiary. This a quite wide definition since control is often guaranteed at a much lower level.

firm needs in order to succeed in its ventures. Firstly, the fact that the affiliate is in a different industry than the parent increases the probability of a joint venture, as opposed to full ownership. Secondly, the probability of joint venture increases when the parent has little experience in international operations.[45] The other factors depend on the characteristics of the industry. Joint ventures are more likely in natural resource intensive industries and in low growth industries. In the first case, foreign firms can use joint ventures to obtain inputs more easily. In the second case, joint ventures may be required due to overcapacities.

These results correspond to those obtained by other authors with respect to the attitudes of American or European multinational firms. The lack of experience in international operations or in a particular country tends to tilt the balance in favor of joint venture since the need for local knowledge and cooperation is more acute. Several studies have also shown that joint ventures are quite often used in natural resources based industries (Caves, 1982; Stuckey, 1983). This is due in particular to the need for high and risky investment. Actually, when dealing with the type of operation chosen by multinational companies, one has to allow for interactions with both the type of industry and the characteristics of the host country. Indeed, natural resource based activities are often located in developing countries, where governments tend to insist on some local control of international operations. In the 1970s, Japanese firms appeared more prone to joint ventures than American firms (Caves, 1982), but one should recall that Japanese firms' foreign operations were heavily geared to resource based industries and were mostly located in developing countries at that time.

The role of sectoral characteristics also clearly appears in the case of Japanese direct investment in Europe. According to Dunning's survey (1986), the most important determinant in the choice for an equity investment is the difficulty of guaranteeing quality control for both the group of electronic industries and for the second group. However, the score of this motivation is significantly higher for the electronic sectors. For them, the second most important motivation is the need to maintain full product, process or market flexibility. For other industries company specific policy to prefer 100% equity ranks second (the third for firms from group 1) and the difficulty of enforcing

---

[45] Proxied by the number of years since the establishment of the Japanese parent's first U.S subsidiary.

Table 9: Distribution of the Japanese Firms in Europe According to the Type of Investment

	Internal investment & full control	Acquisition	Joint venture with local interests	Capital partici- pation	Total (number of firms)[1]
Processing and assembly	56.6	18.6	19.4	5.4	129
Electronic & electric appliances	69.6	10.1	15.9	4.3	69
Transport equipment	28.6	14.3	57.1	0.0	14
General machinery	34.4	37.5	18.8	9.4	32
Precision machinery	71.4	21.4	0.0	7.1	14
Parts & components	54.4	14.6	22.3	4.9	103
Chemicals	37.1	22.6	33.9	4.8	62
Raw materials	23.9	30.7	36.4	6.8	88
Design and R&D centers	69.6	4.3	17.4	0.0	23
Total[2]	47.6	20.0	24.9	5.2	441

[1] Apart from the types mentioned in the table, there are 10 units of other types.

[2] Apart from the sectors mentioned in the table, there are 36 firms in other sectors.

Source: (JETRO 1992b)

patent and trade mark rights also appears as one of the most important motivations. Table 9 shows that more recent data confirm the influence of the sectoral characteristics.

The propensity to use joint ventures is clearly higher for raw materials and even for chemicals than for processing and assembly industries. Within the latter, transport equipment shows a high proportion of joint ventures. This should be related to the geographical distribution of the units. According to the general data collected by JETRO (1992, Table 1–2), 50% of the production units of this sector are located in Southern Europe, where there is a general tendency towards joint ventures.[46] Moreover, there may be a problem of insufficient scale in the case of

---

[46] 52.3% of the production units are joint ventures in Southern Europe (JETRO 1992a, Table 2–6).

a number of autocomponent units.[47] At the opposite, electronic and electric sectors exhibits a low proportion of joint ventures (Table 9). Table 9 also shows that there are sectoral differences in the propensity to acquire companies. This should be related in particular to the possibility of overcapacity and thus to the rate of growth of the sector. The two sectors in which the rate of acquisition is the highest are general machinery and raw materials.

The different results on the motivations of Japanese foreign multi-nationals tend to show that they react according to the same lines as their American and European counterparts. In particular, the determinants which are identified by the eclectic paradigm are valid for Japanese firms. Japanese firms also react in conformity to transaction cost analysis with respect to the choice of the mode of entry. But Japanese multinationals show specific features with respect to the role of marketing and research expenditures in the decision to set up production abroad.

Foreign direct investment has often been related to the role of marketing and research expenditures because it is supposed to occur for sophisticated and innovative products. It was the case in particular for American multinationals, which have been the typical cases of application for the product cycle model.[48] Both goodwill and innovation are difficult to trade on markets because they largely constitute an accumulation of intangible assets (Teece 1981). Empirical studies show that high marketing or research investment tend to favor full control of foreign units as opposed to joint ventures.[49] The importance of advertising expenditure does not seem to influence the occurence of Japanese foreign direct investment in the United States (Drake, Caves 1992). It does not influence the choice between full control and joint venture either (Hennart 1991a). In both cases, it seems that the "cultural distance" between the United States and Japan would reverse the analysis in terms of goodwill and experience in managing advertising campains; the intangible assets resulting from high marketing expenditures by the parent company in Japan would not be transferable to Western countries.

The research factor is more difficult to interpret. According to an empirical analysis of Japan's share of foreign investment in the U.S over the period 1976–1986 (Drake, Caves 1992), research intensity (re-

---

[47] See Chapter 4 on the automobile industry.

[48] See above.

[49] See in particular (Caves, 1982; Porter, Fuller, 1986).

search outlays by industry) has had no measurable influence. However, the authors conclude that in the 1980s Japan's growing research efforts have probably come to have a positive influence on its investment in the United States. According to this analysis, the evolution would be quite logical since Japan has grown from an imitating country to an innovative country with high R&D outlays. J-F. Hennart (1991a) uses data on Japanese subsidiaries in the United States at the end of 1985 to examine the determinants of choice in favor of full control. According to his analysis, the Japanese parent's ratio of R&D expenditures to sales has no significant influence on this choice. This could be due to the fact that innovation is not an important source of ownership advantage for Japanese multinationals; Japanese firms would have relatively little innovation-related intangible assets to defend, which would explain that R&D is not a determinant in the choice in favor of fully owned subsidiaries. This explanation is compatible with the fact that the competitive advantages of Japanese firms are often located in the fields of production management. Another explanation relates to the fact that Japanese firms invest in the United States in part to secure access to technology.[50]

To summarize these results, it would appear that when Japanese multinational companies exhibit specific attitudes, these attitudes can largely be explained by differences in the sources of their competitive advantages.

2.4 COMPETITIVE ADVANTAGES AND FIRMS' STRATEGIES

The analysis of the competitive game in an industry complements the examination of the motivations of Japanese firms to invest in Europe. Such an approach confirms the relevance of the motivations proposed by the eclectic paradigm, but also contributes to the understanding of their development and their timing. In the case of Japanese direct investment, both in the United States and in Europe, the sectoral competitive game perspective is thus very useful to analyse the formation of the ownership advantages and the role of protectionist pressures. The sectoral perspective also quite naturally deals with all the motivations to delocalize production be it in the United States or in Europe.[51]

---

[50] On this point, see Chapters 5 and 7.

[51] In a recent paper, H. Yamawaki (1992) noted that little attention had been paid to possible strategic links between Japanese FDI in the US and in Europe.

This section draws on the sectoral chapters of this volume to discuss the importance of the competitive game perspective.[52]

2.4.1   *The automobile and electronic industries*

The sectoral picture is similar for the electrical and electronic equipment and in the transport equipment industries, which have received a large share Japanese investments.[53] Japanese firms are strongly competitive on a worldwide basis and have gained large market shares in foreign countries through exports. These inroads have triggered protectionist measures of various kinds, which have in turn been strong incentives to start production in the United States and in Europe.

Sectoral analyses of both the electronic and automobile industries have showed that the source of Japanese competitiveness rests on the production system. The superiority of the system is particularly obvious in assembly industries and where the product cycle is relatively short and rapid adaptation to the market is important. Productivity and adaptability to the market are crucial for consumer electronics and cars. In the case of electronic components, competitiveness rests on the exploitation of economies of scale and on the capability to be first mover for the successive generations of products. In all cases the high and consistent level of quality has been one of the major assets of Japanese firms. This ability to consistently achieve high levels of quality also results from the organization of the production system which goes beyond the firm itself[54] to include its relationships with its suppliers. These relationships are long term and demanding for both parties. They are not pure market transactions by which products are traded, but rather contractual relationships through which both products and knowledge are exchanged.

The competitiveness of the Japanese cars and electronic products largely result from organizational features which tend to be internalized, either within firms or within networks, usually centered on a core firm. Such an organization is not conducive to foreign production. Indeed, the main worry of the firm is its ability to replicate

---

[52] This section uses the conclusions of these chapters and the reader is referred to them for details and statistical data.

[53] See Chapter 1 (and Chapters 3 and 4) for detailed data.

[54] Where the specific characteristics of the Japanese system have to do with team work (assembly) and with simultaneous engineering (product development).

its production system in foreign countries where both the industrial structures and the work practices are quite different and hence, protectionist pressures have been the mightiest incentive to lead them to produce abroad. Otherwise, they would have retained their export strategy much longer.

The importance of protectionist pressures is also clear in the progressive increases in the level of local value added. Japanese firms have tended to locate in Europe the productions which were under threat; firstly the final assembly and then various components or operations.[55] Actually, the fears about the transplantability of the Japanese system were quite well-founded; estimates in the automobile industry for example have shown that, at least for a period, Japanese foreign production units are not as productive as the domestic ones.[56]

The localization of component production units is one way to increase the local content of final products. However, assembly industries tend to have lower local content ratios than manufacturing operations as a whole. This is quite logical given the characteristics of the Japanese production system which have been recalled above. Another route is to deal with local partners. In order to do so, transplants assist the local firms, in particular with technical and human support.[57] At the end of the 1980s, there has been a steady increase in the local content of Japanese production units in both the automobile and electronic sectors.[58] But, at the beginning of the 1990s, electronics remains the sector in which local supplies from the EC is the lowest (JETRO 1991).

The specific organization of the relationships between carmakers and their suppliers has led to a wave of direct investment in the United States by the latter, which have been following the former. It seems that these investments have been favored by the low competitiveness of the American automobile equipment sector, and in particular to quality problems. It is also due to the worries of the Japanese

---

[55] The Chapters (3 and 4) on the automobile industry and the electronic industry give the evolution of the protectionist pressures from the final product to the components or the process of production.

[56] Firms have worked at transplanting the production system, but they have had to adapt a number of its characteristics according to local conditions. See Chapter 4 on the automobile industry and on the management of Japanese multinational companies in this volume.

[57] See (JETRO 1988) and Chapter 4 on the automobile industry.

[58] See the sectoral chapters in this volume. The number of manufacturing subsidairies has increased dramatically in the electronic component sector (Chapter 3 on electronics, Tables 4, 11).

carmakers about the replication of their ownership advantage in a very different context. In Europe, investments from Japanese carmakers have not induced so many delocalizations from their suppliers. This is largely due to the fact that the European automobile equipment sector is more competitive. Moreover, numerous competitive firms are independent from the makers, while in the United States, carmakers have traditionally been more integrated. But one should also take into account the experience which the Japanese carmakers have gained in international operations over the 1980s. In this respect, the European investments benefit from the American experience.

2.4.2   The Chemical Industry

The sectoral analysis gives a different picture in the case of chemicals. Japanese production and sales units are also quite numerous in Europe, but they exhibit specific characteristics as compared with those which assemble electronic and transport equipment products. They tend to be older and/or linked to investments in other industries. Moreover, the ownership advantage is much more difficult to identify than in assembly industries. Actually, in a number of cases, it seems that investment has been triggered by the very weakness of the Japanese chemical industry.

The average age of Japanese chemical production units is higher than the overall average (all industrial sectors). A number had been set up during the 1970s with the objective to obtain raw materials at low costs (Nations Unies 1991). Indeed, the Japanese petrochemical industry has undergone a period of severe crisis after the oil shocks, which passed through the price of naphta.[59] Numerous more recent units have been set up to supply Japanese subsidiaries from other industries. This is particularly true of the units producing ink which can supply the owners of Japanese photocopiers and printers. This dependency upon other industries is due to the position of the chemical industry as a provider of intermediate products.

Europe offers a number of location advantages for chemical operations, but the Japanese firms do not exhibit any obvious ownership advantage. Actually, the Japanese chemical industry in general has a relatively weak competitive record. Moreover, Japanese firms tend to export less and to be less internationalized than their competitors.

---

[59] See Chapter 5 on the chemical industry in this volume.

There is no general ownership advantage, be it for chemicals or for pharmaceuticals, even if there are exceptions and some Japanese firms aim at becoming global competitors.

European investment from Japanese chemical companies is not explained well by the different theories of foreign production. Instead we should take into account the evolution of the sectoral competitive game and in particular the high degree of internationalization. Chapter 4 on the chemical industry claims that the high degree of internationalization of the American and European firms, and in particular their presence in Japan, constituted an incentive for Japanese firms to set up foreign production units. The pharmaceutical industry is becoming globalized, in particular because the very high costs of R&D require world markets. In such a context, all firms try to have their products distributed world wide.

One of the indicators of the high degree of internationalization of the chemical industry is the existence of numerous delocalized R&D units. Some of these research units are a result of the need to adapt products to market demand and local regulations. But others aim at getting or staying in contact with research in the different technologically advanced areas. In this context, some Japanese units in Europe and the United States can be interpreted as a strategic move to access specific competitive resources.

2.5   CONCLUSION

The experience of Japanese firms in Europe generally supports the relevance of the general determinants of the decision to set up foreign production abroad. This chapter has shown that the analysis of the sectoral competitive game offers an interesting complement. It enables us to deal with a number of important issues which are related to foreign production. Firstly, the development of the competitive advantage, secondly, the question of the evolution of foreign production once a firm has become international, and finally, the influence of the degree of internationalization of the sector.

The assembly industries, which represent the majority of Japanese manufacturing units in Europe, clearly show the combination of the different types of determinants which the eclectic paradigm has identified. The Japanese firms have a strong ownership advantage in terms of production and product management. Protectionist measures and pressures have threatened the possibility to exploit this advantage through exports and have constituted strong location advantages, leading to production in the United States and Europe. Finally, the nature of the ownership advantage which is linked to the organization of the production system explains that the first choice of the Japanese firms has been to look for a relatively high degree of internalization. In a number of cases, this tendency has been countered either by risk considerations or local institutional constraints, which explain a number of joint ventures.

Once the first foreign production unit has been set up, the process of decision is modified. This is due to learning processes within the firm and to spillovers within industries. At the firm level, learning mainly concerns the foreign environment. For Japanese firms from the automobile and electronic sectors, the objective was to reproduce the specific features of their production system. In particular, they had to deal with the local workforce and component suppliers. Learning about these features of the environment can be seen from the increasing local content rates. Part of this increase is due to higher sourcing from European firms, which are considered as partners and taught Japanese methods. Experience is also reflected in the evolution of the type of transaction which is chosen to set up the production units. In the automobile sector for example, a number of firms have preferred cooperative solutions for their first investment and dared to venture alone later on.

Spillovers within industries mainly concern suppliers. Some theoretical studies of multinationals have insisted on the oligopolistic aspect of foreign production and on interactions between firms. In actual fact, the occurrence of such oligopolistic reactions depends on the structure of the sector. In the case of Japanese investments in assembly industries, the clearest spillover has been from suppliers which have followed their clients either to keep its business or because the client felt more comfortable with a well known partner than with foreigners.[60] For the supplier, foreign production by its client constitutes a location incentive, its ownership advantage being its close and successful past relationship with that client.

Contemporary foreign investments have to be analyzed in their context.[61] In particular, the process of globalization should be taken into account. Generally speaking, globalization tendencies lead to relate the analysis of direct investment, of the decisions to extend

---

[60] The performance of which were often considered as insufficient.

[61] What follows applies to foreign units in general and not only to the Japanese case.

multinational operations, and the analysis of the competitive game at the international level. Such an approach, as well as various empirical observations does not single out the behavior of the Japanese multinational companies. The "Japanese model" of multinational may have existed in the 1950s and 1960s, but it is not relevant for analysing Japanese investment in European in the 1980s. During the 1980s, protectionism has been a major incentive in Japanese firms' decisions, since they wanted to access the dynamic European markets.[62] In the 1990s, development of globalization and the growing experience of multinational operations by Japanese firms modifies the decision processes. The sectoral chapters of this book provide elements to deal with these evolutions.

APPENDIX: SELECTED RESULTS FROM SURVEYS

2.1 The survey by J. Dunning (1986).

The sample

23 of the 26 Japanese affiliates known to be operating in the British manufacturing industries by mid-1983. The survey was conducted between between July 1983 and March 1984.

The sample has been divided into 2 groups: 1. 9 producers of consumer and industrial electronic products, 2. 15 firms from different industries (light engineering, chemicals...).

Questionnaires

For the different evaluations, the Japanese affiliates were asked to assess on a 1 to 5 scale the significance of the different factors which were listed (1 indicating no significance).

Results

Table A1 present the results with respect to the relative competitive advantage of Japanese firms.

---

[62] Other empirical studies have reached the same conclusions as this chapter on this point, see in particular (Heitger, Stehn 1990; Fabry 1992).

Table A1:   Competitive Advantages of Japanese Firms' Affiliates[1]

	Group 1	Group 2	Total
1. Advantages based on particular assets			
1.1 Product related variables			
Nature of product	3.2	3.6	3.4
Patent protection	2.3	2.1	2.3
Product quality & reliability	4.7	4.7	4.7
Product price	3.1	3.3	3.2
Keeping delivery dates	3.6	4.0	3.8
After sales servicing	2.3	2.6	2.6
Advertising	1.6	1.6	1.6
Marketing methods	2.5	2.0	2.2
Product adaptation	1.9	2.2	2.0
1.2 Production related variables			
Process technology	4.0	3.9	4.0
Work organization	4.3	3.0	3.4
Industrial relations	3.7	2.7	3.0
Materials usage	2.1	2.3	2.2
Incentive schemes	1.2	1.7	1.5
Management philosophy	4.3	2.9	3.5
Quality of inputs	4.2	1.5	2.7
2. Common governance advantages			
More dynamic entrepreneurship	2.3	2.6	2.4
Favored access to parent's inputs	2.1	2.5	2.3
Favored addess to R&D	3.5	3.5	3.5
Favored access to parent's administrative services	2.2	1.9	2.0
Economies of scale	2.0	1.8	1.9
Product diversification	1.5	1.8	1.7
Market diversification	1.6	1.7	1.7
Favored access to markets	1.5	1.2	1.4

[1] As perceived by the management of affiliates.

Source: (Dunning 1986)

2.2 The JETRO surveys

Since 1983, the JETRO issues an annual survey of European operations of Japanese companies in the manufacturing sector. JETRO identifies the Japanese units in Europe and then sends them questionnaires on various subjects.

2.2.1 The categories of motivations used in the 1983 survey

JETRO asked the following question of the firms which were surveyed: what were the motive and purpose of starting to produce in Europe? Please select 3 answers from A to F below, in order of importance. Circle the sub-items if they were particularly important as the motive(s).

A. *In order to obtain production factors (for cost saving investment).*

–   As it is easy to secure raw materials and parts.

–   As the costs of energy such as electricity and gas are low.

–   As it is easy to acquire a large tract of land at low cost.

–   As it is possible to secure abundant labor at low cost.

–   As costs for preventing pollution and coping with excessive concentration are low.

–   As it is possible to reduce transportation costs.

B. *In order to develop new markets (export substitution investment).*

–   As it helps expand the local markets.

–   As it helps expand markets in third countries.

–   As it offers greater chances of obtaining orders beyond the limit of doing business on the basis of affiliations in Japan.

–   As our corporation was recommended by its importer (s). (As it was given a facility for getting products delivered).

– As it is possible to strengthen repair and after-sales services.

– As it is possible to avoid high import duties.

– As it helps avoid exchange risk.

C.   *In order to avoid trade friction.*

– As trade friction has arisen due to an increase in our corporation's market share.

– As there exists a fear of trade friction occuring though it has not taken place as yet.

D.   *In order to acquire information.*

– As it is easy to obtain technical information.

– As it is easy to obtain market information (including that of consumers' preferences and fashion trends).

E.   *In order to raise funds.*

– As it is easy to raise funds.

– As it is possible to take advantage of high yen exchange rate.

F.   *Others.*

2.3 JETRO's 1990 survey

The question asked to Japanese affiliates in Europe was the following: What were your company's motivations and/or reasons for advancing into Europe? Firms could choose up to 3 answers from the list below.

(1) To shift from exports to local production to meet increased demand

(2) To reduce production cost

(3) To avoid discriminatory quantitative restrictions on Japanese imports

(4) To secure raw materials at lower cost

(5) To avoid exchange fluctuation risks

(6) Part of a globalization strategy

(7) Concern about a rise in protectionism as a result of the EC's market integration

(8) To benefit from the expansion of economic activity resulting from the EC's market integration

(9) Strategy in anticipation of expanded European markets resulting from the realization of the European Economic Sphere (EES) initiative, as well as the liberalization of East European market

(10) Presence of parent company in Europe

(11) Investment incentives such as tax credits

(12) To meet consumers' needs

(13) To avoid infringement of anti-dumping regulations

(14) To avoid infringement of anti-dumping regulations on parts and components

(15) Effective use of European designs

(16) To carry out R&D activities in Europe

(17) To supply parts, components and raw materials to affiliates of Japanese manufacturers operating in Europe

(18) Establishment of manufacturing base in Europe resulting from M&A of American firms

(19) Other

These items have been grouped into categories according to their content. The objective was to regroup similar motives. These categories appear in Table 3 in the main text of this chapter. The categories have been constructed as follows (the figures correspond to those appearing in the columns of Table 3): 1 corresponds to item 6, 2 to items 3, 7, 12 and 13, 3 to items 1, 8 and 9, 4 to items 11 and 14, 5 to item 16, 6 to item 10, 7 to items 2 and 4, 8 to item 5, 9 to item 15 and 10 to items 17 and 18.

2.4 JETRO's 1992 survey

The question asked of Japanese affiliates in Europe was the following: What were the motives and/or purposes for your advance into Europe? Firms could choose up to 3 answers from the list below.

(1) To meet expanded demand

(2) To reduce production cost

(3) To avoid discriminatory quantitative restrictions on Japanese imports

(4) To secure raw materials at lower cost

(5) To avoid exchange fluctuation risks

(6) To meet a rise in trade protectionism resulting from the EC's market integration

(7) To benefit from the expansion of economic activity resulting from German unification, the realization of the European Economic Area (EEA) initiative, as well as from the liberalization of East European markets

(8) Treading on the heels of parent companies that have already advanced in Europe

(9) Investment incentives such as tax credit

(10) To meet consumers' needs

(11) To avoid infringement of anti-dumping regulations

(12) To avoid infringement of anti-dumping regulations on parts and components

(13) To implement design and development operations in Europe

(14) To carry out R&D activities in Europe

(15) To supply parts, components and raw materials to affilitiates of Japanese manufacturers operating in Europe

(16) Other

These items have been grouped into categories according to their content. The objective was to regroup similar motives. These categories appear in Table 4 in the main text of this chapter. The categories have been constructed as follows (the figures correspond to those appearing in the columns of Table 4): 1 corresponds to items 1, 7, and 8, 2 to items 3, 6, 12 and 13, 3 to items 10 and 14, 4 to item 16, 5 to item 11, 6 to item 15, 7 to items 2 and 4, 8 to item 9, 9 to item 5, and 10 to item 17.

REFERENCES

Cantwell, John, "A survey of theories of international production" in Christos N. Pitelis & Roger Sugden (ed.), *The nature of the Transnational firm*, London, Routledge 1991.

Caves, Richard, E., *Multinational enterprise and economic analysis*, Cambridge University Press, 1982.

Contractor, Farok, J., Lorange, Peter, *Cooperative Strategies in International Business, Joint Ventures and Technology Partnerships between Firms*, Lexington Books, New York, 1988.

Drake, Tracey, Caves, Richard, "Changing Determinants of Japanese Foreign Investment in the United States", *Journal of the Japanese and International Economics*, no. 6, 1992.

Dunning, John. H., *Multinational enterprises and the global economy*, Addison-Wesley Publishing Company, 1993.

Dunning, John. H., "The eclectic paradigm of international production: a personal perspective", in Christos N. Pitelis & Roger Sugden, *The nature of the Transnational firm* London, Routledge 1990.

Dunning, John. H., *Explaining international production*, Unwin Hyman, 1988.

Dunning, John. H., *Japanese participation in British Industry*, Routledge, London 1986.

Emmot, Bill, *Japan's Global Reach*, Century, London, 1992.

Fabry, Nathalie, "Le protectionnisme et les investissements directs manufacturiers dans la CEE", *Revue d'économie politique*, September-October 1992.

HEC, *Le Japon en Europe. Prochaines mutations dans le pays économique européen*, HEC EURASIA Institute, Jouy-en-Josas, 1990.

Heigter, Bernard, Stehn, Jrgen, "Japanese Direct Investments in the EC. Response to the Internal Market 1993?", *Journal of Common Market Studies*, September 1990.

Hennart, Jean-Franois, "The transaction costs theory of joint ventures: an empirical study of Japanese subsidiaries in the United States", *Management Science*, April 1991a.

Hennart, Jean-Franois, "The transaction cost theory of the multinational enterprise", in Christos N. Pitelis & Roger Sugden, *The nature of the Transnational firm*, London, Routledge, 1991b.

Hood, N., "European Locational Decisions of Japanese Manufacturers: Survey evidence on the case of the UK", in *Japan Multinationals: Strategies and Management*, Manchester Business School, June 7–9, 1992.

Hymer, S., *The international operations of national firms: a study of foreign direct investment*, MIT Press, 1976.

Jacquemot, Pierre, *La Firme multinationale: une introduction économique*, Economica, 1990.

JETRO (Japanese External Trade Organization), *8th Survey of European Operations of Japanese Companies in the Manufacturing Sector*, Tokyo, 1992.

JETRO (Japanese External Trade Organization), Current Management Situation of Japanese Manufacturing Enterprises in Europe. *7th Survey Report*, Tokyo, 1991.

JETRO (Japanese External Trade Organization), *Current Management Structure of Japanese Manufacturing Enterprises in Europe. 4th Survey Report*, Tokyo, 1988.

JETRO (Japanese External Trade Organization), *Japanese Manufacturing Companies in Europe*, Tokyo, 1983.

Knickerboker, F., *Oligopolistic reaction and the multinational enterprise*, Harvard University Press, 1973.

Kogut, Bruce, Zander, Udo, "The knowledge of the firm in the choice of the mode of technology transaction", *Proceedings of EIBA 18th Annual Meeting*, Reading University, 13–15 December 1992.

Monteverde, K., Teece, D., "Supplier switching costs and vertical integration in the automobile industry", *Bell Journal of Economics*, 1982.

Mowery, D., "Collaborative ventures between US and foreign manufacturing firms: an overview", Mowery, D. (ed.) International collaborative ventures in US manufacturing, Ballinger, 1988.

Mucchielli, Jean-Louis, *Les firmes multinationales: mutations et nouvelles perspectives*, Economica 1985.

Nations Unies, *Les sociétés transnationales japonaises en Europe. Structures, stratégies et nouvelles tendances*, Nations Unies, New York, 1991.

Ozawa, Terutomo, *Multinationalism, Japanese style, The political economy of outward dependency*, Princeton University Press, Princeton, 1979.

Ozawa, Terutomo, "Cross-Investments Between Japan and the EC: Income Similarity, Technological Congruity and Economies of Scale", Cantwell, J., (ed.), *Multinational Investment in Modern Europe*, Edward Elgar, London, 1992.

Porter, M., Fuller, M., "Coalitions and global strategy", Porter, M. (ed.), *Competition in global industries*, Harvard Buisiness School Press 1986.

Sachwald, F., *Ajustement sectoriel et adaptation des entreprises. Le cas de l'industrie automobile*, Document de travail, CEPII, Paris, June 1989.

Sachwald, Frédérique, "Les accords dans l'industrie automobile: une analyse en termes de coûts de transaction", *Economie prospective internationale*, CEPII, La Documentation française, Paris, 2e trim. 1990.

Sachwald, Frédérique, "Cooperative agreements in the world automobile industry", European International Business Association (EIBA), Proceedings of the 18th Annual conference, University of Reading, 13–15 December 1992.

Sachwald, Frédérique (ed.), *Europe integration and competitiveness. Acquisitions and alliances in industry*, Edward Elgar, London 1994.

Stuckey, J., *Vertical integration and joint ventures in the aluminium industry*, Harvard University Press, 1983.

Tejima, S., "Japanese foreign direct investment in the 1980s and its prospects for the 1990s", *EXIM Review*, vol. 11 no.2, 1992.

Thomsen, Stephen, Nicolaides, Phedon, *The Evolution of Japanese Direct Investment in Europe. Death of a Transistor Salesman*, Harvester Wheatsheaf, 1991.

Vernon, Raymond, "The product cycle hypothesis in a new international environment", *Oxford Bulletin of Economics and Statistics*, November 1979.

Vernon, R., "International investment and international trade in the product cycle", *Quarterly Journal of Economics*, May 1966.

Volpato, G., *L'industria Automobilistica internazionale*, Cedam, Pavoda, 1983.

Williamson, O. E, *The Economic Institutions of Capitalism*, The Free Press, 1985.

Yamawaki, Hideki, "Japanese Multinationals in US and European Manufacturing Industries: Entry, Strategy and Patterns", *Japanese Direct Investment in a Unifying Europe: Impacts on Japan and the European Community Conference*, INSEAD/Euro-Asia Centre Fontainebleau, 26–27 June 1992.

$89-167$

$Japan$
$Europe$
$F24$
$F23$
$L63$

3

The Role of Investment in Europe in the Globalization Strategy of Japanese Electronics Firms

René A. Belderbos

3.1   INTRODUCTION

The Japanese electronics industry is the most important contributor to Japanese Direct Foreign Investment (FDI) in manufacturing with a share of 25% of cumulative FDI as of March 1991 (Ministry of Finance 1991). The electronics industry is also a major exporter, responsible for 27% of exports to the European Community (EC) and 22% of exports to the US during 1991 (JETRO 1992). In terms of the relative importance of foreign production, the industry ranks second after the transport machinery industry: according to the latest MITI survey among Japanese Multinational Enterprises (MNEs), sales of foreign production subsidiaries amounted to 11.4% of production in Japan in Fiscal Year 1990 (ending March 1991); this foreign production ratio stood at 12.6 for the transport machinery industry (MITI 1992).

Although FDI by Japanese electronics firms has been an important vehicle to increase foreign production, in particular since the mid-1980s, the foreign production ratio still is only about a third of those of the US and European electronics industries.[1] Japanese firms'

---

[1] The foreign production ratios are estimated to be 32 and 37% for the US and European electronics industry, respectively, in 1983. See John H. Dunning and

89

foreign involvement has long been limited to export dependence and investment in overseas distribution networks, and the recent surge in FDI in manufacturing is an effort to 'catch up' with their US and European rivals. In the second half of the 1980s, Japanese firms embarked on a 'globalization' drive, striving to have manufacturing bases and ultimately R&D centers in the three major markets of the world: Japan/South-East Asia, Europe, and North America. While manufacturing FDI in South-East Asia was mainly governed by the need to transfer manufacturing activities for which Japan has lost comparative advantage, FDI in Europe and North America has been largely a response to trade practises restricting Japanese exports. Trade restrictions in the electronics industry have been particularly severe in the EC. Since Japanese firms were less well represented than in their most important foreign market, the US, they have pursued their catching up strategy here with special vigor.

This chapter will analyze the recent state of FDI by Japanese electronics firms in the EC. It will give a detailed description of the Japanese firms' presence by country in manufacturing as well as in distribution. Investment strategies in the EC will be discussed by highlighting modes of entry (greenfield plants, joint ventures, acquisitions), procurement and local content, and destination of sales, among others. Based on these and other characteristics of Japanese FDI in the EC, such as R&D activities and localization of management, effects on the EC economy are assessed.

However, in order to get a proper understanding of Japanese electronics firms' activities in the EC, it is imperative to view them in the broader perspective of firms' globalization strategies. This in turn necessitates a detailed analysis of the role of restrictive trade policies in the US and the EC in spurring Japanese FDI. Furthermore, it will often prove useful to compare characteristics of Japanese firms' FDI in the EC with those of FDI in the US.

The first section of this chapter starts with a brief description of factors determining the recent trend in globalization of Japanese electronics firms and provides some key figures on the foreign involvement of these firms. Section 2 provides a detailed analysis of the role of trade policy in governing FDI and export patterns. Interesting observations can be made by comparing trade policy measures and FDI in the EC and the US. Section 3 provides data on Japanese

---

Robert D. Pierce, 1985, *The World's Largest Industrial Enterprises, 1962–1983*, (Gower Aldershot).

electronics firms' manufacturing and distribution subsidiaries in the EC by country, product group, and firm. Special attention will be given to the mode of market entry chosen and the degree of integration of European activities as illustrated by procurement and sales behavior by subsidiaries. An effort to assess the effects of Japanese FDI on the EC economy and the EC electronics industry in particular is made in Section 3.4.

Before turning to the next section, a note concerning the definition of the electronics industry is in order. This chapter uses a broad definition covering heavy electrical equipment, telecommunications equipment, household electrical goods, components and semiconductors, audio and video equipment, computer, office machines, and measuring equipment. This definition can be used for Japanese FDI in the EC by drawing on the detailed information on overseas Japanese subsidiaries as published by Touyou Keizai in the *Kaigai Shinshutsu Kigyou Souran* (*Directory of Multinational Corporations*). The definition has to be narrowed down when drawing on two other sources of information on Japanese FDI: MITI's survey under Japanese MNEs, *Kaigai Toushi Toukei Souran* (*Basic Survey on Foreign Direct Investment*) and the Ministry of Finance figures on notifications of direct investments abroad (Ministry of Finance 1991). In both cases, the electronics industry does not include copiers (classified under 'precision machinery') and other office machines (classified under 'general machinery'). For further remarks concerning the various data on Japanese FDI the reader is referred to the general Appendix of the book.

3.1 THE GLOBALIZATION OF JAPANESE ELECTRONICS FIRMS AND THE ROLE OF THE EC MARKET

3.1.1 The Globalization of Business and Japanese Electronics Firms' Strategies

The electronics industry is one of the industries in which a clear trend towards globalization of business has been observed after the world recession of the early 1980s. Developments in the 1980s can be characterized by surging R&D costs, rapidly changing technologies, shortening product life cycles, and the increasing uniformity of global consumer tastes.[2] These increasingly prompt electronics firms to sell on all major markets, to be able to recoup R&D costs in a short

---

[2] See the seminal work of Ohmae (1985).

time-span and to reap economies of scale. Furthermore firms try to gain a strong foothold in the major markets of the 'Triad' (Japan, Europe and the US) to be less vulnerable to protectionism and exchange rate volatility, and to have reliable and quick access to technological and market developments. Technological developments such as flexible manufacturing techniques and advances in telecommunication facilitate international production and control over a globally operating company.

The need for globalization of business has been, and still is, most distinct for Japanese electronics firms. Firstly, as noted above, they are less internationalized in terms of foreign production than their European and US competitors. Secondly, the rise in protectionism in the electronics industry has been largely directed against Japanese firms' exports to the US and the EC, giving strong inducements to 'jump' tariffs, anti-dumping duties, and Voluntary Export Restraints (VERs), and to attain the status of 'insider' to alleviate threats of future protectionism. Thirdly, the comparative advantage of production in Japan has been declining due to the strong appreciation of the Yen since 1985 and with increasing labor shortages in Japan.

The underlying conditions for globalization through FDI were also favorable to Japanese firms. Japanese electronics firms' export successes were based on competitive advantages which were strongly related to the home market. Japanese firms excel in management of large scale, automated production processes churning out high quality goods at low costs. Quality control through quality circles and sophisticated testing procedures, just in time deliveries of components through close cooperation with subcontractors, and the ability to foster the commitment of employees through life time employment systems are all part of the highly successful production and engineering management in Japanese companies (Belderbos 1991; Franko 1983). Japanese firms had been reluctant to become multinationals because it was not at all evident that these firm-specific advantages could be transferred abroad successfully. However, by the mid-1980s, the major Japanese electronics firms had gained valuable experience in operating CTV and VTR manufacturing plants in the US and the EC and Japanese firms' skills and knowledge had proved to be, at least to a certain extent, transferable abroad.[3]

---

[3] Dunning (1986), surveying Japanese CTV plants in the UK in 1984, found that Japanese plants could operate at roughly 5–10% below the productivity level of

Furthermore, the competitiveness of Japanese companies evolved from strengths based on production processes and management to clear technological advantages in new products, the latter having much weaker links to the home market. In addition, since the mid-1980s, host governments in South-East Asia as well as in the US and in the EC changed their attitudes towards inward FDI to a liberal and often supportive stance. Export processing zones were set up in Malaysia, Thailand, and Taiwan, for instance, and local authorities in the US and the EC were eager to attract Japanese FDI and subsidized plant establishments.

Japanese firms thus embarked on a globalization strategy generally incorporating the following two features. Firstly, in the US and the EC, firms set up assembly plants for electronics goods which had been hit by import restrictions and anti-dumping actions. Pressures to increase the local content of goods produced in Japanese plants (particularly strong in the EC), and fear of future protectionism after the formation of the EC internal market and the North American free trade zone, consequently prompted firms to increase the value added of local production in the regions, deemed necessary to become an 'insider' and to alleviate future protectionism. These investments are mainly defensive, market-oriented, and generally substitute for exports.

A second type of FDI in the EC and the US is strategic in character and concerns the acquisition of a controlling or minority stake in US and EC firms. The goal is to acquire specific technological skills, software, or access to markets. Sony's takeovers of CBS records and Columbia Pictures, Matsushita's takeover of MCA, Toshiba's participation in Time Warner, Fujitsu's acquisition of ICL, and Ricoh's participation in Gestetner (a major distributor of office machines in Europe), are all major transactions that fit into this pattern. In addition, Japanese firms have been active acquirers of small and medium sized innovative electronics firms, in particular in the US (Genther and Dalton 1992).

Secondly, in South-East Asia, Japanese firms set up so-called 'regional core networks' of interdependent manufacturing plants making use of comparative locational advantages in labor costs and skills in different countries (Nakakita and Urata 1991; Gold *et al.,* 1991). Investments in South-East Asia are predominantly cost-oriented and

---

plants in Japan. In a more recent study, Abo (forthcoming) reports that Sanyo's CTV plant in the UK has reached a productivity comparable to its Japanese plant in final assembly.

lead to intra-firm, intra-industry trade between Japan and South-East Asian countries.[4] Regional core networks are set up to establish an efficient division of labor. Products manufactured with standardized and mature technologies, such as radios, headphone stereos and black and white televisions, and standardized parts are produced in ASEAN countries where cheap labor is relatively abundant. Products of intermediate technology such as simple VTRs are produced in the NIEs where labor is more expensive but also more skilled. High technology products and newly introduced products, such as camcorders, high-resolution VTRs and crucial components are manufactured in Japan, where production can be cost-effective by investments in manufacturing automation. A typical example would be labor-intensive assembly of CTVs in Malaysia making use of cathode ray tubes (CRTs) and integrated circuits (ICs) from Japan and other parts from Taiwanese affiliates (Nakakita and Urata 1991).

Regional core networks also provide opportunities for smaller Japanese subcontractors and independent component suppliers which can lower costs and shorten delivery times by relocating production near the Asian production sites of their Japanese client firms. For small and medium sized firms, the Japanese government has been instrumental in promoting FDI in Asia through tax breaks and assistance by institutions such as the Export-Import Bank since the 1960s and 1970s. Ozawa (1979, 1991) argues that Japan regarded (and still regard) the relocation of manufacturing activities for which Japan has lost comparative advantage an indispensable part of industrial policy.

Gold *et al.* (1991) argue that regional core networks in electronics, machinery and automobile industries are contributing to the creation of a South-East Asian trade and investment block. Some evidence is provided by Urata (1992), who finds that Japanese manufacturing subsidiaries are more specialized in Asian trade than Asian manufacturing industries at large, while Japanese subsidiaries are estimated to be responsible for 20% of total Asian manufactured exports. In addition, the findings in Belderbos (1992) suggest that Japanese electronics firms are not trully hindered by national borders in setting up manufacturing plants in South-East Asia (as distinct from setting up plants in the US and the EC), pointing to the importance of cumulative economic ties between Japan and South-East Asia.

---

[4] See Urata (1991) for a discussion of Japanese FDI in Asia. Japanese FDI in Asia is found to be significantly higher in Japanese industries with both high export and import intensity, supporting the idea that FDI in Asia promotes intra-industry trade.

Japanese firms' globalization strategies have required changes in organisation and management. In the late 1980s, virtually all major electronics firms established regional headquarters in the Triad markets of the US, the EC, and Japan; some firms assigned South-East Asia as a special region as well. These headquarters are assisting regional sales and production subsidiaries, by performing functions such as communication with authorities, monitoring of advertising and coordination of regional sales, training of employees, and procurement of local funds; they are also meant to show Japanese firms' commitment to become 'insiders' in the EC and the US. In the EC in particular, many firms also set up financial subsidiaries linked with the regional headquarters to procure funds at Euro-currency markets.[5] Regional headquarters in South-East Asia are usually located in Singapore and are mainly assigned the task of coordinating components procurement from Asian components plants for further processing and assembly in Asia, the EC, the US, or Japan. In some cases, the organizational structure of the firm was adapted more fundamentally. For instance, Matsushita Electric Industrial, the second largest Japanese electronics firm, altered the divisional structure and regrouped divisions by type of customer instead of product in 1987; in 1988 it merged with its overseas sales division to unite control of overseas sales and manufacturing.

The emerging global strategies of Japanese electronics (and automobile) firms were presented as 'overseas cooperation programs' in the second half of the 1980s. MITI had come under increasing pressure of foreign governments to help reduce Japanese trade surpluses and pressured Japanese firms to be cooperative to meet this end. Firms typically announced that they would reduce the share of exports in total sales, increase foreign procurement, and increase the share of locally manufactured goods in overseas sales. Since these resolutions are all compatible with the necessary strategy changes outlined above, compliance with MITI's request in this way did not pose many difficulties.[6]

---

[5] For instance, in the years of booming Japanese share prices, Japanese firms could attract billions of dollars at the Euro-currency market at low interest rates by issuing corporate bonds with attached warrants (giving creditors the right to buy future shares at fixed prices).

[6] By implication, it can not be ruled out that MITI was more concerned about presentation than about contents. See Yamazawa (1992) and Furlotti (1991) for discussions of the 'international cooperation programs'. Furlotti notes that with burgeoning domestic demand and a rising Yen, exports can still rise significantly in volume without the targets being missed.

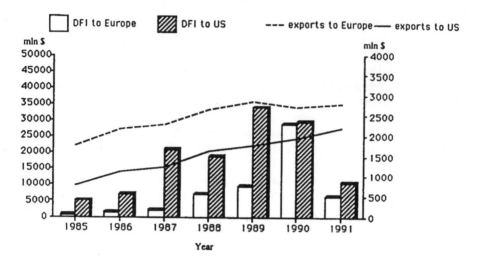

Sources: Ministry of Finance (1991), JETRO (1986–1992), Kaburagi (1992).

Figure 1: Developments in FDI and Exports by the Japanese Electronics Industry: The EC versus the US.

3.1.2   The Extent of Overseas Involvement and the Role of the EC Market

After the brief sketch of the emerging globalization strategies of Japanese electronics firms since the mid-1980s, this paragraph examines the extent of foreign involvement by 1991 and some observable trends in the second half of the 1980s and the early 1990s.

Figure 1 shows the development in Japanese electronics exports and FDI to the EC and the US since 1985.[7] Electronics exports to both the EC and the US generally have been increasing up to 1989, while the appreciation of the Yen led to a temporary growth slowdown in exports measured in dollars in 1987. From 1989 to 1991, exports to the EC grew steadily, while, in contrast, exports to the US did not show

---

[7] Electronics exports include the sectors 'electrical machinery', 'precision machinery', and 'office machines' in the JETRO classification.

any growth. Exports to the EC reached more than 27 billion dollars in 1990, an 180% increase during 1985–1991. Exports to the US increased by only 58% over the same period, from 22 to 35 billion dollars. By 1991, exports to the EC amounted to more than three quarters of exports to the US, up from 44% in 1985. All this signifies a clear trend towards increasing dependence of Japanese electronics firms on the EC market.

The increasing importance of the EC relative to the US is also seen in the case of FDI flows. FDI by Japanese electronics firms to the EC increased exponentially from less than 100 million dollars in 1985 to 2.4 billion dollars in 1990 — the first year that FDI flows to the EC were comparable to FDI in the US.[8] In terms of cumulative FDI, however, the EC is still considerably less important, with FDI stocks reaching only a quarter of FDI in the US. The historical highs in FDI in 1989 and 1990 have not been maintained in 1991. FDI to the EC decreased to 501 million dollars, an amount comparable to FDI in 1988. The decline in FDI to the US has been stronger, from 2.3 billion dollars in 1990 to 868 million dollars in 1991.

There are reasons to believe that FDI flows during 1989 and 1990 have been exceptional, since a few major acquisitions, such as the takeover of the US semiconductor manufacturer AVX by Kyocera and the acquisition of UK computer manufacturer ICL by Fujitsu, were responsible for a major share of FDI (Kaburagi 1992).[9] These and other major acquisitions by Japanese firms during 1989–1990 were easily affordable because of the exceptionally low cost of capital, resulting from high profits on the domestic market, low interest rates, and continuously rising stock prices. FDI in 1991 might have fallen back roughly to a level which is sustainable even under the economic conditions prevailing in 1992, charaterized by falling profits and stock market prices but Japanese electronics firms indicated in a 1992 survey that they had plans to increase FDI compared to the 1991 level (Tejima, 1992).

It is important to note that declines in FDI flows do not necessarily lead to a comparable slowdown in growth of overseas manufacturing activities. FDI flows from Japan finance only a small part of the capital requirements of foreign subsidiaries, and it is possible that subsidiaries

---

[8] Note that FDI flows are not registered during calendar years but during Fiscal Years which run from April to March.

[9] Note that the FDI figures exclude the acquisitions of record and film companies MCA by Matsushita and CBS and Columbia Pictures by Sony, since these are classified under the service industry.

keep on increasing their activities using internally generated or locally attracted funds.[10] A more accurate picture can be obtained by looking at employment and number of subsidiaries abroad, a route which will be followed in the remainder of this chapter.

Another way to look at the growth of overseas activities of Japanese electronics firms is to examine at trends in exports and foreign production for some major products (Figures 2a–2d). Foreign production has been continuously increasing for color televisions (CTVs), video tape recorders (VTRs), microwave ovens (MWOs), and compact disk players (CDs). Figure 2a shows a sharp decline in domestic CTV production in 1986 and 1987, the years in which the Yen's appreciation made itself felt. In contrast, foreign production has been rising every year since 1983, and by 1990 roughly three quarters of CTV production for foreign markets was taking place outside Japan. Production for exports in Japan increased again in 1990, mainly as a result of the successful introduction of LCD CTVs.

About half of foreign sales of MWOs came from foreign production bases by 1989 (Figure 2b). It is worth noting that total Japanese sales abroad have been declining since 1987, which is related to market saturation in the US in combination with strong competition by Korean firms. In case of VTRs, production is still largely concentrated in Japan, although foreign production reached the sizable volume of 7.2 million units in 1990 (Figure 2c). One reason for the relatively small share of foreign production is that Japanese firms are mainly relying on exports to service the US market, where there have been no import restrictions on VTRs. Foreign sales of Japanese CD players, a relatively new product, have been growing rapidly since 1988 (Figure 2d). Foreign production increased from 80000 in 1985 to 5.2 million units, about almost one third of total sales abroad, in 1989.

The results of trends in FDI and exports in the late 1980s and early 1990s are reflected in Table 1, which presents key data concerning the overseas activities of Japanese electronics firms in 1990 and 1991 based on a MITI survey among Japanese MNEs.[11] The table covers the three basic modes of foreign involvement: exports, foreign production, and licensing. The export ratio for the surveyed MNEs (given in the last column) was 26% in 1990, while the ratio of sales by foreign production subsidiaries to domestic production stood unchanged

---

[10] See also Appendix A.

[11] See Appendix A for remarks on the data sources.

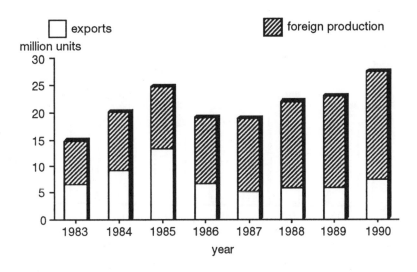

Figure 2a: Exports and Foreign Production of CTV's

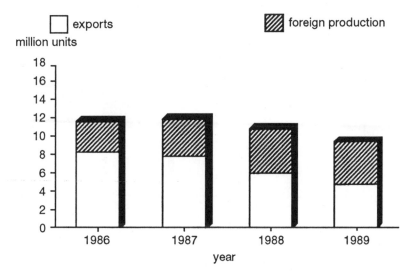

Figure 2b: Exports and Foreign Production of MWOs

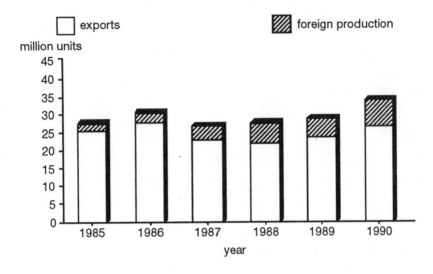

Figure 2c: Exports and Foreign Production of VTRs

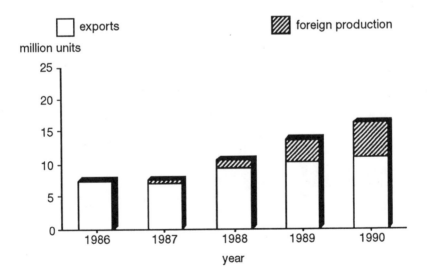

Sources: Jetro (1984–1991), YRI (1991), EIAJ (1992b).

Figure 2d: Exports and Foreign Production of CD Players.

Table 1: Overseas Activities of Japanese Electronics Firms in 1990 and 1991

	EC	US	Asia	Total	Total/ Japan (%)
Exports	[a]2127	[b]3150	1970	7876	[d]26
1990	(27)	(40)	(25)	(100)	
Licensing	[a]76	[b]118	312	592	na
1990	(13)	(20)	(53)	(100)	
Foreign Production[c]					
1990	1084	3433	1987	6777	22
	(16)	(51)	(29)	(100)	
1991	1869	3240	2436	7957	22
	(23)	(41)	(30)	(100)	
Employment					
1990	24447	63820	188104	307039	50
	(8)	(21)	(62)	(100)	
1991	58861	77996	249043	419215	na
	(14)	(19)	(59)	(100)	
# Subsidiaries					
1990	112	130	353	670	na
	(17)	(19)	(53)	(100)	
1991	168	180	442	884	na
	(19)	(20)	(50)	(100)	

Source: Calculations based on MITI (1991, 1992).

Remarks: The figures represent the situation in March 1990 and March 1991, respectively, for the number of subsidiaries, number of licensing contracts, and employment, while exports and foreign production refer to the years ending March 1990 and March 1991, respectively. Exports, foreign sales, value added and assets in million Yen. The licensing variable is the number of independent foreign firms given a licensing contract. Figures between brackets are regional shares in total overseas activities. See Appendix A for further remarks concerning the data sources.

[a] Europe.

[b] North America.

[c] Sales of foreign manufacturing subsidiaries.

[d] Export ratio: value of exports divided by value of production in Japan.

at 22% in 1990–1991. In Fiscal Year ending March 1990, the MNEs exported 2127 billion Yen worth of electronics goods to Europe, 27% of their export total. Exports to Europe are markedly smaller than exports to North America, which absorbs 40% of the MNEs exports.

In foreign production, the EC was poorly represented in 1990, with a share of 16%. Furthermore, the value of foreign production here only reached half the value of imports, whilst foreign production exceeded imports for North America and Asia. Clearly, Japanese firms' FDI in the EC has been lagging behind. The picture of market servicing can be completed by looking at exports from Asian subsidiaries as well. The figures in MITI (1991) show that about 15% of the sales of Asian subsidiaries was directed to the US and the EC in 1990. The share of the US was about three times as large as the share of the EC, with imports by the EC amounting to an estimated 70 billion Yen. In the EC, stronger local content requirements and anti-dumping actions against imports from Asian countries have made exports of final products and components from Asian production bases a less attractive option.

The pattern of overseas production by Japanese electronics firms appears to have changed markedly during 1990 and 1991. Japanese firms have been rapidly expanding production in the EC, and the EC's share increased to 23%, while the share of the US has been declining. The EC's growing importance in the early 1990s is even more pronounced in terms of employment: employment more than doubled during 1990 and early 1991, reflecting, among others, some major acquisitions and new ventures in the components sector. While the EC's share of total overseas employment increased to 14 percent, Asian subsidiary employed almost 60% of Japanese firms' overseas employees. The latter fact reflects the high labor intensity of production in this region. The total number of overseas employees of the MNEs in the survey also saw a sharp rise from just over 300,000 to 419,000.

In terms of number of subsidiaries, the EC's shares increased slightly to 19% of a rapidly increasing total number of overseas subsidiaries. Licensing contracts, the third mode of servicing foreign market along with foreign production and exports, tend to be more often concluded with Asian firms, which are responsible for 53% of all contracts). Licensing contracts with Asian firms provide a way to capitalize on knowledge of standardized low technology products which Japanese companies find it difficult to manufacture competitively.

An additional way to analyze Japanese electronics firms' overseas activities is to look at FDI and exports of individual firms in 1989. Table 2 presents data on the value of sales by foreign manufacturing subsidiaries as a percentage of total consolidated sales,[12] export ratios and EC and US shares in exports, and the number of foreign manufacturing plants with the corresonding EC and US shares. Integrated electronics manufacturers such as Hitachi and Toshiba are least internationally involved. Both foreign production ratio (5–9%) and export ratios are relatively low. Of course, by their sheer size these firms are important exporters and foreign investors in absolute terms. The strongest export dependence is recorded for producers of office machines and cameras, and producers of audio and video products, with export ratios around 50% and even up to 70–80%. Audio and video manufacturers combine export dependence with relatively high foreign production shares. The pattern of foreign involvement for component manufacturers is diverse. The larger firms Murata, TDK and Alps are strongly internationally oriented, both in terms of exports and foreign production. Yet the smaller components manufacturers are the leaders in globalization in terms of foreign production: Tabuchi, Tamura, and Mitsumi produce more abroad than they export. The highest foreign production share is recorded for Akai, which employs almost as many people in the EC as in Japan.

For the larger integrated and consumer electronics firms, the share of exports directed to Europe is generally smaller than the share going to the US, reflecting the traditional importance of the US market. Audio and video producers with strong brand names in Europe such as JVC, Pioneer, Aiwa and Akai export more to Europe. For component manufacturers, the combined share of Europe and North America tends to be smaller; their exports are more oriented to Asia where they mainly supply Japanese assembly plants.

The information on the number of foreign manufacturing subsidiaries has to be interpreted with care. Differences in regional markets within Europe have often compelled Japanese firms to set up more than one manufacturing subsidiary for products such as VTRs and CTVs, while in the US one large subsidiary typically sufficed.

---

[12] Note that the definition of the 'foreign production share' differs from the definition of the 'foreign production ratio' in Table 1. In the latter, the denominator is the value of production in Japan only.

Table 2:   Foreign Involvement of Japanese Electronics Firms in 1989

Company	Sales mln Yen	F. Prod share %	Exports			Foreign Manf. Subs		
			ratio %	EC %	US %	#	EC %	US %
Industrial/Integrated								
Hitachi	6401	5	25	[b]23	[b]36	17	18	12
Toshiba	3800	9	31	[b]30	[b]40	16	31	6
NEC	3082	8	22	na	na	22	14	18
Mitsubishi Electric	2716	7	21	na	na	16	19	6
Fujitsu	2387	na	18	na	na	9	22	22
Omron	372	na	15	35	45	7	29	14
Consumer								
Matsushita	5504	14	34	26	38	58	16	14
Sharp	1258	25	48	28	41	14	29	7
Sanyo	1255	27	32	na	na	37	14	27
Audio/Video								
Sony	2201	20	61	[b]35	[b]39	18	28	11
JVC	1641	20	47	49	37	8	38	13
Pioneer	449	30	47	44	40	3	67	0
Kenwood	157	16	53	31	49	2	50	0
Aiwa	99	[a]15	64	33	29	2	50	0
Akai	71	45	82	60	10	1	100	0
Office Machines, Cameras								
Canon	1106	10	74	41	48	11	27	18
Ricoh	729	na	34	na	na	5	40	20
Minolta	306	na	75	42	43	5	20	20
Brother	204	14	64	39	34	7	14	14

Thus, the relatively large number of foreign production subsidiaries located in the EC relative to the US, does not imply that the share in foreign production is higher in the EC than in the US. Still, some interesting observations can be made. Firstly, most firms have set up more manufacturing subsidiaries in Asia than in the developed markets (the combined share of the EC and the US often only reaches 50%),

Table 2: *Continued*

				Exports		Foreign Manf. Subs		
Company	Sales mln Yen	F. Prod share %	ratio %	EC %	US %	#	EC %	US %
Components								
Murata	486	ᵃ15	30	19	28	7	29	29
TDK	418	23	35	na	na	14	7	43
Alps	376	ᵃ12	30	24	27	12	25	25
Kyocera	338	7	45	na	na	6	50	17
Nitto Denko	191	9	15	10	23	3	33	0
Mitsumi	131	29	37	4	32	12	8	0
SMK	53	11	12	23	24	5	20	0
Tamura	51	20	16	na	na	6	17	0
Tabuchi	35	40	7	69	12	3	33	0

Sources: Touyou Keizai (1989-1991), Dempa (1990, 1991), Dempa (1990b), Japan Development Bank (1990), Company Reports.

Remarks: Sales on consolidated basis in billion Yen in Fiscal Year 1988 (ending March 1989), foreign production ratio = sales of foreign manufacturing subsidiaries divided by total consolidated sales (1988/1989), Export ratio is exports of parent firm divided by unconsolidated sales in Fiscal Year 1988.

ᵃ 1987.

ᵇ Share in overseas sales.

in line with the distribution of the number of subsidiaries presented in Table 1. Secondly, several (mostly smaller) audio, video and components manufacturers have set up manufacturing subsidiaries in the Europe but not in the US. This must be attributed to differences in trade policy measures between the US and the EC. Anti-dumping measures have hit Japanese exports of CD players and VTRs to Europe, but not exports to the US. Measures to increase the local content requirement of Japanese assembly plants in the EC have created a market for EC-produced components to which several components suppliers responded by setting up manufacturing plants in the EC. The effect of differences in trade policy between the US and the EC on Japanese exports and FDI is analyzed further in the next Section.

3.2   TRADE POLICY, EXPORTS, AND FDI

The most salient feature of the surge in Japanese electronics firms' FDI in the EC as well as in the US in the second half of the 1980s has been the role of trade policy. Specific trade policy measures such as anti-dumping actions and Orderly Market Arrangements (OMAs) have often urged Japanese firms to respond by setting up local manufacturing plants to 'jump' trade barriers. Such defensive export-substituting FDI dominated at least until the end of the 1980s, and Japanese FDI in the EC and the US can not be analyzed meaningfully without paying broad attention to trade policy. In the next paragraph, an assessment of the role of trade policy measures in shaping export and FDI patterns is made by comparing trade policy, FDI and exports in the EC and the US. In paragraph 3.2.1, EC trade policy and its impact on Japanese FDI will be discussed in more detail.

3.2.1   *Trade Policy, Exports, and FDI: The EC and the US Compared*

Trade friction over Japan's electronics exports to the US and the EC reached its first peak in the beginning of the 1970s, when cheaply priced Japanese CTV exports gained market share rapidly. In the EC, several countries threatened to use safeguard measures against Japanese imports, and in 1972 MITI responded by unilaterally restraining exports of CTVs and Cathode Ray Tubes (CRTs) to ensure an 'orderly working of markets'. In addition, several EC countries restricted Japanese CTV imports through national quota, to which an industry-to-industry VER in the UK was added in 1974. In the US, CTV manufacturers filed anti-dumping suits against Japanese CTV imports in 1970 and the Treasury Department determined anti-dumping duties up to 60% in 1971.[13] Eventually, in early 1977

---

[13] See Burton and Saelens (1987) and Van Marion (1992). Although Japanese firms' export advance was based on superior production processes, design, and quality, there also is convincing evidence that dumping was taking place in the early 1970s. Prices in Japan were substantially higher than in export markets, because the major Japanese firms prevented price competition on their home market through their control over vast networks of captive retail networks. Informal agreements on production and prices under the auspices of the Electronics Industries Association of Japan were recorded at least until the mid-1970s (Yamamura 1987; Blair *et al.* 1991; Holmes *et al.* 1992).

an Orderly Market Arrangement (OMA) was negotiated limiting Japanese CTV exports to the US.

As a response to these impediments to exports, Japanese firms set up CTV assembly plants in the US and the UK, their first manufacturing plants in developed countries. Sony led the industry and set up assembly plants in the US in 1972 and in the UK in 1974. Matsushita followed suit and established plants in the US and the UK in 1974. Other CTV manufacturers followed in the second half of the 1970s. The first Japanese manufacturing investments were thus of a defensive nature — deemed necessary to secure market share — and were substituting for exports.

The parallel in trade policy and FDI between the US and EC as witnessed in the CTV industry, has only been repeated for trade friction over Japanese exports of MWOs, and DRAM and EPROM chips. For other products, such as VTRs, plain paper copiers (PPCs), printers and CD players, Japanese exports were the only target of anti-dumping actions or import restrictions in the EC. In contrast, anti-dumping actions were taken only in the US against Japanese imports of pagers (1982) and floppy disks (1988), while in 1987 tariffs were slapped on imports of laptop personal computers (PCs), among others, as a retaliation for non-adherence by Japan of the US-Japan semiconductor agreement. These differences allow for an assessment of the effects of trade policy by comparing exports and FDI for the EC and the US for these products. Table 3 presents data on the volume of Japanese exports, the number of manufacturing plants, and trade policy measures for specific products in the EC and the US. The products are ranked by the relative importance of the EC for Japanese exports in 1990. For comparison, the value of total exports of electronics (broadly defined) to the EC and the US is included.

While the ratio of exports to the EC over exports to the US stood at 0.72 in 1990, the EC/US ratios for individual products differ markedly from this average. Although differences between ratios are related to differences in market size and market share of Japanese firms (which in is turn related to the competitiveness of local firms), the role of differences in trade policy measures and export-substituting FDI can be clearly discerned. Above average ratios of Japanese shipments to the EC relative to the US are found for CTVs, PCs, facsimiles, and camcorders. These are products for which no overt trade policy measures have been taken in the EC and the US, exports to both markets have been restricted (CTVs), or only exports to the US have been targeted by trade policy

Table 3:   Japanese Firms' Exports and Local Manufacturing in 1990 Compared for the EC and the US: The Role of Trade Policy

Product	Exports (1000 units)			# Plants			Trade Policy	
	EC	US	ratio	EC	US	ratio	EC	US
CTVs[a]	313	167	1.87	15	[b]11	1.4	VERs	AD/OMA
PCs	[c]356	[c]190	1.87	2	4	0.5	–	tariff[d]
Facsimiles	1111	1017	1.09	5	3	1.7	–	–
Camcorders	2667	3473	0.77	0	0	–	–	–
PPCs	456	726	0.62	11	3	3.7	AD	–
MWOs	[e]500	866	0.58	6	3	2	AD	AD
Printers	2855	6242	0.46	10	2	5	AD	–
CD Players	2198	4955	0.44	10	1	10	AD	–
ICs	[f]1138	[f]2627	0.43	7	12	0.6	AD/OMA	AD/OMA
VTRs	3171	8610	0.37	16	2	8	VER/AD	–
All Electronics	[g]24603	[g]34131	0.72	140	141	1.0		

Sources: JETRO (1991), EIAJ (1992), Dempa (1991-1992).

Remarks: Ratio's are exports (local plants) in the EC divided by exports (local plants) in the US; Products are ranked by the relative importance of exports to the EC; AD = Anti-Dumping, OMA = Orderly Market Arrangement.

[a] excluding LCD CTVs.

[b] four more plants are located in Mexico and two in Canada.

[c] 1989.

[d] Temporary 100% tariff levied in 1987 as a retaliation for non-complicance by Japan of the US-Japan semiconductor agreement.

[e] Source: Eurostat (1990).

[f] in million dollars.

[g] in million dollars; includes 'precision machinery' and 'office machines'.

measures (PCs). The number of Japanese manufacturing plants for these products is roughly comparable in both regions, or clearly higher in the US (PCs).

From the lower end of Table 3, below average exports to the EC are found for VTRs, CD players, printers, and PPCs, which were hit by trade policy measures in the EC only. The number of manufacturing plants in the EC is several times higher than the number of plants in the

US (although it has to be taken into account that production volumes in EC plants tend to be smaller than those in US plants). VTRs are a case in point, with 16 plants in the EC versus only 2 plants in the US. It is estimated that the volume of Japanese exports to the EC was roughly equal to Japanese production in the EC in 1987, with Japanese exports serving roughly one third of the market; on the other hand, production by Japanese firms in the US was negligible, while Japanese exports took 90% of the market (Belderbos 1992b). For MWOs and integrated circuits (ICs), exports to both markets have been target of trade policy measures and the picture is more mixed. The relatively low level of IC export to the EC is likely to be related to the small size of the EC market for ICs compared to the US.[14]

While Table 3 gives strong support for the idea that the most important motive for manufacturing FDI by Japanese electronics firms in the EC and the US is to 'jump' trade barriers, it is also clear that FDI has been taking place without overt trade policy measures. In some cases, such as facsimiles, the *threat* of import restrictions have been real, and FDI has been undertaken to pre-empt trade policy measures. In general, Japanese firms have accepted the need to localize production of more mature products as part of their commitment to become 'insiders' in the EC and US markets. Yet it also seems evident that locational advantages of the EC and the US have increased vis-à-vis Japan. Japanese firms' cumulative experience in managing manufacturing operations, continuous fluctuations in exchange rates, the advance in automation and flexible manufacturing techniques, and the need to adapt products quickly to rapidly changing local consumer demands, have made production in the EC and the US more attractive.

3.2.2   The Role of EC Trade Policy[15]

The beginning of the 1980s marked the starts of a second round of increasing trade friction between the EC and Japan after the friction over CTV imports in the early 1970s. In 1982, EC producers of VTRs, among which Philips had developed its own VTR standard (the

---

[14] The market for active components in the US is roughly 1.6 times the size of the EC market (CEC 1991a).

[15] This paragraph draws heavily on Belderbos (forthcoming) and Belderbos (1992b), to which the reader is referred for further details.

V-2000), filed a dumping complaint against Japanese firms with the EC Commission. Furthermore, in October France took administrative action to limit VTR imports, by requiring all VTR imports to be handled by the customs office of Poitiers, which became known as the 'Poitiers incident'.[16] Both the dumping complaint and the French measure were finally withdrawn when the EC Commission negotiated an EC-wide VER with Japanese industry through MITI, restricting imports of Japanese VTRs.

During 1982 and 1983, JVC, Sony, Matsushita and Hitachi, the major VTR producers, were the first to begin VTR manufacturing in the EC. Two of these four establishments were joint ventures: JVC started a joint venture with Thorn EMI and Telefunken, as described above, and Matsushita teamed up with Bosch/Blaupunkt in Germany. While the need to be less vulnerable to trade policy measures was the major reason for these investments, the establishments of joint ventures were also part of a successful strategy by Matsushita/JVC of licensing VTR production to EC competitors to gain an early lead for their VHS standard.

The relationship between EC trade policy concerning VTRs and Japanese FDI is illustrated in Figure 3, which sets out the EC's trade policy measures concerning VTRs on a time scale and orders Japanese VTR manufacturing plants by the date of establishment. Other Japanese VTR manufacturers such as Sanyo, Mitsubishi, and Toshiba, followed with plant establishments in 1985. All these investments were located in the UK and Germany; in France only Sony started small-scale VTR manufacturing operations. After the 'Poitiers incident' France definitely was not perceived to have a positive stance towards Japanese firms and was avoided. In 1986 when the VER expired, the EC raised the tariff on VTR imports from 8 to 14%. One year later, trade friction rose again and European producers filed another dumping complaint against two Japanese producers, Funai and Orion, and Korean exporters. One can discern a second wave of plant establishments around this time. Not only Funai and Orion set up VTR assembly plants to avoid paying dumping duties, NEC set up its first VTR plant in the EC as well, and several other producers set up second plants. Presumably, the new anti-dumping investigation signaled a threat of possible future trade restrictions and prompted Japanese firms to pre-empt such measures by setting up manufacturing plants. When in August 1988, the EC Commission decided on 18%

---

[16] See Ishikawa (1990) for a discussion of the events.

anti-dumping duties to be levied on VTR exports by Funai and Orion, both firms' EC plants were well in operation.

What is striking in Figure 3 is the number of (small-scale) plants in different EC countries set up by Japanese firms: in 1989 there were 22 Japanese plants, operated by only 12 firms. On the one hand, this indicates that Japanese plants were mostly handling the simplest assembly and packaging tasks, so that logistics played a more important role than economies of scale in assembly. On the other hand, it indicates a fragmentation of the EC market. This may stem from differences in tastes and culture, and different technical standards. There are, however, other factors that are only relevant to Japanese firms: the remaining national quota for Japanese electronics imports and political factors. The need to appease the French government may have been the most important reason for Matsushita to set up an extra VTR plant in France. The number of plants operating in Spain is clearly related to the fact that Spain limits Japanese VTR imports by a national quota. Japanese firms can not bypass the quota by exporting VTRs assembled in another EC country, if at least 45% of the value added is not generated in the EC, the origin rule applying to VTRs in the EC (see below). Japanese firms have thus opted for a country-based investment strategy instead of an EC-wide strategy, sacrificing economies of scale and efficiency in production. In the next paragraph it becomes clear that this changed in the late 1980s: Japanese firms gradually developed EC-wide strategies and EC activities of Japanese firms have become more integrated.

Trade friction over Japanese VTR imports set the stage for an impressive range of trade policy measures against Japanese electronics exporters taken by the EC Commission during the 1980s, as illustrated by Table 4. The most popular instrument has been the anti-dumping measure. European producers have filed dumping complaints concerning 10 Japanese electronics export goods such as electronic typewriters, Plain Paper Copiers (PPCs), MWOs, CD players and audio cassettes. In several cases, the EC Commission, after investigating, judged that Japanese firms had dumped their exports on the EC market and calculated substantial dumping duties. In all cases, Japanese firms have set up assembly plants in the EC around the time of the anti-dumping investigation to try to avoid having to pay duties: a prime example of what is called 'tariff-jumping FDI'. This even happened in the cases of MWOs and car telephones, in which no actual duties were levied. Apparently the threat of anti-dumping actions has been sufficient to prompt Japanese firms to invest.

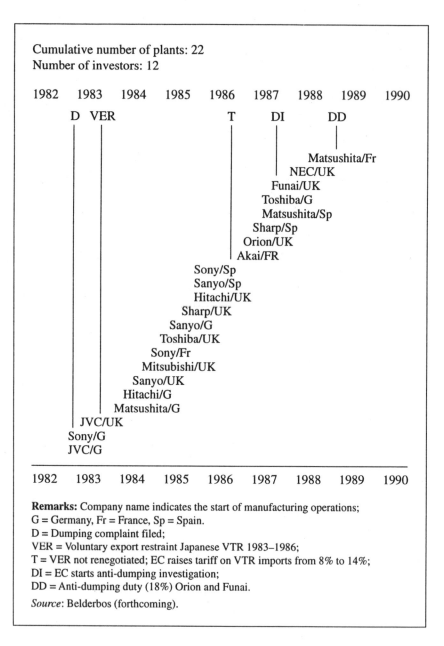

Cumulative number of plants: 22
Number of investors: 12

| 1982 | 1983 | 1984 | 1985 | 1986 | 1987 | 1988 | 1989 | 1990 |

D   VER   T   DI   DD

                                                    Matsushita/Fr
                                              NEC/UK
                                          Funai/UK
                                         Toshiba/G
                                       Matsushita/Sp
                                     Sharp/Sp
                                    Orion/UK
                                   Akai/FR
                      Sony/Sp
                      Sanyo/Sp
                      Hitachi/UK
                   Sharp/UK
                 Sanyo/G
               Toshiba/UK
             Sony/Fr
          Mitsubishi/UK
         Sanyo/UK
       Hitachi/G
     Matsushita/G
   JVC/UK
 Sony/G
 JVC/G

| 1982 | 1983 | 1984 | 1985 | 1986 | 1987 | 1988 | 1989 | 1990 |

Remarks: Company name indicates the start of manufacturing operations;
G = Germany, Fr = France, Sp = Spain.
D = Dumping complaint filed;
VER = Voluntary export restraint Japanese VTR 1983–1986;
T = VER not renegotiated; EC raises tariff on VTR imports from 8% to 14%;
DI = EC starts anti-dumping investigation;
DD = Anti-dumping duty (18%) Orion and Funai.
Source: Belderbos (forthcoming).

Figure 3:   EC Trade Policy and the Start of Japanese VTR Manufacturing

Table 4: EC Trade Policy Targeting Japanese Electronics Exports

Voluntary Export Restraint (VER)

period	*products*
1983–1986	VTRs (monitoring CTV, CRT)

Tariffs and Tariff Changes

year	*product*	*tariff % (previously)*
	CRTs	15
	CTVs	14
1985	ICs	14 (17)
1984	CD Players	19[a] (9.5)
1986	VTRs	14 (8)

Anti-Dumping

start investigation	*product*	*decision, duty %*
1982	VTRs	canceled (VER)
1983	Electronics Scales	1 - 27, undertakings
1984	Electronic Typewriters	17 - 35
1985	PPCs	7.2 - 20
1986	Microwave Ovens	canceled
1987	DOT Matrix Printers	4.8 - 47
1987	CD Players	8.3 - 32
1987	Car Telephones	canceled
1987	VTRs	13, undertakings
1987	DRAMs, EPROMs	undertakings
1989	Audio Cassettes	1.9 - 25.5
1992	CD Players[b]	pending
1992	CTVs	canceled/pending[c]

Table 4: *Continued*

Anti-Dumping Against Assembly Plants		
start investigation	*product*	*decision*
1987	Electronic Scales	duties
1987	Electronic Typewriters	duties/undertakings
1988	PPCs	duties/undertakings
1988	Printers	canceled
1989	VTRs	canceled
Product-Specific Rules of Origin		
year	*product*	*requirement*
1989	ICs	wafer etching
1989	PPCs	major processes

Source: Belderbos (1992b).

[a] 16.5% in 1987, gradually brought back to 9.5% in 1989.

[b] Indirect Japanese Imports from South-East Asian countries.

[c] Investigation of direct imports from Japan canceled, imports from South-East Asian countries still under investigation in early 1993.

The question of to what extent Japanese firms have been dumping is difficult to answer. There have been cases of markedly higher prices for consumer electronics in Japan, which could be ascribed to the market power Japanese firms possess through their size and control over wholesaling and retailing networks (see Van Marion 1992; Holmes *et al.* 1992). On the other hand, most observers conclude that the EC anti-dumping rules are flawed and can even lead to the finding of dumping when prices in Japan are higher than in the EC. The anti-dumping instrument has been used to give EC producers protection against Japanese competition, making it an instrument of industrial policy, besides protecting against possible dumping (Van Bael and Bellis 1990; Hindley 1988; Ishikawa 1990; Messerlin 1989). For instance, Tharakan (1991) finds that factors such as the state of the trade balance and the economic power of the complaining EC producers influence the decision process significantly. Furthermore, the largest number of anti-dumping cases have been brought forward against Japanese firms, and most concern products for which the competitive strength of Japanese firms is undisputed. Once dumping is established, duties tend to be substantial and extend at least five years, so that they have a strong influence on competitive conditions in the industry.

A further indication that anti-dumping policy served as an instrument of industrial policy, may be given by the response of the EC Commission to the wave of tariff-jumping investments by Japanese firms. In 1987, when it became clear that Japanese firms could still threaten to increase market shares by investing in assembly plants in the EC, the EC commission responded by amending its anti-dumping legislation to make it applicable to Japanese assembly plants as well.[17] The new rule stipulated that firms that had been target of anti-dumping actions and had reacted by setting up assembly plants in the EC, were required to procure at least 40% of components used in assembly from other countries than Japan. If Japanese firms did not clear this requirement, anti-dumping duties were to be levied on Japanese products assembled in the EC. The amendment should have impeded Japanese firms from circumventing anti-dumping measures by setting up simple assembly plants, but in practice it forced Japanese firms to increase manufacturing activities in the EC. The relationship with anti-dumping was rather obscure since, according to the new law, it was not necessary to prove that Japanese firms were still dumping and that this was causing the EC industry 'material injury'; just the fact that they set up or increased assembly in the EC was sufficient. Anti-dumping actions against assembly plants were taken five times (see Table 10) and led to additional duties or undertakings[18] by which Japanese firms agreed to increase the local content of EC production.

However, in March 1989, the GATT panel ruled against the new legislation, mainly because it is applied in a discriminatory way to Japanese producers.[19] The EC Commission has not invoked the law since then, although the Commission refused to withdraw its legislation. These events will not give Japanese firms much of an assurance that local content rules will not affect their EC activities

---

[17] EC legislation Council Regulation No. 1761/87, published in the Official Journal of the EC, 26 June 1987. See Ishikawa (1989) for a discussion.

[18] An undertaking is an agreement between the filing (EC firms) party and the anti-dumping authority (the EC commission) on the one hand, and the exporter under investigation on the other, by which the authority ends the anti-dumping investigation without levying duties, while the exporters agrees on specific conduct, which in case of anti-dumping against assembly plants usually meant increasing local content.

[19] In fact, there are EC producers who would not be able to pass the 40% test. See Vermulst and Waer (1990). Also note that the law has only been invoked in seven cases, all of which concerned Japanese firms (Van Bael and Bellis 1990).

in some form in the future. In fact, the EC Commission used another unconventional instrument of trade policy, the rule of origin, apparently to strengthen the effectiveness of anti-dumping actions, but effectively forcing Japanese firms to extend manufacturing operations in the EC. Rules of origin state what national origin should be attached to a product, and gain importance when trade policy measures are country- or firm-specific, as is the case with anti-dumping policy.

In February 1990, a new product-specific rule of origin was accepted for PPCs, stipulating that some minor manufacturing operations are not sufficient to confer origin. The new rule was directly aimed at impeding Ricoh to bypass anti-dumping duties on PPC imports from Japan by importing PPCs assembled in its US plant in California (Vermulst and Waer 1990). It must have assured Ricoh (and other Japanese PPC manufacturers) that the only way to secure sales in the EC was by expanding EC manufacturing operations. In July 1989, a new origin for ICs was adopted, stating that the country of origin is that where the etching of silicon wafers takes place. This new rule was likewise directed specifically at Japanese firms, which were still under investigation in an anti-dumping case concerning DRAM and EPROM memory chips. At the time, the major Japanese IC manufacturers operated IC plants in the EC, but these plants mostly engaged in assembly, packaging and testing. Without the new rule of origin, EC-assembled ICs would be considered of European origin, and anti-dumping actions could have been avoided by increasing EC assembly activities. As a response to the new rule, all major Japanese manufacturers (NEC, Fujitsu, Hitachi, Toshiba, and Mitsubishi) have extended their EC operations to include wafer etching or established new integrated plants.[20] It is estimated that cumulative investment in Japanese IC manufacturing plants in the EC amounted to 3 billion ECUs by 1991 (CEC 1991b, p. 12–15).

Eventually, no anti-dumping duties were levied, but an EC-Japanese semiconductor agreement was concluded which set minimum prices for Japanese IC exports to the EC. However, Japanese IC manufacturers have still another reason to have their ICs labeled 'European'. The drive to increase the European content of EC-manufactured products by Japanese producers of products such as PPCs and VTRs, led to a growing demand for 'European' ICs, necessary to clear local content

---

[20] See CEC (1991b, p. 12–14), Furlotti (1991), and Electronics Business, September 17, 1990, p. 79. Note that US firms which had no wafer etching facilitates in the EC followed a similar investment strategy.

rules. It also led to demand for other EC-made components such as printed circuit boards, power supply units, tuners, capacitors, magnetic heads, magnetrons and the like. This has been an important factor determining a wave of investments in components manufacturing. Firstly, major Japanese components suppliers such as Alps, Murata, Tabuchi and Tamura, which are important suppliers of components to Japanese electronics firms in Japan, have set up and expanded manufacturing activities in the EC, primarily to supply Japanese firms. Table 5 demonstrates the rapid increase in EC operations by Japanese components manufacturers during 1986–1991. Kyocera, which did not have any presence in the EC in 1986, became the largest manufacturer in the EC among Japanese components firms through the acquisition of the US based AVX Corp., which had important European operations (see also Section 3.4.2). Alps, TDK, and Murata grew rapidly by investments in greenfield plants. Secondly, Japanese electronics firms increased in-house production of key components in the EC. Matsushita, for instance, chose this route more than other Japanese firms, and operates EC plants manufacturing magnetrons for MWOs, transformers, relays, electric motors for office equipment, and magnetic heads, among others, and has set up a joint venture with Siemens in passive components. Trends in investment in the EC will be discussed in more detail in Section 3.4.

From the above, it might be concluded that virtually all manufacturing investments by Japanese firms in the EC in the 1980s were in some way induced by EC trade policy measures. In the eyes of Japanese electronics firms, the threat of a 'fortress Europe' has materialized well before the establishment of the Internal Market in 1993.

After the rule of origin measures in 1989, there has been a relative calm in trade disputes between the EC and Japan in 1990 and 1991 although there have been some indications of trade friction. The EC Commission has attempted (but failed) to get camcorders reclassified as VTRs at customs, which would increase the import tariff by 10% points. Several Japanese producers of facsimiles are reported to have set up manufacturing activities in the EC because of anti-dumping threats, which apparently have never materialized in an official investigation (Japan Society for the Promotion of Machinery 1989) and EC manufacturers of PPCs (Xerox UK and Olivetti) applied for an extension of the five-year period during which duties were levied on Japanese PPC imports.

In 1992, however, two important anti-dumping cases arose (see Table 4). In June, EC producers filed anti-dumping suits against

Table 5:   Japanese Electronic Components Suppliers in the EC

Company	Plant Location	Products	EC Employment 1991	1986
Kyocera/AVX	UK, G, Fr	ceramic components, capacitors	1866	29
Alps	UK, G, Ire	keyboards, tuners, switches, magnetic heads	1146	329
TDK	G, Lux	audio tapes, coils, magnets	1210	180
Murata Electronic	UK, G	condensors, filters, resistors	730	na
Tabuchi	UK	power supply units	520	190
Munekata	UK, Ire	plastic molded parts	413	0
Nitto Denko	Bel	insulating tapes	398	274
Tamura	UK	power supply units, transformers	312	0
Mitsumi	UK, Ire	coils, tuners, switches	234	5
SMK	UK	keyboard switches, remote controls	178	13
Terasaki	UK	power switch boards	160	0
Nihon CMK	Bel	printed circuit boards	140	0
JST	UK, G, Fr	connectors	104	0
Teikoku	Neth	switches, resistors	100	0

Sources: Touyou Keizai (1987, 1992), EIAJ (1992).

Remarks: G=Germany, Bel=Belgium, Fr=France, Ire=Ireland, Neth=Netherlands, Lux=Luxembourg.

Japanese imports of CD players which were allegedly routed via trading firms or assembly plants in Malaysia, Taiwan, and Singapore; direct imports from Japan are already subject to duties. In July, another anti-dumping complaint was filed against Japanese CTV imports from Japan and several South-East Asian countries.

Both actions come at a time of low demand and overcapacity in the EC as well as in the Japanese consumer electronics market. Both EC and Japanese firms have reported losses or steep declines in profits. Sony reported a first-time loss on its Japanese operations, Toshiba and Hitachi have decided to pull out of the audio market altogether, and Shintomu, a medium-sized Japanese OEM producer of VTRs, closed its factory in Japan to concentrate production in Singapore. In Europe, Philips took a multi-billion loss in 1991 and embarked on an ambitious restructuring plan and Thomson consumer electronics has not been profitable during several years.

Against this background, the filing of anti-dumping complaints by EC firms appears to be an effort to gain relief from harsh competition. There are also reasons to believe that anti-dumping actions might not lead to favorable conclusions for EC producers. Firstly, Japan refused to accept the EC Commission's May 1991 ruling on the dumping of audio cassettes and in October 1992 asked the GATT dispute settlement panel whether anti-dumping duties had been levied unfairly. The possibility of a negative GATT ruling might make the EC Commission more cautious in pursuing anti-dumping cases, especially, since the last time Japan went to the GATT to ask for a ruling on the EC's anti dumping legislation against assembly plants, it won. Furthermore, Japanese firms by now have become important producers of CD players and CTVs in the EC and must be able to use their economic leverage to protect their interests at the EC Commission.[21]

Recent events in the CTV anti-dumping case may illustrate the leverage of Japanese firms: the EC Commission in November 1992 decided to take Japan off the list of countries under investigation for allegedly dumping CTVs on EC markets. Japanese firms can still be affected, since some firms export part of production by their manufacturing subsidiaries in South-East Asian countries such as Malaysia and Singapore to the EC, and these exports are still under investigation. Nevertheless, it is clear that the major target of the EC's anti-dumping actions is no longer Japanese firms but rather firms from South-Korean, Hong Kong, and Taiwan.

The CD player case is somewhat different, since competition from the NIEs is not very strong in this sector. Here, Japanese exports from South-East Asian plants have been the major target of the EC's anti-dumping action. Just as the new rule of origin for PPCs, it signals to Japanese producers that only production within the EC can secure free access to the EC market.

While trade policy measures thus still affect Japanese firms operations in the EC in the early 1990s, Japanese investments in the

---

[21] It is interesting to note that as early as 1987, established Japanese VTR producers in the EC joined in the anti-dumping complaints against Funai, Orion and Korean VTR exporters.

EC are evolving from mere responses to trade policy measures to a more balanced 'insider' strategy to secure market access in the longer term and to exploit local advantages. In the next section, it will be shown that recent acquisitions of computer firms Apricot computer and ICL fit into this pattern, as well as the recent establishments of software engineering centers and greenfield establishments of production plants for products such as PCs and disk drives.

3.3   JAPANESE DIRECT FOREIGN INVESTMENT IN THE EC

This section will describe patterns of Japanese electronics firms' investments in the EC by country, product group, and company. Paragraph 3.4.1 presents a detailed picture of Japanese subsidiaries and employment in 1986 and 1990. Paragraph 3.4.2 looks at modes of entry into the EC market. Paragraph 3.4.3 takes up the issue of possible pan-EC strategies adopted by Japanese firms, while in paragraph 3.4.4 an attempt is made to put Japanese investment in the EC in a broader perspective.

3.3.1   *Manufacturing and Sales Subsidiaries in the EC in 1990*

Tables 6 through 9 show employment and subsidiaries in the EC in 1986 and 1990 by country and product group. The figures represent the situation around May of the year. The subsidiaries are classified according to activity (manufacturing or sales)[22] and product group: consumer electronics (including MWOs), industrial electronics and office automation equipment, and components (including ICs). The main source of information is Touyou Keizai (1987, 1991), which provides a near complete listing of Japanese subsidiaries abroad.[23] As a rule, only subsidiaries in which Japanese firms hold an equity stake of more than 40% are included in the tables in this chapter.

Table 6 shows the location of Japanese electronics firms' manufacturing subsidiaries in the EC in 1990 and 1986. The total number of subsidiaries in the EC grew by 141% in 1986–1990, from 70 in 1986 to 169 in 1990. The number of components subsidiaries (77)

---

[22] Subsidiaries which combine manufacturing functions with some sales activities are classified as manufacturing subsidiaries.

[23] See Appendix A for a discussion of the data sources.

Table 6: Japanese Manufacturing Subsidiaries in the EC in 1990 and 1986 by Country

country	1990					1986	
	cons	indu	compo	all	(%)	all	(%)
UK	28	13	32	64	(38)	21	(30)
Germany	4	9	16	38	(22)	23	(33)
France	15	9	7	26	(15)	6	(9)
Spain	6	2	4	9	(5)	7	(10)
Italy	3	5	3	8	(5)	1	(1)
Holland	0	4	3	6	(4)	2	(3)
Belgium	10	4	6	11	(7)	6	(9)
Ireland	0	0	6	6	(4)	4	(6)
Denmark	0	1	0	1	(1)	0	(0)
Total	7	47	77	169	(100)	70	(100)
1986	38	16	23	70			
% incr	76	193	234	141			

Source: Calculations based on Touyou Keizai (1991, 1987).

Remarks: cons= consumer electronics, indu= industrial electronics, compo= electronic components; multiple classification is possible if a subsidiary manufactures products in more than one product group; consequently the sum of the number of subsidiaries in cons, indu, and compo can be greater than the total number of subsidiaries. Figures represent subsidiaries with manufacturing function; these may be combined with sales functions.

surpassed the number of subsidiaries which manufacture consumer electronics (67), growing by 234% against a 76% growth for consumer electronics. Since the number of subsidiaries producing industrial electronics also increased by almost 200%, the pattern of manufacturing investment has clearly shifted away from consumer electronics to industrial electronics and components in the second half of the 1980s.

The products manufactured reflect both Japanese firms' strengths and trade policy measures against exports: consumer electronics: (CTVs, VTRs, MWOs, CD players, car audio, electronic typewriters, PC printers, magnetic tapes), office automation equipment (PPCs, facsimiles), car telephones, ICs (DRAMs and EPROMs, mostly), and various components for office automation equipment and consumer electronics (magnetrons for MWOs, power sources, transformers,

Table 7: Employment in Japanese Manufacturing Subsidiaries in the EC in 1990 and 1986

country						1986	

country	cons	indu	compo	all	(%)	all	(%)
UK	15673	2666	10094	22569	(47)	4149	(43)
Germany	3952	1726	3848	9176	(19)	1868	(18)
France	4805	1630	963	6328	(13)	482	(5)
Italy	1120	786	0	1236	(3)	na	(na)
Spain	5131	2152	221	5344	(11)	1495	(16)
Netherlands	0	261	96	290	(1)	15	(0)
Belgium	388	658	959	2005	(4)	1268	(13)
Ireland	0	0	1205	1205	(2)	522	(5)
Denmark	0	160	0	160	(0)	0	(0)
total	31069	10039	17386	48313	(100)	9671	(100)
1986	6501	886	3027	9671			
% incr	378	1033	474	400			

Source: Calculations based on Touyou Keizai (1991, 1987).

Remarks: cons= consumer electronics, indu= industrial electronics, compo= electronic components. Multiple classification is possible if a subsidiary manufactures products in more than one product group; consequently the sum of employment in cons, indu, and compo can be greater than total employment. Figures represent employment in subsidiaries with manufacturing function; these may be combined with sales functions. Note that the figures for 1986 do not include manufacturing employment of Sony, Canon, Hitachi, Ricoh, JVC, Mitsubishi, and Minolta, for which firms no information was available. The increase in employment 1986-1990 thus is overestimated.

switches, connectors, printed circuit boards, capacitors, condensers, magnetic heads for VTRs, etc). These products, cover virtually all manufacturing activity by Japanese firms in 1990.

By country, the UK is by far the most important host of Japanese FDI, attracting 38% of all subsidiaries. Factors promoting investment in the UK are its large home market, the accessible English language, business attitudes and culture which are similar to those in the US where Japanese firms have gained experience in operating manufacturing plants, and the forthcoming attitude of national and local governments, which have actively invited (and subsidized) Japanese investors. The relative attractiveness of the UK only seems to be increasing, as its share has been rising by 8% points since 1986. This increase is mainly due to the UK's attractiveness for components manufacturing; in industrial electronics, the UK is much less dominant. Germany and France host another 64 plants, bringing the share of the three largest markets to three quarters. Although the number of subsidiaries in Germany increased from 23 in 1986 to 38 in 1990, its share declined from 33 to 22%.

France, on the other hand, has become much more important as a manufacturing base for Japanese electronics firms: in 1990 it hosted 26 subsidiaries, 15% of the EC total, while the country was still clearly under-represented in 1986 (9%). Companies such as Hitachi and Matsushita, the two largest Japanese electronics firms, have largely ignored France because of the perceived hostility and intrusiveness of the French government. Although Sony's Akio Morita has also voiced complaints about the 'administrative guidance' of the French government affecting its operations in France (Morita 1987), it has steadily increased manufacturing subsidiaries in France and currently employs 2000 personnel in manufacturing plants alone. The same positive attitude can be ascribed to Canon, which operates a sophisticated PPC plant in Bretagne has recently established an R&D center in Rennes.

The French government's stance on Japanese FDI changed radically in 1984 from open hostility to accommodation, when Laurent Fabius visited Tokyo and openly invited Japanese investors. Political relations were further improved upon the visit of MITI officials to France in 1986 (HEC Eurasia Institute, 1989). Still the need to appease the French government and avert protectionist pressures is often cited as a major reason to invest in France, all the more because the French government is seen to have a great influence on decisions by the EC commission.[24] Although France hosts four PPC plants, investment has mostly concentrated on consumer electronics (manufacture of VTRs and CD players). Special technical specifications for French consumer products, such as those related to the SECAM broadcasting system, play a role, and so does the attractiveness of the French consumer electronics market, where prices tend to be high relative to other EC countries (Mackintosh 1985).

Other European countries host the remaining quarter of Japanese

---

[24] This view was supported by a Matsushita official in an interview in 1990.

subsidiaries. Belgium is relatively important (11 subsidiaries), whereas Italy has only recently attracted Japanese investments, its number of subsidiaries increasing from 1 to 8. Denmark (1 subsidiary), Greece and Portugal (no production) are barely considered as locations for electronics manufacturing within the EC if at all.

Most of the observations are strengthened by the data on employment in manufacturing subsidiaries presented in Table 7. The number of employees in Japanese manufacturing subsidiaries almost reached 50,000 in 1990, a 400% increase over 1986. These figures exclude the acquisition of ICL by Fujitsu, which was finalized in the end of 1990, and a large joint venture between Siemens and Matsushita in components, among others.[25] In terms of employment, consumer electronics is still by far the most important sector. Employment in components plants has been rising rapidly to more than 17,000 persons, in the wake of local content regulations and rules of origin, as was also illustrated by Table 5 above.

The dominance of the three largest EC countries is even more pronounced than in term of numbers of subsidiaries: 79% of manufacturing employment is located in the UK, Germany and France. The UK hosts almost half the total number of employees. Germany's share increased by 1% point during 1986–1990, implying that growth in investment here was for a large part achieved by expansion of existing subsidiaries. The investment position of France improved impressively in 1986–1990: its employment share increasing from a mere 5 to a substantial 13%. In France, the concentration on consumer electronics is pronounced, while components manufacturing is not well represented. The other manufacturing location of importance is Spain, attracting 11% of the total number of employees in 1990. However, it has lost some ground to the larger countries.

Investments in extensive distribution channels is often cited as a major strength of Japanese firms. The major Japanese electronics firms, lead by Matsushita, have vertically integrated into wholesaling and retailing in Japan, controling thousands of electronics retail shops throughout the country. In the US and the EC, Japanese firms have set up extensive distribution networks as well, at the wholesale level. This to increase customer services such as repair and product guarantees, to take care of advertising and foster the brand name of the company, and to feed back valuable information on consumer tastes and market

---

[25] In 1990, Matsushita still had only a 35% stake in the venture; in 1991 it increased its stake to 50%. See also Section 3.4.2.

developments. Yamawaki (1991), for instance, finds empirical evidence that investments in distribution networks in the US have enhanced the export performance of Japanese firms. Belderbos (1992b) finds similar results for exports to Europe by Japanese electronics manufacturers.

Tables 8 and 9 show that Japanese electronics firms expanded their distribution networks in the EC in 1986-1990. In 1990 the number of sales subsidiaries reached 416 (Table 6), employing more than 27,000 people (Table 8). The number of sales bases increased by 43%, while the increase was stronger for the components and industrial sectors than for consumer electronics. Sales networks for consumer electronics date from the 1960s when Sony and Matsushita established their first subsidiaries, and the distribution networks in consumer

Table 8: Japanese Sales Subsidiaries in the EC in 1990 and 1986 by Country

country	1990					1986	
	cons	indu	compo	all	(%)	all	(%)
UK	41	58	26	101	(24)	68	(23)
Germany	58	66	42	138	(33)	114	(39)
France	17	25	14	48	(12)	30	(10)
Spain	9	13	2	17	(4)	8	(3)
Italy	10	16	8	29	(7)	15	(5)
Netherlands	14	13	6	32	(8)	21	(7)
Belgium	12	15	5	26	(6)	19	(7)
Ireland	5	4	0	5	(1)	4	(1)
Denmark	8	6	2	13	(3)	9	(3)
Portugal	2	4	0	6	(1)	1	(0)
Greece	1	0	0	1	(0)	0	(0)
1986	148	144	57	290			
% incr	20	57	84	43			
Total	177	226	105	416	(100)	290	(100)

Source: Calculations based on Touyou Keizai (1991, 1987).

Remarks: cons= consumer electronics, indu= industrial electronics, compo= electronic components; multiple classification is possible if a subsidiary distributes products in more than one product group; consequently the sum of the number of subsidiaries in cons, indu, and compo càn be greater than the total number of subsidiaries; Figures represent sales subsidiaries without any manufacturing activity.

Table 9:   Employment in Japanese Sales Subsidiaries in the EC in 1990 and 1986

country	1990 cons	indu	compo	all	(%)	1986 all	(%)
UK	6051	5611	1442	8868	(32)	5247	(32)
Germany	5134	4207	1992	9081	(33)	5927	(36)
France	890	2998	307	3802	(14)	2899	(18)
Italy	671	966	92	1469	(5)	648	(4)
Spain	832	892	15	1023	(4)	172	(1)
Netherlands	614	1183	181	1531	(6)	709	(4)
Belgium	618	701	76	1192	(4)	590	(4)
Denmark	173	151	7	264	(1)	152	(1)
Ireland	93	93	0	93	(0)	0	(0)
Portugal	91	21	0	112	(0)	9	(0)
Greece	19	0	0	19	(0)	12	(0)
Total	15186	16823	4112	27454	(100)	16429	(100)
1986	9176	9073	1623	16429			
% incr	65	85	153	67			

Source: Calculations based on Touyou Keizai (1991, 1987).

Remarks: cons= consumer electronics, indu=industrial electronics, compo= electronic components. Multiple classification is possible if a subsidiary distributes products in more than one product group; consequently the sum of employment in cons, indu, and compo can be greater than total employment. Figures represent employment in subsidiaries with only sales activities. Figures for do not include employment of Sony, Ricoh, JVC, and Minolta, for which firms no information was available. The increase in employment 1986-1990 thus is overestimated.

electronics are relatively complete. Most Japanese component suppliers, on the other hand, have not been active in the EC for very long and they have increased their sales efforts markedly in the second half of the 1980s.

The country distribution of the number of subsidiaries largely reflects the size of the market in the different countries. Germany hosts the largest number of sales subsidiaries, followed by the UK and France. On the other hand, the Netherlands and Belgium have received relative large shares of investments in distribution due to their geographical location, excellent infrastructure, and facilities for distribution centers.

In terms of employment (Table 8), the expansion of distribution networks is even more obvious. Employment increased by an impressive 153% in the components sector, while growth in consumer electronics still reached 65%. The distribution among countries is roughly similar to that in Table 6; the UK hosts comparatively large sales subsidiaries and is equally important as Germany in terms of sales employees.

Data on employment and the number of subsidiaries by individual firms are provided in the Appendix to this chapter, which lists all Japanese electronics firms employing more than 100 people in the EC by 1990. Companies are, if relevant, grouped by membership of *keiretsu* company groupings.[26] The biggest investor in terms of employment is the Matsushita group. The parent firm Matsushita Electric Industrial employed more than 6000 people in the EC in 1990. In addition, various subsidiaries of the parent firm have invested in the EC. JVC, 50% owned by Matsushita but run relatively independent from its parent firm, is the largest and employs more than 2400 in manufacturing only. Other big investors are Sony (6765 employees in manufacturing subsidiaries only), Canon (nearly 8000 employees), Toshiba (4709), and Hitachi, NEC, Sanyo, Kyocera, and Sharp (all around 3000 employees). Employment in sales subsidiaries is relatively high for Canon, with an impressive 6000 employees devoted to its sales, service and repair of its PPCs, office machines and cameras. Most of the large investors have increased employment in the EC rapidly over 1986–1990, for example: Matsushita (184%), Canon (110%), Toshiba (84%), NEC (140%), and Sharp (116%). Towards the end of the list, there is an important number of (mostly small or medium-sized) Japanese firms which set up subsidiaries in the EC for the first time in 1986-1990. Investment in the EC clearly is no longer reserved for large Japanese electronics firms.

Trends in Japanese investment during 1991–1992 show several characteristics which are distinct from the pattern of investment in the 1980s. Acquisition became a popular instrument to secure access to markets and to complement Japanese firms' skills. Besides some major acquisitions, a large number of smaller firms were acquired, as will be discussed below in paragraph 3.4.2. Greenfield investments took

---

[26] Only the so-called vertical *keiretsu*, in which there is a clear hierarchical relationship between parent and subsidiaries, are considered here, and not the diversified, bank-centered horizontal *keiretsu*.

place at a lesser pace than before. Two major new plant establishments concern manufacturing plants for disk drives: Matsushita Kotobuki set up a plant in Ireland in 1992 (250 employees planned), and Hitachi set up a plant in Ardon in France in 1991 (440 employees planned). In addition, Toshiba started production of laptop PCs in its Regensburg plant in Germany in 1990. Another major investment was the establishment of a joint venture by TDK and Germany's Robert Bosch to manufacture ferrite magnets (700 employees planned). These investment are less obviously related to trade policy measures, and investment is shifting to components and computer- and software-related areas, including the setup of software engineering centers. Information on the pattern of Japanese investments during 1991–1992 lead an estimate that the total number of employees in manufacturing subsidiaries in the EC at the end of 1992 reached at least 60,000.

3.3.2   Modes of Entry in Manufacturing

The lion's share of Japanese electronics firms' manufacturing subsidiaries in the EC until 1990 was wholly or majority owned and established as greenfield plants. A major competitive advantage of Japanese firms is the ability to produce high quality products at low costs through expertise in manufacturing technology and production management. These advantages are best transferred abroad by exercising strict control over management and production abroad. Japanese firms are furthermore keen to maintain the technological lead they achieved in the development of products such as facsimiles and PPCs. Investments in wholesale distribution subsidiaries (likewise mostly wholly owned) are set up to exercise control over after-sales service, spare parts deliveries, repair and marketing, which Japanese firms tend to see as critical to their market position in the long run.

In several cases, however, Japanese firms have set up manufacturing joint ventures with EC firms. The first joint ventures were set up in CTV production in 1978 by Hitachi and Toshiba, with the UK firms GEC and Rank, respectively. An earlier attempt by Hitachi to set up a greenfield plant had been canceled after vigorous opposition by the UK television industry and labor unions (Cawson *et al.* 1990). The major purpose of the joint ventures was to fend off this hostility, although another important advantage was the acquired right to produce CTVs for the EC market under a PAL license. Both joint ventures eventually ended in a takeover by the Japanese firm. The

Japanese firms complained that they did not get any cooperation in introducing their efficient production and management methods. The UK side disputed the necessity to use Japanese components, and some hinted (e.g. Van Marion 1992) that the Japanese firms willfully let the joint ventures collapse to be able to take full control.

The next major Japanese-EC joint venture was established in 1982, when JVC teamed up with Thorn-EMI in the UK and Telefunken in Germany to form an alliance in VTRs. It appeared a successful strategic move by JVC, which acquired access to the important distribution channels (among which VTR rental shops) of Thorn and Telefunken and the video software produced by EMI. This proved crucial in the battle for market share between JVC, which had developed its own VHS standard for VTRs, Sony (Betamax), and Philips (V-2000). The VHS standard eventually became the industry's standard. Thomson, the French state-owned consumer electronics firm, had opted to join the joint venture as well, but was blocked by the French government (Cawson *et al.* 1990). In 1984, however, it acquired Telefunken and automatically became JVC's main joint venture partner. Thorn left the venture in 1987 and since then production has been concentrated in Germany and France. In Tonnerre, France, mecadecks are manufactured which are shipped to Berlin where J2T produces around a million VTRs per year, which makes it by far the largest among Japanese VTR plants in the EC. The VTRs are distributed separately by Thomson and JVC under their own brand names.

Table 10 lists the major joint ventures between Japanese and EC firms in the electronics industry by 1991. Until the end of 1989, the J2T joint venture was the largest with more than 1600 employees in its two establishments. By far the largest joint venture was established by Siemens and Matsushita in October 1989 in Germany: 5200 employees work in the new subsidiary. The goal is to manufacture and develop passive components. Matsushita initially held a minority stake of 35% (the reason why the joint venture is not included in the employment figures in other tables), but this stake increased to 50% in 1992.

Even without this major joint venture, employment in Japanese-EC joint ventures amounted to around 12% of total employment in Japanese manufacturing subsidiaries in the EC in 1990. This percentage was substantially higher in Italy (two thirds) and, to a lesser extent, France (around a quarter), the two countries which have been most antagonistic with respect to Japanese investment in the past. The main goal of joint ventures is to secure market access and a more forthcoming government attitude. On the other hand,

Table 10:   Main EC-Japanese Joint Ventures in Electronics by Country

Subsidiary Name	Japanese Firm (%) / Partner Firm (%)	Estbl	Empl (J)	Products
United Kingdom				
Lucas-Yuasa Batteries	Yuasa (50) / Lucas Industries (50)	1988.08	654 (0)	car batteries
Gooding Sanken	Sanken Electric (49) / Gooding (51)	1989.10	240 (7)	transformers, power switches
Germany				
J2T	JVC (50) / Thomson (50)	1982.05	758 (1)	VTRs
MB Video	Matsushita (65) / Robert Bosch (35)	1982.12	875 (14)	VTRs, CD players
Siemens-Matsushita Components	Matsushita (50) / Siemens (50)	1989.10	5448 (4)	passive components
BT Magnet Technology	TDK (50) / Robert Bosch (50)	1991	700 (2)	ferrite magnets
France				
J2T	JVC (50) / Thomson (50)	1982.03	519 (1)	mecadecks for VTRs
Toshiba Systems	Toshiba (74) / Rhone Poulenc (26)	1986.06	602 (7)	PPCs, fax
CEFEMO	Toshiba (33) / Thomson (33), AEG (33)	1987.09	408 (2)	MWOs
Italy				
Olivetti-Canon Industrial	Canon (50) / Olivetti (50)	1987.04	642 (5)	fax, laser printers
Olivetti-Sanyo Industrial	Sanyo (44) / Olivetti (56)	1990.01	162 (1)	fax
Belgium				
Philips-Matsuthita Battery	Matsushita (50) / Philips (50)	1970.09	335 (1)	lead dry batteries

Table 10: *continued*

Subsidiary Name	Japanese Firm (%) Partner Firm (%)	Estbl	Empl (J)	Products
Netherlands				
Noble Europe	Teikoku Tsushin (51)	1991.10	100	variable resistors, switches
	Philips (49)		(2)	

Sources: Touyou Keizai (1991-1992), EIAJ (1992), Jetro (1990b).

Remarks: (%)=percentage capital stake, Estbl=establishment time, Empl=number of employees, (J)=number of Japanese employees.

the Siemens-Matsushita and Olivetti-Canon joint ventures are broader alliances which extend to the joint development of new products.

At the firm level, it is interesting to note that there are important differences between strategies of Japanese firms. On the one hand, Matsushita, Japan's largest electronics firm and investor in Europe, operates joint ventures with all major European competitors except Nokia: Siemens, Bosch, Philips, and Thomson (through JVC). On the other hand, two of the largest Japanese investors, Sony and Hitachi, do not operate any joint ventures in the EC. Sony, probably the most innovative Japanese consumer electronics firm, finds strict control over manufacturing, marketing and product design essential for its long term competitive position. It is also the firm which is most devoted to the principle "manufacture where you sell", and this is probably why it largely managed to avoid friction with EC governments; it became the largest investor in France and set up a greenfield plant for the manufacture of audio tapes in Italy's Rovereto in 1989.

The third mode of market entry, acquisition of EC firms, has gained remarkable importance recently, while being a neglected mode of investment during most of the 1980s. In Table 9, the major acquisitions of Japanese electronics firms in the EC are ordered by year of acquisition. The first Japanese acquisition was the takeover by Sony of the German audio manufacturer Wega in 1975. In the 1980s, there were some smaller acquisitions, among which the joint venture buyouts by Hitachi and Toshiba of their partners Rank and GEC, respectively.

Breaking with past trends, the year 989–1992 saw a range of takeovers, two of which involved EC firms occupying a major place in EC industry. With the acquisition of AVX in the US, Kyocera acquired AVX's operations in the EC. AVX is a major producers of capacitors, among others, and holds a market share of 9%, equal to Siemens and just below Philips (CEC 1991b). The most important and ardently discussed acquisition is also the most recent one: Fujitsu's takeover of ICL for 700 million pounds in 1991. With this acquisition, Fujitsu at once became an important player in the EC market for large computers. Both Kyocera and Fujitsu had a relatively small presence in the EC before, and acquisition is a major means to reach a critical market share in the EC quickly. The timing suggests that firms found it opportune to invest before the planned completion of the Internal Market in the beginning of 1993.

Japanese firms also acquired several medium sized firms in Europe in areas ranging from PCs and software (Matsushita's acquisition of Office Workstations and Mitsubishi's acquisition of Apricot Computers) to cabinets for CTVs (Munekata's acquisition of Plastronics in Ireland), components (Hoshiden-Besson and Omron-Schoenbuch), and measuring equipment (Sanyo-Gallenkamp and Advantest-Giga Instrumentation). Besides these takeovers, joint venture buy-outs became popular again in the years 1990–1991, with Funai, Tamura, and Kenwood buying out their respective joint venture partners. In addition, there were two major capital participations by Japanese firms. Matsushita acquired a 25% stake in the German CTV producer Loewe Opta, and Ricoh bought a 24% stake in major European distributor of office machines Gestetner, to which Ricoh supplies office machines on an OEM basis.

The importance of acquisitions as a mode to enter the EC market, suggests that investments have evolved from direct responses to trade policy to strategic investments to secure market access and to acquire specific technological skills. This pattern in the EC follows the trend in investments in the US, where Japanese electronics firms have acquired a range of small and innovative firms (see Genther and Dalton 1992).

Finally, it is important to note the dominance of UK firms as targets for Japanese acquisition. This may reflect a business culture in which acquisition as a means of firm expansion is generally accepted, and the relatively positive stance of the UK government and industry towards Japanese firms and investments. French firms, on the other hand, have not been a target of acquisition by Japanese firms in the 1980s. The increasingly open environment for Japanese firms in France is again illustrated by the fact that during 1990–1991 Japanese firms for the first time acquired French firms: Advantest acquired Giga Instrumentation

Table 11:   Main European Acquisitions by Japanese Electronics Firms

Japanese Company	Target Firm	Year	Cap Stake	Empl 1991	Activity
Acquisitions					
Sony	Wega (G)	1975	100	654	audio, video
King	Chubb Cash Registers (UK)	1983	100	230	cash registers
Minolta	Develop Dr. Eisbein (G)	1986	83	500	PPCs
Shimadzu	Kratos Group (UK)	1989	100	290	analytical equipment
Munekata	Plastronics (Ire)	1989	100	372	cabinets for CTV
Matsushita	Office Workstations (UK)	1989	100	65	software
Kyocera	AVX (US/UK)	1990	100	1398	components
Hoshiden	Besson (UK)	1990	100	434	telephones, components
Mitsubishi El.	Apricot Computers (UK)	1990	100	431	PCs, software
Sanyo	Gallenkamp Plc (UK)	1990	100	312	measuring equipment
Advantest	Giga Instrumentation (Fr)	1990	100	90	measuring & testing eq
Fujitsu	ICL (UK)	1991	[a]80	na	computers
Omron	Schoenbuch Electronics	1991	95	85	sensors, switches
Capital Participations					
Matsushita	Loewe Opta (G)	1990	25.1	1430	CTVs, car electronics
Ricoh	Gestetner Holding (UK)	1991	24.2	12000	distibution of office equipment

Table 11: *Continued*

Japanese Company	Joint Venture	Buy-Out	Setup	Empl 1991	Activity
Joint Venture Buy-Outs					
Toshiba	Rank-Toshiba (UK)	1980	1978	na	CTVs
Hitachi	GEC-Hitachi (UK)	1983	1978	na	CTVs
Funai	Funai-Amstrad (UK)	1990	1987	116	VTRs
Tamura	Tamura Hinchley[b] (UK)	1991	1989	312	power sources
Kenwood	Sofradore Trio-Kenwood[c] (Fr)	1991	1985	112	CD players, car stereos

Sources: Touyou Keizai (1992), EIAJ (1992), Jetro (1990b), Burton and Saelens (1987).

Remarks: Fr=France, G=Germany; Ire=Ireland; Estbl=year of acquisition; Cap=Capital; Empl= number of employees.

[a] The cost of acquisition was 700 mln.

[b] previously 49% owned by Cambridge Electronics.

[c] previously 50% owned by Sofrel and Delta Dole.

and Kenwood bought out its Japanese partners in a joint venture established in 1985.

3.3.3   EC Investment Strategies and Integration of EC Activities

In order to be able to assess the effects of Japanese electronics firms' investments in the EC on the EC electronics industry, it is important to examine possible EC-wide investment strategies adopted by Japanese firms and the degree of integration of EC activities. In the case of VTRs, it was shown that investment has been country-specific rather than part of an EC-wide strategy. This was mainly due to national quota, rules of origin, and political factors, which kept the EC markets fragmented for Japanese firms and induced the establishment of multiple small-scale plants. A similar pattern had emerged in the 1970s in CTV production, with several firms operating plants in Germany or Spain, as well as a main plant in the UK. Still in 1989, only production at Sony's UK plant surpassed the minimum efficient scale level estimated to be around 500,000 units a year (Van Marion 1992).

This has been particular to CTV plants in the EC, since Japanese CTV plants in the US reached the minimum efficient scale not long after the establishment (Burton and Saelens 1987). Dunning (1986) in his survey of Japanese plants in the UK in the early 1980s finds no evidence for an integration of EC activities.

However, there is abundant evidence that Japanese electronics firms have adopted pan-European strategies and are moving towards greater integration of EC production and sales activities. Japanese firms' operations are acquiring a sufficient scale and integration to allow for a more efficient organisation of production in Europe. With locally manufactured products sufficiently 'European' to clear origin requirements, and with the movement towards the Internal Market in 1993, Japanese firms perceive fewer obstacles to intra-EC flows of final goods and components. Several trends point to an increasing integration of EC activities. Firstly, several firms have taken steps to rationalize VTR production in the EC towards the end of the 1980s. A good example is the joint venture of JVC and Thomson, which consists of the production of components in France which are used in a large scale assembly plant in Berlin; small scale production of VTRs in the UK was discontinued in 1989. Sanyo, which until recently operated three VTR plants in the EC, stopped production in the UK and Spain in 1987 and concentrated production in Germany. A similar move has been reported for Sharp, which concentrated production in the UK. The proliferation of plants is still notable for some other VTR manufacturers and to a lesser extent for PPC production (Canon, for instance, operates three PPC plants in the EC), but clearly less for other products such as CD players, and printers.

Secondly, the major Japanese electronics firms have set up European headquarters to improve coordination in EC sales and procurement activities, among others. However, the role of these headquarters should not be overestimated since the responsibility for plant investments, products lines and the appointment of executive personnel usually still lies with the product division headquarters in Japan (Takaoka and Satake 1991, p. 25).

Thirdly, developments in procurement and sales patterns of Japanese subsidiaries in the EC suggest a move towards greater integration of EC activities. Table 12 shows the destination of sales by electronics subsidiaries in 1988, 1990, and 1991, as recorded in MITI surveys under Japanese MNEs. While the share of sales on the local market (the country hosting the plants) at 62% was still high in 1991, reflecting the persisting preference of Japanese electronics firms to

Table 12:   Destination of Sales by Japanese Electronics Subsidiaries in the EC

	Local Market %	Other Europe %	Japan %	Other %	Total mln Yen
1988	85	14	1	0	694
1990	73	25	1	0	1084
1991	62	34	2	1	1869

Source: MITI (1990–1992)

concentrate manufacturing plants in the large EC countries, this share has been declining by 23% points during 1988–1991. Instead, sales have been directed more towards other EC countries.[27]

Procurement behavior also has become more 'pan-European' during 1988–1991, as is illustrated by Table 13. Japanese firms have become less reliant on imports of components from Japan: the share of these procurements declined from 62 to 46%. In contrast, procurements from other EC countries than the country invested in increased to 24% in 1991 from a mere 4% in 1988. Furthermore, in 1990, more than three quarters of components sourced from other EC countries were supplied by subsidiaries of the same firm or affiliated firms (intra-group deliveries).[28] These figures suggest a development towards product specialization by Japanese electronics firms' plants, with some plants located in country A specializing in components destined for an assembly plant in country B, which in turn may export to various EC countries.

Other trends that can be distiled from Table 13 are an increasing reliance on the EC for procurements (the combined share of the local market and other EC countries increased to 49% in 1991 from 35% in 1988), and to some extent a move towards greater in-house production (procurements as a percentage of sales declined to 66% in 1990 but increased slightly to 69% in 1991). Both developments imply

---

[27] Sazanami (1992) reaches similar conclusions for the manufacturing industry as a whole.

[28] Some caution should be exercised in interpreting the figures on intra-group deliveries. The definition of company group is not given in an unambiguous way by MITI, but presumably only refers to vertical *keiretsu*. Secondly, it could be that procurements from other countries include procurements from a central European components distribution center operated by the Japanese firm, which would obscure the actual origin of procurements.

The Globalization Strategy of Japanese Electronics Firms 137

Table 13:   Procurements of Japanese Electronics Subsidiaries in the EC by Region of
Origin

| Year | Region of Origin | | | | Total mill Yen | % of sales |
	Local %	Other Europe %	Japan %	Asia %		
1988	31	4	62	4	521	75
1990	22	22	50	4	711	66
of which:						
intra-group (%)	36	77	96	71		
1991	25	24	46	6	1286	69

Source: MITI (1990-1992).

an increasing local content ratio of EC-made Japanese electronics products, a subject that will be dealt with further in Section 3.5.

Fourthly, there is evidence that a European strategy as opposed to a country perspective is already prevailing in the organization of distribution networks of Japanese electronics firms. In Tables 6 and 7, it was shown that Belgium and the Netherlands, countries with a small national market but characterized by a strategic geographical location in the EC, a highly developed infrastructure and a standing tradition in international trade, have received a relatively large share of distribution activities. Williamson and Yamawaki (1991) analyzed the determinants of the location of Japanese sales subsidiaries empirically and found that these locations are not much related to national markets, but reflected the availability of physical and telecommunications infrastructure and distance to concentrations of consumers with high purchasing power. They concluded that the Japanese distribution system in Europe is 'ready and waiting for the Internal Market'.

3.3.4   Japanese Firms' Presence in the EC in Perspective

This last paragraph attempts to put the EC activities of Japanese firms into some perspective through comparisons with sales and production activities by EC and US firms. Table 14 shows the EC shares in total worldwide electronics sales and employment for major Japanese electronics firms in 1989. For comparison, world and EC electronics sales are presented for important EC and US sellers in the EC. Electronics sales data are taken from CEC (1991b), which uses a narrow definition of the electronics sector. Therefore, sales figures are usually smaller than total consolidated sales of the firms.

There are marked differences in the share of the EC in electronics sales of Japanese firms. For the biggest seller on the EC market, Hitachi, EC electronics sales represent 10% of total worldwide electronics sales. Marginally smaller percentages are recorded for Matsushita and Toshiba, while NEC's EC sales amount to less than 5% of global sales. Most dependent on the EC market are Sony for which EC sales represent 15.6% of global sales, and presumably Canon. The EC market was already relatively important for Fujitsu (12%) in 1989; with the acquisition of ICL in 1991 it has become the biggest Japanese seller in the EC. However, the advance of Japanese firms in terms of sales, has not been followed, or at least not to the same extent, by a 'localization' of production, measured by the EC share of firms' worldwide employees. The number of people employed by Hitachi in the EC only represents a little more than 1% of its total number of employees. This implies that Hitachi's manufacturing operations are still largely concentrated in Japan with the EC market mostly served by exports. Similar observations can be made for Matsushita, Toshiba and Fujitsu, although the gaps between EC sales and employment shares are less pronounced. Sony and Canon are the firms that are most 'localized' in the EC. Since manufacturing employees are less well represented in Canon's employment, this leaves Sony as the one maverick among the major Japanese electronics MNEs, having made progress in the implementation of its strategy to produce where its sells. It should be noted, however, that several smaller firms are at least as 'localized' as Sony. Firms such as Alps, Murata, Pioneer, Akai, to but a few, have substantial manufacturing operations in the EC relative to both Japanese and other foreign manufacturing activities.

Table 14 also shows that EC sales of major EC firms are in general several times higher than sales by Japanese firms. Only Nokia's sales are outstripped by the top-three Japanese sellers. The EC firms sell 50 to 70% of their total output in the EC. This figure is roughly one third for the three major US electronics firms listed. Sales levels of DEC and Hewlett Packard are comparable to sales of EC firms such as Bull and Olivetti. The largest seller on the EC market is IBM, with sales of almost 18 billion ECUs. IBM employs an estimated 100,000 people in the EC, twice the number of all Japanese firms' employees in the EC.

Table 14:   The Japanese Presence in the EC Consumer Electronics Industry in 1989

	# Plants	Employment	Empl/Plant
European Firms	106	105,000	991
Japanese Firms	58	19,000	328
Other Firms[a]	10	2,200	220
Total	174	126,200	725
Share Japanese Firms	33	15	

Sources: Estimates based on CEC (1991), EACEM (1991).

[a] Korean and Taiwanese firms.

IBM's experience in internationalization has resulted in a high degree of 'localization': it employs 26% of its total number of employees in the EC, roughly comparable to its dependence on EC sales.

Although electronics sales on the EC market by major Japanese firms are relatively modest, Japanese firms have gained important market shares for specific products. Japanese firms supply the larger majority of DRAMs and EPROMs in the EC,[29] and have made significant inroads in the gate array market as well. With the acquisition of ICL, Fujitsu became a major player on the market for business computers. Canon holds 7% of the office equipment market (CEC 1991b, p. 12–32) and Kyocera's acquisition of AVX launched it into the top-three EC capacitor producers. Japanese firms are also the major suppliers of MWOs, PC printers and small PPCs in the EC.

Yet the biggest advance has been in the consumer electronics market. In 1987, the EC's main producer Philips still held 15% of the EC market, followed by Thomson of France (13%), and at some distance by Matsushita (8%), Sony (6%), and Hitachi (4%) (Bowen 1991). Since then, Japanese producers have gained substantial ground. Japanese firms hold roughly 80% of the VTR market, probably a third of the CTV market, and have a virtual monopoly in camcorders. In the EC audio market, sales of Sony, Matsushita and Pioneer have surpassed those of the former market leader Philips. The consumer electronics industry is also the sector which has received most Japanese manufacturing investments, mostly prompted by EC trade policy measures.

---

[29] Although for the EC semiconductor market as a whole, Toshiba and NEC only reached the seventh (4.9%) and eighth (4.1%) place, respectively, in terms of EC markets share (CEC 1991b, p. 12–11).

Table 15 presents figures concerning plants and manufacturing employment of Japanese and EC firms in the industry. The definition of consumer electronics used by the EACEM is stricter than the definition used in this chapter (e.g. MWOs are not included), which makes the figures less comparable with those in Tables 4 and 5. Japanese firms were responsible for 15% of total manufacturing employment in the EC consumer electronics industry in 1989, which has made them a factor of economic and political importance. The Japanese share in the number of plants was more than twice as high at 33%, once more highlighting the fragmentation of Japanese manufacturing activities in the EC. The average number of employees per Japanese plant was 328 against almost a 1000 for the EC firms. While this difference will reflect a higher degree of integration and higher value added within plants of EC firms, it also points out that the rationalization of EC production activities was further advanced by EC firms than by their Japanese rivals by 1989.[30]

As for the broad electronics industry as a whole, the 50,000 jobs in Japanese manufacturing subsidiaries constitute approximately 5% of total manufacturing employment in the EC in 1990. On this count as well, the Japanese presence is relatively greater in the US than in the EC: a recent study by the US Department of Commerce (Genther and Dalton 1992) found that Japanese manufacturing plants provided jobs to 86,000 employees in 1990, which constituted 8% of the total number of production workers in the broad US electronics industry.[31] For the subsector audio and video, which in the US mainly consists of CTV production, this percentage reached 30%.

3.4   JAPANESE FDI AND ITS IMPACT
ON THE EC ECONOMY

The impact of Japanese manufacturing FDI on the EC economy in general and the EC electronics industry in particular, is not easily assessed. Possible positive effects (such as transfer of technology) or negative effects (such as the extent to which FDI substitutes

---

[30] The restructuring efforts by EC consumer electronics firms in the 1980s is indicated by the rapid decrease in the number of EC plants: in 1987, consumer electronics plants operated in the EC by EC firms still numbered 181 (CEC 1991b).

[31] Note that the figures are limited strictly to factory employment, measured at the plant level. Total US factory employment reached just over 1 million in 1990, while total employment in the electronics sector was over 2.5 million.

Table 15: The Importance of the EC Market for Major Japanese, EC, and US Firms in 1989

Company	Electronics Sales			Employment		
	EC	World	EC %	[a]EC	World	EC %
Japanese Firms						
Hitachi	1,900	18,790	10.1	3.3	264	1.2
Matsushita	1,790	19,775	9.1	7.7	193	4.0
Sony	1,560	10,020	15.6	[b]8.0	79	10.1
Toshiba	1,360	15,080	9.0	4.7	125	3.8
NEC	910	19,820	4.6	3.1	115	2.7
Canon	[c]859	na	na	7.8	37.5	20.5
Fujitsu[d]	830	6,910	12.0	3.1	115	2.7
EC Firms						
Siemens	10,050	16,830	59.7		353	
CGE Alcatel	8,000	12,000	66.7		204	
Philips	6,960	14,760	47.2		310	
Thomson	5,400	10,020	53.9		104	
Olivetti	3,570	5,880	60.7		58	
Bull	3,190	5,820	54.8		46	
Nokia	1,410	2,620	53.8		45	
US Firms						
IBM	17,840	57,010	31.2	[b]100	387	25.8
DEC	3,950	11,590	34.0		121	
Hewlett Packard	3,350	10,820	31.0		87	

Sources: Based on CEC (1992), company reports, and the Appendix.

Remarks: Electronics sales do not include sales of (heavy) electrical equipment, electric household goods, and lighting.

[a] 1990, see the Appendix.

[b] estimation.

[c] sales of computer-related equipment and office machines.

[d] Does not include sales of the UK firm ICL, which Fujitsu acquired in 1991.

for investments by EC firms) are hard to quantify. The effects on the sectoral trade balance and employment are usually considered important by authorities and policy makers, while economists adopting a general equilibrium framework tend to argue that an economy's trade balance is determined by the macroeconomic balance between saving and investment and that unemployment in the longer term can only be solved by reducing mismatches between supply and demand. Both economists and policy makers, however, usually agree that FDI on balance has favorable effects on the host economy.[32]

This section attempts to provide insight into the effects of Japanese FDI on the EC economy by reviewing the available information on the characteristics of Japanese FDI. It will briefly discuss likely effects on EC employment and the electronics trade balance, since these have been focal points of attention. Then the value added of Japanese manufacturing activities in the EC is assessed by reviewing the evidence concerning local content, procurement, and the shift from assembly to components production. The extent to which expertise and technology are diffused to the EC industry and labor force is discussed by looking at joint ventures, R&D activities, and the localization of personnel. Lastly, some remarks are made with respect to efficiency of production, consumer welfare, and the competitiveness of EC firms.

3.4.1   Employment

Japanese electronics firms have been increasing employment in the EC rapidly and have become a factor of importance in the economic landscape. As mentioned above, total manufacturing employment reached almost 50,000 persons in 1990, which amounted to approximately 5% of total employment in the EC electronics industry in that year. Employment by Japanese firms in the consumer electronics industry reached a share of 15% in 1989, and is likely to have increased since.

Japanese investment in general has not been accompanied by increases in employment in the electronics industry, but it may have helped to stem the employment decline which began in the early 1980s. For instance, employment in the consumer electronics industry

---

[32] See Graham and Krugman (1990) for a useful discussion of the effects of FDI on host economies. Micossi and Viesti (1991) and Thomsen and Nicolaides (1991) give assessments of Japanese FDI in Europe.

declined from 160,000 in 1980 to 123,000 in 1988, but showed its first increase to 126,000 in 1989 (CEC 1991b). A slight increase in employment was also recorded in 1989 in the EC components industry, with employment reaching an estimated 233,000.

For an assessment of the employment effects of Japanese FDI, however, one should not only look at mere employment figures, but also at the quality of employment. Japanese plants set up in the EC as a response to trade policy measures often limited activities to simple assembly and packaging tasks and tended to use only low skilled labor. Recent trends towards integrated production, investments in components manufacturing, and emphasis on product design and software engineering suggest that employment provided by Japanese firms is reaching a more balanced distribution over assembly-type low skilled and more highly skilled labor. A thorough assessment, however, can not be made on the basis of the data available. Further remarks concerning the valued added of Japanese production in the EC are made in Section 3.5.3.

Japanese electronics firms, in addition to manufacturing employ-ment, provided some 30,000 jobs in their distribution subsidiaries in the EC. Part of these jobs consist of simple warehousing and administrative tasks, but the share of qualified service functions and staff functions in marketing and planning may be relatively large. Staff functions requiring qualified personnel are also relatively important in the recently established European headquarters of Japanese electron-ics firms.

A positive effect of Japanese FDI stems from the location of Japanese firms' plant establishments. Encouraged by financial and other incentives, Japanese electronics firms have shown a inclination to locate manufacturing plants in areas in the UK and France which are characterized by high structural unemployment. With labor relatively immobile, such investments are likely to help reduce regional mismatches on the labor market.

3.4.2   The Electronics Trade Balance

Most Japanese FDI has been of the 'tariff-jumping' type and has led to export substitution at the final product level. Table 3 shows evidence of substitution of local production (indicated by the establishment of plants) for exports where EC trade policy has been more restrictive than in the US.

Further evidence of export substitution is shown in Belderbos (1992b), where a clear relationship is found at the product level between Japanese plant establishments in the EC, declining exports, and increased local production. For example, Figure 4 illustrates these developments for the case of PPCs. It shows that the number of Japanese PPC manufacturing plants quickly rose to 11 after the start of the anti-dumping investigation in 1985. As result, local production reached an estimated 650,000 units in 1989. In contrast, imports declined from 840,000 units in 1985 to 470,000 in 1989. An empirical analysis of export behavior by individual Japanese electronics firms in Belderbos (1992b) also provides evidence that FDI has been substituting for exports: the growth in the number of EC manufacturing subsidiaries during 1986–1989 is found to have a significantly negative effect on the level of a firm's exports to Europe in 1989. On the other hand, the evidence also points to a partially offsetting growth in components imports from Japan.

The fact that Japanese FDI lead to increased imports of components from Japan was also illustrated in Table 13: roughly half the procurements of Japanese electronics firms' subsidiaries in the EC in 1990 originated in Japan. However, the declining importance of Japan as a source of procurements and the wave of investments by Japanese components suppliers suggest that components imports are of decreasing importance.

In sum, the evidence suggests that the effect of Japanese manufacturing investments on the electronics trade balance of the EC vis-à-vis Japan has been positive. An indication for this is given by developments in the consumer electronics trade balance of the EC as compared with Japan in the late 1980s: in 1989, the trade deficit of the EC vis-à-vis Japan showed a year on year decline for the first time, be it only marginally, from 5.5 to 5.3 billion ECUs.

3.4.3   Value Added and Local Content

The growth in Japanese components manufacturing in the EC, both through investments by (independent) component producers and through increased in-house production by final goods producers, signifies the shift from mere assembly activities to integrated production with increased value added. This is an important trend, since the manufacture of components tends to be more technology intensive than product assembly and requires more skilled labor and training of employees.

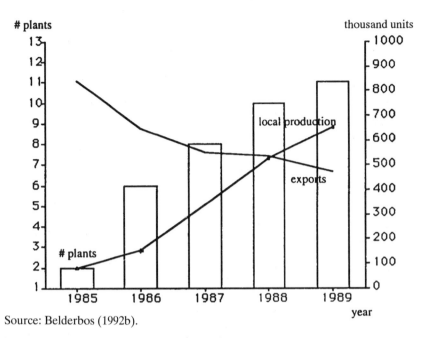

Source: Belderbos (1992b).

Figure 4: Trade Policy, Japanese Plants, Exports, and Local Production in the EC PPC Industry.

The trends towards greater value added generated in Japanese electronics plants and greater reliance on procurements in the EC was illustrated by Table 13. Additional information concerning the local (EC) content ratio of Japanese electronics subsidiaries in the EC is presented in Table 16. Definitions of local content leave ample room for interpretation and Japanese firms will prefer to show high local content levels for their operations abroad. Nevertheless, the figures provide evidence that a substantial number of Japanese electronics subsidiaries reach very satisfactory local content levels.[33] Almost one third of the subsidiaries reported levels between 90 and 100% and approximately another third reached levels above 45%, necessary to have products such as CTVs and VTRs labeled 'European made'.

---

[33] Another rough check on local content levels is to add EC procurements to in-house value added in Table 13, which gives a weighted local content ratio of 63%. On the other hand, a survey among Japanese electronics firms undertaken by the Export-Import Bank of Japan reported an average local content ratio of only 41% in Europe in 1989–1990 (Takaoka and Satake 1991).

Table 16:   Local Content of Japanese Electronics Subsidiaries in the EC in 1990

Local Content Ratio	% firms
0–2	8
20–30	9
30–40	11
40–50	16
50–60	5
60–70	8
70–80	3
80–90	9
90–100	31
Reasons to Increase Local Content[a]	% firms
Cost effectiveness	29
Local content regulations	48
Procurements from local subsidiaries	29
Local in-house production	14

Sources: MITI (1990, 1991).

[a] percentage of subsidiaries for which the reason is valid; multiple answers were possible.

However, high local content levels appear to be forced upon Japanese firms by local content requirements: almost half the subsidiaries reported that the reason they raised or were planning to raise local content levels was the existence of local content regulations. Only 29% of the subsidiaries increased local content because this was more cost effective.[34] Thus, the possibility exists that increases in local content lead to increases in production costs, which may in turn may be passed on to consumers through higher prices. Further remarks on this issue are made in Section 3.5.5.

On two counts, Japanese manufacturing FDI has not had such favorable effects on the EC economy. Firstly, it was shown (see Table 13) that a substantial share of components procured by EC subsidiaries of Japanese electronics firms were supplied by affiliated subsidiaries in the EC. If we also take into account the rapidly increased production by independent Japanese components manufacturers in the EC, this suggests that Japanese firms do not procur components produced by

---

[34] In contrast, these percentages were 4 and 48, respectively, for Japanese electronics subsidiaries in the US.

EC firms frequently. Indeed, Japanese firms regularly complain about insufficient quality and reliability of components supplied by EC firms (e.g. see JETRO 1990b).

The reliance on Japanese components (be they EC-made or not), however, also reflects the importance of long-term supplier-client relationships between Japanese firms. These relationships with sub-contractors and long-standing suppliers are part of an organisation of production characterized by 'lean production' methods, just in time deliveries of components, and joint development of components for new products. Since this type of production management constitutes a major competitive advantage of Japanese electronics firms, firms pursue a strategy to transfer the system abroad (Dunning and Gittelman 1991).

This has been most clearly demonstrated by the experience of Japanese automobile manufacturers, which were followed by a great number of Japanese components suppliers (usually member of the vertical *keiretsu* of Japanese car manufacturers) in setting up manufacturing plants in the United States. This lead to the creation of geographically concentrated networks of interrelated Japanese manufacturing plants, also dubbed 'little Japans'. In the EC, a movement towards the creation of Japanese networks is evident in the electronics industry, spurred by trade policy measures and local content requirements. This development harbors some possible dangers. Long-term supplier-client relationships between Japanese firms may be difficult to break for EC components producers. In that case, an increasing dominance of Japanese final goods producers leads almost automatically to falling demand for EC components producers. It is therefore of interest to encourage the active involvement of EC components manufacturers in component supplier networks of Japanese electronics producers in the EC. Some Japanese firms already report that they provide EC suppliers with technological assistance to meet this end (JETRO 1990).

A second count on which Japanese electronics firms do not score well is production of high margin, high value-added products in the EC. Japanese firms tend to transfer only the manufacture of more mature products. For instance, Japanese IC producers manufacture the before-last generation of DRAMs in the EC, while production of the newest generation is concentrated in Japan (Furlotti 1991).[35] Similarly, the latest generation of VTRs and camcorders are largely

---

[35] A recent exception is NEC, which reportedly plans to start production of 16-megabit DRAMs at its Livingstone facility in the UK in March 1993 (Nikkei Economic

imported from Japan. A survey by the Export-Import Bank of Japan in 1991 revealed that the transfer of production of high value-added products to the EC had a very low priority for Japanese electronics firms (Takaoka and Satake 1991). Japanese firms' innovative base is Japan, where they create new products, test the appreciation of demanding Japanese consumers, and try to reach satisfactory efficiency levels in manufacturing by increasing the scale of production and through 'learning by doing'. The globalization strategies of Japanese firms have not gone so far as to reduce this kind of reliance on the home country.

3.4.4   Diffusion of Know-how and Technology

The most undisputed positive effect of Japanese manufacturing FDI on the EC economy is the diffusion of technology, efficient management practises and know-how. Japanese firms introduce new management and engineering methods which can be emulated by EC firms. Workers and local managers get acquainted with Japanese-style production methods, quality control, and labor-management relations. Engineers and researchers learn Japanese product development techniques. Although it is inherently difficult to assess the extent and importance of such diffusion, an attempt is made to gain some insight into the matter by looking at EC-Japanese joint ventures, Japanese R&D activities in the EC, and the localization of management.

Diffusion of technology and emulation of best production and engineering practises are most likely to take place within Japanese-EC joint ventures. In Section 3.3.2 it was reported that joint ventures are a factor of importance in Japanese manufacturing activities in the EC. While the first experience with EC-Japanese joint ventures in CTV production was clearly unfavorable for EC firms, more recent joint ventures seem better matched and might enable EC firms to regain some competitiveness in the manufacture of products (PPCs, facsimiles, VTRs) for which Japanese firms have an efficiency and technological lead.[36]

Besides joint ventures, other forms of cooperation and business tie-ups are at least as important, but much less well documented.

Journal, 14 December, 1992).

[36] In addition, there are joint ventures between EC and Japanese firms elsewhere. For instance, Thomson operates a VTR plant with Toshiba in Singapore and Philips manufactures VTRs in a joint venture with JVC in Malaysia.

For example, Siemens regained a position as DRAM manufacturer through a tie-up with Toshiba in 1 megabit DRAMs. Grundig (controlled by Philips) in Germany has a tie-up with Matsushita in VTRs: with technological assistance by Matsushita, Grundig manufactures key components such as magnetic heads, which Matsushita uses at its German VTR assembly plant. Links between Philips and Matsushita date from the 1950s when Philips acquired a minority stake in a core Matsushita subsidiary in Japan (Matsushita Electronics Corporation). Marketing agreements and technological corporation between the world's two largest consumer electronics firms cover lighting, semiconductors and components.

R&D activities, especially basic R&D, are generally considered to have positive spillover effects on economies, besides providing employment opportunities for highly skilled labor. However, 'localization' of R&D activities by Japanese electronics firms has not been a strong point until recently. In 1990, the MITI survey counted a total of 2732 people engaged in R&D in foreign subsidiaries of Japanese electronics firms (MITI 1991). This is no more than 2.4% of the more than 112,000 R&D personnel in Japan (Management and Coordination Agency 1991). In the EC, Japanese firms reported 461 R&D personnel, which implies an EC share (17%) commensurate to the EC's share in manufacturing activities. However, R&D personnel amounts to a mere 1% of Japanese firms' manufacturing employees in the EC. In contrast, the ratio of R&D to manufacturing employees reached 10% in Japan.

The lack of foreign R&D activities may be partly related to the relatively late internationalization of Japanese firms. On the other hand, economies of scale in R&D in high-tech industries and the need for close communication between the research department and decision centers generally favors centralization of R&D in the home country. Concentration of R&D in the home country, although to a lesser extent, can also be observed for US MNEs which generally have more experience in overseas operations. For instance, US MNEs in the consumer electronics and electrical appliances industry had 6.9% of US personnel dedicated to R&D, while this ratio was only 2.5% abroad. Interestingly, foreign R&D personnel was more concentrated in the EC, where the share of R&D to total personnel reached 5.4% (Japan Development Bank 1988).[37]

---

[37] The ratio of foreign to US R&D personnel was 12.9%, reflecting extensive overseas operations of these US MNEs.

A list of Japanese R&D and design centers operated by Japanese electronics firms in the EC is presented in Table 17. Since reliable information on R&D facilities is scarce, the list is incomplete and limited to R&D facilities that are set up as a separate subsidiary. A first observation is that R&D centers are small in scale: Japanese R&D centers in general employ 10–40 personnel. The one exception is Canon Information Systems, which reportedly plans to put about a hundred people to work on software development and image processing systems research. In addition, there are, probably fairly large scale, R&D activities attached to two Euro-Japanese manufacturing joint ventures (not in Table 17): Siemens-Matsushita Components develops passive components and Canon-Olivetti develops laser printers (Japan Development Bank 1988).

What stands out in Table 17 is the marked increase in the number of establishments in the early 1990s: at least eight separate R&D centers were set up during 1990–1991, which is probably more than the total number up to 1990.[38] The take off in R&D investments in the 1990s is even more pronounced if we take into account the R&D centers for which more accurate information is lacking. For instance, Hitachi reportedly started R&D activities at three different locations in the EC during 1991: ASIC design Maidenhead, UK, basic research in submicron production technology in Cambridge, UK, and product design in Munich, Germany (*Electronics Business*, 17 September 1990); Fujitsu established a design facility for large scale ICs near Heathrow Airport, UK in June 1990; and NEC began audio and video design activities in its Telford plant in the UK in 1990.

The two most important R&D activities are product design and software development. Product design and development is undertaken to adapt products to European requirements and tastes, a prime example being the design of application-specific ICs (ASICs) which have to be customized according to the demands of client-firms in Europe. Also, European (re)design of products is often necessary to encompass European components in Japanese products and to reach satisfactory levels of local content. This type of R&D in particular is likely to gain more importance in the near future. Takaoka and Satake (1991) report that 57% of Japanese electronics firms surveyed by the

---

[38] A parallel trend in R&D activities by Japanese firms can be observed in the US, where Japanese firms increased the number of greenfield R&D subsidiaries to 70 by 1991, mostly in product design and software engineering. Japanese electronics firms spent an estimated 770 million dollars on R&D in the US in 1989, up from 307 million dollars in 1987 (Genther and Dalton 1992).

Table 17: R&D and Design Affiliates of Japanese Electronics Firms in Europe

Company	Ctr	Subsidiary name	Estbl	Empl (J)	Activity
Sony	UK	Sony Broadcast	1978	30	digital VTRs, software
Fujitsu	UK	Fujitsu Microelectronics	1983.8	8 (0)	ASIC design
Ricoh	G	Ricoh Deutschland	1986	8 (3)	Fax design
Canon	UK	Canon Research Europe	1988.2	10 (2)	software development
Sony	G	European Technology Center	1988.4	41	satelite CTV and communication R&D
Sharp	UK	Sharp Laboratories of Europe	1990.2	30 (3)	software development, basic R&D, language systems
Fujitsu	UK	Fujitsu Europe Telecom R&D Centre	1990.5	na	telecommunications software, product development
Matsushita	UK	D2B Systems[a]	1990.6	15 (0)	software development
NEC	G	(Dusseldorf)	1990.6	40	semiconductor design
Canon image	Fr	Canon Information Systems	1990.6	[b]100	software development, processing research
Dainippon Printing	De	DNP Research Denmark	na 1990.10		optoelectronics product development
Toshiba	UK	Toshiba Cambridge Research Center	1991.1	na	basic research
Matsushita	G	Panasonic R&D Center	1991.9	na	CTV, VTR design

Table 17 notes:

Sources: JETRO (1990b), EIAJ (1992), Touyou Keizai (1992), Japan Development Bank (1990), Electronics Business, 17 September 1990, Furlotti (1991).

Remarks: Ctr = country; Estbl = time of establishment; G = Germany; De = Denmark; Fr = France; Empl (J) = number of research employees (number of Japanese employees between brackets).

[a] Joint venture of Philips (75%) and Matsushita (25%).

[b] Planned.

Export-Import Bank of Japan in 1990 regarded the localization of product development in the EC as a major priority in their strategy for the EC market.

Software development is a field in which Japanese firms are often said to be relatively behind. Technology sourcing seems to be the main purpose of these R&D centers, while an additional reason to develop software in the EC is the scarcity of software engineers in Japan (Genther and Dalton 1992). Expertise in software development has also played a role in the acquisitions of Apricot computers by Mitsubishi and ICL by Fujitsu and Office Workstations by Matsushita (see Table 11). The D2B Systems venture is a joint effort by Philips

Table 18:   Japanese Expatriates (percentage) in Management Positions at Electronics Subsidiaries in the EC and the US

Position	EC %	US %
President	79	84
Vice-president	71	55
Finance	64	62
Sales	46	40
Procurement	42	39
Planning	40	45
R&D	[a]27	43
Personnel Affairs	22	31
Total Management	53	51
All Employees	3.0	3.1

Source: MITI (1991).

[a] based on only 8 EC subsidiaries reporting.

and Matsushita to develop a software standard for remote controls for audio and video systems.

A characteristic of Japanese R&D is the concentration of centers in the UK and Germany. Product design needs feedback from manufacturing and marketing and the UK and Germany are the two largest markets for Japanese electronics where most of Japanese firms' manufacturing plants are located. In contrast, the facility in Rennes set up by Canon is the only R&D affiliate located in France, although Ricoh is also reported to undertake R&D activities, i.e. components development for office automation equipment, in its Wettolsheim plant (Japan Development Bank 1988).

A final area for discussion is the appointment of EC personnel to management positions in Japanese electronics subsidiaries. Japanese MNEs have often been accused of failing to train and promote local personnel of overseas subsidiaries. Table 18 shows that these allegations have some substance. It shows the percentage of Japanese electronics firms' subsidiaries in the EC where Japanese expatriates are appointed to management positions; for comparison figures on the situation in the US are also presented.

Japanese nationals were appointed as president of Japanese subsidiaries in the EC in 79% of all cases in 1990; this percentage was even slightly higher in the US. More remarkable is that 71% of vice-presidents were Japanese as well. This is much higher than for subsidiaries in the US and partly reflects the longer experience Japanese firms have in operating subsidiaries there. Japanese firms also prefer to appoint expatriates as head of the finance division because of the need to keep strict control over crucial activities such as investments and financing, and to facilitate close relationships with the parent firm and the main bank. In total, local managers were appointed to less than half the management positions available, the favorite being the position of head of personnel affairs, which has a relatively low status. This compares with an expatriate ratio of only 3% for all employees. On both counts, the differences between the EC and the US are negligible.

3.4.5 Efficiency, Competition, and Consumer Prices

A specific characteristic of Japanese electronics firms' FDI in the EC is its strong relationship with EC trade policy. It was shown that in the absence of VERs and anti-dumping measures, Japanese firms would have mostly preferred to concentrate manufacturing in their 'regional core networks' in Japan and South-East Asia, and to export to the EC. Similarly, local content rules have forced Japanese producers to increase the value added of EC production activities and has prompted components firms to manufacture in the EC. In both cases, manufacturing in the EC is a 'second best' option and is likely to lead to higher production costs.

In the literature on strategic trade policy (see e.g. Krugman 1986), trade policy measures are regarded as a means to put domestic firms at an advantage against foreign rivals to ensure that 'home' firms capture a larger share of surplus profits in international oligopolistic markets. In Section 3.3.3 it was argued that EC anti-dumping measures indeed reflect elements of industrial policy designed to shield EC firms from Japanese competition. Anti-dumping measures and local content requirements, by directly or indirectly increasing the costs of Japanese producers, may help to blunt the competitive edge of Japanese firms. If fostering an indigenous EC electronics industry is considered a legitimate policy objective, for instance to ensure positive spillovers to other industries and to preserve pluralism of competition in the long run, this must be judged as a positive effect. However, this is achieved only by decreasing allocative efficiency and increasing the average production costs in the industry. An upward pressure on consumer prices is likely to result. While this effect is potentially serious, steady price declines of products such as CD players and VTRs do not suggest that consumers have been paying the bill. On the other hand, it does not appear that EC electronics firms have gained strength although Japanese firms are competing more and more on a 'level playing field' in the EC. Japanese firms' recently gained experience in transferring production abroad and advances in flexible manufacturing and labor saving production techniques have presumably enabled them to manufacture in the EC without substantial cost increases. In this regard, Ozawa (1991) argues that Japanese FDI in the US and the EC is developing from a 'second best' to a 'first best' strategy.

3.5   CONCLUSION

The investments by Japanese electronics firms in the EC are part of a globalization strategy adopted in the mid-1980s spurred by the rise in global protectionism, the appreciation of the Yen, and emerging trends in the electronics industry at large. The EC attracted increasing shares of both exports and FDI by Japanese electronics firms during the second half of the 1980s, reflecting the renewed interest in the EC market stemming from the unification program and the relative neglect of the EC by Japanese firms in the past. Manufacturing investment in the EC is strongly induced by a range of trade policy measures against Japanese electronic imports and EC assembly plants taken by the EC Commission since the beginning of the 1980s, which by 1990 essentially had made the threat of a 'fortress Europe' materialize for Japanese electronics firms.

During the period 1986–1990, employment in manufacturing subsidiaries in the EC rose four-fold to reach almost 50,000 people in 1990. This amounted to approximately 5% of total employment in the EC electronics industry. The contribution of Japanese firms to manufacturing employment reached 15% in the consumer electronics industry where investments have been most concentrated. At the same time, Japanese electronics firms increased their distribution networks in the EC, increasing the number of distribution subsidiaries to 416, employing at least 27,000 people. While manufacturing investments in the early 1980s were still oriented towards individual countries, Japanese firms have increasingly adopted pan-European investment strategies, characterized by specialization of production by manufacturing plants and intra-EC flows of components and final goods. However, by the end of the 1980s, the EC still was more important as an export market than as a production base for Japanese firms.

The distribution of Japanese electronics firms' manufacturing investments across countries shows a distinct concentration of facilities in the UK, and, to a lesser extent, Germany, the two most important markets for Japanese products. However, another salient feature of Japanese investment in the late 1980s and early 1990s is the growing importance of France as an investment location, reflecting foremost a more cooperative attitude of the French government towards Japanese firms. Japanese sales subsidiaries are more evenly distributed over EC countries, with a more important role for the smaller countries Belgium and the Netherlands.

Japanese electronics firms' FDI in the EC has probably helped to stem the decline in manufacturing employment in the EC electronics industry and has had a positive effect on the EC trade balance with Japan. Further favorable effects on the EC economy are arguably following from a shift from assembly activities to technology intensive components production, emulation of best production and management practises by EC firms and diffusion of Japanese technological and managerial know-how, in particular through joint ventures and tie-ups. On some counts, however, Japanese FDI scores less well. Japanese firms show a reluctance to transfer production of high value added products and R&D activities abroad and are not inclined to appoint local personnel to management positions. Japanese firms also show a strong preference for procurement of components in the EC from their own EC plants and from plants of related Japanese suppliers, while hesitating to include EC components manufacturers in their supplier networks.

In the 1990s new developments in Japanese firms' strategies towards the EC can be discerned. Japanese firms had by and large refrained from acquisitions as a means to penetrate the EC market until the late 1980s. In contrast, the years 1990 and 1991 brought a number of acquisitions of which the Kyocera-AVX and Fujitsu-ICL deals gave the Japanese side substantial market shares in the EC. In the same two years, a range of R&D and design centers were established by the major Japanese electronics firms. Both phenomena reflect a shift in Japanese firms' investments strategies from direct responses to trade policy measures to a more long term commitment to the EC market. The ultimate goal of Japanese firms is to be recognized as 'insiders' in the EC, to assure the preservation of market shares in the long term and to decrease the vulnerability to EC trade policy measures.

Although Japanese electronics firms' FDI outflows have fallen back in the early 1990s from the historical highs in 1989 and 1990, investments have still been substantial. Furthermore, electronics firms have predicted a rebound in their overseas investment from 1992 (Tejima 1992). As for the EC, Japanese firms reported that their first priority in the 1990s is to further extend manufacturing capacity and sales networks (Takaoka and Satake 1991). Japanese electronics firms' investments in the EC are thus projected to continue their growth, though probably at a slower pace than in the late 1980s.

APPENDIX A

Glossary

ASIC	application-specific integrated circuit
ASEAN	countries in the Association of South-East Asian Nations: Indonesia, Malaysia, Philippines, Brunei, Thailand; Singapore is a member of ASEAN but is usually grouped under the NIEs
CD	compact disk player
CEC	Commission of the European Communities
CRT	cathode ray television tube
CTV	color television
FDI	direct foreign investment
DRAM	direct random access memory chip
EACEM	European association of electronics manufacturers
EC	European Community
EIAJ	electronics industries association of Japan
EPROM	erasable programmable read-only memory chip
IC	integrated circuit, chip
LCD	liquid crystal display
JETRO	Japan external trade organization
LTCB	long term credit bank of Japan
magnetron	core part of a microwave oven, generator of microwaves
mecadeck	mechanical parts of a video tape recorder
MITI	Japanese ministry of international trade and industry
MNE	multinational enterprise
MOF	Japanese ministry of finance
MWO	microwave oven
NIEs	Newly Industrialized Economies: S'pore, Hong Kong, S. Korea, Taiwan
OEM	original equipment manufacturing: occurs when company A agrees to manufacture products according to the specifications of client-firm B, which procurs them from A to sell them under the B brand name
PC	personal computer
PPC	plain paper copying machine
OMA	orderly market arrangement
Touyou Keizai	independent Japanese publishing company specialized in economic databases and books
VER	voluntary export restraint
VTR	video tape recorder
YRI	Yamaichi research institute

Appendix B: Subsidiaries and Employment of Japanese Electronics Firms in the EC in 1990 by Company

Company (group)	products	# subs all	manf	employment all	manf	sales	incr % 86–90
Matsushita group							
Matsushita[a]	consumer	17	10	6097	4255	1842	87
JVC	audio, video	17	5	na	2413	na	na
Mats. Components	component	2	2	528	528	0	456
Kyushu Matsushita	tel, prn	1	1	500	500	0	est
Mats. Elec. Works	electr. relais	3	1	318	238	80	47
Mats. C'municat'n	car-audio, tel	2	2	198	198	0	est
Matsushita Denso	fax	1	1	65	65	0	est
Mats. Denshi Oyo	magnetrons	1	1	16	16	0	est
total		44	23	+10135	8231	+1922	184
Sony group							
Sony	audio, video	135	na	6240	na	na	
Aiwa	audio	3	1	587	516	71	94
Sony Magnescale	scales	1	0	6	0	6	est
total		17	6	na	6765	na	na
Canon group							
Canon	ofm, cameras	17	3	7848	1861	5987	110
Copyer	PPCs	2	0	24	0	24	200
total		19	3	7872	1861	6011	110
Toshiba group							
Toshiba	cons, indu	20	5	3954	2122	1832	93
Tokyo Electric	scales, prn	7	3	571	320	251	18
Topkon	medical eq	4	0	80	0	80	63
Onkyo	audio	3	0	55	0	55	129
Toshiba Litec	halogen lamps	1	1	49	49	0	est
total		35	9	4709	2491	2218	84
Hitachi group							
Hitachi	cons, indu	4	3	1950	1520	430	na
Hitachi Sales	cons, indu	9	0	625	0	625	15
Hitachi Maxell	tapes	2	1	na	530	na	na

Appendix B: *continued*

Company (group)	products	# subs		employment			
		all	manf	all	manf	sales	incr % 86–90
Nissei Sangyo	compo	2	0	80	0	80	23
Hitachi Denshi	meas eq	2	0	49	0	49	0
Hitachi Koki	power tools	4	0	0	0	na	na
Hitachi Medico	medical eq	1	0	5	0	5	est
Kokusai Electric	wireless eq	1	0	18	0	18	100
total		25	4	+3259	2050	+1207	na
Fujitsu group							
Fujitsu[b]	indu, ICs	11	4	2757	2515	242	372
Fujitsu Isotec	prn	1	1	200	200	0	est
Advantest	IC testers	3	1	80	40	40	900
Fujitsu General	consumer	3	0	50	0	50	22
Fujitsu Ten	car-audio	1	0	7	0	7	133
total		19	6	3094	2755	339	392
NEC group							
NEC	cons, indu	13	3	2998	1608	1390	135
Anritsu Electric	meas eq	3	0	71	0	71	87
Ando	IC testers	1	0	11	0	11	10
total		17	3	3080	1608	1472	140
Sanyo group							
Sanyo Electric	consumer	9	4	1669	1249	420	-18
Sanyo Denki Boeki	consumer	4	2	1199	913	286	est
total		13	6	2868	2162	706	41
Kyocera	components	15	3	2842	2313	529	9700
Sharp	cons, PPC	6	4	2818	2152	666	116
Konica	PPC, cameras	6	1	2342	138	2204	130
Ricoh	ofm, cameras	8	2	na	931	0	na
Mitsubishi group							
Mitsubishi Electric	cons, indu	8	5	1525	984	541	na
Akai	audio	4	1	657	457	200	46
total		12	6	2182	1441	741	na

Appendix B: *continued*

Company (group)	products	# subs all	# subs manf	employment all	employment manf	employment sales	incr % 86–90
Brother group							
Brother	cons, prn	3	3	990	990	0	560
Brother International	cons, prn	11	0	869	0	869	18
total		14	3	1859	990	869	109
Pioneer	audio	10	2	1372	471	901	28
Alps group							
Alps	components	4	3	1246	1006	240	299
Alpine	car-audio	3	0	71	0	71	est
total		7	3	1317	1006	311	322
Yuasa Battery	batteries	4	2	1165	1133	32	442
Omron	indu, PCBs	16	2	1059	185	874	91
Seiko group							
Seiko Epson	printers, PCs	9	3	1041	674	367	178
Seiko Denshi Kogyo	compo, LCDs	3	2	22	8	14	100
Hattori Seiko	watches	3	0	400	0	400	176
total		15	5	1463	682	781	176
Oki	indu, compo	10	1	964	499	465	1653
Murata	components	7	2	640	360	280	na
TDK	tapes	3	1	539	350	189	205
Tabuchi Denki	power units	1	1	520	520	0	174
Minolta	ofm, cameras	10	2	na	500	na	na
Shimadzu	meas eq	2	2	468	468	0	1571
Tamura	transformers	1	1	457	457	0	est
Star Micronics	meas eq, prn	4	1	449	306	143	580
Hosiden	tel and -parts	2	1	440	434	6	11000
Clarion	car audio	3	2	416	395	21	179
Orion	VTRs	1	1	400	400	0	est

Appendix B: *continued*

Company (group)	products	# subs		employment			
		all	manf	all	manf	sales	incr % 86–90
Citizin group							
Citizin Trading	watches	3	1	214	54	160	-4
Citizen	watches, prn	4	2	162	116	46	853
total		7	3	376	170	206	57
Nitto Denko	components	4	1	385	334	51	41
Olympus	cameras, PPCs	3	1	+366	na	366	est
Janome	sewing eq	2	1	351	217	134	-6
Terumo	medical	1	1	350	350	0	1
Kenwood	audio	6	1	348	49	299	47
Funai Denki	consumer	3	2	340	330	10	11000
Dainippon Screen	optoelectric eq	4	0	315	0	315	111
Makita Electric	power tools	7	0	313	0	313	52
Mita	PPCs	7	0	304	0	304	111
Casio	consumer	3	0	286	0	286	30
Mitsutoyo	meas eq	4	1	237	59	178	est
Mitsumi	components	3	2	234	224	10	4580
King Kogyo	cash registers	1	0	230	0	230	0
Nippon Columbia	audio	2	1	177	141	36	est
Aisin Seiki	home electr eq	3	0	173	0	173	82
Terasaki Denki	power switches	1	1	160	160	0	est
Dainippon Printing	projection screens	1	1	160	160	0	est
Daikin Kogyo	airconditioners	1	1	149	149	0	60
Nippon Denso	car parts	4	0	148	0	148	est
SMK	components	2	1	141	124	17	985

Appendix B: *continued*

Company (group)	products	# subs all	manf	employment all	manf	sales	incr % 86–90
Rohm	semiconductors	2	0	132	0	132	136
Nihon CMK	PCBs	1	1	130	130	0	est
Horiba	meas eq	3	3	126	126	0	62
JEOL	medical	4	0	120	0	120	21
Nihon Seiki	meas eq for cars	1	1	114	114	0	est
Amano	time recorders	1	1	109	109	0	est
JST	connectors	5	5	104	104	0	est
Yamauchi Electric	rubber compo	1	1	100	100	0	est
Showa Plastics	audio cabinets	1	1	100	100	0	est

Sources: Touyou Keizai (1987,1991); JETRO (1990b); EIAJ (1990); EACEM (1991).

Remarks: # subs = number of subsidiaries, empl = number of persons employed, manf = subsidiaries with manufacturing function; sales = subsidiaries with only sales function; incr % = percentage increase in total employment 1986-1990, est = subsidiaries newly established in the period 1986-1990: no employees in the EC in 1986; + = actual number of employees is higher.

Products: indu = industrial electronics, cons = consumer electronics, comm = communication equipment (including tel = telephones, fax = facsimiles), tel = telephones, ofm = office machines (including Plain Paper Copiers = PPCs), scales = electronic scales, meas eq = measuring equipment, prn = printers, PCs = personal computers, compo = components, ICs = integrated circuits, PCBs = Printed Circuit Boards, LCDs = Liquid Crystal Displays.

[a] Does not include Siemens-Matsushita Components.

[b] Does not include the acquistion of ICL.

REFERENCES

Abo, Tetsuo, 1991, Sanyo's Overseas Production Plants, in: Helmut Schütte, ed., *The Global Competitiveness of Asian Firms*, Macmillan, London.

Bael, Ivo van, and Jean-Francois Bellis, 1990, *Anti-Dumping and other Trade Protection Laws of the EEC*, second edition, CCH Editions, Bicester.

Baragiola, Patrick, and Karin Bogart, 1990, *The Japanese in Europe: EC-Japan Relations* (volume II), Club de Bruxelles.

Belderbos, René A., forthcoming, On the Advance of Japanese Electronics Manufacturers in the EC: Companies, Trends, and Trade Policy, in: Helmut Schütte, ed., *The Global Competitiveness of Asian Firms*, Macmillan, London.

Belderbos, René A., 1992b, *Tariff Jumping FDI and Export Substitution: The Case of Japanese Electronics Firms in Europe*, Paper Prepared for the 1993 Japanese Business Studies Meetings, Columbia University, New York, January 8–10, 1993.

Belderbos, René A., 1992a, *Firm Determinants of Japanese Direct Foreign Investment in South-East Asia, Europe, and the United States*, mimeo, Erasmus University, Rotterdam.

Belderbos, René A., 1991, *Japanese Industrial Investments in the EC: Facts and Factors*, mimeo, Erasmus University, Rotterdam.

Blair, D., *et al.*, 1991, An Economic Analysis of Matsushita, *The Antitrust Bulletin*, 355–381.

Bowen, Harry, 1991, Consumer Electronics, in: David Mayes, ed., *The European Challenge: Industry's Response to the 1992 Programme*, Harvester Wheatsheaf, London.

Buigues, Pierre, and Alexis Jacquemin, 1989, Strategies of Firms and Structural Environments in the Large Internal Market, *Journal of Common Market Studies*, 1 (28), 53–67.

Bürgenmeyer, B. and J.L. Mucchielli, 1991, *Multinationals and Europe 1992*, Routledge, New York.

Burton, F. N., and F. H. Saelens, 1987, Trade Barriers and Japanese Foreign Direct Investment in the Colour Television industry, *Managerial and Decision Economics*, vol. 8, 285–293.

Caves, Richard E., 1982, *Multinational Enterprise and Economic Analysis*, MIT Press, Cambridge.

Cawson, Alan, *et al.*, 1990, *Hostile Brothers: Competition and Closure in the European Electronics Industry*, Clarendon Press, Oxford.

Commission of the European Communities (CEC), 1991a, *The European Electronics and Information Technology Industry: State of Play, Issues at Stake and Proposals for Action*, DG XIII.

Commission of the European Communities (CEC), 1991b, *Panorama of EC industry*, Luxembourg.

Dempa, 1991–1992, *Japan Electronics Almanac*, Dempa, Tokyo.

Dempa, 1990, *Japan Electronics Buyers Guide*, Dempa, Tokyo.

Dunning, John H., and Michelle Gittelman, 1991, *Japanese Multinationals in Europe and the United States: Some Comparisons and Contrasts*, Discussion Papers in International Investment and Business Studies, Series B, No. 154, Department of Economics, University of Reading.

Dunning, John, H., 1986, *Japanese Participation in British Industry*, Croom Helm, London.

Dunning, John H., 1981, *International Production and the Multinational Enterprise*, London.

European Association of Electronics Manufacturers (EACEM), 1990, *Consumer Electronic Industrial Plants in Europe by Far-East Manufacturers*, edition 5.

Electronic Industries Association Japan (EIAJ), 1990–1992, *Kaigai Houjin Risuto* (*List of Overseas Affiliates*), Tokyo.

Electronic Industries Association Japan (EIAJ), 1992b, *Minseiyou Denshi Kiki Deitashuu* (*Handbook of Consumer Electronics Statistics*), EIAJ, Tokyo.

Euro-Jerc Research Centre, ed., 1990, *Japanese Presence in Europe*, Catholic University of Louvain.

Euromonitor, 1991, *Consumer Europe 1991*, 8th Edition, Euromonitor Publications, London.

Eurostat, 1985–1990, *Harmonized External Trade Statistics*, Luxembourg.

Flamm, Kenneth, 1990, Semiconductors, in: G. Hufbauer, ed., *Europe 1992: An American Perspective*, The Brookings Institution, Washington.

Franko, Lawrence G., 1983, *The Threat of Japanese Multinationals: How the West can Respond*, Wiley, Chichester.

Froot, Kenneth A., 1991, *Japanese Foreign Direct Investment*, Working Paper No. 3737, National Bureau of Economic Research, Cambridge, MA.

Furlotti, Marco, 1991, *Japanese Foreign Direct Investment in the Electronic Industry and the European Community*, unpublished MA dissertation, Hitotsubashi University.

Genther, Phyllis A., and Donald H. Dalton, 1992, *Japanese-Affiliated Electronics Companies: Implications for US Technology Development*, US Department of Commerce, Washington, DC.

Gold, David, Persa Eonomou and Telly Tolentino, 1991, *Trade Blocs and Investment Blocs: The Triad in Foreign Direct Investment and International Trade*, Paper presented at the annual meeting of the Academy of International Business, Miami, October 19, 1991.

Graham, Edward M. and Paul Krugman, 1990, *Foreign Direct Investment in the United States*, Institute for International Economics, Washington DC.

Gregory, Gene, 1986, *Japanese Electronics Technology: Enterprise and Innovation*, John Wiley, Chicester.

HEC Eurasia Institute, 1989, *Corporate Challenges for Japan and Europe 1992*, HEC Eurasia Institute.

Hindley, Brain, 1988, Dumping and the Far East Trade of the European Community, *The World Economy*, 445–464.

Holmes, Peter, René Belderbos and Alasdair Smith, 1992, *Strategic Trade and "Unfair" Business Practices in Global Information Technology and Electronics Markets: Problems and Policy Responses*, University of Sussex, Brighton.

Ishikawa, K., 1990, *Japan and the Challenge of Europe 1992*, Royal Institute of International Affairs, London, Pinter Publishers.

Japan Development Bank, 1989, *Kyuuninen EC Tougou to Wagakuni seigyou no Mondai: Jidousha to Denshi meikah no Taiou* (*The 1992 EC Unification and the Problems faced by our Country's Industries: the Case of the Automobile and Electronics Industries*), Nihon Kaihatsuginkou Chousa 131.

Japan Development Bank (Investment Research Institute), 1989b, *Kigyou Zaimu Deita* (*Corporate Financial Data*), Tokyo.

Japan Development Bank, 1988, Douki Hajimeru Wagakuni Kigyou no Kaigai Kenkyuu Kaihatsu (Japanese firms' R&D Activities Abroad), *Nihon Kaihatsuginkou Chousa*, 115.

Japan Machinery Export Council, 1992, *Kikai Yushutsu Shijou Kankyou Seibi Taisaku Suishin Chousa Houkokusho* (*Report on Developments in Policies Dealing with Localisation in Machinery Export Markets*), mimeograph, Nihon Kikai Yushutsu Sougou, Tokyo.

Japan Society for the Promotion of Machinery, 1989, *Nichi-ou on Kyouei* (*Co-existence and Co-prosperity of the Japanese and European Machinery Industry*), Kikai Kougyou Keizai Kenkyuujo 63–5.

JETRO, 1986–1992, *White Paper on International Trade*, JETRO, Tokyo.

JETRO, 1990b, *The Current Management Situation of Japanese Manufacturing Enterprises in Europe*, JETRO, Tokyo.

Kaburagi, Shinji, 1992, 1991 Nendou no Wagakuni no Kaigai Chokusetsu Toushi Doukou (Trends in Japanese FDI in Fiscal Year 1991), *Kaigai Toushi Kenkyuushohou*, 11, 110–130.

Kojima, Kiyoshi, 1978, *Direct Foreign Investments: a Japanese Model of Multinational Business Operations*, Croom Helm, London.

Komiya, R., 1987, *Japan's Foreign Direct Investment: Facts and Theoretical Considerations*, Discussion Paper 87-F-13, University of Tokyo.

Krugman, Paul, ed., 1986, *Strategic Trade Policy and the New International Economics*, MIT Press, Cambridge MA and London.

Long Term Credit Bank of Japan (LTCB), 1989, *Entry in the Internal Market of the European Community by Japanese Manufacturers*, LTCB, Tokyo.

Mackintosh International, 1985, *The European Consumer Electronics Industry*, Office for Official Publications of the European Communities, Luxembourg.

Management and Coordination Agency, 1991, *Report on the Survey of Research and Development in Japan*, Nihon Toukei kyoukai, Tokyo.

Marion, M.F. van, 1992, *Liberal Trade and Japan: The Incompatibility Issue in Electronics*, Ph.D. thesis, University of Groningen.

Messerlin, Patrick A., 1989, The EC Anti-Dumping Regulations: A First Economic Appraisal, 1980–1985, *Weltwirtschaftliches Archiv*, 125, 563–587.

Micossi, Stefano, and Gianfranco Viesti, Japanese Direct Manufacturing Investment in Europe, in: L. Alan Winters and Anthony J. Venables, eds., 1991, *European Integration: Trade and Industry*, Cambridge University Press.

Ministry of International Trade and Industry (MITI), 1990, 1992, *Wagakuni Kigyou no Kaigai Jigyou Katsudou* (*Report on the Foreign Activities of Japanese Corporations*), Okurashou Insatsukyoku, Tokyo.

Ministry of International Trade and Industry (MITI), 1991, *Dai 4-kai Kaigai Toushi Toukei Souran* (*Directory of Foreign Direct Investment*), Okurashou Insatsukyoku, Tokyo.

Ministry of International Trade and Industry (MITI), 1990b, *Denshi Kougyou Nenkan* (*Electronic Industry Yearbook 1990*), Dempa Shinbunsha, Tokyo.

Ministry of Finance, 1991, *Zaisei Kinyuu Toukei Geppou* (*Financial Investment Statistics Monthly*), no 476, December 1991.

Morita, Akio, 1987, *Made in Japan*, Fontana/Collins, London.

Nakakita, Toru, and Shujiro Urata, 1991, *Industrial Adjustment in Japan and its Impact on Developing Countries*, presented at the conference on "Industrial Adjustment of Developed Countries and its Impact on Developing Countries, Ajia Kenkyuujo, Tokyo, february 1-2, 1991.

National Consumer Council, 1990, *International Trade and the Consumer: Consumer Electronics and the EC's Anti-Dumping Policy*, National Consumer Council, London.

Ohmae, Kenichi, 1985, *Triad Power: the Coming Shape of Global Competition*, the Free Press, New York.

Ozawa, Terutomo, 1991, Japan in a New Phase of Multinationalism and Industrial Upgrading: Functional Integration of Trade, Growth, and FDI, *Journal of World Trade*, 43–60.

Ozawa, Terutomo, 1979, *Multinationalism, Japanese Style: The Political Economy of Outward Dependency*, Princeton University Press, Princeton.

Sazanami, Yoko, 1992, *Globalisation Strategy of Japanese Manufacturing Firms and its Impact on Trade Flows Between Europe, Asia and North America*, mimeograph, Keio University.

Sazanami, Yoko, 1991, *Determinants of Japanese Foreign Direct Investment: Locational Attractiveness of European Countries to Japanese Multinationals*, Paper presented at the French Economic Society Meeting, Paris, 24–25 September, 1991.

Takaoka, Hirobumi, and Takanori Satake, 1991, Report on Results of Fiscal Year 1990 Foreign Direct Investment Survey, *EXIM Review*, 1 (11), 2–25.

Takaoka, Hirobumi, 1991, *The Results of a Survey on Global Management and Overseas Direct Investment*, The Export-Import Bank of Japan, Research Institute of Overseas Investment, Tokyo.

Tejima, Shigeki, 1992, Japanese Foreign Direct Investment in the 1980s and its Prospect for the 1990s, *EXIM Review*, 11 (2), 25–51.

Thomsen, S. and P. Nicolaides, 1991, *The Evolution of Japanese Direct Investment in Europe: Death of a Transistor Salesman*, Royal Institute of International Affairs, London.

Touyou Keizai, 1987, 1991, 1992, *Kaigai Shinshutsu Kigyou Souran* (*Directory of Japanese Multinational Corporations*), Tokyo.

Urata, Shujiro, 1992, *Japanese Foreign Direct Investment and Its Impact on Foreign Trade in Asia*, mimeograph, Waseda University.

Urata, Shujiro, 1991, The Rapid Increase of Direct Investment Abroad and Structural Change in Japan, in: Eric D. Ramstetter, ed., *Direct Foreign Investment in Asia's Developing Economies and Structural Change in the Asia-Pacific Region*, Westview Press, Boulder.

Vermulst, Edwin, and Paul Waer, 1990, European Community Rules of Origin as Commercial Policy Instruments?, *Journal of World Trade*, 55–99.

Watanabe, Soitsu, 1988, Trends of Japan's Direct Investment in Europe, *EXIM Review*, 1 (9), 43–97.

Williamson, Peter J., and Hideki Yamawaki, 1991, *The Japanese Distribution Network in Europe: Ready and Waiting for the Single Market?*, mimeo, London Business School.

Yamaichi Research Institute (YRI), 1991, *Sangyou no Subete* (*Industry Yearbook*), Yamaichi Shouken, Tokyo.

Yamamura, Kozo, and Ulrike Wassmann, 1989, Do Japanese Firms Behave Differently?: The Effects of Keiretsu in the United States, in: Kozo Yamamura, *Japanese Investment in the United States: Should We Be Concerned?*, Society for Japanese Studies.

Yamawaki, Hideki, 1991, Exports and Foreign Distributional Activities: Evidence on Japanese Firms in the United States, *Review of Economics and Statistics*, 2, 294–30.
Yamazawa, Ippei, 1991, The New Europe and the Japanese Strategy, *Rivista Di Politica Economica*, 81 (5), 631–653.
Yoshitomi, Masaru, ed., 1991, *Japanese Direct Investment in Europe*, The Sumitomo-Life Research Institute and the Royal Institute of International Affairs, Avebury, Aldershot.

4

The Automobile Industry: The Transplantation of the Japanese System Abroad

Frédérique Sachwald

The forceful entry of the Japanese producers on international car markets has been one of the major factors which have unsettled the competitive game in the automobile industry since 1970s.[1] These major new entrants have threatened the positions of traditional American and European producers, which have reacted with two types of answers. Firstly a set of protectionist measures and secondly a vast movement of restructuring and upgrading in Western car industries.

Since the end of the 1970s, the sucesses of the Japanese carmakers on world markets have been a fundamental factor in the growing internationalization of the industry. This chapter explores one aspect of this process, namely the Japanese strategies of direct investment in the United States and Europe. Indeed, in the context of the automobile industry, it is important to consider both sides of the Atlantic since strategies tend to be conceived at a global level.

The first part of this chapter emphasizes the role of international markets for Japanese carmakers as one strong motive to go and produce abroad. The second part explains the determinants of the decisions by Japanese producers to locate in the United States and in Europe and examines the different types of investment which they

---

[1] For a more general perspective on the factors of evolution of the competitive game in the industry (which include both demand and supply factors), see in particular (Sachwald 1994b).

have chosen according to the specific circumstances of each operation. The third part explores how Japanese carmakers have worked at "transplanting" their specific production system in Europe. Indeed, their success abroad largely depends on their ability to reproduce in the United States and Europe the conditions of their strong competitiveness.

4.1   THE NEED FOR INTERNATIONAL MARKETS

Japanese carmakers have achieved a high level of productivity which has been a powerful weapon to penetrate foreign markets. At the same time, Japanese producers have become very dependent on international sales, which has constituted a strong motive for their investment in foreign production units.

4.1.1   Japanese Inroads

Japanese carmakers have made rapid inroads on international markets from the 1970s onwards. Japanese automobile production was negligible until the 1960s (100,000 vehicles in 1956 (Roos 1990)); moreover, it was essentially directed at the domestic market until the end of the 1960s. Japan really became the third pole of world automobile production in the 1970s. During that decade, Japanese automobile production increased much more rapidly than production from other regions. In 1980, Japanese car production exceeded that of the United States; this was the case again until 1983, and then from 1987.[2]

From the 1950s onwards, trade was progressively liberated. This movement first benefited the Europeans which traded between themselves and with the United States. American producers were already multinationals and exports from the United States were low. Figure 1 shows the evolution of the structure of automobile exports; the larger share taken by Japanese producers has largely been compensated by the reduction in the European share. It also underlines the fact that, as for production, there are really only three important regions.

For a long period, the industry was moderately internationalized. By the 1920s, Ford and General Motors had production units in

---

[2] Statistics from the annual bulletin from CCFA (see bibliography).

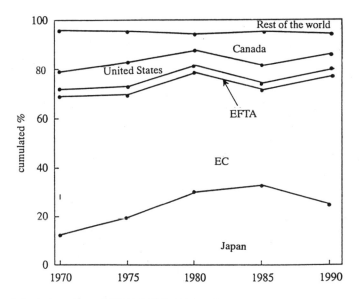

Source: Calculations from CHELEM/CEPII data base

Figure 1:   Regional Origin of Automobile Exports, in Cumulated Percentage

numerous countries; this internationalization of the American producers was reinforced in the 1930s as European countries tried to
protect their infant automobile industry (Sachwald 1989). European
producers also built international operations, but on a much smaller
scale. Producers from industrialized countries had manufacturing
operations in developing countries, but here again, the importance
of these operations remained rather limited. So, until the 1970s,
national markets were relatively protected from foreign cars, be it from
exports or from multinational production units. Moreover, in Europe,
automobile imports often came from other European countries.[3]

From the 1970s, part of the Japanese production is exported;
the share of Japanese producers in world automobile exports grows
rapidly from 1970 to 1985 (see Figure 1 above). Table 1 shows the
evolution of the rate of penetration by Japanese brands into the main
car markets.[4]

---

[3] The automobile sector was thus a clear example of intra-industry trade.

[4] At the beginning of the 1990s, the market share of Japanese carmakers has tended

Table 1: Share of Japanese Brands in Total Registrations, in %

Countries	1970	1975	1980	1984	1988	1991	1992
US	3.7	9.4	21.3	18.3	21.3	30.2	30.0
Germany	0.1	1.7	10.4	11.6	15.5	15.3	13.7
UK	0.4	9.0	11.9	11.1	11.4	10.7	12.3
France	0.2	1.5	2.9	3.0	2.9	4.0	4.1
Spain	–	–	–	0.6	0.9	2.3	2.7
Italy	a	a	0.1	0.2	0.9	2.6	3.0
Portugal	10.7	20.5	7.5	8.5	7.8	9.2	n.a
Greece	-	-	49.2	30.9	38.9	31.6	n.a
Belgium	4.9	16.5	24.7	20.1	21.0	22.3	21.3
Netherlands	3.1	15.5	25.7	22.0	27.7	27.8	27.0
Norway	11.4	28.3	39.1	33.5	39.3	45.1	42.5
Sweden	0.7	6.5	12.1	15.0	25.5	25.3	24.6
Austria	0.9	5.4	19.2	27.0	33.1	28.7	29.7

[a] Less than 0.1%

Sources: CCFA, *Les Echos* 6/2/1991, *Le Journal de l'Automobile* no. 337, *La lettre de l'Automobile* av. 1992

The rate of penetration by Japanese cars has grown earlier in the United States and has reached higher levels; in 1980, it was already over 20%. This is due to the weak competitiveness of the American industry and to the good fuel performances of the Japanese cars in a period when gas consumption had become an important preoccupation.

In Europe there are clearly two categories of countries. In countries where there is no national automaker such as Austria or Greece, the Japanese market share has quickly reached very high levels. In countries where there are national companies the progression has been much slower. This is due to two types of factors. Firstly, automobile markets were traditionally characterized by a relatively high level of brand loyalty, which tended to benefit national producers. In turn, this brand loyalty interacted with the fact that markets were relatively protected and fragmented. Secondly, a number of European markets were protected by non-tariff barriers in the 1970s. On average, figures in Table 1 confirm Japanese competitive strength but the differences in

---

to stagnate or diminish, especially in the U.S.

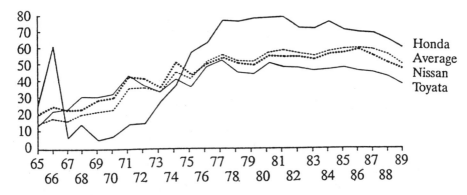

Share of exports as a percentage of the total production of cases.

Source: (Bélis-Bergouignan, Lung 1992)

Figure 2: Rate of Export of the Japanese Automobile Industry

trade policies between countries makes it difficult to compare relative positions.

The Japanese inroads on international markets has been one of the important sources of increased competition in the automobile industry. Measures of concentration of sales show that the degree of concentration has decreased on the most important automobile markets since the end of the 1970s (Sachwald 1994b).

4.1.2 Dependency upon Foreign Markets

Exports have been important for the Japanese automobile industry quite early in its development. On average, the Japanese automobile industry exported 20% of its production at the end of the 1960s. The rate of export grew rapidly in the 1970s and reached nearly 60% in 1980 (Bélis-Bergouignan, Lung 1992). Figure 2 shows that there were large differences between carmakers, with Honda exporting a much larger share of its production.

Table 2:   Geographical Distribution of Japanese Exports of Automobiles, in %, from Data in Value

Exports to:	1970	1975	1980	1985	1990
United States	57.6	47.3	49.3	60.7	48.2
EC	5.8	16.9	17.4	11.2	22.0
EFTA	3.8	3.6	4.0	3.4	5.8
Total Western Europe	9.6	20.5	21.4	14.6	27.8
Total US and Europe	67.2	68.8	70.7	75.3	75.0

Source: Calculations from the data base CHELEM (CEPII/GSI)

The geographical distribution of Japanese car exports has been strongly influenced by the successes on the American market during the 1970s mentioned above. Table 2 shows that the American market is by far the first export market. It also underlines the significance of exports to industrial countries which are by far the most important markets.

It was thus logical that the efforts to maintain the market share in the United States would be of first strategic importance. More generally, Japanese carmakers needed foreign markets in order to fully benefit from their productive efficiency. Given the crucial importance of international markets and the difficulties met in continuing massive exports,[5] Japanese producers have chosen to produce abroad. Table 3 shows that foreign production has rapidly increased during the 1980s. Production in North America started before production in Europe and remains much more important, even if the progression has been particularly rapid in Europe.

Japanese carmakers have also made a number of arrangements to produce or assemble light commercial vehicles in Europe. Nissan produces vans, trucks and buses at its Barcelona complex. IBC, a UK joint venture between GM and Isuzu, produces a number of Isuzu badged vans. Volkswagen assembles the Toyota Hi-Lux under licence at its Hanover plant.[6] A number of Japanese commercial vehicles are also assembled in Italy and Portugal (EIU 1992).

---

[5] See section 2 below.

[6] In 1990, prodution was 10,528, in 1991, 12,017 (German statistical source VDA, quoted by CCFA). VW sells two thirds of the production through its network, under the name Taro.

Table 3: Japanese Production of Passenger Cars in North America and Europe (Number of Cars)

Carmaker	1985	1988	1990	1991
United States				
Toyota	–	18 527	218 195	192 000
NUMMI (GM/Toyota)[a]	64 604	129 978	205 287	206 000
Nissan[b]	43 810	109 897	95 844	133 000
Honda	145 337	366 355	435 437	449 000
Mazda	–	167 205	184 428	166 000
Mitsubishi	–	2 409	148 379	169 000
Subaru/Isuzu[b]	–	–	32 461	58 000
Canada				
Honda	–	50 430	104 572	98 000
Toyota	–	200	60 804	68 000
CAMI (GM/Suzuki)[b]	–	–	44 606	85 000
Total North America	253 751	845 001	1 381 634	1 465 000
Europe				
Nissan (UK)	–	56 541	76 190	124 666
Nissan (Spain)[c]	7 872	19 552	27 332	22 431
Santana (Suzuki, Spain)[d]	9 238	22 362	21 203	25 505
IBC (GM/Isuzu)[e]	–	–	–	11 000p
Honda (UK)[f]	–	5 044	26 454	35 952
Total Europe	17 110	102 449	151 179	219 554

[a] Also produces a few pick ups since 1991

[b] Also produces small utility vehicles (pick ups, vans).

[c] Ebro trucks are not counted.

[d] Land Rover vehicles are not counted.

[e] Only the off-road vehicle (Frontera), IBC produces mostly utility vehicles

[f] Honda cars which are produced by Rover are not counted.

Source: CCFA, Répertoire various editions pour les années antérieures à 91, EIU 92 pour 91

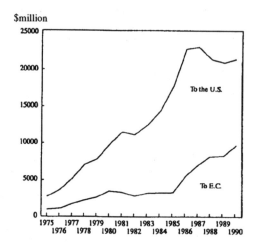

Source: Calculations from the data base CHELEM (CEPII/GSI)

Figure 3: Japanese Exports of Cars to Europe and the United States

From 1992 the evolution of Japanese production abroad had slowed down as a result of the recession. At the beginning of 1993, Mazda has shelved its project to localize in Europe in cooperation with Ford. One reason for this decision was the development of overcapacities in Europe. In these conditions, it seems that Japanese carmakers may not reach the production level of one million vehicles per year by the end of the 1990s, as some forecasts had predicted.

The substitution effect between exports and foreign production is evidenced by the relative decline in automobile exports from Japan at the end of the 1980s. Figure 3 shows that this decline is quite clear for exports to the United States; exports to Europe, where Japanese production is still low, have continued to increase until the beginning of the 1990s.

Figure 4 clearly shows an inverse relationship between the rate of export by Japanese carmakers and their rate of production abroad. The substitution between exports and local production has thus exerted a positive effect on the trade balance for cars.[7] The favorable

---

[7] Which is not necessarily the case for the entire automobile sector (including components); see below.

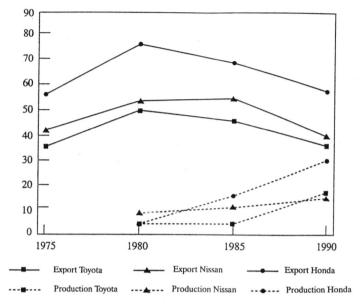

In 1975 the rate of production abroad is near to zero

Source: Own calculations from CCFA data.

Figure 4: Rate of Export and Rate of Production Abroad by the Main Japanese Carmakers (1975–1990, in %)

effects on the balance of trade for cars can be reinforced by the fact that the Japanese production units in North America and Europe export to other regions of the world. Table 4 shows that exports from Japanese foreign production units are still relatively limited. Moreover, they are not targeted at Japan.

Exports from Japanese transplants have increased rapidly from 1989, but volumes remain quite limited. In particular, these exports are quite small in comparison with imports from Japan; in 1991, the EC countries have imported 1.2 million cars from Japan and the United States about 1.7 million. Exports from European locations are substantially higher than from North America. But most of these exports are intra-European, and more precisely, intra-EC because the British and Spanish production units supply various markets.[8]

---

[8] See below, section 4.2.1.

Table 4:   Exports by Japanese Carmakers from their North American and European
Production Units (Number of Cars)

	1987	1988	1989	1990	1991	1992
To	From the United States and Canada					
Japan	0	6650	3432	15300	15026	26395
Total Asia	725	9025	12072	36249	47180	84849
Europe[a]	0	0	0	0	8623	27712
Total	725	9025	12072	37951	59678	114962
To	From the EC[b]					
EC	1556	779	9620	97165	154179	
Total	1748	782	10353	113319	180016	
To	From the UK					
Total Europe	1748	779	10353	73462	139944	
To	From Spain[b]					
Total Europe	n.a	n.a	n.a	39857	40072	

[a] Does not include the Ford Probe, which Mazda produces for Ford in the US

[b] Exports from Spain are included only from 1990 though Santana did export a number
of cars from Spain between 1987 and 1989. In 1990, exports from Spain in this table
total 25,199.

Sources: For North America, US and Canada export shipments (passenger cars),
MVMA, Detroit. For the UK, SMMT Motorstatistics and CCFA. For Spain, CCFA.

4.2   RAPID INCREASE OF PRODUCTION ABROAD

In the United States as in Europe, the first answer to the Japanese challenge has been protectionist measures, which in turn have constituted
a strong incentive to direct investment (4.2.1). Japanese carmakers had
not expected to increase their foreign production so rapidly and on
such a large scale, so they have had to resort to various solutions in
order to do so without taking too much risk (4.2.2).

4.2.1   Why?

American and European producers have identified the central problem, which was the evolution of the production paradigm, quite

slowly and have had difficulties in both deciding and implementing adequate strategies. For some time, the hypothesis (sincere or not) was that Japanese producers operated under such different conditions that confrontation was unfair. Consequently, a number of countries resorted to protection.

4.2.1.1 Neo-protectionism in the automobile industry

Since the post-war period, the organization of trade in the car industry has been quite exemplary. Indeed, after tariff liberalization, it has experienced an important neo-protectionist move from the countries which were threatened by new competitors.

In 1950, cars were protected by high tariffs in most countries, and in a number of cases also by quotas. These protectionist measures have been lowered by the GATT rounds;[9] at the beginning of the 1980s, the American tariff on cars was below 3% and Japan had no tariff at all. The EC common external tariff was 10% and there was no tariff for intra-European trade in cars (since 1968).

But while trade in cars was being freed from tariff protection, it became subject to new forms of non-tariff protection. The term neo-protectionism has been coined to designate new and non-orthodox (with respect to the GATT) practices.[10] In the automobile industry, neo-protectionism has mainly taken the shape of *voluntary export restraints against* Japanese imports. The term itself is typical of neo-protectionism, since it is a actually a euphemism to designate new forms of quantitative restrictions. The export restraint is voluntary because it is negotiated with the exporting country, which means that it is a discriminatory quota. Its main interest is that it is not explicitly forbidden by GATT, and thus belongs to the grey area in which neo-protectionism has thrived.

In Europe, trade protection in the automobile industry resulted from national measures which were of different nature. Italy, Spain and Portugal have applied quantitative restrictions on car imports from Japan early on. In 1955, Italy and Japan had negotiated a limited reciprocal penetration of their markets; it seems that at the time, Japan feared competition from FIAT. Since then Italy has had a quota of Japanese automobile imports, which has been recognized by the

---

[9] Especially in the 1950s and 1960s, see (Bourdet 1987, Sachwald 1994b).

[10] On this general question, see (OCDE 1985, Sachwald 1990b, Nicolas 1992).

EC. At the beginning of the 1980s, Italy imported about 2,500 cars and 750 commercial vehicles from Japan (GATT 1991). Italy actually imports more Japanese cars indirectly, that is through other European countries, but these are also limited (*Europolitique* 25/1/1992). Spain authorizes 1,000 cars from Japan a year and Portugal, which has no national carmaker, has limited imports from extra-EC countries to 20,000 (GATT 1991).

Other car producing European countries have restricted Japanese imports when the latter threatened local production. It seems that the first voluntary export restraint was that of the United Kingdom in 1975. It was actually negociated between the *Society of Motor Manufacturers and Traders* and the *Japanese Automobile Manufacturers Association*. This producers' agreement is not acknowleged by the two organizations, but, since then, the Japanese market share has been stabilized at around 11% (see Table 1). In 1977, the French government has arranged that Japanese imports would be limited to 3% of the car market.[11]

The American restriction on Japanese car imports has been an important step in the build up of protectionist reactions.[12] The first American voluntary export restraint was negotiated between the Reagan administration and the MITI at the beginning of 1981; Japanese car exports were not to exceed 1.68 million units between April 1981 and March 1982. This limitation has been renewed in 1982 and in 1983 the Japanese government announced that the ceiling was increased to 1.85 million. President Reagan did not renew the VER in 1985, but Japan announced that it would maintain exports to 2.3 million cars. From 1987 to 1991, Japanese car exports were below the ceiling of 2.3 million, largely because of the increasing local production by Japanese automakers. In 1991, Japanese exports to the United States had dropped to about 1.7 million cars (*Financial Times* 11/9/1991). At the beginning of 1992, the MITI announced that it would lower the ceiling on Japanese auto exports to the U.S to 1.65 million (for the fiscal year 1992-93). This decision has been interpreted as an attempt to ease relationships with the United States (*Mainichi Daily News* 20/3/1992). In fact, because of increasing Japanese production in North America, exports were expected to decline to about the

---

[11] The share of Japanese cars registrations is higher in Table 1 because of intra-European imports of Japanese built cars, see below.

[12] For details on the American case, see in particular (Cowley, Long 1983, Hufbauer *et al.* 1986).

level of the new ceiling. Canada has also negotiated Japanese export restrictions at the beginning of the 1980s. Japanese imports were limited to 23% of the Canadian market from 1981 to 1986, and to 18% from 1986.

In 1981, the EC protested because the protectionist stand of Washington frustrated its own efforts to obtain a similar restriction from Japan. The European Commission continued to negotiate with Japan, which announced a voluntary export restraint to EC markets in 1983. This arrangement was to be revised in order to prepare for the Single market (see below). In 1981, Japan announced its decision to limit car exports to Germany and the Benelux. Germany always protested that there was no VER, but the Japanese share of the German market has been stabilized during the 1980s at around 15%.[13] Swedish carmakers had begun to feel threatened by Japanese products at the end of the 1980s and a voluntary export restraint for the Swedish market was agreed upon in 1988.

4.2.1.2   Fortress Europe?

Since the first reaction of the industry has been to seek protection, it was logical that it would resist further internationalization. This explains the protracted negotiations about EC external trade policy after the completion of the Single market. Indeed the different national trade policies which have been explained above meant that there was no real common market for cars. As a result, a common external policy and more open markets were the most important prospective consequences of the Single market for the car industry.

The Single market scheme aimed at the free circulation of goods within the Community. In the case of cars, it meant that, in fact, no national market would be able to benefit from stricter access conditions than other EC members. Let's take an example. As seen above, France was protected from Japanese exports by a very low quota. Germany was much more open. If cars had traveled freely between France and Germany,[14] the solution would have been obvious: export cars to Germany... and then from Germany to France. Worries from the protected countries have induced delays in the completion of the

---

[13] On this point, see (Cowley, Long 1983, Sachwald 1994b).

[14] Free trade already exists, and the Single market provides for technical harmonization (which did not effectively exist before within the EC).

Single market, which depended on the adoption of harmonization measures on numerous technical matters.[15] In particular, the French, Italian and Spanish governments have blocked the achievement of the European technical harmonization as long as the Community had not adopted a common external trade policy vis-à-vis Japan for the post 1992 period (Sachwald 1989).

Negotiations between the European Commission and Japan started in 1988 and lasted over three years. In July 1991, Japan and the Commission agreed on a voluntary export restraint of European scope to open the Single market progressively.[16] From 1993 to 1999, imports of Japanese cars and light commercial vehicles in EC markets should be limited to 1,230,000 vehicles per year and access should be totally free from 2000 on. Besides, Japanese imports should not target the markets which are the most protected and their situation will be examined specifically in order to evaluate what level of import they can bear. Finally, the "elements of consensus" provide that Japan should take the evolution of demand into account and adapt the volume of their exports accordingly. A system of information is to observe the evolution of the market and the MITI and the Commission meet twice a year to discuss these matters.

In actual fact, the agreement remains quite unclear. The uncertainties focus on the treatment of the cars which will flow out of the Japanese assembly lines in Europe. The Japanese and Europeans did not agree on the question of transplants and they chose to remain vague about it. According to the agreement, Japanese brands should not exceed a 16% market share in the EC, which means that, given the forecast on the size of the market which served as a basis (15.1 million), apart from the allowed imports (1,230,000), Japan producers could sell 1,200,000 cars from their transplants. But this is not explicit in the agreement. Moreover, Japanese and Europeans diverge on this question; according to the former, the transplants are not affected by the agreement, and cars produced in the EC should be considered as European and not subjected to any limitation. The agreement between Japan and the EC remains quite unclear and offers new grounds for quarrels. Discussions between experts from the EC and Japan in 1992 and 1993 prove that the evolution of demand in Europe constitutes a

---

[15]The car industry has been identified as one in which the technical barriers to intra-community trade were among the highest (Cecchini 1988).

[16] On what is more exactly called, "elements of consensus" and on the details of the negotiations, see (*Europolitique* 17/7/1991, 31/7/199, 3/8/1991, *Les Echos* 17/10/1991, Gandillot 1992).

major bone of contention; given the recession the Commission wants a lower level of Japanese imports.

Protectionist measures from major export markets have created an insecure environment for the Japanese carmakers and have accelerated their internationalization.[17] The sheer size of the Japanese automobile industry and the appreciation of the Yen have certainly contributed to the evolution towards a growing share of international production. But trade impediments have been strong incentives to go ahead in a large scale quite soon. It appears that the decision to produce in Europe has been largely motivated by two interrelated movements: the persistence of protectionist pressures and the prospective growing importance of the European market. Indeed, the Single market was considered as leading both to more dynamic European economies and to more inward looking markets.[18] A further indication that investments have been strongly motivated by barriers to trade is the fact that exports from European production sites are targeted at the most protected markets.

Table 5 shows that the sales of European produced Japanese cars are more concentrated in the protected countries. In this respect, it should be noticed that in 1991, the two categories of countries each represented about 50% of the total EC car sales (CCFA 1992). This focus on the protected markets of the EC could account for the faster penetration of Japanese brands on Southern markets, as compared to Northern Europe, at the beginning of the 1990s.[19]

4.2.2 How?

In 1985, Japanese car production in Europe was negligible. Between 1985 and 1990, the number of cars and light commercial vehicles produced in Europe by Japanese manufacturers has been multiplied by 6.3, the corresponding figure is 3.83 for production in the United

---

[17] This has been a major consequence of the protectionist measures, but not the only one. Other important aspects have been the increase in the price of Japanese cars and the development of top of the range models. On these points, see (Dixit 1987, OCDE 1987, Digby *et al.* 1988).

[18] The role of these factors have been emphasized by several other analyses for the automobile and electronic sectors, see in particular (Dourille-Feer 1992, *Wall Street Journal Europe* 8/1/92). See also Chapters 2 and 3 in this volume.

[19] (*Le Journal de l'Automobile* 22/11/1991) compares the evolution of the rate of penetration of Japanese brands on various European markets. It also notices that the rates of penetration on EFTA markets is relatively stable.

Table 5:   Distribution of Sales of Cars[1] Produced by Japanese Firms in the UK and Spain, in 1991, %

Japanese cars produced in	Sold in protected countries: F, I, Sp, P, UK	Sold in open countries: D, B, L, NL, Dk, Ir, G
UK	55	45
Spain	89	12
UK and Spain	67	33

[1] The table includes, the production by Santana and two Nissan models for Spain (Patrol and Vanette), the Nissan Primera and the Honda Concerto for the UK.

Source: Calculations from data collected by CCFA

States, which started earlier. This section shows that in order to increase rapidly foreign production and to overcome their relative inexperience with international production, Japanese carmakers have resorted to various solutions. Greenfield investments are the best known and most spectacular ones, but Japanese firms have also resorted to various cooperations with local firms.

4.2.2.1   Greenfield investments

Greenfield investments designate the instalation of new units of production. Table 6 lists Japanese manufacturing operations in Europe and the United States and gives a number of their characteristics. A large majority of the operations in Table 6 are new units of production under total Japanese control, but the table also includes 50/50 joint ventures.

In 1982 Honda was the first Japanese carmaker to operate a production facility in one of the large automobile producing country. This early start can be explained by the peculiar situation of Honda which, given its relatively weak domestic position as a latecomer, badly needed international markets.[20] Honda founded Honda of America Manufacturing as early as 1978. The firm started to produce motorcycles in 1979 and cars in 1982. In 1985, it complemented the assembly

---

[20] Honda started car production quite late. At the beginning of the 1980s, it was already a strong exporter (see Figures 2 and 4) and had a cooperative agreement in Great Britain, see below.

Table 6: Greenfield Japanese Automakers Investments in Europe and the United States

Firm	Location	Start-up/ Founded date[1]	Products	Production capacity, in 000	Employees (number)	Local value added in %
Honda	Marysville/US	1982/ 78[2]	Accord, Civic, TRX	89:360, 91:500	6200 (auto)	88:60, 91:75
	Anna/US	1985–6	Engines, parts	500	2000	n.a
	Alliston/Ca	1986/84	Civic	88:50, 89:80	1400	75
	East Liberty/US	1989	Civic, Acura	150	1800	75
	Swindon/UK	1989/85	Engines	92:240	300	n.a
		1992	Accord	94:50, 97:100	1500, 95:2000	60, 95:80
Toyota/GM (NUMMI)	Fremont/US	1984/83	Corolla/Geo Prizm, pick up, parts	250, 91:320	2800	65, 91:77
Toyota	Cambridge/Ca	1988/86	Corolla	75	1000	50
	Georgetown/US	1988/86	Camry	220, 94:400	3500, 93:5000	68, 92:75
		1990	Engines, parts	500	n.a	n.a
	Burnaston/UK	1992/89	Carina	100, 95:200	3000	93:60, 95:80
	Deeside/UK	1992	Engines	100 (later 200)	200 (later 300)	n.a
Nissan	Smyrna/US	1983– 85[3]/80	Light trucks, Sentra	240, 92:440	3900, 93:5500	88:50, 91:70, 93.75
		1992	Engines	150	n.a	n.a
	Sunderland/UK	1986/84	Bluebird, 89: Primera, 92: Micra	93:270	4700	88:60, 9a 0:>80, 60/Micr
	Decherd/US	1996	Engines, parts	300 (engines)	500, (later 1000)	n.a

Table 6:   *Continued*

Firm	Location	Start-up/ Founded date[1]	Products	Production capacity, in 000	Employees (number)	Local value added in %
Mazda[4]	Flat Rock/US	1987/85	MX6, 89: 626, Ford Probe	240	3100	90:68, 92:77–78
Mitsubishi/ Chrysler (Diamond Star)[5]	Bloomington/US	1988/85	Laser, Eclipse, Eagle, Talon, 90: Mirage	240	2900	65
Suzuki/GM (CAMI)	Ingersoll/Ca	1989/86	Cars, 4X4	200	2000	60
Fuji Heavy/ Isuzu (Subaru/Isuzu Automotive)	Lafayette/US	1989/87	Car, pick-up	150, 93: 240	1925	65

[1] The second date corresponds to the date of the foundation of the company; hence it is indicated only once for each company in each country, even if there are several locations.

[2] In 1979, Honda started to produce motorcycles at Marysville. In 1985 it started to produce engines for motorcycles at Anna.

[3] In 1983, the factory produced only pick-ups and started to produce cars in 1985.

[4] In 1992, Ford has taken a 50% participation into the Auto Alliance International Inc., which controlled the Flat Rock unit.

[5] Mitsubishi bought Chrysler's share back in 1991 and now completely controls the Diamond Star, which continue to provide Chrysler with cars though.

Sources: CCFA, JAMA press

plant with an engine and component plant. Honda also started production in Canada in 1986. Nissan came second by opening a factory in the United States in 1983. The Smyrna unit only produced light trucks in 1983 and 1984, and started the production of cars in 1985.

Toyota has also operated a production facility quite early in the United States, however, it has chosen a less risky solution by creating a 50/50 joint venture with General Motors, NUMMI (New United Motor Manufacturing Inc.), in 1983 for a period of 12 years (after 1996 Toyota should control the venture). The objective was to produce Toyota cars, with Toyota's method of production, in a GM facility.[21] Production started in 1984. This joint venture has constituted an important learning experience for Toyota which has been in charge of the management; managers have gained an experience in teaching Toyota's production techniques to American employees. Toyota has decided to go it alone for its next American ventures, and in Europe with greenfield investments. Both Toyota Motor Manufacturing USA and Toyota Motor Manufacturing Canada were founded in 1986 and started production in 1988. Production has rapidly increased and, taking into account both the different production units, including the joint venture, Toyota is second behind Honda for the size of its production in North America (Table 3). In Europe, production of cars and engines started in late 1992, at two British sites.

Toyota has pioneered the joint venture solution to produce cars abroad. The two other joint ventures in North America have created new units of production. Mitsubishi and Chrysler, which have had a broad alliance since 1971 (Sachwald 1994b), have agreed to the constitution of a 50/50 production joint venture in 1985, the Diamond Star. The Diamond Star started production in 1988 and supplied cars to both Chrysler and Mitsubishi. In 1991, partly because of Chrysler's financial difficulties, Mitsubishi has taken full control of the venture. In 1986, General Motors and Suzuki agreed to create a 50/50 joint venture (CAMI) to produce cars in Canada. The factory has started production in 1989.

The most numerous production facilities only started during the second half of the 1980s, both in North America and in Europe. Nissan started production in Great Britain in 1986. It also complemented its car factory with a engine production unit in the United States in 1992. Mazda has started production in the US in 1987; it has been able to decrease the risks to some extent since Ford, its partner, has been buying part of the production of the Flat Rock unit (Table 6).

Honda has continued to actively invest abroad. It started to produce in Canada in 1986 and opened an other unit to produce cars in the United States in 1989. As a result, Honda is the first Japanese producer of cars, both in the United States and Canada (see Table 3). Honda has opened an engine facility in 1989 to support the production of

---

[21] The agreement enables each of the companies to distribute part of the production.

both Rover and Honda cars in the UK. The car factory has started production in 1992, also in Swindon.

4.2.2.2   A variety of means

During the 1980s, carmakers concluded numerous cooperative agreements. This kind of transaction, as opposed to either internal growth or mergers and acquisitions, matched the evolution of the global competitive game in the automobile industry.[22] An observation of the patterns of cooperation shows that the Japanese producers have been the most active in concluding international alliances (Sachwald 1994b); they have resorted to cooperative agreements both to export more cars and to produce locally.

Japanese car manufacturers had to rapidly transfer part of their production abroad during the 1980s, first in the United States and then in Europe. They basically had to choose from three types of solutions: build greenfield operations and run them as part of their world businesses, buy existing facilities, or collaborate with local producers. Because of the sheer size of the necessary investments and of the risks which they represented, they largely chose the collaborative solution, at least as a first step. It is thus insufficient to observe the sole greenfield investments to analyze the evolution of Japanese production abroad. As mentioned above, Japanese carmakers have created joint ventures to set up new large production facilities in North America. They have also resorted to various cooperative agreements with American producers to rapidly penetrate the market and produce some models (Sachwald 1994b). In Europe, Japanese carmakers have largely used the cooperative solution to start production. Table 7 lists the cooperative ventures which the Japanese carmakers have used as a way to produce cars and light commercial vehicles in Europe.[23]

The agreements listed in Table 7 are of different types and significance. Typically, the joint ventures with a local partner are the most important transactions. Capital participations can have a similar importance when they eventually lead to the control of a local firm. The other types of agreements (licenses for example) are less costly and

---

[22] For a detailed analysis of cooperative agreements in the automobile industry, including the agreements which the Japanese have used to penetrate foreign markets with exports, see (Sachwald 1990a, b, 1993).

[23] The table does not include the production of trucks by Japanese producers (Hino, Isuzu, Mitsubishi, Nissan).

Table 7: Production Cooperative Ventures and Capital Participations of Japanese Carmakers in Europe, as of November 1992 (Cars and Light Commercial Vehicles[1])

Automaker	Location	Start-up/ Date of the agreement date[2]	Type of agreement/ participation	Products	Capacity (effective product'n), in 000	Employee
Toyota/ Salvador Caetano	Portugal	1971	27% capital participation in Salvador Caetano	Toyota Land Cruiser, light commercial vehicles, trucks	(14)	2200
Nissan/ Teocar	Volos/ Greece	1980	Assembly under license by Teocar	Pulsar, Pick-ups	36,(91:16)	700
Suzuki (Santana Motor)	Spain	1985/ 82–84–91	Agreement in 82, capital participation in 84, control in 91	4 WD (Suzuki and Land Rover)	50 (92: 32)	3000
Nissan Motor Iberica	Spain	1983/ 80–82[3]	Capital participation and control in 1982	Commercial vehicles, 4WD, components	(92:172, including trucks)	6870
Honda/ Rover	UK	1986/ 83–86	Development and production agreements[4]	Legend, Ballade, Concerto	30	–
Isuzu/ GM (IBC)	Luton/UK	1987/87[5]	Joint-venture (60% Isuzu)	Light commercial vehicle	130 (92:48)	2000
Toyota/VW	Hanover/ Germany	1989/87	Production agreement	Toyotal Hi-Lux assembled by VW	30 (92:12)	–
Daihatsu/ Bertone	Italy	1989/88	Assembly by Bertone	Daihatsu 4 WD	10 (3)	–

Table 7: *continued*

Automaker	Location	Start-up/ Date of the agreement date[2]	Type of agreement/ participation	Products	Capacity (effective product'n), in 000	Employee
Nissan/ Ford	UK/Spain	1993/89	Conception and production agreement[6]	4 WD	50	–
Daihatsu/ Piaggio (P&D SpA)	Pisa/Italy	1992/90	Joint venture (51% Piaggio)	Daihatsu Hijet minivan	35	–
Magyar Suzuki Co.	Hongrie	1992/91	Joint venture (Suzuki 40%, Autokonszern 40%, Itoh 11%, World Bank 9%)	Cultus	93:15 95:50	420
Mitsubishi/ Volvo/Dutch Government (Nederland Car)	Born/NL	1995/91	Joint venture (33% each partner)	Cars	100 to 200	n.a
Suzuki/ VW-SEAT[7]	Spain	1995/92	Development and production agreement	Small car (Suzuki and VW brands)	150	n.a

[1] Unless otherwise indicated. Isuzu, Mazda, Mitsubishi and Nissan also assemble commercial vehicles (pick-ups, trucks, industrial vehicles) in Portugal. In some cases with a local partner.

[2] The second date(s) indicates when the agreement was signed or when the participation began (or augmented).

[3] Nissan participated in Motor Iberica in 1980 and acquired control in 1982. As part of a wide cooperation, including a 20% participation of Honda in Rover, see box 1.

[4] As part of a large cooperation, dating back to 1979.

[5] The factory was previously part of Bedford (GM), and already produced Isuzu vehicles.

[6] Production will take place at Nissan Motor Iberica.

[7] The project was abandoned in July 1993.

Sources: Own data-base (Auto-A) (Sachwald 1994b), CCFA, JAMA, Toyota (1992), EIU (1992), press

more reversible; they may well be a quite temporary solution to produce abroad. The type of transactions depend both on the strategy of the Japanese automakers and on the potential partners. In particular, capital participation implies that the local firm, and in a number of cases the government, are willing to let the Japanese carmaker take a stake in the company.

Capital participations have concerned modest firms in countries with a small or weak automobile industry. The first case has been in Portugal, for assembly operations. Then came Spain at the beginning of the 1980s. Nissan has taken the control of a Spanish firm which is now called Nissan Motor Iberica. It produces cars, light commercial vehicles as well as trucks. After a first cooperative agreement with Land Rover Santana, another Spanish small specialist producer, in 1982, Suzuki had a participation in 1984. In 1991, Suzuki gained control of the firm, which has become Santana Motors. Santana originally produced Land Rover models under license and agricultural machinery; from 1982 on, it started to produce Suzuki models. The proportion of Suzuki models has progressively augmented, while that of Land Rover diminished. These are the only cases of acquisitions of automobile producers in industrial countries by Japanese firms.

Joint ventures have occured later in Europe than in the United States, like the greenfield investments. Moreover, they concern smaller and more specialized units of production. Finally, they use existing facilities, while in the United States joint ventures have created new factories.[24] In 1987, Isuzu and General Motors, which had been partners since 1971, created IBC as a joint venture. IBC has inherited a production facility from Bedford (GM) where it assembles light commercial vehicles and a 4WD model (Frontera). The local content goes from 60 to 80% according to the models. IBC produces Isuzu and Suzuki models. The other European joint venture includes three partners, each controling a third of the capital: Mitsubishi, Volvo and the Dutch government. In 1995, they agreed to create Nederland Car to operate the previous facilities of Volvo Car BV. Production should start in 1995. The capacity should be doubled to 200,000 and production will be shared between Volvo and Mitsubishi.

In order to produce in Europe, Japanese carmakers have also resorted to various cooperative agreements. The most important ones are part of the wide alliance between Honda and Rover, which

---

[24] With the notable exception of NUMMI, but the GM factory was closed before NUMMI re-opened it.

developed progressively and now includes a 20% participation of Honda into Rover (Box 1).

Box 1:   Cooperation between Honda and Rover

Cooperation started in 1979 with a license agreement for production of a car developed by Honda, production of the Triumph Acclaim began in 1981.

In 1983 they agreed to develop a new model in common. The executive car was to have two versions with some common characteristics. Both versions were to be produced by Honda in Japan and Rover in Great Britain. Common production of the Rover 800/Honda Legend, which started in 1986, actually stopped in 1988 and objectives were not reached. In 1985 they decided to develop a new car in common, along similar lines as the previous agreement; the Honda Concerto/Rover 200-400 which were launched in 1989.

In 1986, Rover started to build the Honda Ballade on a commission basis in its Longbridge factory in order to use spare capacity; the contract has been renewed in 1989 for the Honda Concerto. The objective was 40,000 cars a year. In 1990, Rover delivered 26,500 Concerto to Honda.

In 1989 Honda took 20% of Rover.

In 1991 the companies signed a memorandum of understanding which provides for a number of new common projects:

- collaboration on the development of three new models;

- organization of a common strategy of component supply for models manufactured in Great Britain by both companies;

- establishment of formal relations by which Rover will access to Honda's production unit in Japan and North America in order to learn engineering and production techniques;

- Rover will set up a stamping unit at Swindon which will become Honda's main European supplier for metallic panels.

At the end of 1992, Honda's Swindon factory started to produce the Accord, which is the first project from the 1991 agreement. The output is scheduled to rise to more than 100,00.

At the beginning of 1994, BMW acquired 80% of Rover, which means that the cooperation with Honda has to evolve, even if the Japanese carmaker keeps its 20% participation.

Rover and Honda have developed and produced several models together. Production by Rover of the Honda versions and vice-versa was part of the cooperative agreements on these models. The level of production of the Legend by Rover was small (about 6,000 from 1986 to 1988), but much higher for the Honda Concerto (30,000 since 1990). In addition, Rover has been producing the Honda Ballade in its Longbridge facility between 1986 and 1991 (about 5,000/year) for distribution by Honda's British network.

At the beginning of the 1980s, Nissan had also tried the cooperative way, but has been less successful with its Italian partner. The Italian market has been protected by a stringent quota from the 1950s[25] and Italy has also been quite opposed to Japanese investment. In 1980, Nissan created a joint venture with Alfa Romeo (AARNA) in order to produce about 60,000 cars in Alfa Romeo's facility in Naples, which were to be split between the two partners. This objective was not met, and the experiment was stopped. In 1986, when Fiat acquired Alfa Romeo, it bought back the share of Nissan in the venture. From then on, the domination by Fiat seriously limited the possibilities of cooperation in Italy.

At the end of the 1980s, Japanese carmakers concluded agreements to produce in Europe specialized and niche vehicles. Their partners are quite diverse, including European or American generalists and European specialist producers. In 1987, Toyota, which had no yet decided to build a production facility in Europe concluded an agreement with Volkswagen. Since 1989, the German carmaker produced Toyota Hi-Lux (a pick-up) from imported parts. Two thirds of the production are sold through the VW network (under the name Taro). In 1988, Daihatsu and the small Italian producer, Bertone, agreed that the latter would assemble a 4 wheel drive model for the Japanese carmaker (Table 7).

Two cooperative agreements of larger importance are located in Spain. In 1989, Nissan and Ford agreed to cooperate on the conception and production of a 4 wheel drive vehicle. Production, starting in 1993 is located in Nissan's Spanish subsidiary (Table 7), and should reach to reach 50,000 units a year. In 1992, Suzuki and Volkswagen reached an agreement to develop and produce a small car in Spain from 1995. Suzuki has vast experience in very small cars and it should be able to benefit from it without investing large sums of money in Europe. Production should take place in SEAT's facilities in Spain;

---

[25] See above.

the forecasted volume of production is 150,000. Finally, Ford and Mazda, which are already partners and cooperate on a wide range of activities, have had lengthy discussions about producing a common vehicle in Europe, but the project was abandonned at the beginning of 1993 because of the overcapacities and disagreements between the partners.[26]

The Japanese carmakers have also used cooperative ventures to produce in the United States, but relatively less than in Europe. This can be explained in part by the fact that Europe is more difficult to penetrate because of the numerous and diverse local producers. Again, one should underline the fact that most of the Japanese production in Europe takes place in Spain and Great Britain, where the local producers were the weakest. This relationship between the weakness of the local industry and the localization of Japanese production is observed both in the case of Greenfield investment and cooperative agreements.

To summarize, the different types of cooperative agreements into which Japanese automakers entered in order to either sell or produce in the United States and Europe answer three large sets of preoccupations. The first one is related to the learning process about local conditions and the second one to the risks attached to large new operations. The third set of motivations includes the constraints on Japanese investments in certain European countries. In such cases, the first two preoccupations are reinforced, and a local partner may actually be the only solution.

4.3   ORGANIZING PRODUCTION ABROAD

Once a firm is located in a foreign country, protectionist considerations become less relevant, at least for the final product. Generally, the objective of the host country is to attract as much value added and employment as possible. The objective of Japanese carmakers has been double. Firstly to set up an efficient production system and secondly to be recognized as "good corporate citizens" in the different countries where they operate. At the beginning, when a firm settles in a new country, the two objectives may be contradictory since the *transplantation* of the production system is not

---

[26] On the cooperation between Ford and Mazda in general, see (Bélis-Bergouignan *et al.* 1991, Sachwald 1994b).

immediate, even if it is in their interest.[27] In the case of Japanese carmakers, the problem is all the more difficult given the source of their competitive advantage. They have made a triumphal entry in an industry which was considered as mature and frought with barriers to entry, but this collective entry on international markets did not directly flow from the national factor endowments of Japan. Their competitive strength resulted instead from a specific capability; the Japanese challenge was essentially organizational (Box 2). These considerations largely explain both that the local content question has become contentious, and that the Japanese carmakers have worked at adapting their production system to the European environment.

Box 2:   The system to be transplanted

Japanese automakers tend to simultaneously achieve high levels of productivity, quality and product mix complexity. These achievements are reflected in the characteristics of the products they offer: since the 1970s, Japanese cars have been praised for their moderate prices, their high quality standards and model diversification. Japanese producers do more with less; which led researchers to label the Japanese system 'lean production'.[1]

As for mass production, lean production is actually a whole system relating strategy, product, organization and management.[2] It can be characterised by its strong ability to harness workers' skills and knowledge (as opposed to the Fordist system) (Florida, Kenney 1993). The objective is to provide the right product, at the right time and at right quality level, which implies an organization which is capable of producing relatively short series at acceptable costs. Flexibility is the name of the game, but this objective is quite dependant on high quality components. Moreover, good quality all along the production chain is the best way to save on costs (repair costs and lower stocks). The search for quality and flexibility have entailed a high degree of cooperation along the entire production chain, including between the automaker and its suppliers. Coordination extends beyond production itself, to conception. Japanese producers have been able to produce new car models more rapidly than their competitors thanks to a process of development which associates the different parts of the production and engineering process very early on.

Japanese carmakers have traditionally been much less integrated than either their American or their European counterparts;[3] they typically buy 70% of their components from external suppliers. This structural feature combined with the fact

---

[27] B. Emmott (1992) emphasizes this point. He notes that this question is quite general for multinational companies. In particular, American firms have had to transplant their production and organization system when they massively located in Europe during the 1960s.

that the quality of a car largely relies on that of its components, led to the organization of specific relationships between Japanese carmakers and their suppliers, where the partners have traditionally been much closer than was the case in the United States or in Europe. The supply system of Japanese carmakers is organized as a hierarchical pyramid. Suppliers from the first tier have a direct and demanding relationship with the carmaker. They themselves deal with the second tier of suppliers, which in turn orders from the third and lower tiers of suppliers.[4] This organization has proved efficient, increasing the productivity and innovativeness of both the carmakers and their first tier suppliers. These relationships are strengthened by two organizational mechanisms. Suppliers usually belong to a sort of producer organization led by one carmaker (*kyorukokai*); moreover, in a number of cases the carmaker has a participation in the capital of the supplier.

[1]This term was originally coined by the MIT International Vehicle Program which has constituted a quite comprehensive effort at understanding the international differences between automobile production systems; see in particular (Altshuler *et al*. 1984, Krafcik 1988, Womack *et al*. 1990).

[2]What follows is not a definition or a precise description of the lean production process, but rather a broad description in order to contrast it to mass production. On these questions, see (Abernathy 1978, Altshuler *et al*. 1984, Jacot 1990, Womack, *et al*. 1990, Abe 1991).

[3]Vertical integration rates are difficult to calculate, on this question, see in particular (Banville, Chanaron 1991, Ruigrok *et al*. 1991, *News from JAMA* No 5 1992).

[4]In the 1980s, first tier suppliers were about 170, second tier, about 4,700 and lower tier establishments about 31,600 (Ozawa 1991).

4.3.1   The Contentious Question of Local Content

The tight relationships along the process of production appear *a priori* as an obstacle to location abroad. Indeed, the Japanese carmakers could hardly set up new production facilities abroad and, at the same time, get a cut from their traditional suppliers. However, it was also difficult to replicate the whole system abroad in countries with such different practices. When they first set up production operations abroad, and especially in the United States, Japanese carmakers largely resorted to imports from the home country to supply their new factories. Then, progressively, a number of their suppliers followed them abroad. In both cases, supply from local producers is very limited, hence the contentious question of the local content.

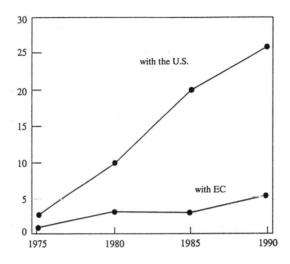

Source: Calculations from CEPII/CHELEM

Figure 5: Balance of Trade for the Automobile Sector[1] with Japan

Japanese investments in the automobile sector have both a positive and a negative effect on the trade balance of the sector. The effect is positive in terms of cars, as the result of two evolutions. First, local production partly substitutes for imports and second, Japanese carmakers may export cars from the host country. These evolutions have been observed in the United States and Canada, and to a lesser extent in Europe.[28] On the contrary, trade effects tend to be negative in terms of components since the Japanese carmakers import a substantial part of their components from the home country. The net effect thus depends on the degree of integration of the Japanese operations of production in the local economy.

Figure 5 shows that Japan continued to increase its surpluses vis-à-vis the United States and Europe throughout the 1980s. In the case of the United States, this is due to the increase in imports of components since there has been a reduction in car imports.[29] In 1990,

---

[28] See Section 4.1 above.

[29] See (University of Michigan 1991) and Section 4.1.

Japanese production in Europe was still quite limited, and imports of components had been increasingly very slowly since 1987. Yet, the question of a similar evolution to that of the United States was considered in earnest. Hence the heated debates on the degree of local content.

As Japanese carmakers have invested in production facilities abroad, the related questions of local content and trade in autocomponents have become more contentious. The local content question has become contentious because of the protectionist context. Indeed, since the barriers to Japanese imports aimed at protecting the European markets, the objective has been to make any turnaround of the barriers as difficult as possible.[30] Debates have been heated both in United States and in Europe. They have underlined the problems of definition of a national product in a globalized economy. In the United States, the threshold which is most commonly mentioned is 75% of local content, but then comes the problem of calculation. In the EC, generally speaking, a product is considered European if its local content reaches 60%, but in the automobile industry, Japanese producers have been firmly invited to aim at a higher level (80%). Box 3 explains the difficulties encountered in calculating the ratio of local content.

Box 3:   What is an indigenous car?

How to calculate the level of local content in a car? This question has raised serious methodological problems. The first one relates to the type of operations which should be taken into account, and the second one to the difference between the country of assembly of the components themselves and the nationality of the supplier.

Let's take the example of the Civic built by Honda in the United States in 1989. Honda claimed that the car had a local content of 75% (i.e. was 75% American). According to a study of the University of Michigan quoted in (*Courier International* 5/12/1991), the local content was at most 36%. What is the source of this important difference? According to this study, the total cost of the car ($10,030) had the following composition: 38% of imported components, 26% of components sourced from Japanese suppliers operations in the US (wholly owned or joint ventures with American firms), 16% of components sourced from American suppliers and 20% of other costs (salaries, depreciation allowances, etc . . .). According to this example, an important source of disagreement is the "nationality" of the components which are bought from foreign production units of Japanese suppliers.

The calculation of the local content ratio of the Civics built in Canada by Honda has

---

[30] In this respect, see also the chapter on electronics.

given rise to a contentious debate between the firm and the US custom services. The latter has ruled that the car had not reached the threshold of 50% of North American content which would have qualified it to enter the US duty free, as provided under the US-Canada free trade agreement. This calculation concerned the 91,000 cars exported from Canada to the US between January 1989 (when the agreement went into effect) and March 1, 1990. According to Honda, the North American content was 69%, but only 45.9% according to the American authorities (*Nikkei Weekly* 14/4/1992). The source of disagreement lies in the local-content formula — in particular, the American formula does not take into account the upstream part of the fabrication of the engines (aluminum and mechanical fabrication).

In Europe, there have also been disagreements as to the exact level of local content of the cars produced by the Japanese owned factories. This has been more particularly the case for the Nissan facility in the UK. France and Italy have refused to import the Bluebirds produced there because they did not achieve an 80% level of local content, especially if the calculation was made by the Europeans and not the Japanese. However, from the point of view of the European authorities, a good was considered European if it had a 60% local content.

One route taken by the Japanese carmakers to increase local value added has been to increase their degree of vertical integration, and in particular to produce engines. Indeed, in order to reach an 80% local content ratio, carmakers have to produce some major components locally.[31] Table 6 (Section 2) shows that there are now a number of engine production units both in the United States and Europe; they have followed the first assembly units with some delays.

4.3.2   Relationships with Suppliers

Mounting pressures from the United States and European countries as well as efficiency considerations have led Japanese carmakers to increase their sourcing from local supplies. In this respect, the evolutions in Europe and in the United States have been quite dissimilar.

Japanese component suppliers have followed the carmakers to the United States early and on a large scale. At the beginning of the 1990s, about 300[32] Japanese suppliers were producing in North America (Greenfields sites, acquisitions, cooperative ventures with

---

[31] See for example, *Asian Automotive Business Review*, Oct. 1992.

[32] Depending on the sources, see in particular the survey in (*Nikkei Weekly* 9/11/1991, *Financial Times* 14/7/1992, EIU 1992, Kenney, Florida 1993).

local partners). And of course, Japanese carmakers have been sourcing from them. This evolution can be traced to two characteristics
of the American autocomponent industry. Firstly, as the carmakers
have traditionally been quite integrated, in a number of cases the
Japanese would have had to source their components from competitors. Secondly, the independant component industry was considered as
insufficiently competitive by Japanese clients. They found the quality
of components particularly low, which constituted a major problem for
them (Kenney, Florida 1993).

In Europe the autocomponent industry is generally quite competitive[33] and some of the European firms are among the first in the
world. In particular, the leading European autocomponent firms
have important research and engineering capabilities. Moreover,
as in the case of the carmakers, national divisions and diversity
constitute obstacles to massive penetration. The relative strength of
the European component autocomponent firms and the fact that
Japanese carmakers produce less in Europe than in the US, should
result in less foreign investments from the Japanese suppliers. At
the beginning of the 1990s, there were about 60 production units of
Japanese autocomponent firms in the EC,[34] and they covered about
60 of the 250 relevant supply lines (*Les Echos* 16/10/1991). Their
geographical distribution corresponds to the location of the Japanese
carmakers; Great Britain counts nearly 30 units, Spain 10, France and
Germany less than 10 (Banville, Chanaron 1993). They have chosen
a cooperative venture with local partners in about half of the cases,
as opposed to about 20% North America (*L'Usine Nouvelle* 8/3/1990).
Apart from the case of tires, where Bridgestone[35] and Sumitomo have
acquired large companies, the European production units of Japanese
suppliers tend to be quite small. Table 8 lists the largest Japanese
autocomponent units in Europe (more than 200 employees).

The Japanese carmakers have increasingly resorted to local autocomponent firms. The difficulties in this respect are linked to the
specific organization of the Japanese automobile production process

---

[33] It does not mean that all firms are competitive; it seems in particular that
British firms have relatively weak performances. On this question, see (NEDC 1991,
Financial Times Survey 17/7/1992, Chanaron, Banville 1993). The European supply
of electronic components may also be insufficient.

[34] (Banville, Chanaron 1993) have identified 64 investments between 1970 and 1991.
According to different sources, the figures vary between 50 and 60 units in operation,
some are still under development (EIU 1992).

[35] On the acquisition of Firestone by Bridgestone, see Chapter 2.

Table 8: The Largest[1] Japanese Automotive Component Units in Europe

Name of the company	Partners[2]	Date[3]	Activity	No. of employees
		UK		
SP Types UK	Sumitomo (80%) other Japanese firms	1984/85	Automotive tires	2530
Ikeda Hoover	Ikeda Bussan (51%) Hoover Universal (49%)	1986	Automotive parts and components	447
Dunlop-Topy Wheels	BTR (85%) Topy Industries (15%)	1987	Automotive wheels	550
Nissan Yamato Engineering	Nissan Motor (80%) Daiwa Kogyo (20%)	1987/90	Automobile sheet panel components	350
Calsonic Int'l	Calsonic (100%)	1989	Automotive parts and components	1150
ND Marston	Nippondenso (75%) Magneti Marelli (25%)	1989	Aluminium and copper radiators	947
Lucas SEI Wiring Systems	Lucas Industries (70%) Simitomo (30%)	1989	Wiring systems	670
Birkbys Aerials	Marubeni (85%) Sanko plastics industries (15%)	1990	Automotive and electrical appliance parts and components	700
		France		
Dunlop France	Sumitomo (100%)	1984	Tires, beds, car sheets, sporting goods, precision rubber parts	2675

Table 8: *Continued*

Name of the company	Partners[2]	Date[3]	Activity	No. of employees
Firestone France	Bridgestone (100%)	1988	Production and sale of tires	1400
Société de Mécanique d'Irigny	Renault (65%) Koyo Seiko (35%)	1991	Steering systems	741
		Germany		
SP Reifenwerke	Sumitomo (100%)	1984/85	Tire tubes	3500
		Spain		
Firestone Hispania	Bridgestone (99%)	1988	Tires, wheels, industrial rubber products	4000
Yazaki Monel	Yazaki Sogyo (100%)	1988	Automotive wire harness	206
		Italy		
Bridgestone Firestone Italia	Bridgestone (100%)	1988	Tires	1116
Borletti Climatizazzione	Magneti Marelli (75%) Nippondenso (25%)	1990	Automotive air-contitioners	1008
		Portugal		
Firestone Portugauesa	Bridgestone Firestone (100%)	1988	Automotive tires	558

[1] Only firms with more than 200 employees have been retained, which gives a lot of weight to tire companies.

[2] The share of the capital of each partner is in parenthesis.

[3] When there are two dates, the first one is that of establishment and the second one that of the beginning of production; when there is only one date, both events happened the same year.

Source: (JETRO 1992), press

which has been recalled above. Typically, the Japanese carmaker has to select the potential foreign suppliers and then teach them its way of working.

The number of US companies supplying the Japanese automakers in North America rose from 309 in 1990 to 372 by early 1992. Government figures show that in 1991, the transplants bought $1.54 of US parts for every $1 of parts they imported, up from $1.04 in 1989 (*Financial Times* 14/7/1992). Numerous European suppliers have also successfully achieved the different steps of the Japanese selection process. By the late 1990s, about £2bn worth of components from European origin are expected to be flowing into the plants of Nissan, Toyota and Honda.[36] In 1992, Nissan UK had 195 suppliers in Europe, 10 of which were controlled by Japanese firms and 8 were joint ventures between Japanese and European partners (*News from JAMA*, May 1992).

In the UK, about 70% of the components bought in Europe by Japanese carmakers are being sourced from either UK groups (Lucas, GKN, T&N, etc.). or the British subsidiaries of continental European groups (Bosch, Valeo, etc.). Thus orders to European companies have largely increased since the mid 1980s. This is due to the fact that Japanese carmakers are more numerous and produce more in Europe, but also because that both sides have grown to know each other better. The Japanese carmakers have assessed the European autocomponent firms and the latter have become acquainted with Japanese methods and have largely accepted them. The Japanese carmakers have imposed a stringent selection process to the European component manufacturers,[37] but they have also proposed them long term contracts, including fruitful cooperation on the improvement of efficiency.

For European autocomponent firms, Japanese carmakers may have quite positive spillovers. At first, the fear has been that they would bring their suppliers along, which would create more competitors. Such new competition does exist. For example Sumitomo and Bridgestone directly compete with Michelin, while Bosch and Valeo have to face Nippondenso on the markets for air systems. But the threat of the

---

[36] In 1991, Nissan bought £600m worth of components to European suppliers. Toyota forecasts that in full production, it will buy about £700m in Europe. Honda has indicated that spending with European suppliers will be £500m annually at the 100,000 cars-a-year level (*Financial Times* 14/7/1992).

[37] For an account of the selection process by Toyota for its Derby plant, which lasted for nearly 2 years, see (*Financial Times* 10/4/1991).

Japanese suppliers does now seem less worrying. On the other hand, the growing size of Japanese car production constitutes an attraction for European suppliers who feel that they should supply the Japanese lest they would lose market share.[38]

One of the most important aspects of European autocomponent firms supplying the Japanese is the qualitative spillover. The demanding relationships with the Japanese carmakers constitute a learning experience which has favorable effects, both on quality and productivity. For example, Nissan has dedicated substantial resources to implementing a partnerhip with its European suppliers. Since 1987, a team has been in charge of relationships with suppliers. It deals with various problems and sets objectives on matters such as quality, delays or stocks. It seems that this organization has been fruitful for the European suppliers in these different fields (*News from JAMA* May 1992). It is for example the opinion of Sommer-Allibert which supplies Nissan in the UK. Sommer-Allibert aknowledges that Japanese criteria in terms of quality are particularly stringent and that there is a quasi-obligation to achieve gains in competitiveness. But communication with the carmaker is frequent, extensive and efficient (*La Tribune* 22/10/1991).

The experience of the British supplier Unipart constitutes an example of collaboration with a Japanese carmaker. Unipart, which had been created in 1974 to group all the component operations of British Leyland, became independent in 1987 and decided to restructure its production organization. It became a supplier of Honda and has been able to benefit from advise from some of the other suppliers of the carmaker adopting a number of "Japanese" methods. In particular, employees from Unipart have received training from Yachiyo Kogyo in Japan (Emmott 1992).

The influence which Japanese carmakers can have on local suppliers depends on the complexity and the importance of the components which are bought locally. In the United States, it seems that Japanese carmakers mainly buy from local suppliers for basic components or those which are difficult to transport. Honda's American suppliers for example fabricate steel, paint and body parts, while their Japanese counterparts supply complex equipments and electronic components (Mair 1993). As a consequence Japanese firms still constitute the majority of first tier suppliers, while American firms are rather second

---

[38] See in particular the interview of the President of the automotive division of Sommer-Allibert in (*La Tribune* 22/10/90).

and third tier suppliers. This tendency could diminish as the rate of local supplies increases. For example, 61 American suppliers have been associated with the development of the latest Accord (*The Nikkei Weekly* 6/9/1993).

4.3.2 R&D and Design

R&D activities are another increasingly important component of the process of automobile production. Such activities can be considered as a source of value added, which explains why they have been caught in some kind of local content argument.

For multinational companies, decentralization of R&D activities in their foreign locations has traditionally been quite rare for reasons of efficiency and the automobile industry is no exception in this respect. Firstly, there exist economies of scale and economies of learning in R&D activities; it follows that there are minimum sizes for laboratories and for the activity as a whole.[39] Secondly, central functions of the firm need to interact with R&D. Indeed, the future of the carmaker crucially depends on R&D activities, which not only search for innovation, but also conceive the new models. The tendency towards globalization entails some delocalized R&D, but so far automobile R&D remains concentrated in home countries.[40]

In the case of the Japanese carmakers, three types of factors induce R&D foreign investments. Firstly, it is important for all carmakers to establish engineering and design surveillance outposts to follow competitors and markets.[41] Secondly, Japanese carmakers have now substantial manufacturing bases abroad. As a result, it becomes logical to pursue a number of developing activities near the foreign units. Such activities are needed in particular to adapt the new models to the regional tastes and demands. Thirdly, the Japanese carmakers have become quite sensitive to pressures from host countries to locate as much value added as possible in the countries where they have chosen to invest – R&D are part of the activities which "good citizens" should have in foreign countries.

---

[39] The precise size depends on the type of cars being produced and on the type of R&D (Miller 1992).

[40] On this question from a general point of view, see Chapter 7.

[41] According to (Miller 1992), this is the most important factor which fosters the international dispersion of R&D and design units by carmakers in general.

The efforts of the Japanese carmakers to set up fully fledged companies is more advanced in the United States than in Europe. This means that design, technical and research centers are less numerous in Europe. All the Japanese carmakers which have manufacturing operations in the United States now have affiliated R&D or technical centers. They actually have quite a number of R&D and design units.[42] Design is concentrated in California (Honda, Toyota, Nissan, Mazda) while technical centers can have more diverse locations, although Michigan is a popular one (Toyota, Nissan).

Until the end of the 1980s, Japanese cars appeared to be more adapted to the American taste than to the European one. Hence the importance of Europeanizing the design in order to increase sales and to be able to produce more in Europe.

Table 9 shows that the size of the R&D and technical units is generally quite small; much smaller than in the United States in the case of Honda and Toyota. With Nissan, the number of employees is similar in Europe and in the United States (about 450). This corresponds to the relative importance of the manufacturing operations.

It is difficult to know precisely what is done in these research units, and what their role is in the research effort of the companies.[43] The number of employees and the relatively small size of the manufacturing activities of Japanese carmakers in Europe indicate however, that the surveillance activities should be relatively important. The roles of the delocalized R&D units will evolve according to two factors. Firstly, the willingness of the Japanese automakers to increase the local content and to appear as good corporate citizens in Europe and the United States. Secondly, their more general strategy in terms of globalization. Indeed, car companies have different ideas about the adaptation of their models to local markets and about the possibility to adopt a "world car" strategy.[44]

4.4   CONCLUSION

Japanese investments in production units in the United States and Europe since the 1980s have constituted a major step in the process

---

[42] Toyota has opened its first R&D center in California in 1973.

[43] This question would require a specific research; for a general framework of analysis in the case of the automobile industry, see (Miller 1992).

[44] This question of the evolution of the general strategy of firms is not dealt with here as such. On this question, see in particular (Ruigrok *et al.* 1991) and (Sachwald 1994) for a comparison between Ford and Honda.

Table 9: R&D and Technical Centers of Japanese Carmakers in Europe

Company-Centre/ Country	Date of establishment	Main activities	Employees
Honda			
Honda R&D Europe/Germany	1985 1990 extension	Design	55 (29 Europeans)
Toyota			
Technical centre for Europe/Belgium	1987	Design, material testing	50
Europe Office of Creation/Belgium	1989	Design, marketing analyses	27 (15 Europeans)
Nissan			
European technology centre/ UK (Sunderland)	1988 1992 extension	Development of components	1991: 280 (260 Europeans) 1992: 350
European technology centre/Belgium	1989	Pollution, noise and vibration reduction, European road conditions	55 (about 30 Europeans)
Nissan Motor Iberica/Spain	1990	Unit attached to the manufacturing operations in Spain	380 Europeans 4 Japanese
Mazda			
R&D Representative office/Germany	1990	Design, clay modelling, exhaust analysis	80 (about 45 Europeans)
Mitsubishi			
Germany	1989	Test laboratory (engines)	57 (27 Europeans)
Germany	1992		

[a] As of mid 1990

Source: JAMA, JETRO, press

of internationalization of the automobile industry. This chapter has shown that protectionism has been a very strong determinant of these investments, on both sides of the Atlantic, but now that the Japanese carmakers have started foreign production, the set of problems are different.

For Japanese carmakers, there are two main challenges. Firstly, the successful transplantation of their production system abroad and secondly the organization of their multinational operations. This chapter has shown that the transplantation process is well under way, even if it does not mean a complete reproduction of what exists in Japan and a number of problems are to be dealt with. In this respect, the comparison of the American and European experiences of the Japanese carmakers is instructive in that it underlines both a learning effect and the fact that the differences in the industrial context, and in particular with respect to suppliers, implies different strategies of adaptation.

For American and European producers, the main challenge during the 1980s has been to increase efficiency, and, more exactly, to learn a quite different mode of production. In this respect, Japanese direct investments have had two effects. Firstly, as these investments have been largely aimed at jumping trade barriers, they have increased the degree of competition faced by the American and European producers. Secondly, these investments have been instrumental to knowledge transfers from Japanese to American and European carmakers and suppliers. In the case of carmakers, a number of cooperative agreements have been quite important in this respect.[45] In Europe, it seems that a number of transfers may be quite successful through local suppliers which have both Japanese and European clients. In these circumstances, the number of jobs which are directly generated by the Japanese locations is but one aspect to take into account.

REFERENCES

Abernathy, William, The Productivity Dilemma: Roadblock to Innovation in the Automobile Industry, Johns Hopkins University Press, Baltimore, 1978.
Altshuler, Alan, Anderson, Martin, Jones, Daniel, Roos, Daniel, Womack, James, The future of the Automobile, Cambridge, MIT Press, 1984.

---

[45] Apart from the fact that when a foreign firm settles in a foreign country, its very presence, and in particular through the mobility of its employees, generates, more or less quickly, some transfer of its technologies and management practices.

Banville, Etienne, de. Chanaron, Jean-Jacques, Sachwald, F., (sous la direction de), L'Europe et la globalisation. Acquisitions et alliances dans l'industrie, IFRI/ MASSON, 1993.

Banville, Etienne, de., Chanaron, Jean-Jacques, Vers un systme automobile européen, Economica, 1991.

Bélis-Bergouignan, Marie-Claude, Lung, Yannick, "L'internationalisation dans la trajectoire du modèle productif japonais", Actes du GERPISA-Réseau international no 4, GERPISA, Avril 1992.

Bélis-Bergouignan, Marie-Claude, Bordenave, Gérard, Lung, Yannick, "Ford: une stratégie trans-régionale", Annales des Mines, Octobre 1991.

Bourdet, International integration, market structure and prices, Lund Economic Studies, 1987.

CCFA, L'industrie automobile en France 1991. Analyse et statistiques, Comité des Constructeurs Français d'Automobiles, Paris, 1992.

Cecchini, Paolo, 1992, le défi, Flammarion, 1988.

Cowley P., Long E., "Testing Theories of Regime Change: Hegemonic, Decline or Surplus Capacity", International Organization, Spring 1983.

Digby, C., Smith, A., Venable, T., "Counting the cost of VERs in the European car market" European research workshop in international trade, mimeo, University of Sussex, 4–7 July 1988.

Dixit, A., "Tariffs and subsidies under oligopoly: the case of the US automobile industry", in Kierzkowski, M., (ed.), Protection and competition in international trade, Basil Blackwell 1987.

Dourille-Feer, Evelyne, "L'Europe sur l'échiquier productif du Japon, le cas des industries électronique et automobile", Economie Prospective Internationale, no 49, 1er trim. 1992.

EIU, "A review of Japan's automotive presence in Western Europe: Outlook to 1999", Japanese Motor Business, European Intelligence Unit, London, June 1992.

Gandillot, La dernière bataille de l'automobile européenne, Fayard, 1992.

GATT 1991.

Hufbauer, G., Berliner, D., Elliot, K., Trade Protection in the United States, 31 Case Studies, Institute for International Economics, Washington, 1986.

Jacot, Jacques-Henri, (sous la direction de), Du Fordisme au Toyotisme, La Documentation française, 1990.

Kenney, M., Florida, R., Beyond Mass Production, Oxford University Press, London, 1993.

Krafcik, J., Comparative analysis of performance indicators at world auto assembly plants, mimeo, Massachusetts Institute of Technology, 1/1988.

Mair, A., "Honda et ses founisseurs en Amérique du Nord", Actes du GERPISA Réseau international no 7, Paris, juillet 1993.

Miller, Roger, D.Sc., Competitive dynamics and the location of R, D&E facilities: the case of the world automobile industry, Université du Québec, Montréal 1992.

NEDC, The experience of Nissan suppliers: lessons for the UK engineering industry, The National Economic Development Council, London, 1991.

Nicolas, Françoise, "Multilatéralisme: le GATT en crise?", Ramses 1992, IFRI/ DUNOD, 1992.

OCDE, Le coût des restrictions à l'importation, OCDE, Paris 1987.

OCDE 1985.

Porter, Michael, "Competition in Global Industries: a Conceptual Framework" in Michael Porter (ed), Competition in Global Industries, Harvard Business School Press, London, 1986.

Roos, Philippe, L'Automobile, Economica, 1990.

Ruigrok, W. Van, Tulder, R., Baven, G., Cooperation, competition, coalitions and control. Globalisation and localisation processes in the World car industry, FAST, EC, 1991.

Sachwald, Frédérique (ed.), *Les défis de la mondialisation. Innovation et concurrence*, Masson, Paris, 1994a.

Sachwald, Frédérique, "The automobile industry", Sachwald, F., (ed.), *European Integration and Competitiveness. Acquisitions and Alliances in Industry*, Edward Elgard, London, 1994b.

Sachwald, Frédérique, "Les accords dans l'industrie automobile: une analyse en termes de coûts de transaction", Economie prospective internationale, CEPII, la Documentation française, Paris, 2e trimestre 1990a.

Sachwald, Frédérique, "Les accords dans l'industrie automobile: la poursuite de la concurrence par d'autres moyens" Economie prospective internationale, CEPII, La Documentation française, 1er trimestre 1990b.

Sachwald, Frédérique, " De la libéralisation au néo-protectionnisme. Le cas de l'industrie automobile", *Politique Etrangère*, no 4 1989.

Stuckey, John, Vertical Integration and Joint Ventures in the Aluminium Industry, Harvard University Press, 1983.

Toyota, The Automobile industry, Toyota and Japan, Toyota Motor Corporation, Tokyo, 1992.

Womack, James, P., Jones, Daniel, T., Roos, Daniel, The Machine that changed the World, Rawson Associates, New York, 1990.

Womack, J., Multinational joint ventures in the steel industry, in Mowery, D., (ed) International collaborative ventures in US manufacturing Balinger, 1988.

Japan
F23
L65

5

Japanese Chemical Firms:
A Limited Internationalization

Frédérique Sachwald

The chemicals industry is one of the most important sectors in industrialized countries. Japan's competitiveness has so far lagged behind that of the United States and Western Europe in this sector. Japanese firms are substantially smaller and less internationalized than Western chemical companies. Yet, Japanese chemical companies have strongly invested abroad during the 1980s.

Japanese chemical companies have little ownership advantages over their European competitors, and yet they have launched a series of direct investments in Europe since the mid 1980s. This chapter explores the reasons behind what appears to be a paradox, especially in comparison with other sectors such as automobiles and electronics.

5.1   THE JAPANESE CHEMICAL INDUSTRY IN
A WEAK COMPETITIVE POSITION

The Japanese chemical industry has a quite weak competitive position on the world scene. Japanese firms are relatively less internationalized, while American and European firms have invested substantially in Japan.

211

Table 1:   Main Exporting Countries of Chemicals, in $bn and %.

Exporting countries	Share in world chemical exports		Value of exports	Value of imports	Share of chemicals in merchandise exports
	1980	1990	1990	1990	1990
Germany	17	17	50.6	30.9	12.5
United States	15	13	39.5	23.7	10
France	9.5	9.5	28.3	25.0	13
Great Britain	8.5	8	23.6	19.3	12.5
Netherlands	8	6.5	20.1	13.1	15.5
UEBL	5	5.5	16.5	13.7	14
Japan	4.5	5.5	15.8	15.2	5.5
Switzerland	4	4.5	13.5	7.9	21
Italy	4	3.5	11.0	20.0	6.5
Canada	2.5	2	6.7	7.8	5
Spain	1	1.5	4.7	8.7	8.5
Hong Kong[1]	0.5	1.5	4.4	–	5.5
Sweden	1	1.5	4.3	–	7.5
USSR	1.5	1.5	4.2	10.4	4
Ireland	1	1.5	3.8	–	16
Total 15 countries above[2]	83	82.5	246.8	195.5	–
EC countries above	54.0	50.0	158.6	125.2	–

[1] Including a large amount of re-exports.
[2] 12 countries for imports.
Source: (GATT 1990–91).

5.1.1   *Trade and Competitiveness*

In 1988, Japan represented 14.6% of the world chemical production, while North America represented 23.3% and the EC 28.1% (Commission des Communautés Européennes 1991). Table 1 shows that Japan's share is substantially lower in world chemical exports, even if it increased during the 1980s, from 4.5% to 5.5%. In 1990, Japan's share in world chemical exports was lower than that of the United States, but also that of Germany, France, Great Britain and the

Table 2: Market Position in the Chemical Industry (Trade Balance/World Imports, in %).

Products	Japan		U.S.		EC		OPEC	
	1980	1990	1980	1990	1980	1990	1980	1990
Chemicals total[1]	2.4	1.8	8.9	4.2	13.6	8.9	−7.2	−2.6
Chemicals except plastics[2] Basic inorganic	−0.9	−2.9	3.9	2.6	2.2	7.3	−4.1	−4.1
Fertilizers and pesticides	1.4	−0.2	12.4	9.1	9.6	1.8	−3.7	7.2
Basic organic[3]	1.4	1.6	9.8	5.7	12.5	8.0	−3.5	−1.2
Plastics, fibers and resins[4]	6.2	4.8	12.0	7.2	14.1	5.4	−4.7	−2.4
Paints, varnishes	2.0	2.7	3.4	1.6	26.2	18.1	−8.2	−4.0
Toilet products, soaps, perfumes	−0.3	0.7	15.5	6.9	19.7	17.5		
Pharmaceuticals	−4.6	−4.3	7.4	3.3	20.5	14.6	−11.6	−5.2
Plastic articles[5]	1.8	0.5	2.9	−3.4	9.9	5.4	−7.9	−2.0

[1] Large definition of chemicals, includes synthetic rubber and synthetic continuous yarn (see also note 4 of the table).

[2] Narrow definition of chemicals, excludes plastic materials (SITC 58), synthetic rubber and synthetic continuous yarn.

[3] Excluding plastics and fibers.

[4] Includes synthetic rubber (SITC 233) and synthetic continuous yarn (SITC 266).

[5] Articles manufactured exclusively in plastics, excluding shoes, clothing and compounds.

Source: Calculations from the data base Chelem/CEPII.

Netherlands. Chemicals represent a much lower share of exports in Japan than in most other industrial countries. Table 1 also shows that Japan has a small surplus in chemical trade ($ m 600 in 1990).[1]

The rate of exports (exports/sales) of the Japanese chemical industry is quite low. It has been below 10% since the end of the 1970s, lower than that of the United States (above 10%) and much lower than that of the EC (below 20%, excluding intra-EC trade).[2]

---

[1] The trade balance depends on the definition of the chemical industry; figures from national accounts (Ministry of Finance) show a small deficit in 1990 ($m 212) (CIA 1991, Ward 1992). The source of the difference is the fact that man-made fibers are excluded.

[2] Data from (CIA 1991).

The market position can be used as an indicator of competitiveness (Lafay *et al.* 1989, Sachwald 1994a). It is the ratio between the trade balance for a given product and world imports for that product. Table 2 shows that the Japanese competitiveness is quite weak relative to that of Europe and the United States. Japanese competitiveness varies widely from one segment of the chemical industry to another. It is particularly weak in pharmaceuticals, while it has a good position for plastics, fibers and resins. Japan has also a quite good position in the sector of paints and varnishes, even if the European position is much stronger.

5.1.2   Japanese Firms are Little Internationalized

At the beginning of the 1980s, the Japanese chemical companies were both much smaller and less internationalized than their Western competitors. During the decade, the chemical sector underwent a serious crisis, followed by rationalization and new strategic moves.[3] The latter have been largely achieved through mergers and acquisition (Sachwald 1994b). As a consequence, some companies have grown rapidly and have substantially increased their degree of internationalization. The Japanese companies have followed similar strategies, but remain much smaller than their American and West European counterparts. Table 3 shows the situation of the Japanese companies as compared with their competitors. From the first Japanese company, Mitsubishi Kasei which occupies the 25th position, the table only mentions Japanese firms (and their rank in the general list).

It is quite difficult to evaluate precisely the share of foreign sales for the different countries since the data is not available for some companies. However, the European groups appear to be the most internationalized. Groups from the large countries (Germany, UK, France) realise about a third of their sales in their home country, another third in Europe and about 20% in North America. The United States represent about two thirds in the sales of American groups. Japanese groups remain much more reliant on their domestic market. Sumitomo Chemicals and Mitsubishi Kasei derive about 14% of their sales from abroad (Eurostaf 1991). Toray realized 11.8% of its sales outside Japan in 1991.[4] Sekisui, which is specialized in plastics, runs 6

---

[3] See below, and (Bower 1986, Sachwald 1993b).

[4] Year ended March 31, 1992 (Annual report). This type of data is typically quite difficult to gather from Japanese firms' annual reports.

Table 3:   Position of the Japanese Chemical Companies on the World Scene, 1990
Sales in $ million.

Rank 1990	Rank 1986	Firm/ nationality	Chemical turnover	Chem's in % of total turnover	Total employ't (1990)
1	3	Hoechst/D	29 754	98.2	172 890
2	1	Bayer/D	28 101	100	171 000
3	2	BASF/D	26 399	83.9	134 647
4	5	ICI/GB	25 291	100	132 100
5	4	Du Pont de Nemours/USA	22 268	55.6	143 961
6	6	Dow Chemical/USA	19 773	100	62 100
7	9	Unilever/GB-NL	17 723	41	304 000
8	11	Rhône-Poulenc/F	15 662	100	91 571
9	7	Procter and Gamble/USA	(15000)	55.5	–
10	17	Elf Aquitaine/F	14 556	41.7	89 309
11	8	Ciba-Geigy/CH	14 507	92.7	94 141
12	–	Enichem/I	13 509	100	43 700
13	10	Royal Dutch/Shell/GB-NL	12 897	11	137 000
14	–	Sinochem/China	12 480	100	–
15	37	Johnson and Johnson/USA	11 232	100	82 200
16	12	Exxon Corporation/USA	11 153	9.6	104 000
17	13	Akzo/F	10 329	100	69 800
18	21	Bristol-Myers/USA	10 300	100	52 900
19	16	Monsanto/USA	8 995	100	41 081
20	25	Sandoz/CH	8 751	89.1	52 640
21	19	Solvay/B	8 348	100	45 700
22	26	Henkel/B	8 109	100	38 803
23	65	Eastman Kodak/USA	7 937	41.9	134 450
24	–	SmithKline Beecham/GB/USA	7 889	84.5	54 100
25	32	Merck and Co./USA	7 671	100	36 900
26	14	Mitsubishi Kasei Corporation/J	7 668	85.4	8 964
29	24	Sumitomo chemical/J	7 117	90	14 546
31	23	Asahi Chemical Industry/J	6 853	100	–
34	30	Toray Industries/J	6 511	100	–
51	38	Takeda Chemical Ind./J	4 473	91.1	15 210
53	62	Sekisui Chemical/J	4 381	100	–

Table 3:   *Continued*

Rank 1990	Rank 1986	Firm/ nationality	Chemical turnover	Chem's in % of total turnover	Total employ't (1990)
54	44	Kao Corporation/J	(4 300)	91.4	–
56	51	Showa Denko/J	4 215	100	–
63	–	Kanebo/J	3 747	100	–
66	70	Shiseido/J	3 672	100	–
72	46	Dainippon Inc/J			
76	87	Sankyo/J	3 217	100	–
80	165	Mitsubishi Petrochemical Ind./J	3 084	100	–
83	–	Asahi Glass/J	2 990	32.7	9 935
87	–	Tosoh/J	2 800	100	5 697
90	92	Mitsui Petrochemical Ind./J	2 615	100	5 323

Source: *Chimie Actualité.*

production plants outside Japan, but still realized only 5% of its sales overseas (*Financial Times* 3/12/1990). According to MITI, overseas operations account for 3.8% of the chemical production of Japanese firms, which is much lower than for transport equipment (14.3%) or electrical machinery (11%) (Ward 1992).

5.1.3   *Foreign Investment in Japan*

The strength of the European and American chemical firms and their international ambitions have led them to invest in Japan, which is the second world chemical market. Manufacturing foreign direct investment in Japan is very concentrated on two sectors: machinery and chemicals. Between 1950 and 1991, chemicals accounted for nearly 30% of the value of cumulated inward investment in manufacturing, behind machinery (48.3%).[5] The share of chemicals has rapidly increased since the end of the 1980s.

In fiscal year 1991, chemicals had become the most important sector for foreign investment in Japan, with a value of $ million 902 (47.5% of total inward investment in manufacturing). That year, Europe was

---

[5] All the figures quoted here on inward investment in Japan are based on statistics from the Ministry of Finance of Japan.

Table 4: Forecasts for Demand and Production in World Chemicals, Annual Rate of Growth, in %.

	Production		Demand	
	1989–1985	1995–2000	1989–1995	1995–2000
Western Europe	2.9	3.2	3.0	3.2
North America	3.0	3.1	3.4	3.8
Latin America	6.5	8.9	5.0	7.0
Eastern Europe	3.1	4.3	3.0	5.0
Asia-Australia	1.6	3.3	3.4	3.6
Africa	4.4	4.4	3.5	3.5
Far-East*	5.8	7.8	5.1	5.7
Indian Sub continent	6.3	7.1	6.0	6.5

* Except China.

Source: (Eurostaf 1991).

the first zone to invest in Japanese chemical industry with a total of $ million 386, before North America ($ million 324).

Chemicals account for the highest share of European manufacturing investment in Japan (52.2% in 1991). It is also the case for North America. Chemicals represent 41.7% of North American manufacturing direct investment in Japan, while general machinery represents 38.8% (12.3% for Europe). According to the MITI, in 1988, sales from Western chemical companies located in Japan amounted to more than $bn 13, which represented 9% of sales from total local production.

The importance of foreign direct investment in Japan is not only due to the sheer size of the Japanese market. It is also motivated by the prospects of the whole Asia Pacific region and to the general globalization move. The forecasts in Table 4 shows that Asian regions, along with Latin America, should experience the fastest rates of growth, both for production and demand.

In certain countries, and for basic chemicals in particular, investment is motivated by low costs – and Japanese chemical firms have followed such a strategy themselves (see below, Section 5.2.1). In the case of foreign investment in Japan, two motives seem very important. Firstly, Japan is a sophisticated economy, which is an asset in terms of innovation for an intermediary industry. Chemical companies see Japan as a market of recommendation; success in supplying local firms should constitute a springboard for other markets. Secondly, in certain sectors, automobile and electronics in particular, Japanese companies are becoming global. Given the traditional relationships with suppliers in Japan, it seems that supplying the main company is a strong asset to have its foreign subsidiaries as clients. In such a context, local production in Japan appears as an asset for global operations.

These different considerations explain that R&D activities are important for foreign chemical companies in Japan. There are indeed numerous basic and applied foreign chemical research facilities in Japan. Moreover, it seems that these facilities have a wider mission than suiting local needs, they participate into the global research effort of the multinational companies (Walsh 1992). This may explain why foreign companies often choose to specialize their laboratories in strong Japanese research areas, such as advanced materials.[6]

5.2   JAPANESE DIRECT INVESTMENT IN CHEMICALS

Chemicals is an important sector of direct investment for Japanese firms. It is the third most important manufacturing sector for the value of cumulated direct investment over the period 1951 to 1991. The share of chemicals is actually equivalent to that of transport equipment (13.3 and 13.7%), electric and electronic industries being largely ahead (24.1%).[7]

The chemical industry has followed the tremendous increase in foreign direct investment at the end of the 1980s. Foreign direct investment in the chemical industry during the three years 1989 to 1991 represents 47.8% of the cumulated total from 1951 to 1991 (46.9% for the total industry).

5.2.1   *Geographical Distribution of Japanese Direct Investment*

North America (United States and Canada) is by far the most important destination for Japanese direct investment in chemicals. Table 5 shows that the region represents 44% of the cumulated value of investment between 1951 and 1991. Asia[8] comes second with 25.6% and Europe is far behind with only 13.1%.

---

[6] Du Pont in Yokohama, Hoechst in Kwagoe, Dow Chemical in Gotemba, Rhône Poulenc and ICI in Tsukuba (Walsh 1992).

[7] Data from the MOF, see Chapter 1.

[8] Excluding the Pacific area, for an explanation on the MOF statistics, see Chapter 1.

Table 5: Geographical Distribution of Japanese Foreign Direct Investment in Manufacturing.

	North America			Asia			Europe			Total	
	Cases	Value	%	Cases	Value	%	Cases	Value	%	Cases	Value
Cumulated 1951–91	536	5521	44,0	1195	3217	25,6	229	1640	13,1	2162	12542
Cumulated 1951–88	372	2311	35,3	991	1785	27,3	144	594	9,1	1690	6540
1989	67	1270	60,2	86	292	13,8	33	516	24,5	196	2109
1990	53	1243	54,3	69	564	24,6	31	305	13,3	161	2291
1991	44	697	43,5	49	576	36,0	21	225	14,0	115	1602

Source: MOF.

The geographical distribution differs substantially in terms of number of cases. Table 5 shows that according to this indicator, Asia is by far the first location for Japanese direct investment in chemicals (55.3% of the cases). The difference between the figures in number of cases and in value leads to the conclusion that the average investment in Asia is of relatively low value.

Historically, Asia has been the first destination of Japanese direct investment in the chemical industry. From 1960s on, Japanese firms had been looking for raw materials and cheaper manpower for their basic industries (Ozawa 1979, 1989). These investments in Asia were concentrated on basic chemicals and textile. For example, in 1985, 11 of the 18 most important foreign subsidiaries or joint ventures of Toray were located in Asia and concerned fibers.[9] More recently the objectives for investing in the region have evolved. The attractiveness of Asia is linked to the high prospective growth rate of chemical markets in the region (see Table 4). Japanese firms are also attracted by the development of the electronic industry in Asia and a number of investments are made to produce chemicals for this industry. Nevertheless, the share of investment in Asia has slightly decreased at the end of the 1980s, while the shares of both North America and Europe grew (Table 5).

In Europe, the chemical industry is in fourth position in terms of Japanese direct investment. The cumulated value of Japanese direct investment in chemicals between 1951 and 1991 (March 1992)

---

[9] Annual reports.

amounts to $m 1618, behind electric and electronic industries ($m 4848), transport equipment ($m 2442) and non-electrical machinery ($m 2332).[10] The rapid increase of the value of Japanese direct investment in Europe which we have seen above can also be read from the evolution of the number of new locations in Europe. There were 17 Japanese chemical units in Europe before 1980; at the beginning of the decade, about 2 to 4 new units were created each year. During each of the three years, 1988, 1989 and 1990, more than 10 new units have been created.

Apart from the production, sales and R&D units, Japanese chemical companies have opened about 40 centers of information in Europe during the last few years (*Les Echos* 10/3/1992). These centers aim at collecting information on European markets and firms. Mitsui Toatsu Chemical, Nippon Soda and Kumiai Chemical have teamed to create such an information center on the European agrochemical market.

Looking at the geographical distribution of the Japanese chemical units in Europe, it seems that the choice of location combines three types of considerations: the size of the country and the importance of its industry, the presence of other Japanese units and the strength of the local chemical industry.

According to Table 6, the UK is less strongly represented in Japanese direct investment in chemicals than in manufacturing in general, since Germany and France total about the same number of units.[11] Actually, the hierachy of countries varies according to the sources. Statistics from the Ministry of Finance and from the MITI show that Germany is the most important location for Japanese direct investment in chemicals. According to these sources, the Netherlands comes in second position and the UK only in fourth or fifth position.[12] The difference may be, at least partly, attributed to the size of the production units. Indeed, the JETRO counts production and R&D units while the MOF registers investment flows and the MITI sales by the Japanese units in Europe.[13] It seems thus that Germany and the Netherlands are

---

[10] Data from Table 17 in Chapter 1.

[11] For data on Japanese FDI in manufacturing in general, see Chapter 1.

[12] These conclusions are drawn from tables in Chapter 1 (Table 19a, b and c). The differences between Table 19b from Chapter 1 and Table 6 above are due to two reasons: Table 6 takes into account units which are not mentioned in JETRO's surveys; the definition of chemicals in Table 6 does not include moulded plastics (considered as plastic transformation).

[13] On the different sources of data on Japanese direct investment, see the general appendix at the end of the book.

Table 6: Geographical Distribution of the Japanese Chemical Units in Europe.

Country	Production and sales units		R&D units		Total number of units	
	Number of units	In %	Number of units	In %	Number of units	In %
UK	24	18	5	45	29	20
France	24	18	2	20	26	18
Germany	21	16	3	27	24	17
Spain	16	12	0	0	16	11
Netherlands	16	12	0	0	16	11
Italy	11	8	0	0	11	8
Benelux	9	7	1	9	10	7
Ireland	7	5	0	0	7	5
Portugal	4	3	0	0	4	3
Greece	1	1	0	0	1	1
Total EC	133	100	10	100	144	100
EFTA countries[1]	8	–	1	–	9	–

[1] There are Japanese units in Switzerland, Austria and Sweden.

Source: JETRO's surveys on Japanese investment in Europe (several years) and own data bases (Chem-MA and Chem-JV on M&A and joint ventures of world chemical companies.

relatively more important locations for Japanese direct investments in chemicals than Table 6 shows; conversely, the relative importance of the UK is probably overestimated.

5.2.2 Types of Investments in Europe

Japanese investments in Europe are quite concentrated on a couple of segments of the chemical industry. Table 7 shows that the first two segments, plastics and films (24%) and dying materials and inks (22%) and account for over 45% of the total. Pharmaceuticals accounts for an other 18%.[14]

---

[14] Section 3 below presents a case study on pharmaceuticals.

Table 7:   Sectoral Distribution of Japanese Production, Sales and R&D Units in the European Community[1]

Production and sales units	Number of units	In %
Plastics, films and resins[2]	32	24
Dying, pigments, printing inks	30	22
Pharmaceuticals	24	18
Synthetic fibers	9	7
Cosmetics	8	6
Agrochemicals	5	4
Basic chemicals	6	4
Adhesives	6	4
Others[3]	13	10
Total production and sales	133	100
R&D units		
Pharmaceuticals	10	91
Others	1	9
Total R&D	11	100
Grand Total	143	–

[1] Units in EFTA countries are not included in this table.

[2] Including one unit of high performance plastics.

[3] Comprises units of: fine chemical products, carbon fibers, optic fibers, biotechnology and products for the electronic sector.

Source: JETRO and personal data base.

Japanese chemical companies have opened only a couple of R&D units in Europe. According to JETRO data, there were 11 such units in Europe at the end of 1990. Among them, 10 were in pharmaceuticals, which is the third most important segment for production and sales units. There was none in dying and inks which is the first segment for direct investment in production and sales. R&D units are more concentrated on the three largest EC countries, Germany, France and the UK, than production units (Table 6).

Table 8 shows that a large majority (73%) of European units are controlled by the Japanese parent company.[15] The rate of majority

[15] In some cases, the parent company has teamed with an other Japanese company,

Table 8: Type of Control on the European Units Japanese Parent Companies, in % of the Number of Units.

Chemical segment	Minority holding in %	Joint venture 50/50, in %	Majority holding in %[1]	Total number of units[2]
Dying, pigments, printing inks	3	3	93	28
Pharmaceuticals	14	28	57	21
Plastics, resins, films	23	7	70	30
Synthetic fibers	28	14	57	7
Agrochemicals	0	0	100	5
Cosmetics	13	0	87	8
Basic chemicals	17	33	50	6
Others	12	19	69	16
Total production and sales	14	12	73	121
R&D	14	12	63	9

[1] Most of the cases in this category are actually 100% Japanese owned.

[2] The number here is inferior to the total number of chemical units (Table 6) in Europe because the type of control is unknown in a number of cases.

Source: JETRO and own data base.

holding is extremely high in the case of agrochemicals (100%), dying, pigments and printing inks (93%) and cosmetics (87%). It is quite lower for basic chemicals (50%) and pharmaceuticals (57%). It is also lower for R&D units in general (63%).

5.3   FIRMS' STRATEGIES

5.3.1   The Need to Internationalize

As mentioned above, the Japanese chemical companies are only marginally internationalized. However, as the data on direct investment which has been explored here show, there has been a strong tendency to increase the degree of internationalization since the end of

which may not be from the chemical sector, to invest in Europe.

the 1980s. This tendency is consistent with both the general evolution of the chemical sector worldwide and with the strategy of the Japanese chemical firms. Actually, it seems that they are, in a way, forced to internationalize.

We have already seen that Japanese chemical companies have invested in Asia to get access to cheaper resources. The Japanese chemical industry has been hardly hit by the oil shocks in the 1970, which have led to large increases in the price of naphta and to important overcapacities in Japan (Bower 1986). As a result, some of the investments made in Europe during the 1970s have also been factor based. The appendix to this chapter shows that the 1970s operations have been mostly in the plastics and fibers sectors, and have been quite concentrated in countries where the cost of raw materials (Netherlands), or labor costs (Portugal, Ireland) were relatively low. The relatively recent surge of investment in the United States and Europe results from a different set of incentives, which relate to the tendencies towards globalization of the chemical industry.

The importance of foreign investment from European and American chemical firms in Japan constitutes a threat for the local companies. Not only because they compete for the same local market, but also because the foreign companies may become global suppliers of internationalized firms from the automobile or the electronic sector in particular. This risk is higher since the Japanese productive system favors tight, demanding and long term relationships with the suppliers. In the automobile sector, there are a number of examples where autocomponent firms have gone through an agreement with the parent company in order to facilitate their supplying the Japanese subsidiaries abroad.[16] The threat of the European and American multinational chemical companies exists for example in the sector of automobile paints, where the leaders (PPG, BASF, Du Pont) are keen on supplying as many automakers as possible around the world (Sachwald 1994b). In the sector of automobile paints, and of industrial paints more generally, Western chemical companies have invested in Japan and created a number of cooperative agreements[17] with local firms to penetrate the market (Ward 1992). On the other hand, the internationalization of the Japanese companies is still very limited.[18]

---

[16] See the chapter on the automobile.

[17] Involving technology transfers in a number of cases.

[18] Kansai Paints has entered a joint venture in the United States with Du Pont (1991) and another one in Europe with ICI and Du Pont, both for automobile paints.

Table 9: Japanese Investment in European Units of Transformation of Plastic Parts in 1990, Number of Production Units[1].

Type of firm	Country of location				
	UK	Spain	Belgium	Ireland	Total
Chemical	4	1	1	2	8
Other supplier	3	1	0	0	4
Total by country	7	2	1	2	12

[1] These production units have not been counted as chemical units in Table 6 above.
Source: Calculations from (JETRO 1991, 1992).

One answer from the Japanese chemical firms is to invest abroad to follow the internationalization of their clients. One can thus draw a parallel with the automobile suppliers, which also belong to an intermediary sector.[19] Actually, both chemical companies and autocomponent firms have invested in units of moulded plastic parts. Table 9 includes cases of moulded parts for automobiles and for electronic products in particular. It shows that this type of investment occurs mainly in countries where there are rather numerous Japanese production units, either in the automobile and motorcycle sectors (UK, Spain, Belgium) or in the electronic sector (Ireland).

The Japanese chemical companies have followed similar strategies as their European and American counterparts during the 1980s. They have refocused their portfolio on specialties and high value added products, in particular pharmaceuticals, which, in a number of cases means more internationalization. This is due to the fact that some niche markets are quite narrow and require the chemical company to reach one of the first world positions. Moreover, the specialties incorporate services into the product, which means that proximity to the clients is essential to competitiveness.[20] So, Japanese chemical firms also invest abroad in order to penetrate new markets and progress towards the status of global companies.

Finally, in a number of cases the scientific and technological base of the Japanese chemical companies appear insufficient, and they need technological transfers even to compete in Japan. In such a context, foreign direct investment aims at increasing the technological

[19] see Chapter 2.
[20] On these general strategic moves in the chemical industry, see (Sahwald 1992b).

competence of the companies. As in other sectors, the weaknesses of the Japanese chemical companies are concentrated on the fundamental end of research. So, one of their objectives is to cooperate with other countries in order to speed the transfer of basic research results so that Japanese companies can exercise their strength in development. In order to do so, a number of Japanese chemical companies plan to open fundamental research laboratories in Europe and the US (*ECN* 15/7/92). For example, Eisai, a pharmaceutical company, has established an institute in Boston for basic research in organic chemistry in 1989 and neurosciences research center in London in 1990 (*Financial Times* 3/12/1990).

In the 1970s, Japanese chemical firms have made a number of factor based foreign investments, mostly in developing countries, but also in Europe. Since the 1980s, direct investment in the United States and Europe result from a more complex set of motives. Some of these investment are market based, but a number of them are factor based. However, the factors which are aimed at are now different; it is mostly technological and knowledge resources.

5.3.2   *The Case of Pharmaceuticals*

Japan is the second largest pharmaceutical market in the world after the United States, and the Japanese consume more drugs per head than any other nationals. Yet the situation of the Japanese pharmaceutical companies on the world scene is similar to that of the chemical firms in general. Table 10 shows that they are still relatively small on a world scale.

The pharmaceutical industry is quite internationalized. In 1980, about 13% of the world's pharmaceutical demand were met through imports and 27% through local production by foreign-owned units (Ballance *et al*. 1992). Moreover, during the 1980s internationalization has become even wider with a surge in foreign direct investment and trans-border cooperative agreements (Wolf 1993). Local production is often preferred to exports because of the strong local specific features of markets, and in particular regulations and the necessary relationships with doctors.[21] The United States is the only country to report separately figures for exports and sales by foreign subsidiaries;

---

[21] Which means in particular a sophisticated distribution system. On this question, see (Ballance *et al*. 1992, Wolf 1992).

Table 10: The Leading Pharmaceutical Companies, and the Leading Japanese Pharmaceutical Companies in 1990[1].

	Country	Rank	Sales 1990 ($ m)	Pharmacy in % of sales
The leading pharmaceutical companies				
Merck & Co	US	1	6,365	83.0
Glaxo	UK	2	6,063	100.0
Bristol Myers-Squibb	US	3	5,261	51.1
Hoechst	Ger	4	4,992	18.0
Bayer	Ger	5	4,956	19.2
Ciba-Geigy	Switz	6	4,582	32.3
Eastman Kodak	US	7	4,349	23.0
Smith-Kline Beecham	UK/US	8	4,242	52.8
Sandoz	Switz	9	4,089	45.9
Eli Lilly	US	10	3,700	71.3
American Home Product	US	11	3,463	51.1
Roche	Switz	12	3,459	49.7
Johnson & Johnson	US	13	3,303	29.4
Pfizer	US	14	3,234	50.5
Abbott	US	15	3,161	51.3
The leading Japanese pharmaceutical companies				
Takeda Chemical Industries	J	1	617	n.a
Yamanouchi Pharmaceutical	J	2	468	n.a
Taisho Pharmaceutical	J	3	383	n.a
Daiichi Pharmaceutical	J	4	347	n.a
Sankyo Co	J	5	328	n.a
Eisai Co	J	6	318	n.a

[1] For Japan, fiscal year ending in March 1991.

Sources: PJB Publications, Reveiew Issue 1991 and (Ward 1992) for the Japanese companies.

in 1988, exports represented only 17.5% of foreign sales by American pharmaceutical firms (Ballance *et al.* 1992).

The Japanese pharmaceutical companies are still largely reliant on their internal market, as shown by Table 11, which gives rough estimations of the degree of internationalization of the pharmaceutical companies for a number of countries.

Table 11: Foreign Sales of Pharmaceuticals by Selected Companies, Averages by Country,[1] 1987/88 in %.

Country	Share of foreign sales	Number of firms covered
Denmark	85.2	4
Belgium	82.5	2
Sweden	79.9	4
United Kingdom	72.6	5
Germany	62.7	15
France	60.1	16
United States	42.4	26
Italy	32.3	13
Japan	6.2	28
Korea	5.1	12
Spain	3.0	2

[1] The coverage being limited, the averages are indicative.

Source: (Ballance *et al.* 1992).

Foreign companies have widely penetrated the Japanese market; companies from industrialized countries account for about 25% of the drug sales in Japan (Ward 1992).[22] Foreign companies owe such strong positions to their technological strength. According to M. Ward (1992), Western developed drugs amount to almost 40% of sales in Japan.

Several evolutions explain the relatively recent moves to internationalize of the Japanese pharmaceutical companies. Two factors seem particularly important: firstly the fact that they have chosen a strategy to reinforce their portfolio of R&D drugs (original products developed in-house) and secondly the stronger competition on the home market and the more stringent drug price regulations in Japan. In recent years, the Japanese companies have substantially increased their R&D expenses, but they still spend much less than their Western competitors in real terms. However, the Japanese companies have increased their performance in terms of new drugs (Ward 1992, Wolf 1992). They are being forced to turn to overseas markets in order to offset the

---

[22] This figure is not entirely comparable with the general figure given for chemical production in Section 5.1.3 above.

increasing costs of product development. Especially since they have to face high developement costs while the governement tends to reduce the official prices at home (Walsh 1992). Moreover, as for the chemical industry in general, competition from foreign firms tends to increase. During the 1970s, American and European companies had resorted to joint ventures to get a foothold in the Japanese pharmaceutical market, but they are now dissolving these partnerships and competing on their own (Ward 1992).

These evolutions of the strategy of the Japanese pharmaceutical companies and of their competitive potential emphasize that they have had plans to globalize since the beginning of the 1980s. As in the chemical industry in general, the internationalization moves have first targeted the United States, but Japanese pharmaceutical companies have rapidly increased their investment in Europe since the end of the 1980s. Table 7 above shows that pharmaceuticals has been one of the most important sectors of Japanese chemical production in Europe, and the most important sector for R&D units.

As we saw above (Table 8), investment in pharmaceuticals has taken the cooperative route more frequently than investments in the chemical sector in general. However, there was a number of cases of acquisitions. In 1991, Yamanouchi Pharmaceuticals has acquired the pharmaceutical division of Gist-Brocades in Europe and of Shaklee US in North America. Fujisawa Pharmaceutical has acquired Lyphomed in the US.

In terms of geographical base, pharmaceutical units are concentrated in the same countries as chemical units in general, but the hierarchy is slightly different. Germany has a higher proportion of production and sales units than the UK; but the UK hosts 5 out of the 10 R&D units. This distribution corresponds to the competence which the UK has accumulated in pharmaceutical research, including laboratories of multinationals (Cantwell 1987).

5.3.3 Examples of Firms

As said above, Japanese chemical companies are still relatively little internationalized, even if the largest strongly insist on the global perspective of their strategies. In this respect, it is quite interesting to observe the situation of Mitsubishi Kasei, which is Japan's most important chemical company. It is still heavily reliant on the domestic market and its overseas operations target essentially South East

Asia and the United States. Mitsubishi has set up only a couple of production and sales unit in Europe. Dainippon Ink & Chemicals and Sumitomo Chemicals have been more active in Europe.

5.3.3.1 Dainippon Ink and Chemicals (DIC)

DIC has developed three main activities: inks, organic pigments and thermoset resins. Inks and synthetic resins represent over 50% of its turnover.[23] The firm's strategy is to reinforce its positions in its main fields and to diversify into five high value added activities (reprography and high performance polymers in particular).

DIC has resorted to direct investment since before the Second World War in Asia. After the Second World War, it also used direct investment to integrate foreign technology. In particular, it acquired the synthetic resins technology from Reichhold Chemicals[24] and the technology to mix synthetic resins with pigments from Sun Chemicals (Suzuta 1989, Ward 1992). DIC created its American subsidiary, DIC America Inc. in 1970. This unit was then mostly a technological outpost. DIC made major acquisitions during the 1980s. In 1986, it acquired the graphic arts division of Sun Chemicals ($550 million), and Reichhold Chemicals in 1987 ($540 million). DIC has become the first world producer of printing ink and the third world producer of organic pigment, with a world market share of 13% for both products. DIC is thus quite internationalized by Japanese chemical companies standards, even if it does not export much from Japan.

DIC has really increased its presence in Europe from the second half of the 1980s on. Acquisitions have played an important role in this strategy. Firstly, DIC has gained control of the European subsidiaries of the Graphic Arts operations of Sun Chemical and Reichhold. Subsequently, DIC's European operations have made a number of acquisitions in their main business areas.[25] DIC appears as an exception since Japanese firms have usually been quite reluctant at using acquisitions.

---

[23] Source: Annual Reports.

[24] Before that, DIC was making ink from varnish.

[25] For a list of DIC's operations in Europe, see the Appendix to this chapter.

5.3.3.2 Sumitomo Chemical Co

Sumitomo has strong basic chemicals operations (48% of the turnover in 1991), but wants to diversify more into specialties (Ward 1992). At the end of the 1980s, overseas operations accounted for about 15% of Sumitomo's turnover (annual reports). Most foreign sales are made in Asia, but the relative importance of the region has slightly decreased at the end of the 1980s.

Sumitomo has invested in the United States in basic chemicals, agrochemicals and pharmaceuticals. Investments in Europe are quite recent. The most active area is agrochemicals. Sumitomo Chemical France, which was created as a subsidiary in 1990 is specialized in agrochemicals. That same year, Sumitomo has acquired Pan Britannica Industries in the UK, which is specialized in garden fertilizers and pesticides. In 1991, Pan Britannica Industries has acquired an agrochemical subsidiary of Rhône Poulenc, May & Baker Garde, and in 1992, the agrochemical Spanish company KenoGard. Sumitomo wants to become a major agrochemical producer in Europe, with a view on the Mediterranean markets.

Sumitomo has also invested in European operations in the fields of pharmaceuticals, dying materials and new materials.[26] In 1991, it created Sumitomo Chemical Deutschland which will distribute dying materials throughout Europe. In 1992, it created an other German subsidiary, Sumitomo Specialty Polymer, to distribute plastics and composite materials across Europe.[27] In pharmaceuticals, Sumitomo has rather resorted to joint ventures, as it has been the case for Japanese companies in general.[28]

CONCLUSION

Although no Japanese chemical group operates globally, many companies have significant overseas operations. The leading Japanese chemical companies have ambitious globalization plans for the 21st century, but they will not become as internationalized as either their American and European competitors or the Japanese

---

[26] For a list, see the Appendix.

[27] This subsidiary should include a technical center (ECN 11/5/1992).

[28] See above.

companies in the automobile and electronic sectors within the next generation.[29]

This chapter has shown that the motives for foreign direct investment by Japanese chemical companies are quite diverse. The most important feature is that foreign investment by Japanese companies are both factor- and demand-based – and the distinction is not only between developing and industrial countries.

The Japanese chemical industry started to internationalize in the 1960s when it was obliged to look for cheaper resources.[30] In the 1980s, it was been faced with the globalization of both the world chemical industry and a number of its Japanese clients from the automobile or the electronic industry in particular. In these conditions, establishing commodity production in Asia is not enough. Japanese chemical companies have to gain a share of American and European markets if they are to compete on the global stage. This means an industrial presence in the United States, but also in Europe. It also means an upgrading of their competitive advantage, which in turn requires strong technological resources. These resources have so far been quite concentrated in the United States and Europe in the chemical sector. This set of factors explains why the Japanese chemical companies have invested in industrial countries both to get closer to demanding markets and to tap into rich technological resources.

The mode of foreign involvement varies quite clearly with the needs of the Japanese companies. Traditionally, and in various sectors, they tend to prefer wholly owned subsidiaries and to be reluctant to acquisitions. Nevertheless, they have used joint ventures and cooperative agreements in a number of cases. Joint ventures have been relatively numerous in pharmaceuticals where Japanese companies need both technological and marketing resources to penetrate foreign markets. Acquisitions have not been numerous but they are not to be excluded on principle. During the 1980s, Japanese chemical companies have acquired about 50 firms in the United States and also in Europe.[31] This solution can seem all the more interesting as Japanese chemical companies aim at internationalizing rapidly.

The large Japanese chemical firms have ambitious plans in terms of internationalization, which should lead to continued foreign direct investment. This evolution should be reinforced (or eased) by the need

[29] On this point, see (*Financial Times* 3/12/1990).
[30] And less crowded areas for pollution reasons.
[31] Data from the author's own data base, Chem-MA.

for rationalization of the Japanese chemical industry, which is still quite fragmented, with more than 4,000 companies. The unification of the European market has been an incentive for investment; it should continue to play such a role, along with the perspective to penetrate Eastern European countries. But in the chemical industry, investments by Japanese companies are still far smaller than in Asia and the United States.

REFERENCES

Ballance, Robert, Pogany, Janos, Forstner, Helmut, *The World's Pharmaceutical Industries*, Edward Elgar, 1992.

Bower, Joseph, L., *When Market Quake. The Management Challenge of Restructuring Industry*, Harvard Business School, 1986.

CIA (Chemical Industries Association), *Basic International Chemical Industry Statistics* 1963–1990, CIA, October 1991.

Commission des Communautés Européennes, *Panorama de l'industrie communautaire 1991–1992*, Office des publications officiells des Communautés Européennes, Luxembourg, 1991.

Dunning, John, H., *Multinational enterprises and the Global Economy*, Addison Wesley, 1993.

European Chemical News 15/7/92.

Eurostaf, *Chimie lourde, Chimie de spécialités*, Collection Stratégies Industrielles et Financières, Eurostaf, 4e trimestre, 1991.

Financial Times 3/12/1990.

JETRO, Current Management Situation of Japanese Manufacturing Enterprises in Europe, 7th Survey report, Tokyo, 1991.

JETRO, Current Management Situation of Japanese Manufacturing Enterprises in Europe, 8th Survey report, Tokyo, 1992.

Lafay *et al.* 1989.

Les Echos 10/3/1992.

Ozawa, T., *Japan's Strategic Policy Towards Outward Direct Investment*, Fort Collins: Colorado State University, Mimeo, July 1989.

Ozawa, T., *Multinationalism: Japanese Style*, Princeton University Press, Princeton 1979.

Sachwald, F. (ed.), *Europe integration and competitiveness. Acquisitions and Alliances in Industry*, Edward Elgar, 1994a.

Sachwald, F. "The chemical industry", Sachwald, F. (ed.), *Europe integration and competitiveness. Acquisitions and Alliances in Industry*, Edward Elgar, 1994b.

Ward, Mike, *Japanese Chemicals. Past, Present and Future*, The Economist Intelligence Unit, Business International, Special Report No R 731, London, June 1992.

Wolf, Peter de, "L'industrie pharmaceutique", Sachwald, *L'Europe et la globalisation* 1993.

6

Adaptation of Japanese Companies to Multinationalization

Sophie Garnier

Japanese businesses have set up manufacturing units abroad later than their American and European counterparts. When they international-ized their production, they were faced with a twofold problem. First of all, they needed to organize their various activities, such as finance, marketing, R & D and so on, on an international scale and to define relationships with their foreign subsidiaries. Secondly, they had to set up their production systems in foreign environments.

Could their production system, which had been designed and developed in a Japanese context, be "transplanted" elsewhere? This question began to be asked in the Seventies, as the Japanese firms were beginning to emerge with a new management model capable of replacing the American one which had predominated until then. The Japanese manufacturing and work organization systems were universally adopted because of their performances and aptitude to motivate workers, and they were considered as a model for Western firms.[1] Soon, however, discussion arose as to how the Japanese model could concretely be transposed into other contexts. It was true that success could be explained by the homogeneity particular to Japanese culture, which puts more stress on harmony and cohesion than on

---

[1] See (Drucker 1974, Pascale, Athos 1981, Ouchy 1982, Beaux 1992).

individualism.[2] Thus it seemed doubtful that the model could be trans-posed. However, studies suggested that the Japanese methods were not inextricably bound up with supposed Japanese peculiarities but were in fact pragmatic responses to the post-war Japanese economic and social climate.[3] If this were the case, then the Japanese model would be adaptable to the different environments it was placed in.

The Japanese firms established abroad give an excellent view of how far Japanese methods are transferable. How far have they tried to apply their system in foreign subsidiaries, and how far have they succeeded? Is the Japanese model adaptable to other countries, thus imposing "Japanization" on American and European industry, or is it changed by local conditions? Only if staff and suppliers are in full agreement can new production methods be set up in foreign subsidiaries. As the Japanese success has often been explained by the superiority of their organization, human resource management and supplier-manufacturer relationships are likely to be the important factors of success in Japanese transplants. According to Japanese businessmen (JETRO, 1991), the absence of these two factors was one of the main obstacles to the setting up of factories in the United States and Europe.

This chapter deals with how Japanese businesses have adapted their organization and management methods to their foreign subsidiaries. It is mainly based on the results of various empirical studies of Japanese transplants in the United States and Europe,[4] and also on interviews with two Japanese companies in France, Canon and Panasonic (Matsushita Group). The accent will be placed on the electronics and automobile sectors, in which Japanese investment has been particularly high in Europe and in North America. After an initial outline of organization in the multinationals and the production system set up by their subsidiaries, the chapter will devote its second part to management of supplies and finally, it will examine personnel management in Japanese subsidiaries abroad.

---

[2] The idea has been proposed by (Abegglen 1958) and is present in a number of contributions; see in particular (Ouchy 1982).

[3] See for example (Lévine, Taira 1974, Koike 1988).

[4] These studies are presented in the Appendix.

6.1   THE MULTINATIONALIZATION OF JAPANESE COMPANIES

In practice, direct international investment by a company results in it setting up its own practices in different economic, social and cultural contexts. When it sets up a subsidiary in another country, the company faces a foreign environment and must deal with more than one culture. Management must combine local concerns with overall strategy. It is often torn between local priorities and the necessity to co-ordinate activity centrally. A multinational enterprise must both make full use of its international dimension and adapt to various local conditions. Thus there are two conflicting forces: the first which imposes the parent company's style of management in all foreign subsidiaries, and the second which encourages adaptation to the host country's style. In the first case, the firm may encounter resistance and obstacles arising from socio-economic and cultural differences. In the second, the firm's cohesion may be jeopardized by insufficient integration of its activities worldwide. Thus one of the main tasks of the multinational is to find a balance between centralization and de-centralization of its various activities. Depending on the strategy adopted, the parent company will give greater or lesser autonomy to its foreign susidiaries. A multinational company will thus create communication networks between its different units, and will define methods of controlling subsidiaries, together with procedures for the parent company to accomplish this.

6.1.1   Centralization of Japanese Multinational Companies

Most Japanese multinational companies are characterized by a high degree of centralization.[5] Japanese firms have set up factories abroad mainly to combat protectionist threats. Subsidaries, seen as mere extensions of the parent company's activities, have been entrusted with the mission of applying central decisions. Decision making thus remained centralized within the parent company. Japanese companies correspond to an organization model in which knowledge is developed and retained centrally, and strategy is defined by the parent company. Subsidiaries have little scope for action. This model is unlike that of American and European multinational companies (Bartlett, Ghoshal,

---

[5] Chapter 7 qualifies this with respect to R&D activities.

1989). American companies internationalized after the war based their coordination process mainly on formal, standardized systems. As for European companies, in which the influence of the founding family often remained considerable, management of subsidiaries was entrusted to a member of the family or a few trusted agents. In both cases, the subsidiaries acquired much greater latitude in defining their products and strategies than Japanese ones. Foreign operations then either made use of local opportunities, or adapted and made use of the parent company's knowledge, and the latter simply kept control over the subsidiary's finance.

The centralized nature of Japanese companies is particularly observable in subsidiary management appointments: Japanese expatriates generally hold the important posts, either as managers or as advisers to local managers. According to Noritake Kobayashi's study in 1985, comparing Japanese and Western multinationals, management of Japanese companies is less internationalized overall than that of American and European companies. It is in the recruitment and promotion of local executives that the difference is most marked. It is less obvious, on the other hand, in functional areas of the company, such as marketing or finance.[6] Operations in subsidiaries are therefore controlled and supported by a network of expatriate managers and technicians in direct contact with the parent company. These managers apply the parent company's decisions and communicate information on the subsidiary's activity to the head office.

Due to the centralized nature of Japanese multinational organization, management recruiting policy raised difficulties in the subsidiaries. Locally recruited managers felt excluded from the decisional network. Employees arrive from the parent company with a full understanding of how the organization and staff in the company function, because they have benefited from the "life employment" system.[7] Consensual decision-making, which is a traditional feature of Japanese companies, is based on total communication throughout the company, and is difficult to apply when there is a parent-subsidiary relationship. For the foreign managers, it would mean perfect mastery of the Japanese language and social customs. Local executives thus find themselves excluded from this system and must use Japanese intermediaries to help them communicate with the parent company

---

[6] The question of control remains a sensitive point for multinational companies, whatever their country of origin; see (Emmott 1992) for some international comparisons.

[7] About a third of Japanese employees benefit from life employment.

(Fukuda, 1992). In spite of (or because of?) the difficulty in recruiting and keeping a management team, Japanese firms seem to be convinced that subsidiaries should be directed by executives from the parent company.

Multinational centralization may be due to the fact that Japanese companies abroad are all of recent date. Direct Japanese investment in industrialized countries, it is true, has only developed since the 1970s; in Europe, most Japanese investment dates from the second half of the 1980s.[8] Japanese companies have therefore lagged behind American and European companies in internationalizing their production activities. Perhaps in future Japanese companies will move towards less centralized, more general operations abroad, since such management requires previous experience of international activity. However, the studies on this subject at different times confirm that centralized management predominates and is being maintained in Japanese multinationals (Tung, 1982; Kobayashi, 1985; Barlett, Ghoshal, 1989).

6.1.2 Particuliarities of the Japanese Production System

Japanese companies have developed manufacturing methods which have often been considered as the key to their success. The Toyota production system is a particularly developed form, traditionally used as an example of the Japanese model. Thus, "Toyotism" is quoted to refer to the Japanese production system, which is shared in fact by most other large Japanese companies. The "Toyota" approach is based on a few general principles.[9]

"Just in Time" (or synchronized production) consists of manufacturing and delivering parts and components just before use. Besides the resulting reduction in inventory, JIT allows greater flexibility in manufacturing organization.

"Total Quality Control" is very close, accurate monitoring of product quality at each stage of production.

Team Work is the basis of work organization. The working group, generally led by a team leader, is given goals and is then left to organize itself so as to attain them. Team work is also developed in quality circles

---

[8] See Chapter 1.

[9] The objective is not to give a thorough description of the Japanese production system. See (Ohno 1989, Womack *et al.* 1990, Abo 1991, Coriat 1991) and Chapter 4.

of several workers, in order to improve production methods little by little.

Work Flexibility is possible chiefly because of simplified job classification. A person, whether an executive or a worker, is not recruited for a specific task but will be sent where he is needed according to manufacturing requirements.

Japanese manufacturing methods require unswerving loyalty and considerable capacity to adapt on the part of the workforce and suppliers. Staff must be capable of accomplishing many tasks not only in terms of work stations but also in terms of content: quality control, plant maintenance and cleanliness of the work station are to a certain degree directly associated with the job in hand. Suppliers must, for their part, improve the quality of their production, respect delivery schedules and adapt to their client's needs.

In Japan, these requirements are part and parcel of the relationship between the company and the staff or the supplier.

As regards personnel management, the Japanese production system, as traditionally presented, is grounded on "three pillars":[10] life employment, salary according to number of years worked (*nenko* system) and the company's union. More generally, and more to the point in today's Japan, the company keeps its workforce in full employment and in return expects "loyalty" from its employees, notably embodied in a high capacity to adapt (as regards work schedules and changes of post, for instance) and belief in the company's goals. Although some aspects are being questioned because of the difficulties experienced today by many companies, the principle of lifetime employment seems to have been widely maintained and most companies have avoided laying off employees.[11]

Similarly, there is marked interdependence between the company and its suppliers. The Japanese supply system is based on a supply pyramid, with close collaboration between clients and suppliers on design and manufacture of parts and components.[12] Japanese production methods are thus applied in accordance with their personnel management and supply policies.

---

[10] This notion has been proposed by (Abegglen 1958, Abegglen, Stalk 1985). Given recent evolutions, it is partially wrong. However, life employment constitutes a factor of loyalty for employees and is one important element of the social cohesion of the Japanese firm.

[11] *Financial Times*, 21 December 1992.

[12] See Chapter 4.

The main features of Japanese company operation – flexibility and quality – are also to be found in Japanese subsidiaries abroad. Observers of the transplants nearly all note attention to detail, rigorous discipline in cleanliness and punctuality, simplified job classification, and job rotation.[13] Japanese transplants mostly put the accent on total quality control, flexible work organization, team work, and JIT, but the latter only to a certain degree.[14]

Canon, the electronics firm, offers an example of a transferred production system. It has standardized its production system, which is found in all its factories, whether Japanese, American or European. This system is based on JIT production, marked attention to quality and teamwork. The firm's leitmotif is avoidance of wastage at every stage of manufacture. Quality control combines computer-aided control of parts and components, products in manufacture and finished products, and continuous controls by workers throughout the production line. Work is organized to ensure great flexibility since job classifications only refer to four grades.

6.2   RELATIONSHIPS BETWEEN THE JAPANESE SUBSIDIARIES AND THEIR SUPPLIERS

The long-term success of the Japanese subsidiaries is linked more particularly to their capacity to structure their supply system. Their integration into local industrial fabric via their organization of supplies also depends on their relationships with local firms.

6.2.1   What is Local?

The repercussions of Japanese implants on the economic activity of the country in which they are set up depend on how complex their own operations are and how they choose to be supplied in parts and components: they may opt for imports or buy from the local market, and in the latter case, will choose either local suppliers or Japanese transplants.[15] The percentage of production directly produced by

---

[13] See (Trevor, White 1983, Dunning 1986, Florida, Kenney 1991).

[14] See also (Oliver, Wilkinson 1988, Fukuda 1991), presented in Appendix 2 and (Costa, Garanto 1993).

[15] See also Chapters 2, 3 and 4.

the country chosen was queried when Japanese firms began to set up in Europe and the United States. So, when they started their operations, the Japanese manufacturing units argued that they were merely "screwdriver factories" assembling parts imported from Japan in order to avoid protectionist measures. But in that case, how far were the Nissan cars from the Sunderland factory more English than Japanese, and the Canon photocopiers from their Breton factory more French than Japanese?

Pressure was brought to bear on Japanese industry to increase the percentage of local supplies. In 1987, the EEC adopted a ruling providing for taxation of goods from these firms if over 60% of purchased parts had been directly imported from Japan (ruling no 1761/87). In late 1988, Japan contested the legality of the new EEC provisions before the GATT. This European ruling, later denounced as a discriminatory measure, was suspended in 1990, but it was used in 1987 and 1988 against three office products: electronic typewriters, photocopiers and printers.[16] The Japanese electronics subsidiaries producing them then encountered difficulty in selling their products on the European market. Thus, in 1987, Canon was unable to sell its fax machines made in the Liffré factory, Brittany,[17] and was obliged to export them for two and a half years. During the same period, the Japanese electronics firm also had difficulty with its typewriters in Great Britain.[18]

Another European ruling also stung the Japanese firms into increasing the European content of their products. An original rule has always decreed that European products are not subject to tax or quotas when they are exported to another European country. To benefit under this rule, products from Japanese factories set up in Europe must have a certain percentage of local content.

A minimum European content of 45%, for example, is required for VCRs to be considered as European and therefore exempted from tax (electronic products are, it is true, heavily taxed). These measures have influenced Japanese firms' attitudes. They have been obliged to increase the added value of their European products and to buy more parts in Europe.

---

[16] *Les Echos*, 22 January 1992. See also Chapter 3.

[17] These machines were directly competing with those of French firms such as Alcatel, Matra or Sagem.

[18] *Financial Times*, 13 May 1992.

Table 1:   Evolution of the Percentage of Local Content in Japanese Subsidiaries in Europe (in %).

	At the starting date			In 1990		
	Europe	Japan	Others	Europe	Japan	Others
Process and assembly industries	43.3	54.5	2.2	60.7	33.0	6.3
Mechanics	60.6	38.6	0.8	75.7	23.0	1.3
E'tronic and e'trical equip'ts	32.1	64.7	3.2	52.8	37.0	10.2
Transport equipments	56.2	43.8	0.0	67.3	31.7	1.0
Parts and components	52.3	45.6	2.1	66.7	31.1	2.2
Electronic components	42.2	54.1	3.7	58.8	37.5	3.7
Automobile components	66.1	33.9		77.5	22.4	0.1
Raw materials	68.5	23.5	8.0	75.0	15.3	9.7
Chemicals	72.3	23.3	4.4	83.1	14.7	2.2
Others	43.1	52.4	4.5	70.1	23.4	6.5
Total	53.2	40.9	4.0	68.9	25.6	5.5

[1] Calculations of local content rates are founded on firms' data. Firms have given for 3 important products the origin of their parts and componants. The term local content is considered broadly for Europe: all European countries are considered as "local".

Source: (JETRO, 1991).

According to the 1990 JETRO Survey (JETRO, 1991), the average local content in Japanese manufacturing industry in Europe accounts for some 70% of added value (Table 1).[19] Moreover, according to the JETRO Survey for 1991 (JETRO, 1992), some 73% of Japanese manufacturing companies have a degree of local content higher than 50%, 58% have a degree higher than 70%, and 21% have 100% content. Not surprisingly, the degree of local content is higher in companies which were taken over than in those which were set up or which are held in partnership by Japanese and non-Japanese firms (Table 2). Since companies began to set up in Europe, the local content has increased. Over three-quarters of the Japanese manufacturers have set up in Europe since the early Eighties, with investment in electronics being the most pronounced. Between this period and 1990, the average local content of Japanese companies has increased overall by fifteen points (Table 1).[20]

---

[19] On JETRO's surveys, see the general appendix of the book and Chapter 2.

[20] According to Dunning's survey (1986) on 23 Japanese subsidiaries in 1984, 58%

Japanese Firms in Europe

Table 2: Percentage of Local Content in Japanese Manufacturing Companies in Europe, Per Type of Company.

	Firms with a rate superior to 50%	Firms with a rate superior to 70%	Total number of firms
Firms under total Japanese control	57.3	39.7	100 (136)
Joint ventures	81.5	61.5	100 (65)
Participations	100.0	71.4	100 (14)
Acquisitions	91.0	86.6	100 (67)
Total	73.2	58.3	100 (216)

Source: (JETRO 1992).

In the electronics industry, local content was relatively lower than in the automobile and chemicals industries. Figures progressed from very low at the start of operations to much higher than in other sectors. The electronics companies surveyed have increased local content by an average 30%, increasing to 60% today. They have adopted a strategy of gradual implantation, starting off by assembling parts imported from Japan and then gradually replacing them by products bought locally. Canon Bretagne followed this pattern: at the start of its activity in 1984, their factories mostly assembled parts imported from Japan, then over the years the firm built up a wide network of local suppliers. Its local content now amounts to some 60% of added value.[21]

When North America and Europe are compared, this increased reliance on local suppliers is confirmed. In North America, where Japanese investment started earlier than in Europe, local purchases by Japanese subsidiaries are relatively higher than in Europe. The latest MITI survey on Japanese business operations abroad shows that in Europe in 1990, local purchases amounted to over 70% of all purchases for a third of Japanese electronics firms and to less than 50% for almost half of them. In North America, two thirds of Japanese firms bought 70% of their supplies locally and 15% of firms bought less than 50% (MITI, 1992).

The increase in local content can first of all be explained by more frequent recourse to local supplies. This is partly due to improved

---

of their supplies were bought in the U.K and 42% were imported. That survey also found that the rate of local supply also tends to increase.

[21] *Financial Times*, 13 May 1992.

Table 3: Japanese Subsidiaries in Europe Per Share of Locally Supplied Purchases in 1990.

		0 to 30%	30 to 50%	50 to 70%	70 to 90%	90 to 100%
Manufacturing industries	North America	4.4	5.8	16.9	15.3	57.6
	Europe	7.3	15.9	21.9	17.2	37.7
Electronic industry	North America	9.3	6.1	18.5	21.5	44.6
	Europe	13.6	32.2	22.1	11.9	20.3

Source: (MITI 1992).

quality in supplies, as observed by Japanese companies. According to the JETRO survey of those companies where local content has increased, this is the main reason. Conversely, poor quality and performances in European supplies can be a major factor in choosing a Japanese supplier. This is the case for the Mitsubishi factory in western France. Only 10% of the parts in its portable telephones are made by European manufacturers, because it feels that Japanese suppliers are technically far more advanced.[22]

The increased local content of Japanese production in Europe can also be explained by the fact that new Japanese parts and components manufacturers have set up abroad and Japanese companies purchase from them. In 1991, there were 66 Japanese electronics parts and components manufacturers in the EEC, mostly in Great Britain (19), Germany (18) and Ireland (11). As far as France was concerned, only a small number of these supply-transplants (6) had been set up, considering the number of Japanese electronics firms operating in France.[23] The arrival of supplier transplants in Europe was no doubt encouraged by Japanese companies wishing to avoid the constraints of the aforementioned European Directive on local content, while keeping their usual Japanese suppliers. For the Japanese suppliers, setting up in Europe could be justified by the wish to avoid losing their clients, all the more so as the increased value of the Yen had made imports from Japan more expensive for Japanese subsidiaries.

---

[22] *Les Echos*, 20 May 1992.

[23] About 30, See Chapter 3.

The increased local content could also be due to the replacement of imports from Japan by in-house manufacture, with foreign factories being entrusted with more complicated manufacturing processes after several years' operation. Perhaps Japanese manufacturers were wisely checking the lie of the land before developing more elaborate activities. Sony France is an illustration of this; the firm first set up factories assembling audio and video cassettes, an activity with low added value. The first unit, with little automatization, was opened in 1981, and the second, more modern, in 1984. In the latter half of the 1980s, more complex operations were undertaken. In 1989, a factory specializing in the manufacture of video cameras, VCRs, CD players and car radios was set up. In the same year a new factory producing video cassettes was set up, but unlike the first, it also undertook coating of magnetic supports, which was a more complex upstream task. The most recent Sony factory in France, opened in April 1992, has been designed for production of optical pick-up heads for compact disc players and so-called multi-layer printed circuits, both added value goods. Thus, within the space of ten years, this Japanese electronics firm has developed more sophisticated production in its French factories.

6.2.2   Constitution of Japanese-Style Networks

Traditionally, to obtain supplies of parts and components, Japanese firms use suppliers upon whom they rely heavily and with whom close ties are created. Banri Asanuma (1989) has been able to define the main characteristics of this supply system by making empirical studies of Japanese companies in the automobile and electronics sectors. He shows that Japanese firms do indeed tend to establish long-term relationships with their suppliers; however, these relationships are not entrenched and may evolve depending on the relative competitivity of suppliers and on negotiations between the partners.

Product life-cycle plays a major role in these fluctuating relationships. Companies choose a supplier for one product and generally keep them for the lifetime of the product. Relationships with suppliers are thus all the more stable as the company produces long-lasting products; they will be more stable, for instance, in the car industry than in electronics. For each new product negotiations are undertaken, during which suppliers are in competition. Relationships are generally maintained, but companies will step up or, on the contrary, reduce their reliance on the different suppliers depending on the latter's ranking. The main criteria for selection are product quality and reliable delivery. But the supplier's capacity to change a product according to the company's needs will also be taken into account.[24] The supplier must also try constantly to reduce production costs during the period of manufacture.

Throughout their relationships, the big companies maintain close contact with suppliers and include them informally in the group in various ways: via technical assistance, sending technicians and engineers, and supplier clubs, for example. Relationships are thus built on partnership, which enables information and know-how to circulate frequently. Because suppliers in Japan have one main client giving them technical assistance, their relationships to be weighted somewhat in favor of the big client company. Indeed, the supplier serves the company as a kind of safety margin. This assymmetry, which is not only to be seen in Japan, can be counterbalanced by the fact that, if suppliers have one client, continued relationships between them will lead to an accumulation of know-how for the supplier (which can serve the large companies in their own development) (Asanuma, 1989).

According to a study of 23 Japanese subsidiaries and 20 suppliers in Great Britain (Dunning, 1986), Japanese companies in Great Britain are trying to build up similar relationships with their local suppliers. Japanese companies, particularly in electronics, have attempted to create long-term relationships with their suppliers. In return, they expect acceptance and respect of their quality standards.

In the electronics sector, Japanese requirements for British companies concern not so much price as quality. According to an electronics components supplier interviewed during the survey (Dunning, 1986), Japanese companies keep up the pressure for high quality and delivery standards much longer and more efficiently than British ones. Another difference lies in the technical assistance given to suppliers by Japanese companies.[25] This assistance ranges from product design and production methods to quality control or operator training, including loan of equipment. Even the company's strategy may come under review. Both the Japanese and British firms surveyed recognized these facts. A supplier of integrated circuits commented on his relationships with his client thus:

---

[24] Contracts at established on a quite general basis so that the firm can modify the specific characteristics of products.

[25] For the automobile industry, see Chapter 4.

"We get more help from the Japanese in terms of technical help, drawings and the like. Unlike most UK firms at least, they see us as an extension of their own factory: therefore it is essential we have mutual understanding of their requirements. If we have any problems, they will send specialists to help or advise us and do everything they can to enable us to be a successful supplier"

(quoted in Dunning, p. 130)

The Japanese electronics companies in France also offer examples of partner-type relationships with suppliers. Canon is thus trying to set up partnerships with suppliers in France like those it has in Japan. Its most important initiative has been the creation of a suppliers' club with 80 of its suppliers (out of a total 135 suppliers, 104 of which are French). The aim of this club is to increase information exchanges between suppliers. Because the various suppliers are in a club, they informally belong to the Canon group and adhere to Canon quality and price objectives. According to a Canon sub-contractor, the suppliers' club is also a useful means of communicating with, or lobbying, the Canon management.[26] Toshiba (whose French factory produces photocopiers) offers another example of close relationships with suppliers. Its 125 European suppliers, of which some 100 are French, were recruited after long negotiations. The company also organizes trips to Japan for its most loyal suppliers to meet their Japanese homologues. Finally, it plans to set up training days in its Dieppe factory for some suppliers. These examples show that Japanese firms wish to build up partnerships based on exchanges of information between companies.

6.3 HUMAN RESOURCES IN JAPANESE SUBSIDIARIES

One of the main strengths of Japanese management is its valorization of human resources. It is indeed one of the main reasons for the success of the production system. But Japanese firms must adapt their foreign implants to economic and social conditions and cannot (or will not) import principles such as life-employment. They can and do, however, bring a non-corporate, non-conflictual attitude towards industrial relations.

---

[26] *Les Echos*, 20 May 1992.

6.3.1   Employment in Japanese Subsidiaries

6.3.1.1   Recruitment

As most Japanese companies in Europe are less than ten years old, recruitment has so far been one of their personnel managements' major tasks. On the whole, Japanese companies have chosen young, semi-trained labor. For semi-skilled posts, for example, Canon Brittanny took on young people from school (with elementary technical skills) most of whom had had no professional experience. This choice of young, semi-trained labor can be explained by the often low level of skill required in many Japanese subsidiaries, particularly in the electronics sector where most operations are in assembly. In this way, the company obtains a workforce which has not acquired particular working habits incompatible with the corporate culture. Young people are also less likely to have had previous union experience. Thus, employees are easier to integrate into the company and will accept cooperative relationships with management.

Companies in Japan (at least, the largest ones) recruit staff directly from school and university. Otherwise, they very rarely recruit from other companies. Labor is thus very stable and the labor market limited. This policy is an illustration of the "lifetime employment" ethic which developed in Japan in the post-war years. As employees are destined to remain in the company for years, it will seek not so much particular technical skills as high capacity to adapt and integrate into the company. The main recruitment criteria are thus based on the candidate's personality and his or her general attitude to work. Only then will more technical consideration of professional capacity intervene. Even though Japanese subsidiaries in Europe and the United States recruit differently from in Japan, the objectives and criteria remain similar. A company will precisely define the principles and method of their recruitment, which may be long even for unskilled staff. Selection of candidates will be based on personality and attitude towards the work and the organization. Among the most sought after qualities will thus be communication skills, and the capacity to adapt to highly flexible work methods and to teamwork.

6.3.1.2   Training

The other main task of personnel management has been training. Japanese companies' policy with regard to training is distinguished first by the importance given to employees' integration into the company.[27] Some companies offer integration programs for newly recruited staff, the length and form of which can vary from one company to another. This policy is, for instance, highly developed at Komatsu in Great Britain. Ten-day integration periods are organized, during which new employees learn about the company's activity, its basic principles such as quality control, and working conditions. They also learn about the union-management agreement in their company (Oliver,Wilkinson, 1988). These programs are not merely aimed at giving preliminary training, they also serve to present the company's objectives and operation, thus easing newcomers' integration. New Matsushita employees thus learn about "house principles" described by the company's director. The company's "seven principles", with the help of a few slogans, lay down a certain business ethic and aim at making staff feel responsible and motivated.[28]

Another characteristic feature of training policy in Japanese subsidiaries is the importance given to on the job training. This is set up within the work team. Staff may be assigned different tasks and are not always kept in precisely defined work stations. Staff thus learn several skills and maintain, even develop, their capacity to adapt to change.

Another side of training is trips to Japan, which enable foreign subsidary staff to discover Japanese operating methods. Some companies spend large sums on sending staff to Japan, not just managers and engineers but also lower executives and even skilled workers. Canon Brittanny offers a striking example, with all its executives, engineers, technicians and skilled workers having had at least one trip to Japan lasting for periods from two weeks to three months. These training periods in Japan put them in direct contact with the Japanese production system and help it to be transplanted to subsidiaries. This training policy can be considered as a means of establishing a production and work organization system in all a company's foreign subsidiaries, and of favorizing a feeling of common identity in a group.

---

[27] Training thus complements the other elements of integration of employees; see Section 6.1.2 and Appendix 1.

[28] In most of the large companies there is a couple of offical ethical principles, see (Aoki 1988).

6.3.1.3 Position and Role of Japanese Expatriates

According to the annual JETRO survey, Japanese expatriates always play a considerable role in Japanese subsidiaries in Europe (JETRO, 1991). In the EEC as a whole, an average of five Japanese per company, representing 1.5% of the workforce,[29] can be observed. A similar number of Japanese expatriates is to be found in companies in the electronics sector. Expatriates moreover occupy a large percentage of the management posts. In half the companies, the chairman or managing director is a Japanese. Finance, R&D and marketing divisions are also generally controlled by Japanese. On the other hand, staff administration is usually headed by a person recruited locally. This is not surprising since the post requires perfect knowledge of the national labor regulations and is not directly responsible to the parent company.

Besides being managers and thus in communication with the parent company, the Japanese expatriates, usually on two- or five-year tours of duty, often play an essential role in training and transmission of knowledge and skills developed in the enterprise. When new plant is installed, engineers and technicians from the parent company are present to set it up. More generally, the high number of Japanese in management but also in technical and engineering posts ensures the transmission of Japanese-style management throughout the company. In their role as advisers, expatriates do not necessarily have a clear hierarchical position. In a number of cases they are in double with a local employee, they are "shadows" and their presence can be felt as oppressing (Emmott 1992).

Michael White and Malcolm Trevor (1983) showed in their study on Japanese management in Great Britain that Japanese working methods were all the more present where there were many expatriates, and where they had a hand in the training of the British workforce. Moreover, their survey of British workers illustrated the preponderant role played by the expatriates in introducing Japanese working methods into subsidiaries. Thus, the advising and coordinating role of the Japanese expatriates appears as fundamental, especially in the field of fabrication, as it has been in the United States (Abo 1991).

---

[29] In the United States, in the electronic sector, Japanese employees represent about 3% of the personnel of Japanese subsidiaries. Expatriates also play an important role in the automobile subsidiaries (Abo 1991).

6.3.2   Industrial Relations

6.3.2.1. The Union Debate

Japanese firms have often had an unfavorable view of the American and European social climates and trade unions. They were afraid that they would have to combat several organized unions per trade and profession. Japanese unions, formed by each company, comprise all the employees of the company except the management. Management has a single interlocutor who does not defend a particular group but deals with the company's activities as a whole. Unlike the European or American worker, the Japanese one will be defined less by his profession than by his identification with a given company. Contrary to their initial fears, Japanese companies did not encounter major difficulty with the trades unions, even if the latter had expressed defiance at first.[30] Those which transposed their working methods and organization into their foreign subsidiaries in fact sought to prevent future confrontation with the unions.Where union presence was felt to be indispensable (or inevitable), Japanese companies chose a single interlocutor. This was the case for Hitachi in Great Britain, which bought up GEC's 50% share in their jointly owned company GEC-Hitachi. After the take over, considerable changes were made in union-management relationships. Whereas before it had dealt with six unions, the management announced in June 1984 that it would thenceforth only deal with one, the Electrical, Electronics, Telecommunications and Plumbing Union (EETPU).

The most famous union agreements signed by Japanese companies are to be found in the car industry. Thus the joint venture between Toyota and GM, NUMMI, 22 in the United States concluded an agreement with the American automobile union United Auto Workers (UAW). This agreement was signed less than a year after the first employees had been hired. Nissan Motor Manufacturing (UK) also concluded a similar agreement in the same year with the Amalgamated Engineering Union (AEU). Toyota also concluded an agreement with the AEU in October 1991 for its latest factory in Great Britain, which came into operation in late 1992. On the contrary, Honda has not concluded any union agreement in Great Britain.

While the agreements may be adapted to each company's case, they seem to be virtually identical. They aim to establish simplified union –

---

[30] In Great Britain in particular, see (Emmott 1992, Costa, Garanto 1993).

personnel management relationships. The management recognises a single union as interlocuter in negotiations, while keeping up direct relationships with the staff. Management-union relationships must be grounded on co-operative, peaceable attitudes and on common recognition of the company's main goals. These agreements also draw flexible guidelines for work organization, notably by the use of a simplified job hierarchy. The Nissan UK agreement lays down among its general principles the following:

> "To promote mutual trust and cooperation between the Company, its employees and the Union; to recognize that all employees, at whatever level, have a valued part to play in the success of the Company; to seek actively the contributions of all employees in furtherance of these goals".

The agreement also states the fundamental goals of the company:

> "to establish an enterprise committed to the highest levels of quality, productivity and competititveness using modern technology and working practices and to make such changes to this technology and working practices as will maintain this position"
>
> (Wickens, 1985, pp. 76 and 62).

That Japanese companies in Europe have no serious problems with their labor relations is also due to the fact that union power is relatively diminished. In France and Great Britain unions have a weak presence in Japanese subsidiaries; unions are better represented in the Japanese companies located in Germany and Spain (Costa, Garanto 1993). The unions are present mostly in the car and textile industries. They are also more or less present according to the type of factory. There are relatively few in companies started from scratch, but many more where companies have been taken over. In the former, staff could be carefully selected, with a view to ensuring general attitudes towards the work and the company, as mentioned earlier. Where subsidiaries were created by buying into companies, or where partnerships were created, they fall between these two extremes.

Japanese electronics firms in France have turned out to be relatively barren recruiting grounds for unions. They are mostly creations from scratch. It should also be noted that they employ a great majority of women and young workers, traditionally less union-oriented. In addition, they are often quite small and offer no real possibility of union development. Only Sony, in France, approaches the 2,000-employee-mark. In Great Britain and Germany, Japanese electronics companies form small units, with the notable exception of the Fujitsu-Northern Telecom (ICL PLC), with 22,000 employees. The only other electronics companies with over 1,500 employees are Matsushita Electric and Sony in Great Britain, and two Matsushita joint companies in Germany (Loewe Opta GmbH and Siemens Matsushita). The localities chosed for manufacturing units may also have played a role in the relative absence of the unions; Japanese firms in France chose to set up in regions where union tradition was weak (like Canon or Mitsubishi in Brittany) or in old, formerly industrialized regions such as Lorraine (Victor Co, Matsushita and Sharp). In these areas, where drastic job losses over the last fifteen years have occurred, the spectre of the dole has no doubt contributed to the peaceful labor relations experienced by the Japanese companies. Finally, weak union activity in Japanese companies also corresponds to the phenomenon observed throughout Europe in the 1980s: people are no longer joining unions. The poor showing of the unions in Japanese companies, particularly in the small and medium-sized ones, therefore corresponds to the norm in French industry as a whole.

Japanese companies support a harmonious, co-operative work "philosophy", which seemed difficult for them to apply in the face of American and European unions. They seem to have over-estimated the power of union opposition. Union agreements, recruiting policy and the choice of locations have all contributed to defusing the bomb.[31] Japanese firms also benefited from the general evolution in European industrial relations. They have thus been able to establish a strategy of union relationships whereby they have imposed a new concept of industrial relations, at the same time doing away with the traditional union.

6.3.2.2. Management Participation

To explain the success of Japanese companies, many observers have underlined their capacity to make use of human resources and rally

---

[31] As for other aspects of the management of multinational companies, there is a parallel with the case of American firms in Europe (Emmott 1992) remarks that IBM, which has 20 000 employees in Europe, never had a union.

employees round the company's goals. This strategy is first of all based on an employee integration policy. As explained earlier, the recruitment methods in Japanese subsidiaries put the emphasis on the candidate's capacity to adapt to the company. The company will, moreover, seek to reinforce this notion of belonging. Most foreign visitors to factories in Japan are struck by customs such as uniforms or morning gymnastics sessions. They are no doubt the most widespread images of the Japanese company. In Japanese subsidiaries abroad, some of these customs are to be found in differing degrees: employees and management all wear uniform, all benefit from the same facilities, etc. They are generally well tolerated by staff, particularly by the unskilled workers who thus feel there is no discrimination between different categories. They are meant to show that rank or authority, while respected, confer no social privileges. The essential aim in this policy of not distinguishing rank is to encourage a feeling of belonging to the same organization and supporting its goals.[32]

In Japan, companies have several types of employee participation in constant product and production system improvements. Depending on the company, suggestions, daily information meetings or quality circles may be preferred. The latter, after working hours, will include unskilled workers in attempts to improve the production system under the guidance of a team leader. The way the workers' knowledge and initiative are put to use and considered essential, is one of the basic characteristics of the Japanese model as compared to the American one, where the different functions are separated (Florida, Kenney, 1991). Japanese subsidiaries abroad have sought to introduce this aspect of the Japanese production system.

Employee participation policy is based first and foremost on fully developed communications: information on company activity is regularly circulated. Goals and results are also presented in short morning meetings for each work team. The object of these meetings is both to inform staff on work in progress and to transmit staff requirements or requests to management. The companies encourage workers' initiatives by delegating responsibility to skilled staff. The working groups are relatively free to organize their work. Moreover, workers on an assembly line will be entrusted with peripheral tasks such as routine machine maintenance, in addition to assembly work.

This policy is particularly manifest in the Canon company, and

---

[32] In some cases the non-discrimination policies seem to be emphasized more abroad than in Japan; see (Emmott 1992) and Table A1 in Appendix 1.

can thus be observed in its French factory. Skilled staff are involved in quality control since they check work done previously before starting their own tasks. They may also suspend operation of the line if an incident requiring a technician occurs. Canon is also trying to introduce quality circles. In 1992, only a few employees were involved, but the management is giving them strong encouragement and considerable publicity, and is setting up project competitions between the different circles.

Despite the efforts sometimes made by Japanese companies to introduce quality circles, they have only had limited success up to now. The enthusiasm of the western countries in the late 1970s and early 1980s has since faded and today, quality circles are the management method the least favored by western enterprise. According to Susumu Watanabe, the quality circles failed in western countries because of the low regard in which they were held. In Japan, the activity of the circles is closely linked to total quality control, whereas in western companies, it tended to be separated from overall operation of the company. Furthermore, staff in western companies were not given sufficient motivation to participate in the quality circles, like for example life employment (Watanabe, 1991).

6.3.3   Where are the Limits?

Japanese companies did not encounter major difficulty in introducing their management system. This may first of all be explained by the evolution in the European labor relations climate. In electronics particularly, the fact that most factories were started up from scratch meant that the workforce was prepared to accept the Japanese rules of the game. However, the Japanese system was altered, or could be altered, in certain areas.

Empirical studies show that while the Japanese system is generally well accepted by the employees,[33] considerable differences may be observed between workers and executives. The workers appreciate the lack of hierarchical discrimination, and the communications and participation policies, but non-Japanese executives find it difficult to integrate into companies with a high number of Japanese expatriates.

---

[33] But there are oppositions, in particular in the automobile industry in the United States. After the starting phase in the factories, some workers have mentioned the increasing pressure due to the speed of the line and to team work (Rehder 1989).

Their career prospects are limited because of the centralized nature of the company, in which key posts will remain in the hands of the Japanese expatriates. Supervisory staff also find it more difficult to adapt to Japanese work methods, notably those in intermediary posts. In American car transplants, foremen often experienced considerable difficulty in adapting to Japanese work methods, mostly because of their attitudes towards workers (Florida, Kenney, 1991, 1993). This difficulty, to greater or lesser degrees, is also to be found in British transplants (White, Trevor, 1983).

Recruitment and training policies may also be criticized. They are based on the Japanese management model but they are implemented in different surroundings, with a far more developed labor market. To attain its goals of flexibility and quality, a company's internal training and employee integration policies must be founded on a stable workforce. It seems difficult to improve production quality continuously and durably if the workforce fluctuates constantly. Moreover, the company's investment in training may be wasted if, once the workforce is trained, it leaves the company. The risk is all the greater as these companies have a very youthful workforce, since mobility is greater in young people. A recent study (Job, 1992) shows that Japanese companies in Great Britain encountered this difficulty and that some are now changing their policy. They are now putting the accent on services offered to staff and envisaging recruitment of older, better trained staff.

Japanese companies also consider that while the Japanese working methods can be introduced in Europe, there remain considerable differences as regards work attitudes. According to a manager in a Japanese subsidiary in Great Britain, "by their nature, the Japanese are more cooperative and less individualistic in their approach to work; and they have a far greater committment to the company. They are more anxious to solve problems whatever the cost in time to themselves. Indeed their pride of achievement or fear of failure drives them to do this – and their families understand" (quoted in Dunning, 1986, p. 166). The more individualistic behavior of employees, and also the absence of a life-employment system as practised in Japan, may explain the muted success of quality circles in Japanese subsidiaries, as indeed occurred in previous experiments with quality circles in Europe. However, the fact that Japanese implants in Europe are recent means that any conclusions drawn from present experience of the Japanese companies in Europe are necessarily limited in scope.

6.4   CONCLUSION

Japanese subsidiaries are still mostly recent creations; their supply and human resources management policies are therefore still evolving. However, the number of studies already made on them lead to partial conclusions as to the exportability of the Japanese management system to other countries.

While the Japanese production system has been transplanted to Japanese companies' subsidiaries abroad, their personnel and supply management systems are not exactly copied from those in Japan. With various alterations, hybrid forms of Japanese management have developed. Thus, in Japanese companies set up abroad, the "three pillars" represented by lifetime employment, salary increases according to years worked, and company unions, do not exist. Indeed, they are at present being queried to some extent in Japan itself. The specific nature of Japanese companies is to be found rather in their organization and industrial relations. The main characteristics of their labor relations is the absence of job classifications, and employee participation. Japanese companies are also attempting to set up cooperation with suppliers. According to French managers of Japanese companies, the Japanese contribution is not simply its production system but also its concept of industrial relations. The Japanese are noted for their attention to the individual worker's participation, whatever his role in the company.

The experience of Japanese companies abroad also shows that the cultural and social conditions in which their production system was developed are not necessarily required to apply it. The production system, developed by adapting American methods to the Japan of the 1950s, has slowly adapted to its social and economic environment. Foreign implants cculd constitute a new step in the evolution of the Japanese system.[34] Some conditions, however, have enabled its application in Japanese subsidiaries. The implantation strategies chosen by Japanese companies have facilitated the application of their management system. By creating new, and/or smaller units, and by gradual development of their activities, Japanese subsidiaries have been able to select staff rigorously, avoid conflicts with unions, and gradually adapt to local conditions. Thus their management system has been relatively painless to set up.

---

[34] This chapter has mainly dealt with the European case, but it is interesting to note that American and European subsidiaries of Japanese firms are not always managed in the same way, in particular with respect to human resources.

APPENDIX 1

Management practices of Japanese subsidiaries in Europe according to the JETRO survey

Japanese Management Style in Manufacturing Subsidiaries (by sector) (% of Firms Applying the Type of Measure).

Sectors (size of the sample)	All sectors (379)	Electronics (125)	Automobile (49)	Chemicals (42)
Just in time	14.5	15.2	30.6	9.5
Forms of life time employment	10.8	10.4	4.1	14.3
Seniority system	4.2	6.4	0	7.1
Bonus	28.2	28.8	14.3	26.2
On the job training	56.6	70.4	53.1	59.5
Firm union	14.2	18.4	16.3	11.9
Quality circles	39.1	46.4	63.3	28.6
Morning assemblies and others	28.8	36.0	26.5	26.2
Morning exercices	3.2	5.6	0	7.1
Unique cafeteria	59.4	80.8	67.3	54.8
Open offices spaces	56.2	72.8	61.2	45.2
Organization of social events for employees	67.8	79.2	51.0	73.8
Uniform	43.8	64.8	51.0	42.9

Source: (JETRO 1992).

Japanese Management Style in Manufacturing Subsidiaries (by Mode of Location) (% of Firms Applying the Type of Measure)

Type of location	Total control (174)*	Joint venture (73)	Merger or acquisition (60)
Just in time	10.9	19.2	11.7
Forms of life time employment	14.9	4.1	8.3
Seniority system	4.6	4.1	1.7
Bonus	33.3	23.3	21.7
On the job training	69.9	52.0	28.3
Firm union	15.5	11.0	20.0
Quality circles	39.1	38.3	28.3
Morning assemblies and others	36.2	20.5	16.7
Morning exercices	5.2	0.0	1.7
Unique cafeteria	68.4	49.3	41.7
Open offices spaces	71.8	50.7	26.7
Organization of social events for employees	79.3	53.4	56.7
Uniform	56.9	30.1	18.31

*Size of the sample.

Source: (JETRO 1992).

APPENDIX 2

Presentation of some Empirical studies on the Management of Japanese subsidiaries abroad

Authors	Date of the survey	Japanese subsidiaries surveyed	Other firms studied	Méthod	Thèmes
Fukuda (1992)	1991	57 subsidiaries in Hong Kong (industry, trade and services)		questionnaires (Japanese managers)	selection and training of the expatriates
Gleave, Oliver (1990)	1990?	5 subsidiaries in the UK		case studies (managers)	human resource management
Florida, Kenney (1991)	1988	7 carmakers and autocomponent suppliers in the US		interviews, questionnaires (managers)	investment strategy, production, work organisation, relationships with suppliers
Oliver, Wilkinson (1988)	1987	31 subsidiaries in the UK	British firms applying Japanese management methods	questionnaires (managers)	location, production methods, human resource management, relationships with suppliers
Dunning (1986)	1986	23 subsidiaries in the UK	local suppliers, clients, local firms	case studies	location decision, relationships with suppliers and clients, human resource management
Jain (1990)	1985	subsidiaries in Singapore, Malaysia and India	local firms from the same sector	questionnaire (managers, unions)	human resource management, decision making
	1982–1983	8 subsidiaries in Canada	Parent companies in Japan	questionnaires and interviews	human resource management, decision making

Appendix 2: *continued*

Authors	Date of the survey	Japanese subsidiaries surveyed	Other firms studied	Méthod	Thèmes
Ishida (1986a)	1980– 1982	39 subsidiaries in Asia, 18 in the US, 23 in Germany		questionnaires (Japanese managers)	human resource management, work attitude
Johnson (1977)	1977	12 subsidiaries in the US	12 American firms	questionnaire (managers), interviews (workers)	communication, decision making, performances, work satisfaction

REFERENCES

Abegglen, James C., *The Japanese Factory*, The Free Press, Glencoe Illinois, 1958.

Abegglen, James C., Stalk, George Jr, *Kaisha, la stratégie des entreprises japonaises*, Les Editions d'organisation, Paris, 1985.

Abo, Tetsuo, "Japanese Motor Vehicle Technologies Abroad in the 1980s", Jeremy, D. J., (sous la direction de), *The Transfer of International Technology*, Edward Elgar, Londres, 1991.

Aoki, Masahoki, "Autoportrait de 11 sociétés japonaises particulièrement performantes", *Cahiers du Japon*, numéro spécial, 1990.

Asanuma, Banri, "Manufacturer-Supplier Relationships in Japan and the Concept of Relation Specific Skill", *Journal of the Japanese and International Economies*, mars, vol 3/1, 1989.

Bartlett, Christopher A., Ghoshal, Sumantra, *Managing Across Borders: The Transnational Solution*, Century Business, Londres, 1989.

Coriat, Benjamin, *Penser à l'envers – Travail et organisation dans l'entreprise japonaise*, Christian Bourgois Editeur, Paris, 1991.

Costa, Isabel de, Garanto, Annie "Entreprises japonaises et syndicalisme en Europe", *Mouvement social*, janvier-mars 1993.

Drucker, Peter F., "What we can learn from Japanese business", *Harvard Business Review*, mars - avril, vol. 49/2, 1971.

Dunning, John H., *Japanese Participation in British Industry*, Croom Helm, Londres, 1986.

Emmott, Bill, *Japan's Global Reach*, Century, Londres, 1992.

Florida, Richard, Kenney, Martin, *Beyond Mass Production*, Oxford University Press, 1993.

Florida, Richard, Kenney, Martin, "Transplanted Organization: The Transfer of Japanese Industrial Organization in the US", *American Sociological Review*, juin, vol. 56/1, 1991.

Fukuda, John K., "The Internationalization of Japanese Business – Different Approaches, Similar Problems", *The International Executive*, janvier/février, vol. 34/1, 1992.

Gleave, Simon, Oliver, Nick, "Human Resource Management in Japanese Manufacturing in the UK: 5 Case Studies", *Journal of General Management*, automne, vol. 16/1, 1990.

Jain, Hem C., "La gestion des ressources humaines dans quelques entreprises japonaises, dans leurs filiales à l'étranger et dans des firmes comparables des pays d'implantation", *Revue internationale du travail*, vol. 129/1, 1990.

JETRO, *8th Survey of European Operations of Japanese Companies in the Manufacturing Sector*, 1992.

JETRO, *Current Situation of Japanese Business Operations in Europe, The 7th Survey Report*, 1991.

Job, Bruno, *La formation en Grande-Bretagne et les entreprises japonaises, mimeo*, 1992.

Koike, Kazuo, *Understanding Industrial Relations in Modern Japan*, Macmillàn, Londres, 1988.

Kobayashi, Noritake, "The Patterns of Management Style Developing in Japanese Multinationals in the 1980s", dans *Japan's Emerging Multinationals – An International Comparison of Policies and Practices*, Susumu Takamiya, Keith Thurley, (sous la direction de), University of Tokyo Press, 1985.

Levine S.B., Taira, K., "Interpreting Industrial Conflict : the Case of Japan", dans *Labor Relations in Advanced Societies: Issues and Problems*, Martin B., Kassalow E.M., (sous la direction de), Carnegie Endownent for International Peace, Washington, 1974.

MITI, *Dainijuichikai – Wakaguni Kigyo no kaigai jigyo katsuyo*, Tsusho sangyosho sangyo seisaku kyoku kokusai sangyo kahen, Tokyo, 1992.

MITI (1992), (à compléter).

Ohno, T., *L'esprit Toyota*, Masson, Paris, 1989.

Oliver, Nick, Wilkinson, Barry, *The Japanization of British Industry*, Basil Blackwell, Oxford, 1988.

Ouchy, William, *Théorie Z*, InterEditions, Paris, 1982.

Pascale, Richard T, Athos, Anthony G, *The Art of Japanese Management*, Simon/Schuster, New York, 1981.

Rehder, Robert R., "Japanese Transplants : In Search of a Balanced and Broader Perspective", *Columbia Journal of World Business*, printemps, 1989.

Trevor, Malcolm, White, Michael, *Under Japanese Management*, Heinemann, Educational Books, Londres, 1983.

Tung, Rosalie L., "Selection and Training Procedures of US, European and Japanese Multinationals", *California Management Review*, vol. 25/1, 1982.

Watanabe, Susumu, "Le cercle de qualité japonais : d'où vient son succès?", *Revue internationale du travail*, vol 130/1, 1991.

White, Michael, Trevor, Malcolm, *Under Japanese Management – The Experience of British Workers*, Heinemann Educational Books, Londres, 1983.

Wickens, Peter, *The Road to Nissan*, Macmillan, Londres, 1985.

Womack, James P., Jones, Daniel T., Roos, Daniel, *The Machine that Changed the World*, Rawson Associates, New York, 1990.

7

The Research and Development of Japanese Multinational Enterprises in Europe

Marina Papanastassiou & Robert Pearce

There has recently been a very substantial increase in the number of research and development (R&D) laboratories run by Japanese Multinational Enterprises (MNEs) in Europe. This reflects the view that leading Japanese enterprises, like their key rivals from North America and Europe itself, recognize the importance of an international perspective on both the creation and use of technology as a major element of their global-competition strategies. Thus, changes in the ways in which MNEs have approached their worldwide competition over the past 30 years have implied a much greater commitment to the development of global perspectives on both the creation and implementation of technology. This has not only been reflected in a notable growth in the number of overseas R&D facilities set up by MNEs, but also in an increase in their scope in order to embrace much more ambitious roles.

Thus in the era when MNEs in many industries used their overseas subsidiaries mainly to supply protected host-country markets with their established range of products, there seemed to be only a limited role for overseas R&D. Such R&D facilities would rarely be required to do more than adapt existing products (and their production processes) in relatively minor ways to respond to local needs and conditions. However, with the increase in global competition, MNEs were often forced to restructure their approach towards a more integrated global strategy in which individual subsidiaries took on new, more outward-looking, roles.[1] This change in roles of MNE subsidiaries also had important implications for their R&D activities.

To elaborate the background to the evolution of the wider scope of overseas R&D operations in the strategies of MNEs we firstly draw a distinction between three types of producing subsidiaries that such laboratories might support.[2] The first of these, termed truncated miniature replica (TMR) played the traditional import-substituting role noted above by supplying a host-country market with established products. The declining viability of a TMR-based strategy as the competitiveness of an increasingly interdependent global economy emerged, led to new roles for many subsidiaries. One possibility in this context was that subsidiaries should take on a much more specialized and export-oriented role. In this case they would work within a network of similar facilities by supplying a small part of the MNE's established product range (or perhaps component parts) to wider regional or global markets. We term such facilities rationalized product (RP) subsidiaries.

Where as such networks of RP subsidiaries provide an approach that can supply an established product range in a very cost-competitive way, it does not seem very well oriented to achieving competitiveness through product differentiation and innovation. In technologically-dynamic industries leading MNEs need to be able to regularly innovate new product concepts, and to do so in ways that also respond to different needs of particular regional markets. In this context world (or regional) product mandate (WPM or RPM) subsidiaries play a much more widely creative export-oriented role than RP subsidiaries. Thus a RPM, for example, may play a role in a MNE's global-innovation strategy by taking the broad technology of a new product concept and developing a distinctive variant of the product to meet the particular needs of its regional market. The RPM will then take full responsibility for producing and marketing its product. Thus the RPM will have a laboratory which operates with its production and marketing personnel to enable it to make the best use of new group technology in its target markets, and thus help the group to implement an effective differentiated innovation of its new product concept worldwide.

---

[1] In the terms used by Porter (1986), MNEs moved from a multidomestic to a global strategy, see also (Pearce 1992).

[2] See (Pearce 1992).

In order to use their technological potential to effectively backup the implementation of a global strategy we see MNEs using three different types of overseas R&D laboratory.[3] The first of these, the support laboratory (SL), focuses on assisting overseas operations in effectively utilizing the MNE's current technology. Its work is thus limited to the adaptation of existing products and/or production processes, in order to support the ability of an allied producing subsidiary to implement them in the most effective way. The role of the SL is clearly most relevant in assisting a TMR subsidiary to supply its local market competitively. By contrast, since the host-country market is not distinctively relevant to what an individual RP subsidiary produces, the type of product adaptation that SLs might supply to TMRs would not be relevant to them. The product to be produced is defined by group needs, and the role allocated to a particular RP subsidiary reflects its production capability. Thus the only direct R&D support likely to be provided to a RP subsidiary would be to help it to make the best use of the production potential of its host-country conditions (i.e. process adaptation). It is possible, however, that somewhere within a network of RP subsidiaries, quite ambitious product adaptation might be carried out by a particularly powerful SL, in order to keep the product range competitive in its markets.

The second type of overseas laboratory, the locally integrated laboratory (LIL), works in conjunction with the management, marketing and engineering units of a subsidiary to develop a distinctive product. The subsidiary then takes overall responsibility for the production and marketing of the product, and for its continued competitive evolution. Thus it is clear that LILs will provide key inputs into the WPM or RPM operations described earlier. In doing so their development work may play a role in the MNE's overall innovation strategy in a way that greatly exceeds the adaptation aims of SLs.

As part of the more globally-focused approach to innovation many MNEs are also using overseas R&D units in the more basic research work aimed to provide the new technology which is intended to underpin the derivation of important new product concepts. Thus this precompetitive phase of the work may be carried out by networks of geographically-dispersed, but centrally-coordinated, research facilities. Thus this third type of overseas R&D unit is termed internationally interdependent laboratories (IILs), since they are likely to be more closely linked to similar units in other

---

[3] See (Pearce 1989).

countries than with any production or marketing units in their host countries.

We develop our discussion of Japanese MNEs' R&D operations in Europe against the background outlined above. Two hypotheses can be suggested with respect to possible distinctive elements in Japanese companies' overseas R&D. Firstly, with regard to work directly supporting local production, we would expect LILs to be relatively more prevalent (compared with SLs) in Japanese overseas laboratories than in those from other home countries. This reflects the view that most Japanese MNEs (at least with respect to their operations in developed countries) have emerged during the global-strategy, rather than import-substitution, era. Thus they are most likely to have articulated the role for overseas R&D in the global-innovation (RPM/LIL) context, with relatively little hangover of SLs backing TMR or RP subsidiary operations. Secondly, a perceived weakness in Japan's basic-research capability may have led Japanese MNEs to be especially keen to pursue foreign sources of such work and incorporate them in IIL type facilities.

7.1. THE EMERGENCE OF OVERSEAS R&D IN JAPANESE MNES

7.1.1   Foreign R&D by Japanese MNE is still Limited

The first piece of evidence on the rise of internationalized R&D operations amongst the world's leading enterprises that we review derives from a survey carried out by Pearce and Singh in 1989/90.[4] In this study the role of overseas R&D was investigated through a questionnaire sent to 623 parent laboratories, i.e. either corporate-level R&D units (physically located at corporate headquarters or otherwise distinguished as the corporate unit) or the main R&D facilities of major divisions in diversified firms. Satisfactory replies were obtained from 245 of these.

A question in the Pearce and Singh survey asked responding parent laboratories to list all of their R&D facilities by country.

---

[4] These comprised the 500 largest industrial enterprises in the world as derived from the Fortune listings, plus 30 more which had substantial numbers of overseas laboratories, plus 30 similar companies without overseas R&D (to match the 30 self-selecting overseas R&D oriented enterprises).

Table 1: Location of Laboratories of the World's Leading Industrial Enterprises

Home country of parent company	Laboratories per parent company							Total labs.	Total parents
	Home Country	USA	UK	Other Europe	Japan	Other C'try	Total o'seas		
Japan	5.4	1.6	0.2	1.1	–	1.1	4.0	236	25
USA	3.8	–	0.4	0.7	0.3	0.4	1.7	568	104
UK	2.7	0.9	–	0.8	0.1	0.5	2.3	174	35
Other Europe	3.9	0.9	0.4	2.4	0.4	0.5	4.6	313	37
Other Countries	1.9	0.4	0.1	0	0	0	0.5	24	10
Total								1315	211

Source: (Pearce, Singh, 1992a)

1. Other European countries (excluding UK) except the home country.

This information was provided by 211 of the parent laboratories, covering a total of 1,315 separate facilities, of which 785 were in the MNE groups' home countries and 530 overseas. The results from this question, presented in Table 1, show that, at least in terms of numbers of laboratories,[5] overseas R&D was well established in certain leading Japanese MNEs by the end of the 1980s. Thus the figure of 4.0 overseas laboratories per responding Japanese parent ranks second only to the 4.6 of Other European (i.e. non-UK) companies. Indeed since, as the table shows, the vast majority of the foreign R&D of the Continental European companies is within Europe the distribution of the Japanese laboratories may be

___

[5] Expenditure figures are less indicative of the role for overseas R&D in Japanese MNEs. Thus of Japanese parent laboratories that answered a question on the share of total MNE group R&D expenditure carried out by overseas subsidiary laboratories, 63 % said this was zero, compared with 44 % of all respondents (Pearce, Singh 1992b, Table 1). Similarly none of the Japanese respondents reported overseas R&D as being over 10 % of total, compared with 29 % of all respondents. The contrast between these expenditure figures and the quite substantial overseas orientation suggested by numbers of laboratories probably reflects the recent origins, and therefore relatively small size, of Japanese laboratories abroad.

Table 2:   Share of Foreign R&D units According to the Date of Establishment

	Pre-1940		1940–1959		1960–1969		1970–1979		1980–1990	
	Home	O'seas	Home	O'seas	Home	O'seas	Home	O'seas	Home	O'seas
Japan	5	0	5	0	11	0	4	3	6	31
USA	29	2	39	11	27	14	13	20	25	19
UK	12	3	16	4	8	7	5	12	8	15
Other Europe	10	4	11	3	7	8	4	16	5	14
Other Countries	1	1	5	0	4	0	1	1	2	1
Total	57	10	76	18	57	29	27	52	46	80

Source: (Pearce, Singh 1992a)

indicative of a more genuinely global approach. From an alternative perspective the Japanese respondents had 0.74 laboratories overseas for each one in the home country. Though this again ranked behind Other European firms, with 1.18 laboratories overseas for each one at home, and those from the UK (0.85), it ranked well ahead of the USA firms' figure of 0.45. Industries in which Japanese parent units reported more laboratories overseas than in Japan were pharmaceuticals and consumer chemicals, electronics and electrical appliances, motor vehicles (including components), and industrial and agricultural chemicals.

In the question which asked parent laboratories to list their R&D units by country, they were also requested to provide the dates of establishment of these facilities. Though this information was only available for 452 laboratories the results, given in Table 2, clearly indicate the way in which overseas R&D has generally emerged alongside the expansion of overseas sales and production in leading MNEs. Thus only 15% of the laboratories set up before 1940 had been outside the company's home country, whilst the comparable ratio for the period 1940 to 1959 only increased to 19%.

During the 1960s, 34% of the laboratories established by responding companies were overseas, followed by a major surge to 66% in the 1970s and 63% in the 1980s. The emergence of overseas R&D amongst Japanese firms has been even more dramatic and recent than that for the broader sample. Whilst 67% of the responding Japanese firms' home-country facilities had been set up before 1970, all of those overseas were established after that date. Thus 43% of the Japanese companies' new R&D units were overseas in the 1970s, and 84% of those in the 1980s. This major shift in Japanese companies' location patterns for research laboratories partly reflects the now natural complementarity of such facilities with their expanding overseas production. However, it may also include some response to the already clear implementation of global perspectives on technology of US and European MNEs, as reflected in the rise of their overseas laboratories in the 1970s.

As a further reflection of the process of evolution of overseas R&D the Pearce and Singh survey asked parent laboratories to evaluate the relevance of four possible developments with respect to the international location of R&D in their company. As Table 3 shows almost two-thirds of responses indicated a likely 'increased emphasis on a globally-integrated R&D network', with one-eighth expecting to place 'more emphasis on autonomous overseas laboratories' and one-fifth anticipating 'more use of the centralized facility'. In broad terms this suggests a continued momentum in internationalization of R&D, in direct support of strategies for global competition. These perspectives are most clearly endorsed by Japanese respondents, which had the strongest tendency to favor increased use of globally-integrated R&D networks and by far the least inclination to expect retrenchment to a centralized unit. These replies may be seen as compatible with the view that by coming relatively late to the setting up of overseas R&D facilities, and by doing so when most MNEs have already adopted a global approach to competitive strategy, Japanese firms have avoided the need for the traditional local-market-support role for these units. Newly established Japanese R&D facilities may well have moved directly into the role of either helping the implementation of a globally-integrated approach to innovation, or taking a position in an international network of basic research units.

One last piece of evidence from this survey further supports the view of a relatively strong tendency towards the recognition of a potential role for overseas R&D in Japanese companies. Those companies which currently had no R&D facilities overseas were asked if they had 'recently considered initiating, or permitting the establishment of, a foreign R&D facility'. A positive answer to this question was provided by 44% of relevant Japanese respondents, compared with 36% of those from US, 29% from Other Europe and 18% from UK.

Further perspectives on the role of overseas operations in the creation of technology by Japanese companies can be obtained by the

Table 3:   Parent Laboratory Attitudes to Future R&D Strategy

	% Parent country				
	Japan	US	UK	Other Europe	TOTAL
More use of the centralized facilitiy	7.4	18.1	33.3	21.1	20.2
More emphasis on autonomous overseas laboratories	11.1	8.4	19.4	15.8	12.8
Increased emphasis on a globally-integrated R&D network	81.5	69.9	41.7	60.5	63.8
No change	–	3.6	5.6	2.6	3.2
Total	100	100	100	100	100

Source: (Pearce, Singh 1992a)

use of data on patenting in the USA.[6] The data on each patent granted records the location of the research facility originally responsible for the innovation, and the firm to which the patent has been granted. Work carried out in collaboration between researchers at the University of Reading and the Science Policy Research Unit of the University of Sussex made it possible to establish the ultimate ownership of patents where they had been granted to affiliates of MNEs. This meant that for a large number of the world's leading industrial enterprises[7] data was available on the total number of patents granted to the group in the USA in a particular year, and the number of these that were attributable to research performed outside of the MNE's home country. In Table 4 the growth rates of the overseas patenting and total patenting of these enterprises from 1969/72 to 1987/90 are presented, broken down by the home country of the firm. Table 5 presents the share of overseas patents in total patents by home country of firm over the period.

---

[6] The data on the geographical origins of patents granted in the USA have been compiled at the University of Reading in collaboration with the SPRU (University of Sussex). The data were prepared by the Office of Technology Assessment and Forecast, US Patent and Trademark Office, with the support of the Science Indicators Unit, US National Science Foundation.

[7] The data covers all the firms from the sample of the 792 largest industrial enterprises in the world in 1982 analyzed by (Dunning, Pearce 1985) for which patenting records were available, plus additionnal companies excluded from that sample but where patenting was extensive.

Table 4: Growth Rates in US Patents Granted to the World's Largest Firms, to Between 1969/1972 and 1987/1990

Home country	Overseas patenting				Total Patenting			
	1973/77	1978/82	1983/86	1987/90	1973/77	1978/82	1983/86	1987/90
Japan	163.3	135.2	186.7	210.5	228.5	290.7	389.7	597.6
USA	133.9	117.2	114.2	121.7	112.0	89.8	74.4	75.9
Europe	132.9	111.7	104.8	132.3	147.9	131.1	111.5	129.3
EC	123.9	103.2	104.4	136.7	144.3	129.6	112.2	132.4
UK	107.6	77.7	73.0	88.7	111.2	85.8	69.2	81.9
Germany	144.7	154.8	160.7	221.3	167.3	163.7	141.7	165.7
France	149.3	123.6	145.3	292.0	158.0	140.7	129.3	150.7
Netherlands	137.1	115.8	129.1	177.1	145.9	122.5	120.5	165.6
Other Europe	167.1	143.9	106.1	115.5	166.1	138.7	108.1	113.8
Sweden	161.6	168.8	181.4	174.7	149.2	120.7	113.4	111.0
Switzerland	164.8	133.7	88.8	98.0	167.9	135.8	94.9	101.4
Total	134.2	114.3	109.5	130.1	127.2	111.4	102.1	120.0

1: 1969/1972 = 100

Source: US patent database held at the University of Reading with the support of the Patent and Trademark Office, US Department of Commerce

For Japanese firms the data on growth of total patents presented in Table 4 strongly verifies the view that, over the most recent two decades, their commitment to creation of new technology has greatly outstripped that of their leading rivals. Thus whilst Japanese firms' patenting in the USA increased almost six times over the period 1969/72 to 1987/90, the patenting growth rate only exceeded 50% for Germany, France and Netherlands among enterprises from major competing countries. Reflecting this the Japanese firms accounted for 6.1% of all patents taken out by the leading enterprises in the USA in 1969/72 and for 30.3% in 1987/90.[8] US patents attributed to the overseas R&D operations of Japanese MNEs doubled over the period 1969/72 to 1987/90, which represents a growth rate well in excess of the average for all of the leading firms covered, though it is below

---

[8] The figures for the intervening periods were 10.9 % for 1973/77, 15.9 % in 1978/82, and 23.2 % in 1983/86.

Table 5:   Share of Total US Patents Granted to the World's Largest Firms Accounted for by their Overseas R&D, in %

Home country of firms	1969–72	1973–77	1978–82	1983–86	1987–90
Japan	2.6	1.9	1.2	1.3	0.9
USA	5.0	5.8	6.5	7.6	8.0
Europe	28.8	25.9	24.6	27.1	29.5
EC	27.4	23.5	21.8	25.5	28.3
UK	45.4	43.9	41.1	47.9	49.2
Germany	12.8	11.0	12.1	14.5	17.1
France	8.2	7.7	7.2	9.2	15.9
Netherlands	50.4	47.4	47.7	54.0	53.9
Other Europe	36.2	36.4	37.6	35.5	36.8
Sweden	18.0	19.5	25.2	28.8	28.3
Switzerland	44.5	43.6	43.8	41.6	43.0
Total	10.3	10.9	10.6	11.1	11.2

Source: As Table 4.

that for France and Germany.[9] Of course the growth rate of overseas patenting by Japanese enterprises is still low relative to that for their total patenting, so that Table 5 shows a fall in the overseas share. Table 5 also shows that the share of patents in Japanese companies that are attributed to their overseas activity is still much lower than that of their leading rivals. This may suggest that the emerging overseas R&D in these Japanese enterprises is playing a distinct supporting role within the strong firm-level momentum towards the creation and implementation of competitive new technologies. Thus the expansion of overseas R&D in Japanese enterprises appears to have been playing a role which is complementary to a parallel expansion of R&D operations in Japan. This may well contrast with the developments in firms from other countries (e.g., Germany and France) where the growth rate in overseas patenting clearly exceeds that from home-country operations, so that Table 5 shows a notable rise in the overseas share in recent years. In such cases it seems more likely that some, at least, of the overseas R&D substitutes for

---

[9] In 1969/72 Japanese companies accounted for 1.5 % of the patents taken out in USA as a result of the overseas R&D of leading enterprises. The comparable figures were 1.9 % for 1973/77, 1.8 % for 1978/82, 2.6 % for 1983/86 and 2.5 % for 1987/90.

work that might have been carried out at home. Thus in enterprises from several other countries, where the apparent overall growth of technological activity is much lower than for Japanese companies, it seems plausible that the implementation of overseas R&D operations may often represent restructuring within a program whose overall magnitude is relatively unchanged. This contrasts with our suggestion that in Japanese companies the overseas component is a distinctive increment in a R&D growth program. In any case it seems likely that much of the surge in the setting up of overseas laboratories by Japanese MNEs, that we discussed earlier, is too recent to have resulted in patenting during the period covered, but that it clearly might produce a quite decisive rise in the share of overseas patents in the near future.

As a final part of this review of broad magnitudes in the emergence of overseas R&D in Japanese MNEs we look briefly at some evidence of such activity amongst their subsidiaries in the USA, using data from the US Department of Commerce's 1987 Benchmark Survey. This data shows that in 1987 Japanese subsidiaries accounted for only 4.7% of the total R&D expenditure of foreign firms in the USA in all industries, and for 4.5% of that in the manufacturing sector. Within manufacturing Japanese firms accounted for their highest share of foreign R&D in the USA in machinery (10.8%)[10] and primary and fabricated metals (8.2%) and for particularly small shares in food and kindred products (1.7%) and chemicals and allied products (1.6%). Once these R&D expenditures are expressed as a share of sales some rather different perspectives emerge. Though the overall research intensity of Japanese operations in the US is shown in Table 6 to be very low, this mainly reflects the limited R&D expenditure in the wholesale trade sector which accounts for a large share of Japanese MNEs' sales in the USA. In the manufacturing sector the R&D intensity of Japanese companies is, whilst still clearly below average, rather more in line with that of other investing countries. This is especially true of the machinery industry, whilst operations in chemicals and allied products are also relatively research intensive.

Another perspective on Japanese R&D is illustrated in results quoted by Graham (1992, Figure 6), which express these expenditures as a percentage of total company-funded R&D in USA (i.e. including that of the domestic operations of US-owned companies). From a level

---

[10] Due to reasons of confidentiality, data do not distinguish the electric and electronic equipment sector.

Table 6: Research-intensity[1] of Foreign Subsidiaries' Operations in the USA, by Home Country and Industry, 1987.

Home Country	JAPAN	EUROPE	TOTAL
All industries	0.16	0.99	0.88
Manufacturing	1.61	2.23	2.48
Food and kindred products	0.16	0.28	0.25
Chemicals and allied products	2.39	NAS	4.46
Primary and fabricated metals	0.36	0.68	0.59
Machinery	3.37	3.28	3.92
Other manufacturing	0.36	NAS	0.88
Wholesale trade	0.03	0.23	0.13
Other services	0.04	0.08	0.24
Other industries (incl. petroleum)	0.00	0.48	0.36

[1] Expenditure on research and development as a percentage of sales.

NAS — not available separately (included in relevant totals).

Source: US Department of Commerce, Bureau of Economic Analysis. Foreign Direct Investment in the United States. 1987 Benchmark Survey, Final Results. Tables E-3 and H-4

of only slightly over 0.1% in 1977 the share of Japanese subsidiaries' R&D rose slowly but steadily to reach 0.5% in 1987. In the next two years this share then increased very substantially, to almost 0.9% in 1988 and 1.1% in 1989. Since there was also some rise in all R&D expenditure in USA in those two years, the absolute rise in that of the Japanese subsidiaries was in fact around 2.5 times.

7.1.2   Nature and motivation of overseas R&D in Japanese MNEs

We now turn to the evaluation of the two hypotheses about the R&D activity of Japanese MNEs outlined in the introduction. These were, firstly, that basic research and supply-side influences would be more important to overseas R&D in Japanese MNEs than in those from other countries, and, secondly, that, among market-focused activities, product development (rather than adaptation) would be relatively more important in Japanese MNEs than in the more well established ones.

Table 7:   Relative Importance of Different Types of R&D in Overseas Laboratories[1]

Type of Research	Average response[2] JAPAN	USA	UK	Other Europe	TOTAL
Basic/Original	1.89	1.24	1.50	1.44	1.40
Applied research to derive new products in present industry	1.83	1.80	1.88	2.18	1.89
Applied research to derive new production technology in present industry	2.00	1.80	1.79	1.95	1.85
Improvement of existing products and/or techniques	2.08	2.04	2.04	2.26	2.09
Applied research to derive additional products in new areas of specialization	1.73	1.64	1.67	1.79	1.71

[1] Responding parent laboratories were asked which of the categories of research work they considered to be, (a) relatively more important in overseas R&D units than in the parent, (b) equally important in overseas and parent R&D units, (c) relatively less important in overseas R&D units than in parent's, (d) not performed in either parent or overseas R&D units.

[2] The average response was calculated by giving a value of 3 to a response of type (a), 2 to a response of type (b), 1 to a response of type (c), and averaging over relevant respondents. Responses of type (d) were excluded from the calculation.

Source: (Pearce and Singh Survey)

In Table 7 we present data from the Pearce and Singh survey which address directly the relative role of various types of R&D in MNEs' overseas laboratories. This certainly seems to confirm the distinctive position of basic research in Japanese MNEs' overseas R&D. Thus basic research is seen as being evaluated as much more important in Japanese overseas R&D than in that of MNEs from the other countries or areas. Of Japanese respondents to this question 18 % said that they did not carry out basic research in either overseas or parent R&D units. This was higher than for Other European respondents (14 %), but below USA (25 %) and UK (27 %). Where basic research was carried out 22 % of Japanese respondents said it was "relatively more important in overseas R&D units than in the parent", compared with 5 % for non-Japanese. Further, 44 % of Japanese respondents felt basic research was "equally important in overseas and parent R&D units" compared with 24 % for non-Japanese. According to Table 7, whilst basic research is clearly rated the least important of the five types of work by USA, UK and Other European companies, it ranks third for the Japanese, and thus generally appears to be given relatively equal consideration in a manner that is not likely to be the case for the firms from other countries.

Evidence relating to our second hypothesis is less decisive. Thus 'applied research to derive new products in the present industry' is of comparable importance in Japanese overseas R&D to that in USA and UK firms, though clearly less so than in Other European firms. Perhaps a little surprisingly applied research overseas 'to derive new production technology in the present industry' is slightly more important in Japanese MNEs than in those from other countries. Adaptation work (i.e. 'improvement of existing products and/or techniques') seems to be of conventional importance in Japanese overseas R&D, rather than being distinctively less relevant as speculated.

The manner in which MNE parent laboratories evaluated the extent to which a number of factors have influenced the types of work undertaken in their overseas R&D units are documented in Table 8. The most distinctive result for Japanese respondents is that (along with Other European countries) they are clearly the most responsive to the influence of 'a distinctive local scientific, educational or technological tradition conducive to certain types of research project.' In a manner which is likely to complement the relative importance of basic research in Japanese overseas R&D just noted, this suggests that these laboratories are located where an established high-quality scientific capability can provide inputs that contribute to a specialized facility operating as part of the MNE's longer-term program of technology generation.[11]

Another question in the Pearce and Singh survey also reflected on this influence. Thus parent laboratories that did not yet have overseas R&D, but which had recently considered the possibility of implementing such facilities, were asked to evaluate the relevance of certain factors in provoking this consideration. One of these factors was 'the desire to incorporate foreign located sources of expertise in centrally coordinated international research programs.'

---

[11] The fact that this factor is also particularly important for other European companies (despite their relatively low commitment to basic research, as noted in Table 7), suggests that certain countries in Europe offer exceptional research capability in particular industries. This, in turn, suggests that these supply-side elements are likely to be of particular relevance to decisions with regard to the nature and extent of Japanese MNEs R&D in Europe.

Table 8: Parent Laboratory Evaluation of Factors Influencing the Type of Work Done in Overseas R&D units

| Influencing factor | Home Country (average response)[2] | | | | | |
	Japan	USA	UK	Other Europe	Other Countries	TOTAL
A distinctive local scientific, educational or technological tradition conductive to certain types of research project	2.07	1.85	1.63	2.13	2.00	1.89
Cost factors	1.93	1.87	2.00	1.96	2.00	1.92
Only room for a small number of basic R&D laboratories	1.67	1.68	2.04	1.59	3.00	1.76
Need to adapt product to local market	2.64	2.54	2.48	2.76	3.00	2.60
Need to develop distinctive new products for the local market	2.43	2.29	2.40	2.46	3.00	2.37
Need to adapt production techniques to local conditions	2.43	2.31	2.75	2.30	2.00	2.35

Source: (Pearce, Singh 1992)

[1] Respondents were asked to rate a factor as 'never relevant', 'sometimes relevant', 'nearly always relevant'.

[2] Average obtained by giving a value of 1 to 'never relevant' 2 to 'sometimes relevant', 3 to 'nearly always relevant'.

This accounted for 47% of Japanese replies compared with 26 % of those from non-Japanese companies.[12]

The other results in Table 8 again suggest that Japanese overseas R&D was influenced to a fairly conventional extent by the need to respond to the distinctive needs of foreign markets, and producing environments, with no particular emphasis on development.

These results clearly indicate a more broadly-based approach to global R&D by Japanese companies, in which, in order to support their

---

[12] Japanese respondents had also been quite strongly influenced to consider overseas R&D by 'the desire of foreign producing facilities to upgrade their technological capability' (33 % of replies compared with 21 % of non-Japanese) and 'increased internationalization of R&D by our rivals' (20 % of Japanese replies compared with 31 % of US but only 13 % from the other countries).

increasing global competitiveness, they are less inclined to rely purely on home-country sources of expertise in basic science and more willing to locate and integrate sources of such capability in other countries. This approach then envisages individual overseas laboratories carrying out various specialized parts of an overseas R&D program organized and coordinated by, in probably the majority of cases, the parent laboratory. Where such an integrated approach exists an implication is a high level of project mobility, with an individual laboratory passing a project onto the parent (or another subsidiary facility) for completion or, perhaps, taking up a partly completed project from the parent unit or elsewhere in the group. Further questions in the Pearce and Singh survey investigated these possibilities. The expectation, derived from our earlier analysis, is that such project mobility would be especially strong in Japanese MNEs.

The first question on project mobility asked if promising projects were shifted from an overseas affiliate R&D laboratory to the parent unit at crucial stages of their development. This was clearly much more prevalent in Japanese MNEs. Thus 64% of Japanese respondents said it happened frequently or automatically, compared with 20% of non-Japanese. Further, all Japanese respondents said such project mobility occurred sometimes, though 19% of non-Japanese reported it never occurred. A complementary question investigated the reasons for project movement from overseas affiliate laboratories to the parent where it occured. This again confirmed the particular relevance of the ability to get work done effectively (i.e. supply-side factors) to Japanese R&D decision making. Thus 86% of Japanese respondents to this question indicated the most relevant reason was 'to better complete the research work'. Though this was also a strong motive for Other European respondents (73%) it was less relevant for USA (36%) and UK (54%) firms. By contrast only 14% of the Japanese firms felt projects returned to the parent laboratory because 'the parent country is the most likely market for innovation of a new product'. This was also relatively unimportant for Other Europe (20%) and UK (18%) firms, but of notable relevance for those from the USA (49%).[13]

When the reverse direction of project mobility was investigated 50% of Japanese respondents said promising projects were shifted from the parent R&D unit to a foreign R&D unit frequently (but

---

[13] The remaining replies for Other Europe, USA and UK firms relate to other (unspecified) reasons.

none automatically). This is rather less distinctive than for the other direction, since 42% of non-Japanese replies also suggested such project mobility was either frequent or automatic. However, when the motivation for such 'outward' project movement was investigated the Japanese case did again emerge as quite distinctive. Thus 43% of Japanese respondents who moved projects this way said that 'to better complete the research work' was a key motive, compared with only 12% for non-Japanese. Further 82% of non-Japanese respondents indicated that outward project mobility was implemented 'to ensure that the outcome is best directed to a particular market', which, though still the main motive for such movements in Japanese companies, was only supported in 50% of these replies. Once again this may be interpreted as reflecting a relatively high tendency in Japanese MNEs to react to the research capability of particular countries.

7.2.   JAPANESE MNES' R&D IN EUROPE

7.2.1   Extent

In Table 9 we present the most recent JETRO assessment of the extent of Japanese MNEs' R&D facilities in Europe. Very helpfully the JETRO data divides these facilities into those which are associated with Japanese manufacturing operations in Europe and those which operate independently from such linkages. In line with the distinctions outlined in the Introduction, the associated facilities could have two possible roles. The first would be essentially to support the European manufacturing operations in effectively producing an existing product from within the current range of the Japanese MNE group. Thus the primary role of such a SL would be the adaptation to European conditions of the current product and/or its production process.

The second role likely for an associated R&D facility would be to work closely with manufacturing and marketing operations in order to help implement a particularly European dimension within a global approach to innovation adopted by a Japanese MNE. Thus such an LIL would work in close association with subsidiary management and marketing personnel in order to develop, for the European market, the most effective (in terms of product characteristics and production techniques) variant of a more broadly conceived new product concept which the Japanese MNE is seeking to innovate globally in the most efficient and responsive way. In this case an RPM subsidiary is

Table 9:   Japanese R&D Facilities in Europe, by Country, 1990–1992[1]

	Associated Facilities[2]			Independent Facilities[3]		
	1990	1991	1992	1990	1991	1992
UK	15	33	54	9	15	19
France	7	11	21	4	7	9
Germany	8	17	25	6	12	14
Netherlands	3	4	5			1
Belgium	3	6	7	1	2	3
Ireland	1	1	1		1	1
Spain	11	15	23			
Italy	1	7	6	2	1	2
Finland			1			
Norway			1			
Sweden	1	1	3			
Denmark					1	1
Austria		1				1
Switzerland				1	3	3
Iceland		1	1			
Total	50	96	149	23	42	54

Source: JETRO. 8th Survey of European Operations of Japanese Companies in the Manufacturing Sector. Table 1.1

[1] Number of R&D facilities in January of each year.

[2] R&D facilities associated with manufacturing facilities.

[3] R&D facilities with no direct association with manufacturing operations.

integrating its technological (i.e. the LIL), marketing, engineering, and management capacity in order to fulfil its mandate to take complete responsibility for the creation, production and marketing of the distinctive product variant for the European market.[14]

As Table 9 shows, the number of associated R&D facilities of Japanese MNEs in Europe trebled between January 1990 and January 1992. The UK retained by far the largest share of these with 36% in 1992 compared with 30% in 1990. Germany and France also held their position in this growth, retaining shares

---

[14] In some cases such a Europe-based subsidiary could develop a product which is so successful that its potential market spreads well beyond Europe. In such a case its Japanese parent could then give it a world product mandate (WPM), and allow it full discretion to pursue these larger market possibilities.

Table 10: Associated R&D Facilities as Percentage of Manufacturing Facilities

	1990	1991	1992
UK	11.5	18.2	27.7
France	7.5	9.2	16.4
Germany	9.3	16.8	22.5
Netherlands	9.1	11.1	11.4
Belgium	12.0	18.8	17.9
Ireland	4.5	3.8	3.3
Spain	20.4	23.4	34.3
Italy	3.6	17.9	12.8
Finland	0	0	25.0
Norway	0	0	100.0
Sweden	16.7	16.7	33.3
Denmark	0	33.3	33.3
Austria	0	0	6.7
Iceland	0	100.0	100.0
Total	9.6	14.7	20.7

Source: As Table 9

of around 17% and 14% respectively. Spain's share of associated facilities fell from 22% in 1990 to the still prominent 15% in 1992. Table 10 documents a somewhat different perspective by expressing the number of Japanese associated R&D facilities as a percentage of Japanese manufacturing facilities, thus providing an indication of the proportion of those Japanese operations that could receive R&D support that actually did so.[15] Though the absolute level of this ratio could still be considered to be quite low, its rise from 9.6% in 1990 to 20.7% in 1992 is very notable. Such a rise could reflect two tendencies. Firstly, it could be the case that a particularly high proportion of new manufacturing operations were set up during the period with associated R&D facilities implemented right from the initiation. Since the number of manufacturing facilities reported by JETRO rose from 520 in 1990 to 721 in 1992 there is clearly some scope for such a development to influence the overall figures.

---

[15] Of course where a Japanese MNE has a number of manufacturing subsidiaries in Europe an associated R&D unit could support several, or all, of them. This is most likely to be the case if SLs backed a network of RPs. LILs may be considered to be more likely to have a one-to-one relationship with a RPM operation.

Secondly, the rise in the ratio would also be likely to incorporate a tendency for Japanese manufacturing subsidiaries that had previously operated without associated R&D units to now incorporate them. In any case Japanese MNEs seem to be reacting to increased competition in the European market by providing their European operations with more of the technological support needed to permit a distinctive reaction to the needs and potentials of the new environment.

The independent facilities, also covered in Table 9, have no direct link with any host-country manufacturing facilities, and are thus likely to be IILs. As previously indicated these facilities are likely to be carrying out rather more basic (or precompetitive) research that is integrated into the Japanese MNE group's wider program of original creative work, aimed at deriving the next generation of new products. The motivation for setting up such a facility in a particular country includes a variety of influencing factors, including availability of talented scientists, an accessible university system, cultural factors and previous experience of Japanese investors with the country. Another important element in this may also be the desire to match research moves made by leading rivals from the same globally-competitive industry, in a manner which may perhaps also reflect agglomeration influences on the location patterns of scientific development.

As Table 9 shows, over three-quarters of Japanese companies' independent laboratories in Europe in January 1992 were in the UK (35%), Germany (26%) or France (17%) where technological resources are particularly developed.

An alternative route through which Japanese firms can access European technological expertise is by undertaking research joint ventures with European companies. Table 12 presents some MITI evidence on this for the period 1982–87.[16] These figures indicate that Japanese research joint ventures with European partners are relatively rare in advanced technology sectors,[17] where US firms accounted for 85% of the total and firms from the four European countries accounted for only 11%. In conventional technology sectors the European countries' firms accounted for 43% of the joint ventures and US for 49%. It should be noted that these figures certainly do not imply

---

[16] Mowery and Teece (1992) note that the MITI 'report appears to have employed a fairly narrow, legalistic definition of a joint venture'.

[17] The majority of the research joint ventures in advanced technology sectors were in communications and computers; integrated circuits factory and office automation; biotechnology.

Table 11: International Research Joint Ventures Involving Japanese Firms, 1982–87 by Nationality of Partner Firms

	All technology Fields	Conventional technology	Advanced technology
United States	93	30	63
Canada	4	2	2
United Kingdom	13	8	5
Germany	9	7	2
France	7	6	1
Italy	5	5	0
Other	4	3	1
Total	135	61	74

Source: (Mowery, Teece 1992)

that Japanese companies did not place a high value on the general capability of the European science base in the more advanced areas of technology. Since other results[18] showed that the majority of these joint ventures focused on applied research and development work, the result for Europe may instead reflect a view by Japanese firms that European enterprises were not making an effective job of exploiting the potentials of European science in these areas. In this case it could be that the Japanese MNEs are opting to access European technology in these areas directly, through the establishment of their own facilities for both development work (LILs) and basic work (IILs), rather than being prepared to pick it up as, at least partially, embodied in the firm-level capability of European enterprises. The corollary of this argument would be that the Japanese companies are trusting their US counterparts to have done a better job of accessing the US technological capability in these advanced technology sectors. Again this argument also implies that Japanese enterprises are showing rather more faith in the ability of European enterprises to better realise technical possibilities in more conventional areas of technology.

---

[18] An analysis of a slightly larger number of cases than covered by Table 11 (Mowery, Teece, 1992, Table 7) showed that 46 % of Japanese firms research joint ventures in advanced technology sectors were "product oriented", 28 % were "market specified" (i.e related to "incremental product modifications for new markets") and 22 % involved "applied research". In conventional technology sectors the shares of these three types of work were 35 %, 43 % and 11 % respectively.

Table 12:   The Share of the US Patents Granted to Largest Japanese Firms as a Result of their Research in US or Europe, by Host Country or Region, 1969–90

Research done in	1969–72	1973–77	1978–82	1983–86	1987–90
US	71.5	83.4	89.6	88.5	79.7
Europe	28.5	16.6	10.4	11.5	20.3
EC	24.4	15.9	7.8	10.9	19.1
Germany	10.6	8.7	6.7	2.2	1.7
UK	8.1	2.5	0.4	7.3	15.8
France	0.8	1.8	0.4	0.3	0.2
Other EC	4.9	2.9	0.4	1.1	1.4
Non-EC Europe	4.1	0.7	2.6	0.6	1.2
Total	100.0	100.0	100.0	100.0	100.0

Remark: It should be noted that figures in Tables 12 to 15 exlcude, when relevant, data for the non-metallic minerals industry. This is because exceptionally high patenting attributed to European operations of Japanese firms in this industry in 1969/77 greatly distorts the picture of more pervasive general trends. Thus this industry accounted for 60 % of all Japanese companies' patents from European operations in 1969/77, but for only 17 % in 1978/90. In addition the non-metallic minerals industry accounted for less that 2 % of all patents attributed to the Europe-based overseas R&D operations of all MNEs throughout the period. Source: as Table 4.

7.2.2   Patenting in the USA

To investigate some alternative perspectives on Japanese MNEs' technological operations in Europe we turn now to some additional evidence on leading firm patenting in the USA. As noted in our discussion of this data in Tables 4 and 5 the information available on a particular patent includes the nationality of the parent company that ultimately owns the patent and also the location of the research that created the patented knowledge. In Tables 4 and 5 we looked at the contribution of overseas R&D to leading MNEs' total patenting. We now go beyond this to assess the relative role of Japanese MNEs' European operations.

The patent data in Table 12 shows that in 1969/72 Japanese-owned patents resulting from their MNEs' research in Europe accounted for 28.5% of all patents taken out in the USA as a result of their research in either Europe or the USA. This figure then declined to

16.6% in 1973/77 and further to 10.4% in 1978/82. A very slight rise in the European share to 11.5% in 1983/86 was followed by a much more substantial increase to 20.3% in 1987/90.[19] Table 14 presents information on the European share of the total patents originating from US or European R&D of Japanese MNEs by industry. Though the figures are quite volatile it is clear that instruments and electrical equipment are the two industries where Japanese MNEs have had the strongest tendency to focus their R&D operations in Europe. The traditionally strong European science base in the chemical industry seems to have attracted surprisingly little Japanese R&D.

In Table 13 we show the industry breakdown of the US patenting activity of Japanese firms' R&D operations in Europe and the USA. The most distinctive result for Europe is obviously the position of the electrical equipment industry,which accounted for 45.5% of all patents taken out by Japanese MNEs as a result of European research over the full 1969/90 period. Even against this strong background the rise in European patenting in the industry since 1983 has been remarkable. Thus 78% of all the electrical equipment patents taken out from Japanese firms' European research emerged in the period 1983/90, compared with 54% for all industries. A factor that may have contributed to this focus by Japanese firms could be the persistence of technologically strong European firms in key sectors of this industry. One element in this rise in patenting may then reflect the response to increasingly competitive market conditions in an industry where several major European firms remain viable on the basis of a distinctive innovative competitiveness. Thus Japanese electrical equipment firms may have been stimulated to carry out European research in SL or LIL facilities to adapt or develop products to better meet the market needs that their important local rivals were more naturally in tune with. In addition Japanese MNEs may be setting up IILs in this industry in order to secure access to the same European sources of more basic scientific expertise that may underwrite the long-term competitiveness of the European firms.

---

[19] The fall in European share in 1973/77 mainly reflected a very strong rise in Japanese firms' patents attributed to their US research, which was 262 % of its 1969/72 level in 1973/77 compared with 131 % for patenting from their European operations. The further fall in European share in 1978/82 was more due to a fall in Europe-based patenting, to 80 % of its 1969/72 level, than to further rises in US (to 274 % of 1969/72 level). The rises in the European share up to 1987/90 then reflected growth in European patenting exeeding that from US. Thus Japanese firms' patents attributed to their European research in 1987/90 were 304 % of their 1978/82 level compared with 139 % for patents from their US operations.

Table 13:   The Share of the US Patents Granted to Largest Japanese Firms as a Result of their Research in US and Europe, by Industry, 1969–90.

	USA					Europe				
	1969/ 72	1973/ 77	1978/ 82	1983/ 86	1987/ 90	1969/ 72	1973/ 77	1978/ 82	1983/ 86	1987/ 90
Food	0	0	6.2	2.5	1.2	0	0	0	0	0
Drink	0	0	0	0.6	0.3	0	0	0	0	0
Chemicals	48.9	32.5	36.1	25.0	13.8	11.4	6.5	7.1	2.4	3.5
Pharma'ticals	0	1.3	0	0.6	0.3	2.9	4.3	3.6	0	0
Metals	4.5	1.7	0	0.6	6.6	0	8.7	0	0	3.5
Mechanical	1.1	0.4	3.3	0.6	0.6	0	2.2	3.6	0	1.2
Electrical	23.9	27.3	21.2	24.1	29.9	25.7	13.0	32.1	75.6	61.2
Office equipment and computing	2.3	12.6	14.1	18.7	22.2	25.7	2.2	3.6	0	0
Motor vehicles	6.8	3.0	10.8	20.3	15.6	11.4	10.9	7.1	4.9	7.1
Other transport equipment	1.1	1.3	0	0.6	0	0	0	0	0	0
Textiles	1.1	2.6	0.4	0.3	1.2	0	6.5	0	2.4	0
Printing	1.1	0.4	0	0	0.3	0	2.2	3.6	0	3.5
Rubber	1.1	0	0	0.3	0.9	0	0	0	0	0
Oil	0	0.4	0	0	0.6	0	0	0	0	0
Instrum'ts	5.7	4.8	6.6	5.4	6.6	17.1	43.5	39.3	12.2	17.6
Other	2.3	11.7	1.2	0.3	0	5.7	0	0	2.4	2.4
Total	100.0	100.0	100.0	100.0	100.0	100.0	100.0	100.0	100.0	100.0

Comment: See Table 12

Source: As Table 4

Professional and scientific instruments emerges in Table 13 as the other industry in which Japanese firms seem to have had a relatively sustained and distinctive commitment to Europe-based research. By contrast patenting activity in chemicals and motor vehicles may be considered surprisingly low in Europe, especially as, like electrical equipment, these industries retain significant European competitors. Office and computing equipment is the industry that has shown the most distinctive rise to prominence in the patenting of US-based

Table 14: The Japanese-owned Share of US Patents due to Research in Foreign-owned Affiliates, by Host Country or Region, 1969–90

	%				
	1969–72	1973–77	1978–82	1983–86	1987–90
US	1.6	3.3	4.3	6.3	5.3
Europe	0.6	0.5	0.4	0.5	1.0
EC	0.6	0.6	0.3	0.6	1.0
Germany	0.8	0.9	0.8	0.3	0.3
UK	0.5	0.3	0.1	1.5	3.6
France	0.1	0.4	0.1	0.1	0.1
Other EC	0.5	0.5	0.1	0.3	0.3
Non-EC Europe	0.8	0.2	0.9	0.3	0.6

Comment: See Table 12

Source: As Table 4

Japanese MNEs. This may be attributed to the existence of strong US rivals, and thus strong technological agglomeration factors, in this industry, that are not matched in Europe.

Table 14 indicates the share of patenting due to Japanese-owned R&D facilities in the total patenting of foreign-owned R&D in particular host countries. For example, it is shown that in 1969/72 Japanese MNEs' patenting in the USA as a result of their US-based R&D was only 1.6% of that resulting from foreign R&D in the US (the major contributors obviously being subsidiaries of European and Canadian companies). This ratio rose steadily to 6.3% in 1983/86 and remained at 5.3% in 1987/90. Thus Japanese subsidiaries were a relatively strong growth force in foreign-owned technology operations in the USA in the past two decades. By contrast the comparable ratio in Europe only reached 1.0% in 1987/90. The only clear sign of growth in the share of Japanese subsidiaries' R&D in Europe was in the UK, where the ratio reached 3.6% in 1987/90. Of course it should be underlined again that the notable surge in establishment of Japanese R&D laboratories in Europe in recent years would not be reflected in patentable research in the period covered.

In Table 15 we provide data comparable to that in the previous table for selected industries. In Europe the greatest prominence for Japanese R&D clearly emerges in professional and scientific instruments. Despite the strong role of electrical equipment in Japanese

Table 15: The Japanese-owned Share of US Patent due to Research in Foreign-owned Affiliates in Selected Industries, by Host Country or Region, 1969–90

		1969/72	1973/77	1978/82	1983/86	1987/90
US	Chemicals	3.3	4.7	5.4	6.1	2.4
	Electricals	3.1	8.0	8.1	8.6	7.5
	Office equipment and computers	5.4	53.7	56.7	88.1	43.3
	Motors vehicles	6.4	3.5	14.9	42.1	41.6
	Instruments	55.6	64.7	64.0	65.4	88.0
Europe	Chemicals	0.3	0.2	0.1	0.1	0.2
	Electricals	0.5	0.3	0.5	1.5	2.0
	Office equipment and computers	3.0	0.2	0.2	0	0
	Motor vehicles	1.5	1.2	0.5	0.4	1.0
	Instruments	2.5	11.3	7.6	4.2	12.8
Germany	Chemicals	0.5	0.3	0.5	0.3	0.6
	Electricals	0.6	0.4	0.9	0.4	0.2
	Instruments	1.8	13.3	12.1	6.1	2.4
	UK Electricals	0.5	0.2	0.2	5.8	11.1
	Motor vehicles	1.6	0	0	0	2.6
	Instruments	2.6	7.0	0	0	27.3

Comment: See Table 12

Source: As Table 4

R&D operations that we noted in Table 13, it nevertheless emerges in Table 15 that Japanese subsidiaries only accounted for very small shares of the patenting due to foreign R&D in Europe in this industry. The exception to this does seem to be the rise in relative importance of Japanese R&D in the industry in the UK in 1983/90. One reason why the apparently strong commitment of Japanese MNEs to European electrical industry R&D as shown in Table 13 declines in relative significance in Table 15, may be that the same factors that we suggested attracted these Japanese operations also strongly attract the foreign R&D of other MNEs. This may include not only the activities of US companies but also intra-European R&D networks supporting the technology of the leading European electrical industry firms. In the USA Japanese subsidiaries have established notably strong positions in foreign-firm patenting in professional and scientific instruments,

Table 16: Activities carried out by Japanese Design Centers and R&D Facilities in Europe, by Industry[1]

	Total Replies	A%	B%	C%	D%	E%
Chemicals	28	17.9	35.7	25.0	21.4	–
Rubber products	8	25.0	25.0	25.0	25.0	–
Metal products	9	11.1	33.3	44.4	11.1	–
General machinery	24	4.2	33.3	45.8	8.3	8.3
Electronic and electrical appliances	38	2.6	28.9	42.1	18.4	7.9
Electronic parts	22	–	31.8	40.9	22.7	4.5
Transport equipment	12	–	33.3	50.0	16.7	–
Transport equipment parts	19	15.8	26.8	26.3	10.5	10.5
Precision machinery	8	12.5	25.0	50.0	12.5	–
Design centers & R&D facilities	42	11.9	45.2	19.0	19.0	4.8
Other	15	26.7	33.3	20.0	–	20.0
Total	225	10.2	34.7	33.3	16.0	5.8

A. Basic research; B. Product development; C. Change of product design and specifications; D. Development of production processes and technologies; E. Other.

[1] 105 companies supplied information on their type of research. Since many did more than one type there were 204 replies. Since some of the respondents were allocated to two industries their replies were included in both. Thus the total number of answers reported in the table is 225.

Source: (JETRO, 1991)

office equipment and computers and motor vehicles, whilst their position is also somewhat stronger than in Europe in chemicals and electrical equipment.

7.2.3 Role and Motivation

In this section we look at JETRO survey evidence on the nature of the work done in Japanese R&D facilities in Europe, and the factors that have influenced decisions regarding such units. The type of work carried out by Japanese MNEs' European R&D facilities are analyzed in Table 16. Despite our earlier discussion, which indicated a relatively prominent position for basic research in Japanese MNEs' overseas

Table 17:   Reasons for Conducting R&D Activities Unitarily at Head Office[1]

	Total Replies	A%	B%	C%	D%
Industry					
Chemicals and pharmaceuticals	18	38.9	–	55.6	5.6
Metals and metal products	12	50.0	8.3	41.7	–
General machinery	9	33.3	–	55.6	11.1
Electronic and electric appliances	14	28.6	14.3	57.1	–
Electronic parts	15	20.0	20.0	60.0	–
Transport equipment parts	10	50.0	10.0	30.0	10.0
Other	19	36.8	5.3	52.6	5.3
Total	97	36.1	8.2	51.5	4.1

A. Developing technologies of our own forms the basis of corporate growth. B. Japanese ways of thinking and designing are good enough to get along. C. There is no room for breaking up funds and manpower resources. D. Other.

[1] 68 of the firms that said research was caried out uniquely at head office answered a question indicating reasons why this occured. Several recognized two of the reasons, there were a total of 80 answers. Since some respondents were allocated to two industries, their replies were included in both. Thus the number of answers in the industry section of the table rise to 97.

Source (JETRO, 1992)

R&D, this was the least important of the four types of work specified, accounting for only 10% of replies. However, since respondents often replied that they did more than one type of work, it should be noted that 21% of the units whose answers are reported in Table 16 included basic research amongst their roles.[20]

Nevertheless it is clear that the other types of R&D work are prevalent in Japanese operations in Europe. Thus 35% of replies covered 'product development', the type of activity we attribute to

---

[20] Another factor may also contribute to the undervaluation of basic research in Table 16. Thus the fact that when a facility reported that it did more than one kind of research or development each type was recorded equally means that the table overvalues diversified laboratories and undervalues those that specialize in one type of work. Since it has been shown (Pearce, Singh 1992a) that laboratories doing basic research are much more likely to specialize on this than those doing adaptation and development work, it is likely that there is some systematic tendency for Table 16 to overvalue adaptation and development relative to basic research.

LILs. Matching these LILs, 33% of replies covered 'change of product design and specification', which is the function of SLs, whilst a further 16% covered 'development of production processes and technologies' which, at least when independent of product development, also seems likely to be a SL role.

The results reported in Table 17 essentially present the views of European subsidiaries of Japanese MNEs with respect to their group's approach to R&D strategy. The first result from this analysis is that almost one-quarter of respondents believed that their MNE group centralizes all the key elements of R&D at the head office in Japan. This, of course, means that a considerable majority of these Japanese companies were perceived (by their European subsidiaries) as finding some significant role for overseas R&D. Of the two types of overseas R&D distinguished in Table 17 the more prominent, with almost half the replies, was that 'some designing activities are left in the hands of European units'. This is in line with results from Table 16 and suggests that these design activities may cover SL work (adaptation) or LIL work (development). The second type of overseas R&D, which was covered by 30% of replies, was that 'international bases of basic research, product development or design are established to globalize corporate activities'. This, in fact, combines the two distinct elements of a global approach to innovation that we have observed. Thus it covers both networks of IILs seeking to create new product concepts, and networks of LILs seeking to effectively implement new products globally. This latter type of work is clearly strongest in pharmaceuticals (63% of replies). Though this networked type of operation is absent amongst general machinery respondents this is strongly compensated by a notable commitment to the more locally-focused type. This reflects the localization influence of the high levels of customization in this industry, which has emerged strongly in previous research (Papanastassiou and Pearce, 1992). A strong predominance of local influence over the global innovation approach also emerges in food-stuffs, transport equipment, and precision machinery.

In Table 18 the companies that suggested in the previous table that they kept their R&D centralized provide explanations for this decision. The most prominent explanation (just over half of replies) was that there was 'no room for breaking up funds and manpower resources'. This may reflect the influence of economies of scale in R&D[21] and/or the lack of the resources that would permit the overseas

---

[21] On economies of scale in R&D see (Pearce 1989, Pearce, Singh 1992a)

Table 18:   Reasons for Localizing R&D Facilities as seen by Japanese Operations in Europe[1]

	Total replies	A	B	C	D	E	F	G	H
Industry									
Chemicals	43	34.9	14.0	–	2.3	27.9	16.3	2.3	–
Pharmaceuticals	12	8.3	33.3	–	16.7	16.7	25.0	–	–
Ceramics, stone and clay products	17	35.3	17.6	–	11.8	11.8	11.8	–	5.9
Metals and metal products	24	37.5	8.3	–	4.2	29.2	12.5	–	4.2
General machinery	26	38.5	7.7	3.8	3.8	34.6	7.7	–	3.8
Electronic and electric appliances	105	30.5	17.1	3.8	1.9	20.0	9.5	5.7	11.4
Electronic parts	95	28.4	13.7	4.2	1.0	2.1	14.7	8.4	7.4
Transport equipment	14	35.7	14.3	–	–	28.6	7.1	–	14.3
Transport equipment parts	27	25.9	18.5	–	3.7	25.9	18.5	–	3.7
Precision machinery	15	46.7	6.7	–	–	26.7	–	–	20.0
Design centers and R&D facilities	60	20.0	25.0	1.7	16.7	13.3	11.7	6.7	1.7
Total	509	30.0	15.7	2.0	4.9	22.0	13.7	4.3	5.9

Answers A to H, as a percentage of the number of answers ("other" reasons are not mentioned) A. It is necessary to manufacture products locally according to local consumers' needs; B. Our horizon of research and development in terms of ideas and ways of thinking must be broadened by employing foreign researchers; C. To cope with anticipated friction over technological issues; D. One of the tasks ahead is to implement R&D projects jointly with foreign enterprises and research institutes; E. Information about what is going on in European markets has to be obtained as quickly as possible to meet intensifying competition for technological supremacy; F. We want to shorten lead times from research and development to commercialization of products; G. To make up for a shortage of R&D personnel in Japan; H. As part of efforts to become an insider in the local markets.

[1] 176 of the firms that recognised the need to localize R&D activities answered a question indicating reasons why this occurred. Since some of the respondents were allocated to two or more industries their replies were include in both. Thus the number of answers indicated in the industry section of the table rises to 509.

Source: (JETRO 1992)

extension of such operations. The other quite prominent reason for centralizing R&D was 'developing our own technologies forms the basis of corporate growth'. This suggests the persistence of a home-country-focused view of innovation (as formalized in Vernon's (1966) product cycle) as distinct from the more globally-dispersed approach detected in much recent work on R&D in MNEs. Relatively few respondents endorsed 'Japanese ways of thinking and designing are good enough to get along'. Lack of enthusiasm for this view supports the suggestion that the pursuit of foreign capabilities in technology (including distinctive approaches to product development for host markets) is relatively important in Japanese MNEs' perspectives.

Having dealt with the reasons for centralizing R&D, the JETRO analysis turns, in Table 19, to the reasons for decentralizing (i.e. localizing) R&D facilities. Clearly the most prominent of these (30% of replies) is that 'it is necessary to manufacture products locally according to local customers' needs'. This strengthens the impression from Tables 16 and 17 of an important role for SLs and LILs in enabling Japanese firms to respond fully to the European market. This motive was especially prominent in precision machinery. Two other prominent motives for localizing R&D are also related to the ability to react adequately to the competitive environment. Firstly, 20% of replies indicated that European R&D was a response to the belief that 'information about what is going on in European markets has to be obtained as quickly as possible to meet intensifying competition for technological supremacy'. The particularly local-market-responsive nature of general machinery is shown here. Secondly, 14% of firms replied that their European R&D came about because 'we want to shorten lead times from R&D to commercialization of products.' Pharmaceutical firms were notably responsive to this influence. Taken together these two factors strongly support our view that a growing role for overseas R&D in MNEs is related to the need to respond quickly to market conditions in globally-competitive industries, and, as part of this, to implement internationalized perspectives on innovation. Another relatively important influence (16% of replies) is that 'our horizon of R&D in terms of ideas and ways of thinking must be broadened by employing foreign researchers'. This is in line with the view of overseas R&D as serving a 'listening post' (or monitoring) function in globally-responsive enterprises, and, more directly, as seeing such R&D as being affected by the availability of quality personnel. The strength of Europe in pharmaceuticals is reflected in a strong response to this factor.

Table 19: Extent of Localization of Japanese R&D as Reported by their European Operations

	Number of Replies	A%	B%	C%	Total %
Country					
UK	102	23.5	45.1	31.4	100
France	46	17.4	63.0	19.6	100
Germany	56	21.4	48.2	30.4	100
Sourthern Europe	47	27.7	42.6	29.8	100
Northern Europe	21	28.6	28.6	42.9	100
Benelux	35	31.4	40.0	28.6	100
Total	311	23.8	45.7	30.5	100
Industry					
Foodstuffs	10	20.0	70.0	10.0	100
Textiles, clothing and made-up goods	8	62.5	37.5	22.5	100
Chemicals	40	40.0	37.5	–	100
Pharmaceuticals	8	25.0	12.5	62.5	100
Ceramics, stone and clay products	10	10.0	60.0	30.0	100
Metals and metal products	22	45.5	36.4	18.2	100
General machinery	30	23.3	76.7	–	100
Electronic and electric appliances	60	18.3	48.3	33.3	100
Electronic parts	52	28.8	36.5	34.6	100
Transport equipment	10	10.0	70.0	20.0	100
Transport equipment parts	29	27.6	44.8	27.6	100
Precision machinery	9	22.2	66.7	11.1	100
Design centers and R&D facilities	25	–	28.0	72.0	100
Total[1]	350	25.1	45.1	29.8	100

A. Basic research, product development and design activities are all uniformly conducted at head offices.

B. Some designing activities are left in the hands of European units to cater to local consumer needs.

C. International bases of basic research, product development or design are established to globalize corporate activities.

[1] Include 37 units from other non specified sectors. Since some of the respondents were allocated to two industries their replies were included in both. Thus the total number of replies reported in the industry part of the table excedes that in the country part.

Source: (JETRO, 1992)

7.2.4   Independent Facilities

The JETRO survey results permit us to analyze the particular characteristics of the independent 'design centers and R&D facilities', as distinct from those associated with manufacturing operations, in Europe (see discussion of Table 9). As would be anticipated Table 16 shows that these have a relatively strong tendency to do basic research, with 27% saying they performed such work (compared with 9% amongst associated facilities).[22] Product development was carried out by 33% of these independent facilities, which closely matched the 35% of units associated with manufacturing operations. One fifth of the independent units did work to change product design and specifications (compared with 35% of associated facilities), but none developed production processes and technologies (compared with 17% of associated facilities). A possible reason for the inclusion of product adaptation in such independent centers could be, as suggested in the Introduction to this chapter, to provide such support for a network of RP subsidiaries. In such a case it might not be appropriate (perhaps for group diplomatic reasons) to associate such a facility with any individual subsidiary in the network.

In Table 19 the analysis of reasons for localizing R&D facilities in Europe by Japanese companies shows that the most popular overall influence, the necessity 'to manufacture products locally according to local needs', was supported by only 20% of independent R&D facilities compared with 31% of those associated with manufacturing subsidiaries. Similarly the other highly rated local-market responsive factor, 'information about what is going on in European markets has to be obtained as quickly as possible to meet intensifying competition for technological supremacy', was supported by only 13% of the independent facilities compared with 23% of associated facilities. By contrast the independent facilities are more distinctively responsive to influences relating to the effectiveness of performing their scientific work. Thus the strongest influence on the localization of these units was 'our horizon of research and development in terms of ideas and ways of thinking must be broadened by employing foreign researchers', which was supported by 25% of the independent facilities compared with 15% of associated facilities. Also 17% of independent facilities

---

[22] In addition 20% of design center and R&D facility respondents said that they did work other than the four specified types. This may well refer to less easily classified precompetitive types of research rather than development or adaptation.

(compared with 3% of associated units) believed 'one of the tasks ahead is to implement R&D projects jointly with foreign enterprise and research institutes.

Further evidence on the distinctive focus of the independent facilities can be obtained from a question in the 8th JETRO survey (JETRO, 1992) which asked respondents about their aims and motives for establishing operations in Europe. A total of 386 replies were received, 23 from the independent design centers and R&D facilities and 363 from manufacturing subsidiaries. The question specified 17 possible motives with respondents permitted to endorse more than one. The main result for the design centers and R&D facilities is to confirm their strong focus on doing R&D work that is not directly related to the current needs of European-oriented operations. Thus 19 of the 23 stand alone R&D units (i.e. 83%) said that 'to carry out R&D activities in Europe' was a motive for their establishment, whilst only 8 (35%) endorsed 'to implement design and development operations in Europe'. Amongst manufacturing operations only 22 of 363 (6%) found the former of these to be a motive for their establishment, and 17 (5%) the latter.[23]

The JETRO survey (JETRO, 1992, Table III-17, p. 34) asked respondents to evaluate 9 possible specific measures to cope with the integration of the EC. Of the 18 independent design centers and R&D units responding 12 (67%) endorsed setting up that type of facility as a means of coping with the consequences of integration, which made it the most popular response with these units. Since other evidence from the JETRO survey indicates these facilities do not see their present operations as often directly supporting current Japanese production in Europe, their favorable response to this factor

---

[23] In Table 19 the analysis of reasons for localizing R&D facilities in Europe by Japanese companies shows that the most popular overall influence, the necessity 'to manufacture products locally according to local needs', was supported by only 20% of independent R&D facilities compared with 31% of those associated with manufacturing subsidiaries. Similarly the other highly rated local-market responsive factor, 'information about what is going on in European markets has to be obtained as quickly as possible to meet intensifying competition for technological supremacy', was supported by only 13% of the independent facilities compared with 23% of associated facilities. By contrast the independent facilities are more distinctively responsive to influences relating to the effectiveness of performing their scientific work. Thus the strongest influence on the localization of these units was 'our horizon of research and development in terms of ideas and ways of thinking must be broadened by employing foreign researchers', which was supported by 25% of the independent facilities compared with 15% of associated facilities. Also 17% of independent facilities (compared with 3% of associated units) believed one of the tasks ahead is to implement R&D projects jointly with foreign enterprise and research institutes.

is more indicative of a general belief in the role of these types of activities.[24] Amongst manufacturing subsidiaries 'establishing design centers and R&D facilities in Europe' was endorsed by 76 of 303 respondents (25%), which ranked it fourth of the nine measures offered. By industry, Japanese manufacturing companies were most inclined to favor establishment of design centers and R&D facilities in Europe in pharmaceuticals (33%), electronic and electrical appliances (45%) and precision machinery (33%). Since the latter two of these industries, in particular, are perceived as being ones where Japanese firms do not lack competitive technology, the response of European production units in these industries may well reflect a need to apply it more effectively in the European market, as part of a globally-integrated innovation strategy.

The survey evidence (JETRO, 1992, pp. 13–15) suggests a particularly strong tendency to establish independent design centers and R&D bases as wholly-owned facilities. Thus 16 of 23 responding facilities (70%) were set up as wholly-owned units. By contrast only 172 of 371 (45%) responding manufacturers were established as wholly-owned operations.[25] Of the 23 stand-alone R&D facilities only 4 (17%) were joint ventures with local interests compared with 93 (25%) of the 371 manufacturing facilities. Further only one (4%) of the R&D units was the result of merger and acquisition,[26] compared with 80 (22%) of manufacturing subsidiaries.[27]

When asked (JETRO, 1992, Table 3–7, p. 22) if they had been subjected to requests of any kind from governments (or other organizations) of host countries, Japanese independent design centers and R&D facilities emerged as notably immune to such pressures

---

[24] In Table 19, where we report the views of their European operations on Japanese MNEs' R&D strategy, 72% of responding design centers and R&D facilities perceive this as 'international bases of basic research, product development or design are established to globalize corporate activities'. Only 26% of associated facilities indicated they saw this as the strategy adopted. By contrast, the more locally-responsive approach, 'some designing activities are left in the hands of European units to cater to local consumer needs' was endorsed by only 28% of the independent units, but by 46% of the associated facilities.

[25] However it should be noted that 47 of 80 Japanese acquisitions in the manufacturing sector took on the form of wholly-owned operations, so that 219 (59%) of the 371 manufacturing operations were actually wholly owned.

[26] It is not clear whether it then became wholly owned or involved some sort of partnership.

[27] The 2 remaining independent R&D facilities (i.e 9%) originated in some other (unspecified) way, as did 1% of the manufacturing operations. Compared with 5% of manufacturing operations, none of the R&D facilities involved capital participation.

in Europe. Thus only 9% (2 of 22) of these respondents said they had received such requests, compared with 38% (136 of 362) of responding manufacturers. These R&D units also seemed relatively optimistic about their futures. In reply to a question about employment expectations (JETRO, 1992, Summary Table 7, p. 80) 16 of 22 of these respondents (73%) reported they planned to increase employment and none planned a decrease. By contrast only 148 of 413 manufacturing subsidiaries (39%) planned employment increases, whilst 27 (7%) planned decreases.

7.3. CASE STUDIES

Here we firstly examine four case studies of Japanese companies' operations in Europe. All of them are in high-technology industries. Two of these companies are wholly-owned subsidiaries and report directly to the Japanese parent. The other two companies are joint ventures of Japanese and another foreign parent. One of these reports to the parents, whilst the other reports firstly to the leading European subsidiary of one of the parents. The second group of four cases are of non-Japanese subsidiaries which belong to the same sectors as the Japanese, and are reviewed for purposes of comparison. The analysis in this section is based on answers given to questionnaires from the Marina Papanastassiou data-base.

7.3.1   Case A

This is a company in a high-technology industry, mainly focused on its host-country market, but with a significant portion of exports. Most of its exports are final goods that go to the sales subsidiaries of the company in Europe in general. Thus, though intra-company trade is strong, only a very small share of this are intermediate goods. As noted the main markets for the subsidiary are in Europe.

Although established for quite a long time the company claims to have no R&D laboratories, but just a design center (DC) which is possibly equivalent to a support laboratory. The DC does mostly adaptation of an existing product, but it also develops a new product, possibly through more significant adaptation, which shows a hidden desire to become an LIL.

The unambitious role of the SL-DC, its technological dependence on the parent, and the relative importance of its host-country market, suggest a truncated miniature replica (TMR) subsidiary. However, the intra-group trade, the adaptation to some extent of the product, the desire to become competitive in its international markets and the fact that they did consider important the development of a new product (which they may do by adapting vital characteristics of an already existing product so as to suit the consumer tastes, and thus altering also the production process so as to make full use of factor proportions) show that the company is in a creative transition period where it wants to increase its role in the MNE group, and thus become more independent by having control over its products and technology.

These types of ambitions come as part of the subsidiary company management's perceptions of the growth and survival of the company in a very competitive sector, and then as part of the globalization strategy of the parent group where it should integrate the activities of its companies as a more productive network of subsidiaries, with a hierarchy that is more democratically divided between them and with the parent playing more of a coordinating role.

The apparent ambition of the subsidiary to become a WPM will give it a more prestigious role in the MNE group, which can be achieved due to the pool of capable local scientific personnel. The extent of adaptation done is clearly admirable and beyond what a typical DC or SL would do, which probably shows the tendency of 'rebellion' in the subsidiary aiming to indicate with actions to the parent what it is capable of doing. The company also mentions the pressure from host-country policies as a 'motive' to promote the role of its DC.

By becoming a WPM, marketing and management in the subsidiary will also become more independent because of the sophistication of the new individualized product line. It is, in fact, obvious that the subsidiary suffocates by its current limited role. Although the main source of technology is still named as the parent the technological results of the DC emerge as an already significant secondary source, in a way that would not normally be expected from a mere DC.

The subsidiary's collaboration with local suppliers is also important. It often provides them with technological advice not only relative to their current needs, i.e. specification of components or inputs to be supplied, but also advises them on specifications having to do with future products. This once more is in line with our argument that the subsidiary wants to become more independent. The ambitious management, therefore, gradually develops the necessary local links (with their suppliers) that will help them better to stand on their own feet when they will have their own distinctive line of production. Also, as part of this strategy, it establishes collaborative research linkages with either other firms or local universities, or even other independent (outside the MNE group) overseas companies.

The employment of foreign scientists in the DC and the fact that its scientific personnel are moved around the MNE group laboratories (including the parent) in order to have a wider view of the MNE's technology, when taken with intensive training, shows an aim to improve the capacity of its technical personnel. In combination with its financial independence this once more comes as strong support for a creative transition period that the subsidiary is going through.

7.3.2   Case B

Though with some background similarities to case A, this company has a more well-established competitive profile. An indicator of the importance of this unit in its MNE group is the big turnover and the quite high percentage this represents as a part of the total sales of the group (notably the largest of the cases in this study). Deeply involved in trade, it exports three-quarters of its production, of which all is intra-group in the form of final goods. The largest part of these exports go to other subsidiaries of the company within the EEC, with other markets playing a lesser role as recipients of the exports.

The subsidiary has been established longer than in case A, (initially by a greenfield operation).

The parent company, with strong views on decentralization of hierarchy. Thus when Europe was seen as a significant market, the subsidiary seems to have been set up with clear independence to target that market. Certainly it seems that the location was selected as being viable as a base for supplying the wider European market. Once the company became well established a laboratory was created with a large staff of scientists and engineers. The size of this facility, (many times greater than the SL-DC of case A), indicates its sophisticated role. Indeed this subsidiary has a widely diversified role. It adapts already existing products, but also creates new ones. As a WPM it should be supported by an especially ambitious LIL. As the subsidiary is involved in both adaptation and creation of the product line, the technology used by and at the laboratory is either adapted technology imported from the MNE group or established host-country technology or R&D results carried out by the subsidiary.

The adaptation can be defined as quite significant since it was seen to be taking into account local factor proportions and economies of scale,[28] thus influencing quite fundamentally the productive process which comes inevitably when a new product is created.

These its role in technology creation indicate that the company is a WPM. The size of the and subsidiary with as strong Eu-Emphasis But as Pearce (1989) stated, a WPM does not mean self sufficiency within the MNE. On the contrary, it develops its links with other parts in the MNE group. The fact is that this subsidiary wants to further increase its competitive advantage by making full use of accessible scientific capability, and the extent of its export performance justifies its position within the 'globalization strategy' of R&D of the parent. The aggressive nature of this subsidiary is also depicted in the fact that part of the work carried out by the laboratory is 'basic research' and subsequently that it partially plays the role of an IIL.

The desire and dedication of the company to a high-quality range of products obliges it to require a similarly high-quality performance from its suppliers. The technological advice that they consequently give to their suppliers relates not only to current component or input specifications, but also covers aspects of the wider production process. It thus prepares its suppliers for a highly responsible and demanding role in providing the high quality standards of inputs that it needs in order to maintain its competitive edge.

Although the establishment of external scientific links has been developed by the subsidiary, this is only at a moderate level. There is only occasional participation of Japanese scientific personnel in the R&D laboratory. However, home-country personnel are more frequently moved around the MNE group, and especially to the parent laboratory, with the main objective of improving and widening their knowledge of the MNE group's technology.

7.3.3   Case C

This company, which is by far the longest established of the cases, is a joint venture between two leading international companies, one of which is Japanese. It is very strongly focused on exports, but by contrast with the two previous cases, only about a third of its exports go to other parts of the MNE group and none of this represents intermediate goods trade.

---

[28] Which can be allowed to play a more significant role the wider the target market is.

The company has identified as its basic goal to develop and sell a new product for its large markets, which practically cover all Europe as well as countries outside Europe. As the company is a WPM the laboratory is a LIL. Its R&D laboratory, which was originally set up as a fresh establishment, is as old as the company itself and today numbers several hundred engineers. The basic sources of technology are the results coming out of the laboratory itself, with adapted host-country technology also considered as a source. The basic reasons for adaptation are to make the product more suitable for their markets and economies of scale.

As a WPM the subsidiary aims at a larger market share. Again as a WPM it seeks a role essentially independent from the activities of the rest of the MNE group, though producing within the globalization of innovation policy of the parent. The global approach enables the WPM to operate more efficiently, in terms of avoiding duplication of resources, e.g. efficiency in the use of human resources, effective application of scientific results into viable and competitive products (strong brand names), as part of a long-term-oriented investment and planning strategy.

However, this LIL does not have any evident elements of IIL, in the manner of the one of company B, despite its larger size. This may be explained by the fact that this laboratory is much older than the one of company B and thus may have learnt to itself assimilate spillovers of basic research which are eventually embodied into its own new products. This is supported by the fact that this laboratory has developed links with other bodies, including Universities or Industrial Research Laboratories, and thus is interested in basic research but in its results that will have quicker applications in the industry. By comparison the essential idea of an IIL is to do basic research purely for science, with the time range for application of results more distant.

The scientific links of the LIL are often international, reflecting the role of its export markets. The goal of competitiveness and the commitment to the development of new products drives the company to send its personnel to be trained in other facilities in other countries. It seems that the company wants to acquire as much as possible a wider and deeper knowledge of its market's characteristics which eventually will be embodied in the new products.

In the nature of the firm's products it is important that the quality of its component parts must reflect its standards and expectations. Therefore the firm often offers advice to suppliers, mostly on matters of specifications (EEC regulations and other market regulations make this essential) but also on the production process (supply-side factors). This type of advice can save the suppliers time and resources, thus making the component part cheaper and eventually the product itself cheaper. This reflects an industry where price competition is still vital, alongside quality and innovativeness. Thus, though low-wage-cost production locations are no longer considered as 'cheap-fake' sources, and are developing their own indigenous competitive identity, they still have a cost-edge that Europe-based suppliers need to respond to.

Less than one-third of laboratory personnel come from the home countries indicating, on the one hand the availability of local scientists and engineers, and on the other the need of host-country personnel to get acquainted with the process of creating a successful new product, not only as seen from the production point of view but also with respect to successful management. Although the laboratory's major source of funds comes from its associated subsidiary, host-country government funds and EC supporting funds enable it to be engaged in a wide exchange program of scientists to support its internal training (including seminars and university courses). The fact that this company is the only one amongst these cases that makes use of EC funding may reflect its position as the longest established, indicating that it has learnt a deeper knowledge of the EEC mechanism. In addition, perhaps, its greater experience may have encouraged it to investigate more thoroughly external sources of financing.

7.3.4   Case D

This is another joint venture between a Japanese company and a leading international player in its industry. Though the company has the aims of a WPM it is not supported technologically by an officially established R&D laboratory, with, on the contrary, significant research done by the existing engineering unit integrated in the company. More specifically the company is a regional product mandate operation, focusing on the wider European market (EEC and non-EEC countries). It is thus an export-oriented facility, and 100% of its exports go to other parts of the MNE groups.

The R&D work done by the engineering unit may in fact be classified as that of an LIL. As the aim of the company is to produce a distinctive new product, and to increase its overall competitiveness in its markets, the unit must play an important role. Despite this the basic reason for not formally establishing an R&D unit is financial constraints, with sales not believed to support such an action.

The industry is a very competitive one characterized by broad product differentiation. The main task of the current engineering unit is to adapt either technology imported from elsewhere in the MNE group or established host-country technology. But this is not a superficial type of adaptation; it is an extensive one that thus may create distinctive characteristics in the product in order to make it more suitable for their markets. This demand-oriented adaptation is in line with the nature of the industry.

Once more globalization of R&D plays a significant role, and the RPM is not fully independent. The fact that the company is a joint venture may make its decision process less flexible, thus limiting the development of its full potential. In particular this one seems to be very restrained by the fact that the parent companies are two in number and probably between them are competitive with different approaches to management, production and marketing. As a result of this hybrid situation, this subsidiary may be in the middle of 'friendly fire', where wholly-owned subsidiaries of each parent (and thus competitors of the joint venture) are given more importance than the joint venture. This may be the reason for not establishing a R&D laboratory, reflecting the fear of revealing each others technological advances. Also this suppressed role of the subsidiary is shown by the fact that the parent does not encourage the company to do major alterations to the product or process. Thus the joint venture is limited to relying on the capability of its engineers.

The company has quite often cooperated with its suppliers, mainly on specification of components or inputs to be supplied. Quality thus plays an important role in their production process. For all its less formal R&D performance the company has an adequate level of scientific links either with local universities or through exchange/movement of scientific personnel in order to obtain more concrete ideas of the MNE technology. Relatively high importance is given to the education of the personnel.

As the subsidiary was recently established the joint venture may represent a compromise of the two parents in order for both to gain a market share and still be in the competitive game, by complementing each other's need; one with a well established name and the other with fresh ideas.

7.4   CONCLUSION

The evidence in this paper provides a number of clear indications of distinctive characteristics of overseas R&D in Japanese MNEs, especially with respect to their operations in Europe. Evidence on the formation of overseas R&D laboratories by Japanese MNEs, both worldwide (section 7.2) and in Europe (section 7.3), shows a massive growth of these in recent years. By contrast information on R&D output (patent data) suggests that the Japanese overseas R&D facilities are still relatively small contributors, both as a share of Japanese MNEs' total R&D efforts and as a share of total overseas R&D output of all leading MNEs. However, these later results understate the growing importance of overseas R&D in Japanese MNEs for two reasons. Firstly, the patent data provides a considerably lagged reflection of trends in R&D investment, as indicated by the formation (and even acquisition) of laboratories, and certainly does not incorporate any substantial representation of the surge of new Japanese MNE R&D facilities in Europe and elsewhere. Thus overseas R&D in Japanese MNEs is seen to be emerging later than that of MNEs from more traditional investing countries, but is very much in the process of catching up. Secondly, the apparent relatively small role for overseas R&D in Japanese MNEs hides an already substantial absolute growth in their patenting within the generally massive growth in the group-level technology creation efforts of these companies (Table 4). Thus for Japanese MNEs, growing overseas R&D is interpreted as playing a distinctive complementary role in an overall program of strong commitment to increased technology creation. For MNEs from other countries it seems more likely that much recent growth in overseas R&D has substituted for activity at home, and is thus emerging in programs of restructuring, rather than enhancement, of technology operations. Again a more positive view of such operations in Japanese companies is indicated.

With regard to the role of overseas R&D in Japanese MNEs our evidence confirms a rather distinctive position for basic research. Thus it appears that the need to build global programs of basic work, to underpin the longer-term development of a group's core technology, plays a particularly important role in the emergence of Japanese MNEs' laboratories overseas. In line with this, Japanese companies' decisions on R&D abroad seem to be relatively responsive to the types of distinctive technological capabilities in host countries that are most likely to attract this type of original scientific work. In sections 7.2 and

7.3 there is less clear indication of a particular focus on development work for local markets compared with adaptation, as we felt the later emergence of Japanese firms' overseas R&D in the context of global competition might imply. However, the case studies of section 7.4 do provide impressive indications of a strong awareness of the need to use such facilities to create a strong regional product perspective amongst Japanese subsidiaries in Europe.

REFERENCES

J.H. Dunning and R.D. Pearce (1985) *The World's Largest Industrial Enterprises*, 1962–1983. Aldershot Gower.

E.M. Graham (1992) 'Japanese Control of R&D Activities in the United States: Is this a Cause for Concern?' in T.S. Arrison, C.F. Bergsten, E.M. Graham and M.C. Harris (editors), *Japan's Growing Technological Capability — Implications for the US Economy*. Washington D.C.: National Academy Press, pp. 189–208.

JETRO (1992) *8th Survey of European Operations of Japanese Companies in the Manufacturing Sector.*

JETRO (1991) *7th Survey of European Operations of Japanese Companies in the Manufacturing Sector.*

D.C. Mowery and D.J. Teece (1992) 'The Changing Place of Japan in the Global Scientific and Technological Enterprise', in T.S. Arrison, C.F. Bergsten, E.M. Graham and M.C. Harris (eds), *Japan's Growing Technological Capability — Implications for the US Economy*. Washington D.C.: National Academy Press.

M. Papanastassiou and R.D. Pearce (1992) 'Firm-strategies and the research-intensity of US MNEs' overseas operations: an analysis of host-country determinants'. University of Reading, Department of Economics, Discussion Papers in International Investment and Business Studies, No. 164.

R.D. Pearce (1992) 'World Product Mandates and MNE Specialisation' in *Scandinavian International Business Review*, Vol. 1, No. 2, pp. 38–58.

R.D. Pearce (1989) *The Internationalisation of Research and Development* by Multinational Enterprises. London: Macmillan.

R.D. Pearce and S. Singh (1992a) *Globalising Research and Development*. London: Macmillan.

R.D. Pearce and S. Singh (1992b) 'Global Strategy and Innovation: The Role of Internationalised Research and Development' in World Trade and MNE in the 21st Century. *Proceedings of Fifth International Conference on Multinational Enterprise*, Taipei, May 4–6 1992, pp. 173–200.

M.E. Porter (1986) 'Competition in Global Industries: A Conceptual Framework', in M.E. Porter (ed) *Competition in Global Industries*, Boston: Harvard Business School Press, pp. 15–60.

R. Vernon (1966) 'International Investment and International Trade in the Product Cycle', *Quarterly Journal of Economics*, Vol. 80, pp. 190–207.

Dunning, John. H., *Multinational enterprises and the global economy*, Addison-Wesley Publishing Company, 1993.

Dunning, John. H., "The eclectic paradigm of international production: a personal perspective", in Christos N. Pitelis & Roger Sugden, *The nature of the Transnational firm*, London, Routledge 1990.

Dunning, John. H., *Explaining international production*, Unwin Hyman, 1988.

Dunning, John. H., *Japanese participation in British Industry*, Routledge, London 1986.

Emmot, Bill, *Japan's Global Reach*, Century, London, 1992.

Fabry, Nathalie, "Le protectionnisme et les investissements directs manufacturiers dans la CEE", *Revue d'économie politique*, September-October 1992.

HEC, Le Japon en Europe. *Prochaines mutations dans le pays économique européen*, HEC EURASIA Institute, Jouy-en-Josas, 1990.

Heigter, Bernard, Stehn, Jürgen, "Japanese Direct Investments in the EC. Response to the Internal Market 1993 ?", *Journal of Common Market Studies*, September 1990.

Hennart, Jean-Franois, "The transaction costs theory of joint ventures: an empirical study of Japanese subsidiaries in the United States", *Management Science*, April 1991a.

Hennart, Jean-Franois, "The transaction cost theory of the multinational enterprise", in Christos N. Pitelis & Roger Sugden, *The nature of the Transnational firm*, London, Routledge, 1991b.

Hood, N., "European Locational Decisions of Japanese Manufacturers: Survey evidence on the case of the UK", in *Japan Multinationals: Strategies and Management*, Manchester Business School, June 7-9, 1992.

Hymer, S., *The international operations of national firms: a study of foreign direct investment*, MIT Press, 1976.

Jacquemot, Pierre, La Firme multinationale: une introduction économique, *Economica*, 1990.

JETRO (Japanese External Trade Organization), *8th Survey of European Operations of Japanese Companies in the Manufacturing Sector*, Tokyo, 1992.

JETRO (Japanese External Trade Organization), Current Management Situation of Japanese Manufacturing Enterprises in Europe. *7th Survey Report*, Tokyo, 1991.

JETRO (Japanese External Trade Organization), Current Management Structure of Japanese Manufacturing Enterprises in Europe. *4th Survey Report*, Tokyo, 1988.

JETRO (Japanese External Trade Organization), *Japanese Manufacturing Companies in Europe*, Tokyo, 1983.

Knickerboker, F., *Oligopolistic reaction and the multinational enterprise*, Harvard University Press, 1973.

Kogut, Bruce, Zander, Udo, "The knowledge of the firm in the choice of the mode of technology transaction", *Proceedings of EIBA 18th Annual Meeting*, Reading University, 13–15 December 1992.

Monteverde, K., Teece, D., "Supplier switching costs and vertical integration in the automobile industry", *Bell Journal of Economics*, 1982.

Mowery, D., "Collaborative ventures between US and foreign manufacturing firms: an overview", Mowery, D. (ed.) *International collaborative ventures in US manufacturing*, Ballinger, 1988.

Mucchielli, Jean-Louis, Les firmes multinationales: mutations et nouvelles perspectives, *Economica*, 1985.

Nations Unies, Les sociétés transnationales japonaises en Europe. Structures, stratégies et nouvelles tendances, *Nations Unies*, New York, 1991.

Ozawa, Terutomo, *Multinationalism, Japanese style, The political economy of outward dependency*, Princeton University Press, Princeton, 1979.
Ozawa, Terutomo, "Cross-Investments Between Japan and the EC: Income Similarity, Technological Congruity and Economies of Scale", Cantwell, J., (ed.), *Multinational Investment in Modern Europe*, Edward Elgar, London, 1992.
Porter, M., Fuller, M., "Coalitions and global strategy", Porter, M. (ed.), *Competition in global industries*, Harvard Buisiness School Press 1986.
Sachwald, F., Ajustement sectoriel et adaptation des entreprises. Le cas de l'industrie automobile, *Document de travail*, CEPII, Paris, June 1989.
Sachwald, Frédérique, "Les accords dans l'industrie automobile: une analyse en termes de coûts de transaction", Economie prospective internationale, CEPII, *La Documentation française*, Paris, 2e trim. 1990.
Sachwald, Frédérique, "Cooperative agreements in the world automobile industry", European International Business Association (EIBA) , *Proceedings of the 18th Annual conference*, University of Reading, 13–15 December 1992.
Sachwald, Frédérique (ed.), Europe integration and competitiveness. *Acquisitions and alliances in industry*, Edward Elgar, London 1994.
Stuckey, J., *Vertical integration and joint ventures in the aluminium industry*, Harvard University Press, 1983.
Tejima, S., "Japanese foreign direct investment in the 1980s and its prospects for the 1990s", *EXIM Review*, vol. 11 no. 2, 1992.
Thomsen, Stephen, Nicolaides, Phedon, The Evolution of Japanese Direct Investment in Europe. *Death of a Transistor Salesman*, Harvester Wheatsheaf, 1991.
Vernon, Raymond, "The product cycle hypothesis in a new international environment", *Oxford Bulletin of Economics and Statistics*, November 1979.
Vernon, R., "International investment and international trade in the product cycle", *Quarterly Journal of Economics*, May 1966.
Volpato, G., *L'industria Automobilistica internazionale*, Cedam, Pavoda, 1983.
Williamson, O. E, *The Economic Institutions of Capitalism*, The Free Press, 1985.
Yamawaki, Hideki, "Japanese Multinationals in US and European Manufacturing Industries: Entry, Strategy and Patterns", *Japanese Direct Investment in a Unifying Europe: Impacts on Japan and the European Community Conference*, INSEAD/Euro-Asia Centre Fontainebleau, 26-27 June 1992.

8

Impact of Japanese Direct Investment on European Host-Countries

Françoise Nicolas

8.1   INTRODUCTION

At the end of the 1980s, even though Japanese direct investment in Europe still carried a minor weight in the European economy,[1] mounting protectionist pressures against Japanese investments started to emerge in the business community. This sounds partly like a reorchestration of the worries that were expressed in the US about the explosion of Japanese direct investment in the early 1980s. The concerns have been, however, more muted than in the US so far, partly because worries concerning Japanese investment are confined to a limited number of sectors in each individual country, but above all because of the recency of those investments. Actually, rather than the absolute level of these investments, it is probably both the speed at which they have advanced, the nature of the sectors in which Japanese are involved and the huge asymmetry in those flows between the two regions, which triggered such strong emotions. It must be remembered that Japan has been running a trade surplus with the EC for a number of years, as a result outward investment by Japanese MNCs was immediately regarded as another unfair means of invasion of the EC

---

[1] See Chapter 1 for further details.

market. Be that as it may, the increased stake of Japanese investors in the European community has given rise to a heated debate about the risks and benefits of such foreign involvement on the host-economies.

Traditionally, opponents to FDI argue that the risk is high that existing local producers may be squeezed out, while those in favor of FDI insist on the regenerative economic properties of such investments. A number of people tend to equate the expansion of Japanese direct investments in Europe with a genuine invasion, alleged to destabilize both the trade balance and the job market. At the other extreme some people view those foreign investors as messiahs capable of revitalizing the whole economy through the creation of well-paid jobs as well as through transfers of technology and of management techniques. How excessive these two positions may be, it is difficult to strike a balance between these two extremes; in addition both positions may be partly true,[2] and this is probably the reason why most countries have ambivalent attitudes towards foreign direct investors.

FDI has typically an ambiguous impact as it may boost job creation and productivity on the one hand and undermine national industrial sovereignty (or independence) on the other. As a result, the overall impact of FDI on the host-economy depends on the weight given to each of these two objectives. A classical example of such a dilemma is the British automobile industry: the British government had to give up part of its industrial independence in order to save employment in this sector. In the implementation of an industrial policy, public authorities are often faced with two such contradictory objectives; the policy to be adopted towards FDI is in this respect comparable to an industrial policy issue.

The current debate about the appropriateness of a welcoming policy towards FDI requires a more thorough analysis of the possible costs and benefits of such foreign involvement for the host-economy. The risks to sovereignty or national security are, however, excluded from the present discussion which focuses on purely economic issues.

Apparently, the presumption among governments is that FDI is on the whole beneficial for host-countries. As a result, public policy towards FDI has been increasingly favorable in all European countries. This welcoming attitude is to be related to the standard explanation for

---

[2] To make a similar point, Julius (1991) uses a metaphor: several blind men try to describe an elephant but each of them touches a different part of the animal; they are all right in their description but they at the same time are all wrong as their description is incomplete. The problem with FDI is that it is such a complex phenomenon that it may be misleading to single out one aspect while ignoring the others.

FDI, which says that a firm must have a comparative advantage over its competitors in order to be willing to invest and produce abroad; this advantage must be strong enough to compensate the disadvantage of operating in a foreign environment. The underlying assumption is that the existence of such an advantage may induce spillover effects both within the industry and across industries.[3]

The present chapter first addresses the theoretical aspect of the issue, in other words it tries to shed some light on the channels through which foreign direct investors may impact on the economic performance of the country where they invest. In so doing the risks of and benefits from such investments are underlined. The second section tries to quantify the effects of Japanese FDI on the EC as a whole and on individual countries, with a strong emphasis on France.

8.2. THE IMPACT OF FDI ON HOST-COUNTRIES

The various impacts of FDI on host-countries can be classified into three broad categories; balance of payments effects, employment effects and spillover effects (primarily affecting competitiveness). These various effects are analyzed in turn in the present section.

As the point is eventually to examine the impact of Japanese direct investment on the major European host-countries, the present section focuses on the possible repercussions of FDI in developed economies and leaves aside a number of issues which are specific to developing countries.[4] A major fear in such countries is the possible loss of control over the nation's own destiny when an unduly dominating share of the local economy is owned by foreign interests. Such fears are also sometimes voiced in developed economies but the problem involved is undoubtedly far less acute and confined to a limited number of so-called strategic industries.

---

[3] See Chapter 2.

[4] There is quite an extensive literature on the possible detrimental effects of FDI on developing countries. For a good survey, see Caves (1982).

8.2.1.   Balance of Payment Effects

8.2.1.1.   Impact on the capital account

In the balance of payments statistics, FDI are classified as long-term capital flows, as a result, they have an impact on the basic balance (which includes the current account balance as well as long-term capital flows). FDI flows contribute to the adjustment of the basic balance: the countries with a current account surplus are net exporters of long-term capital and their direct investments abroad help those countries with a current account deficit to keep their basic balance in equilibrium. FDI also impacts on the current account itself since the returns on direct investment are accounted for as "interests, dividends and other capital revenues".

As current account deficits reflect the existence of a gap between savings and investment, FDI may precisely help to correct such imbalances. The benefits of FDI consist in the first place of an inflow of capital with which to finance investment. The role of foreign capital was particularly important in the 1980s in the United States for instance; without foreign capital, a reduction in the US investment rate would probably have taken place, leading to a fall in productivity growth and to a significantly reduced level of GNP. For an economy as a whole, large capital inflows from abroad essentially help filling the gap between domestic saving and investment. From this point of view the form of FDI is wholly immaterial (Greenfield investment or acquisitions boil down to the same thing) as the result is still to provide capital and thus resources for new investment.

To exaggerate this capital account effect is the result of an extremely short-sighted view. The preoccupation with balance of payments impact leads very often to an excessive emphasis on the FDI flow itself. The capital account impact is a one-shot effect: the FDI flow itself is, however, almost incidental to understanding the economic impact of the investment decision on the host-economy. What really matters is what happens once the productive facilities are established. Beyond these purely financial adjustments, FDI may contribute to the overall economic adjustment of an economy. Such is the case because the inflows of direct investment help to revitalize the supply in the country importing this capital. The problem is that such influences are not recorded in the balance of payments.

The behavior of the newly-located MNC impacts on the host-country's efficiency and growth. Trade effects are certainly at the same time larger and longer-lasting than the pure capital account effect. In this respect, the relevant time-horizon extends well beyond the short-term. Subsequent sales by foreign-owned firms may not appear in the balance of payments, yet they are the true raison d'être for FDI and the relevant measure, along with trade, of economic impact and integration.

8.2.1.2. Impact on the trade balance

The influence of FDI on the trade balance is extremely difficult to assess and even more tricky to quantify. The first difficulty pertains to the definition of the counterfactual situation and the second to the extreme diversity of the possible effects. Typically FDI may reduce imports directly (through substitution by locally-produced goods), but it may increase imports indirectly through imports of components and parts used for the production of the final product. These direct and indirect effects are analyzed in turn.

A look at the various motives underlying FDI may be of help in order to better assess the impact of FDI on trade flows. FDI may be classified into three major categories.[5]

- Trade-substituting FDI goes into import-substitution activities aimed at the domestic market. Such flows are so-called market-based or market-seeking.[6] According to some Japanese authors,[7] US investment in the 1950s and 1960s was the typical example of such anti-trade-creating FDI.

- Trade-promoting FDI takes the form of offshore operations producing for the international market. These investments are usually factor-based, which means that the investing firm tries to take advantage of the relatively better conditions of production prevailing in the host-country.[8]

---

[5] This taxonomy is borrowed from Ariff (1989) and quoted in Julius (1991).

[6] An obvious example of this type of FDI is the case of VCRs; the Japanese investments in European VCR production facilities have clearly displaced VCR imports from Japan.

[7] See for instance Cantwell (1991) and Chapter 2 for a presentation of the argument.

[8] This description was obviously supposed to fit initial Japanese FDI in Asia, whereas more recent investment in the US or the EC result from other determinants. This type

- Trade-complementing FDI is directed at providing back-up and intra-industry support facilities in the export markets. FDI in distributional activities typically belongs to this category.

The impact on trade flows and thus on the trade balance differs across these different types of FDI. Trade-promoting FDI will most probably foster exports, while trade-substituting FDI will reduce imports. As a result, the trade balance is likely to improve in all cases. The chances of a trade balance improvement are, however, highest in the case of import-substitution, because the counterfactual situation is easier to define. If everything that is produced by the foreign affiliates had been imported before, then the impact would be undoubtedly positive for the trade balance; alternatively, if it had been produced domestically before, then the impact on the trade balance is indeterminate.[9]

The alternative situation to trade-promoting FDI is all but ill-defined. The crucial factor is whether foreign firms are more export prone than domestic firms or not. A key unknown in any analysis of inward investment is what would have happened in the absence of such foreign involvement. In the present case it is not at all obvious that domestic firms would have behaved very differently from foreign-owned firms (FOFs). The usual presumption is that FOFs move in precisely because they are more dynamic and more aggressive in the international market, but this is a mere presumption. Trade-complementing FDI is by contrast likely to have a negative impact on the trade balance as it may foster imports by the host-economy.

The impact depends heavily on the underlying assumption about the motives for investing abroad but this is obviously not enough, what really matters is whether FDI crowds out domestic production or not.

An additional difficulty is that a single investment may exhibit different characteristics at different points in time. The primary rationale of an investment may be to reach a given market, however the intensification of the relationship between the two economies may eventually foster exports back to the home-country for instance. Another possibility is for an import-complementing FDI to lead over time to a trade-substituting FDI and eventually to a trade-promoting FDI as the foreign affiliates gradually start to export more. In the

---

of investment is not specific to Japan, however, but to any rapidly growing economy.
[9] The additional difficulty is that the likeliest scenario lies most probably inbetween these two extremes.

short term, foreign firms often supply exclusively the local market;[10] once they are well-established, they may start contemplating the expansion of their activities to foreign markets and thus increase their exports. The important point is thus to keep in mind that the time factor definitely affects FOFs' selling and trading behaviors and that a distinction should be made between short-term and long-term behaviors.

Further indirect effects may, however, offset the globally positive direct impacts of FDI on the trade balance of the host-country. A commonly held view is that foreign-owned firms have a higher propensity to source abroad than their domestic-owned counterparts, thus leading to a possible deterioration of the trade balance.[11] Empirical evidence tends to prove that there is some truth behind this concern, especially in the case of Japanese affiliates abroad. In a comparison of the buying behavior of American, European and Japanese-owned affiliates operating in Australia, Kreinin (1988) observes that Japanese subsidiaries exhibit a distinctive behavior: they are tightly controled by the respective parent company, procure their equipment mainly in Japan and own and operate mainly Japanese machinery. The same conclusions were obtained by Graham and Krugman (1991) who examine the behavior of Japanese MNCs in the US. The higher propensity to import on the part of Japanese affiliates may, however, merely reflect a bias in the type of activity in which they are engaged, compared to domestic firms or other foreign firms. The greatest care is thus required in interpreting the results from such studies and a sectoral analysis is certainly warranted.

Moreover, sourcing behaviors are often found to evolve as time goes by and thus the gap between FOFs' propensity to import and that of their local counterparts tends to narrow over time (Lipsey, 1992). The difference in sourcing patterns of Japanese firms may thus simply be due to the extreme brevity of their presence abroad.[12] The local-content ratio typically increases with the presence of the MNC in a given country for a number of reasons. This is first due to the pressure imposed by local authorities for increased local-content requirement[13] and secondly because thanks to positive spillovers

---

[10] In the case of the EC, sales to the local market may involve exports as well since the local market actually encompasses the whole region.

[11] These particular sourcing patterns may also limit the strategic spillovers to the host countries where they set up operations; see section 8.1.3.1. below.

[12] See Chapters 3, 4 and 5.

[13] The point of such pressures is to foster positive spillovers through the establishment

318   *Japanese Firms in Europe*

the quality of domestic suppliers improves. Another possibility still is that the local content will increase as a result of the transfer of vertically integrated systems of production. According to Ozawa (1989), the particular type of industries, now attracted to Europe, are the assembly-based, mass-market-oriented industries (automobile and consumer electronics) with a low degree of integration but transfer of multi-layered system of subcontracting may eventually follow. The advance of downstream firms (final assemblers) and upstream firms (parts/components suppliers) may occur in parallel. As a result the local-content ratio may be increased rather easily and a deterioration of the trade balance may be avoided but additional difficulties are likely to emerge in particular on the labor market.

Another indirect effect is through the increase in the reputation of the product. The transfer of production facilities may contribute to enhance the reputation of a given brand, thus leading to a rise in imports of such products, which cannot be produced locally in sufficient quantity (Vincent, 1990). Such FDI flows are so-called trade-complementing.

Beyond the relationship between the type of FDI and the size and direction of its impact on the trade account, another interesting issue is whether the form of investment matters or not. A common presumption is that Greenfield investment is likely to have a stronger impact on imports than the acquisition of an existing firm. In the former case, FDI is expected to be either import-substituting or trade-complementing, while in the latter case the operation amounts to buying up a market share. This is why the latter form of FDI is less likely to affect trade patterns, at least in the short-term. Yet, even when foreigners move in by acquiring local firms, pre-existing export levels may very well be increased; the overriding factor is thus the motive for FDI rather than the form of investment.

It is worth emphasizing that all these effects are valid at the sectoral and possibly regional levels only; at the macroeconomic level, however, Graham and Krugman (1991) argue rightly that the trade balance has no reason to be influenced by microeconomic factors. These authors dispose of the issue of effects on the balance of payments by emphasizing that these are macroeconomic problems. As a result, these effects must be addressed in terms of the level of saving and investment and of movements in the foreign exchange rate that respond to changes in the host-country's propensities to save, invest

---

of more intense backward linkages with the rest of the economy.

and import. (Lipsey, 1991). At the sectoral and/or regional level, the various impacts referred to above, may be far from negligible. In order to have a precise idea of the impact of FDI on the host-country's economy, it is necessary to examine in more detail the behavior of foreign-owned firms and in particular their propensity to export, to source locally or abroad, etc. Rather than trade balance effects, which may not show up at the aggregate level, especially if the amount of FDI is quite small, the analysis of trade performance by individual firms is more relevant.

8.2.1.3.   Other trade-related effects

Because MNCs are thought to possess some kind of specific advantage over domestic firms, they are likely to affect the structure of trade of host countries. This may arise for instance through a change in the allocation of resources from less to more productive value-added activities or from low to high growth sectors.

   Finally, by providing domestic jobs and improving sectoral balances, FDI is likely to reduce or defuse the threat of protectionism. The imposition of, or the threat to impose, restrictions on trade in order to promote domestic jobs in many large (and often mature) industries, induce foreign firms to set up production facilities in the country and to supply its market with the production of these transplants rather than through exports from their home country. Tariff-jumping FDI is the response to existing protectionist barriers, while quid pro quo FDI is the response to a threat of higher trade protection and an attempt to defuse this threat. (Salvatore 1991). FDI may be the result of trade frictions and may contribute to their reduction.

8.2.2.   Employment Effects

8.2.2.1.   Job-Creation or Destruction?

Employment effects of FDI are a *priori* the most visible impact on the host-economy. The naive view is to believe that all the jobs created by foreign-owned firms in an economy are *net* job-creations. This is naive because these jobs may be the result of job-displacements as well as real job-creations. Job-displacements typically take place when advances by foreign firms reduce employment of existing local businesses, while real job-creations occur when FDI expands the local industrial base. As with trade effects, the impact of FDI on overall employment level is ambiguous.

The linkages between the production by FOFs and the production by domestic firms are again essential determinants of the employment impact of FDI on the host-economy. If everything that is produced by foreign affiliates had been produced domestically before, then clearly FDI displaces employment without creating jobs, at least in the short term. Alternatively, if everything had been imported then the impact is likely to be positive or employment-creating. In the latter case, there is again some kind of job-displacement, but this time the phenomenon operates across countries and not within a given country. The key point is again whether an increase in FDI ends up crowding out local production or not.

Employment effects are also expected to vary widely across sectors. The impact of MNCs on job creations depends on the competitiveness and market structure of the industry in which the investment is made prior to the entry of the foreign firms. For Micossi and Viesti (1991), in the case of the EC, less job displacements are expected in the "younger" industries such as the electronics industry where new products (which were not produced locally) have been introduced (VCRs, camcorders, fax machines,etc.).[14] FDI in ailing industries may, however, also have a positive employment impact as they help maintain or preserve existing jobs that would otherwise disappear because they are not profitable.[15]

The form of investment is also very often said to play an important role. Greenfield investment is theoretically more likely to create jobs than the acquisition of an exisitng firm. The time-horizon is again important in this respect. Greenfield investment may appear extremely attractive in the short-term but it may turn out to crowd out local employment at a later stage and thus to be finally job-destroying rather than job-creating.

The number of jobs may be a highly misleading yardstick under given circumstances for measuring the benefits of FDI. The introduction of labor-saving technologies by foreign investors may lead in the short term to some redundancies but may eventually increase the output of the economy elsewhere. As a result, immediate net

---

[14] In the case of a so-called infant industry, however, competition from foreign producers may defuse opportunities and displace jobs.

[15] See the case of the British automobile industry as described in Chapter 4.

employment changes may lead to completely erroneous conclusions. (Kudrle, 1991).

Here again, in general equilibrium terms, FDI cannot make any difference as equilibrium on the labor market obtains as a result of macroeconomic considerations. As they analyze the case of the US, Graham and Krugman (1991) conclude that the effect of FDI on unemployment is likely to be close to zero at the macro level. This does not mean that FDI should be denied any impact on employment though. The relevant level is not the macro level but again the sectoral or the regional level. Looking at the industrial level, Glickman and Woodward (1989) observe that in the US, net results are negative when decreases in jobs due to layoffs (as a result of restructuring) are set against job increases by plant construction and expansion.

Indirect and local longer-term effects have to be accounted for as well: the introduction of new capital and technology may help to prevent unemployment through the revitalization of some ailing sectors in the host-economy. Moreover, securing jobs in existing companies, although negligible at the aggregate level, is certainly not immaterial for a given region or a given sector.

8.2.2.2.   Job qualification

Securing or creating jobs is only one aspect of possible employment effects, wage levels and productivity are equally important considerations. A common criticism raised against Japanese foreign direct investors is that they tend to create "lower quality" jobs or to shift the quality of employment towards so-called "bad" jobs, as they invest mainly in assembly operations (screwdriver plants) that require lower skills while keeping the highly qualified jobs at home. Obviously, the transfer of skills depends, among other things, on whether managerial positions are held by expatriates or local people for instance. Yet, even though inward foreign investment can theoretically bring managerial and technical jobs, the major employment effect is actually to create blue-collar, relatively unskilled assembly jobs, while most managing positions are usually held by expatriates.[16]

An interesting distinction in this context is that made by Krugman between what he calls "plain" and "fancy" investment. A plain investment brings with it very little in the way of new or advanced technology,

---

[16] On this point see Senker (1991).

while a fancy investment would be one that brings advanced technology or other technical spillovers. The quality of employment is likely to be higher in fancy investments than in plain investments. For the host-country, the appropriate strategy to avoid negative quality effects is certainly to engage into some kind of industrial policy favoring the right kind of investment. The nature of the activities in which foreign investors engage (assembly, research and development, etc) is thus of paramount importance for the assessment of employment quality effects.

The employment effect triggered by FDI is again a purely empirical issue. In the US, no conclusive evidence could be found on this point according to Graham and Krugman (1991) who compared the average compensation per worker in manufacturing FOFs and in US-owned firms.

8.2.3. Spillovers

MNCs do not merely affect the working of the host economy as a whole but also influence the working of local firms, be they competitors, suppliers or customers of foreign investors. Additional effects may arise as a direct consequence of the linkages established between foreign direct investors and other economic agents in the countries in which they operate. The prospect of acquiring advanced technology is no doubt one important reason why governments try to attract foreign direct investors. The establishment of competitive foreign firms in an economy is assumed to constitute an efficient channel for technology transfers. Such is the case because technology is partly a public good (in the sense that it is a nonrival good and a partially nonexcludable good). The incomplete appropriability of knowledge is a main source of externalities. The transfer takes place because the producers of a technological innovation cannot prevent their competitors from making unauthorized use of it.[17]

FDI is also thought to lead to indirect productivity gains for the host country through the realization of further external economies resulting from increased competition among other things.[18] These

---

[17] A number of mechanisms exist that help prevent such unauthorized use of information (e.g., patents) but leakages remain possible. This assumes that getting access to technology is at least as important as the actual control of technology but this is not always the case.

[18] See Blomström (1991).

different impacts are usually refered to as spillovers which may be felt by the competitors, suppliers and customers of foreign investors in the host-country.

8.2.3.1. Horizontal spillovers

Horizontal spillovers refer to the influence of foreign direct investors on the efficiency of their host-country competitors. The underlying assumption is that foreign investors have a comparative advantage over their domestic competitors even though their lack of knowledge of the local consumer and factor markets is at their disadvantage.

A first possible channel is through an intensification of competition. The presence of more competitive and more aggressive foreign producers keeps local producers on their toes, stimulating domestic producers' innovatory capacity, forcing the less inefficient firms to adopt more efficient production methods and driving the most in-efficient firms out of the market. The physical proximity makes the competition more intense than competition with imported products even if the competitors are the same. In other words, FDI does not simply shift competition from imported products to locally-produced ones, but extends it by making it more direct (Julius, 1991).

Foreign competition does not necessarily stifle domestic production altogether but may very well revive it. Such positive effects of increased competition obviously presuppose the ability on the part of domestic competitors to respond to the challenge. Cantwell (1989) observes for instance that the competitive stimulus of the entry of American firms into Europe helped to spur an indigenous revival in areas of traditional technological strength. Such was the case of the UK computer industry which responded successfully to the growing penetration of the UK market by IBM in the 1970s. By contrast, Japanese producers have recently outcompeted European firms in the electronic industry and in particular in the VCR equipment sector.[19] Foreign investors may, however, contribute to the survival of ailing sectors. Some authors argue for instance that the recovery of the consumer electrical equipment in the US would probably have been impossible without the help of foreign companies.[20] Of course, because of the risk for some inefficient producers to be driven out of business, frictions may

---

[19] Dunning (1993).

[20] This is a view defended by Takaoka (1991) for instance.

arise between MNCs' corporate activities and the national objectives of the recipient country. Another risk is the possible emergence of overcapacity.

On the whole, however, the surge in competition generated by FDI can be expected to revitalize the host-economy. Such considerations led some authors to conclude that Japanese FDI can thus be expected to produce the type of gains that were sought with the launch of the internal market program in the EC.[21]

A second impact is that FDI may speed up know-how transfers (including resources management). Foreign firms operating in a country demonstrate that new and better ways of production and management are both possible and successful, thus creating a fruitful emulation for local competitors. The best example of such a "demonstration effect" is probably to be found in the system of high component-reliability that the Japanese brought with them when investing both in the US and in Britain for instance. Japanese are usually thought to provide a qualitative contribution to improving relatively inferior production technology of EC companies through the transfer of advance technology. The Japanese production system is alleged to be highly efficient (total quality control, flexible working, just-in-time inventory control, etc.) thus strengthening European firms' competitiveness. Empirical evidence about the Japanese experience in Britain shows that during the 1980s the proportion of UK firms undertaking or planning to undertake Japanese working practices increased quite dramatically.[22]

Technological spillovers may however be limited by the local environment. For the local competitors to be able to reap all the fruits from FDI, a minimum level of skill is indeed required. When domestic producers are technically too far behind foreign producers, they are in no position to copy or imitate, not to mention improve upon, foreign technology. Reverse-engineering is not necessarily an easy process.

Another major qualification to the likely existence of positive technological spillovers triggered by FDI is the so-called "heaquarters effect". The argument is traditionally that firms tend to keep or shift the most sophisticated activities near their headquarters on the grounds of efficiency. As a result, once these activities are shifted to the MNC's country of origin, the residents of the host-country who were previously able to derive indirect benefit from proximity to these activities, can no longer do so. As a matter of fact, US-based MNCs for

---

[21] Such a position is supported in Micossi and Viesti (1991).

[22] See Dunning (1993) for more details.

instance do tend to locate their R&D activities in their home markets, close to corporate headquarters (Graham and Krugman, 1991).

Again, the time dimension plays a key role in this respect: the behavior of foreign investors apparently changes over time. Experienced MNCs tend to locate R&D in all of the major markets in which they operate. The question is to know for what reasons they do so. It may be to be closer to the market so as to be able to develop products that are better adapted to the the local market. In this case R&D centers are mere design centers and the transfer of technology is necessarily limited.[23]

The distinction between plain and fancy investment may prove useful once again, at least to some extent. Fancy investment is more likely to give rise to technological spillovers than plain investment in which very low value-added or technology is embodied. The situation may not be all that straightforward though; contradictory evidence is provided by the British car industry for instance. As a matter of fact, foreign investment (especially Japanese) in this sector has undoubtedly helped the British economy although this was a fairly plain investment. The benefits were derived from better management techniques rather than sophisticated high-technology. Skills in management are thus as important factors as purely technological assets. Technology should thus be taken in the broadest possible sense, to include not only science-and-engineering-based production but also management methods (Graham and Krugman, 1991). In addition, high skill profiles and skills that are less firm-specific are certainly more able to adapt and innovate and are more able to spin off new firms.[24]

To sum up, FDI may provide competitive, technological and managerial stimuli to domestic competitors.

8.2.3.2. Vertical spillovers

Beyond local competitors, FOFs may also affect their local suppliers and consumers. These impacts are refered to as vertical spillovers, which may operate through backward or downward linkages.

In the first place, FOFs influence both the producing capacity and the productivity of local suppliers; the latter impact is certainly the most important one. A positive contribution to the efficiency

---

[23] See Chapter 7.
[24] Senker (1991).

of the host-economy may derive from assembler-supplier relationships, to the extent that local suppliers are forced to upgrade their
performances in order to meet the higher quality standards, reliability and speed of delivery imposed by the foreign investors for
instance. These beneficial impacts on local suppliers are very often
mentionned in the case of Japanese direct investment in Europe,
because of the extremely demanding procurement requirements of
Japanese affiliates.[25] Here again, the positive contribution may be
purely technological or managerial.

Such spillovers will obviously only take place when vertical backward
linkages are forged between foreign investors and local suppliers,
that is to say when foreign producers do not import intermediate
products nor produce them in-house. The procurement strategy of
MNCs depends to a large extent on the age of the investment. As
explained above,[26] the local content ratio tends to increase over
time as indigenous technological and productive capacity and the
price of indigenous intermediate products get more competitive. The
evolution also depends on the nature of investment and on the
extent to which MNCs are integrated into the national value-added
chain. When complete vertically-integrated systems of production are
transplanted abroad for instance, the impact on local suppliers is
bound to be quite limited (Ozawa, 1989).

Backward linkages with local suppliers are one aspect of the
relationships between foreign investors and the economic agents in
the host country. Downstream linkages established between foreign
investors and their local customers may also affect the latter's competitiveness and innovatory capacities. A typical example of such
downstream spillovers is when new products introduced by FOFs stim-
ulate productivity and competitiveness in the local firms purchasing
these products (Blomström, 1991). Recently emerging technologies
provided by foreign MNCs may open up new opportunities for
local firms that are not necessarily in a position to develop these
technologies themselves because of their costs.

Vertical spillovers (resulting from downstream and upstream linkages) are even more tricky both to trace and assess than horizontal
spillovers. This is because they are by definition extremely diffuse
and may show up after rather long lags. The key to the emergence

---

[25] See Dunning (1986) or Stopford and Turner (1985) for further evidence on this
point, as well as Chapters 4 and 6.

[26] See section 8.1.1.6.

of vertical spillovers is the necessary existence of extremely tight relationships between the foreign-owned firms and the rest of the host-country's economic system. In this respect, a distinction must probably be made between large and small countries. For the former a real control of the new technologies brought in by MNCs may be important; whereas small countries may simply want to have the capability to use advanced technologies rather than to produce them.

8.2.4. Regional impact

Even though the employment balance is determined by a series of local macroeconomic factors, FDI may affect the regional distribution of employment and more generally of economic activity throughout a country. Since gains in employment in one given region usually take place at the expense of other regions, frictions may emerge and the various regions may even engage into competition to attract foreign investors. Such competition may be extremely costly in terms of financial resources. The same type of difficulties may also arise across countries and for instance at the Community level.

Because of the modest share of foreign inward investment in overall employment, production, etc, one must be extremely careful when discussing the possible impacts of such investments on the host-economy. Were it to be evenly spread across all industries and all parts of the country, the effect would most likely be of minor consequence. But such is not the case. Not only is FDI concentrated in a limited number of industries, but the regional dispersion is also highly skewed. As a result, the impact may appear to be negligible at the aggregate level but extremely important both at the sectoral level and at the regional level. These two dimensions must be kept in mind when looking at the case studies.

8.3 THE ECONOMIC CONSEQUENCES OF JAPANESE DIRECT INVESTMENTS IN EUROPE

The general discussion leads first to the conclusion that all the impacts of FDI on the host-country are empirical questions. Secondly, macroeconomic balance of payments and employment effects are deemed to be largely irrelevant concerns. Finally, the major concrete contribution of FDI on host-countries is to revitalize their economies through a number of channels, and in particular through technological spillovers and an intensification of competition. A major difficulty is that these impacts cannot be measured as such, as a result, the only way to get a feel of the possible repercussions of FDI on the host-economy is to examine the extent to which foreign affiliates are integrated in the local industrial fabric and the type of contribution they bring to the host-economy. The absence of backward linkages will result for instance in a number of costs for the host economy.

A further point that emerges from the above discussion is the difficulty to define the so-called counterfactual situation. Nobody knows what would have happened had the foreign investors not shown up. Our approach is not to try to contrast what happened with what could have happened in the absence of foreign investors. In the remainder of this chapter, we will primarily focus on the gross contribution of foreign investments.[27]

The point of the present section is to assess the possible impact of Japanese direct investment in the EC on the basis of the few shreds of statistical evidence at hand. A later section focuses on the specific case of Japanese FDI in France.

8.3.1.   Weight of Japanese Affiliates in the European Economy

Despite the acceleration of Japanese direct investment in Europe since the mid-1980s, Japanese involvement in Europe is still quite small as compared to other foreign presences and to overall investment capacity in this region. As of March 1992, the cumulative flows of US manufacturing direct investment to Europe were still six times larger than Japanese flows (JETRO, 1992). The share of Japanese direct investment is about 5% of overall FDI in Europe.

The share of Japanese investments in Europe is about 1% of overall manufacturing investments; this is obviously too small for the capital inflow to make a difference and to relax the financial constraint imposed on the expansion of productive capacities. This is all the more unlikely since part of these investments imply a destruction of productive capacities as part of an industrial restructuring process.

---

[27] A number of studies such as Strange (1992) or Yoshitomi (1991) compare economic performances in the presence of foreign investors with a hypothetical counterfactual situation.

Table 1: Jobs Created or Secured by Japanese Investors in Europe (as of March 1989)

Country	Number of jobs	Average size of the firm
UK	32612	268
France	18923	184
Germany	16444	198
Spain	23850	555
Belgium	6250	195
Netherlands	2800	98
Ireland	2910	108
Italy	5400	216
Portugal	4920	447
Greece	1128	376
Luxembourg	415	208
Denmark	70	35
EC 12	115722	240
Total Europe	117268	230

Source: DATAR (1989).

Japanese manufacturing FDI in the EC is also quite small as compared to Japanese presence in other parts of the world. It is 17% of Japanese direct investment in the US; considering that the GNP of the EC is slightly larger than that of the US and that EC imports from Japan are more than one half of the US imports from Japan, Japanese investment in Europe is indeed quite small. By contrast, Japanese investment in Europe is quite large compared to European involvement in Japan (it is more than ten times larger).

With all these qualifications in mind, any employment creation effect can at most have an impact at the sectoral or regional level but certainly not at the aggregate level of the community. According to the latest MITI survey, Japanese manufacturing affiliates employed 154,115 people in the EC as of the end of March 1991, compared to approximately 1.8 million in the US. This figure should not be taken as an indicator of net job creations, as explained above. Other data from the DATAR suggest that more than 100,000 jobs had been created or maintained in the EC by Japanese investors (Table 1) as of March 1989, but very little can actually be said about the nature of employment effects.[28]

8.3.2.   The Sales Behavior of Japanese MNCs in the EC

A more promising avenue is to concentrate on the trading behavior of Japanese affiliates once they are established in the EC. The analysis of this behavior may help to get a clearer picture of the extent to which those affiliates are integrated in the local industrial fabric and are thus able to dynamize the local economy.

A first point is to concentrate on the pattern of sales by Japanese affiliates in the EC. Most of them obviously consider the European market to be the biggest outlet for their products, a situation that is comparable to Japanese affiliates' attitude in the US. The share of their local sales, defined as the sales that are directed to the country where the affiliate is located, proves to be extremely high (58%, see Table 2). If sales to the rest of the EC are added to purely local sales, this share rises to 95.5%. This means that no less than 38% of Japanese affiliates' sales are intra-EC operations.

Since 1986, the distribution of sales between the country of location and the rest of the EC has been modified quite significantly. While the overall share of sales in Europe (both local and intra-EC) has remained almost constant at around 95%, the share of the sales directed to other EC countries has increased quite regularly, rising from 25% in 1986 to 30% in 1989 and 38% in 1991. Such a behavior confirms the hypothesis that Japanese firms envisage the EC as one large market and not so much as separate national markets. This trend has also probably been enhanced both by the desire to substitute local production in the EC for exports to the EC so as to avoid trade frictions and by the desire to take full advantage of the Single market effect.[29] Japanese affiliates acted in a way as catalysts to the process of integration within the EC through the strengthening of intra-EC trade flows.

Of course, the evolution in the behavior of Japanese affiliates may also have to do with the "age" of the companies. Relatively young firms tend to focus more on the local market than more mature enterprises. Alternatively, this change in behavior may be due to the emergence

---

[28] Possible employment spillovers are discussed indirectly in the section 8.2.3 on the relations between Japanese affiliates and local suppliers.

[29] JETRO (1992b), see also Chapter 2.

Table 2: Evolution in the Pattern of Sales of Japanese Affiliates in the EC (1986–1991)

	Total sales bill. Yen	Local (%)	Europe (%)	Japan (%)	Other (%)
1986	1655	70.3	25.6	1.2	2.9
1989	3110	66.5	29.6	1.7	2.2
1991	2917	57.6	37.9	1.2	3.3

Source: MITI, *21st survey of overseas business activities of Japanese companies*, 1992.

of a stronger tendency towards vertical integration. In the latter case, the various European locations are chosen according to their specific advantages or areas of specialization, giving rise to a regional division of labor, with parts producers in one country and assembly plants in another. These explanations are all valid but vary across sectors.

Table 3 shows significant discrepancies in the sales pattern of Japanese affiliates according to their sector of activity. The foodstuff sector exhibits the highest proportion of exports to Japan (19%); at the other extreme, sales in the textiles sector are exclusively directed to the regional market. A potentially more interesting feature is the heavy orientation of the transport equipment sector towards the EC market, as opposed to the purely local market.[30] The sales to the EC account for 55% of the total; such is also the case for the chemical sector, but to a lesser extent, with 45% of total sales. This should not come as a surprise: Economies of scale are particularly important in the transport equipment sector and this explains why production is concentrated in large units and in a limited number of locations. The hypothesis of a regional division of labor does not fit this sector, however.

The reverse situation is observed for the precision machinery sector, where more than 75% of the sales are directed to the local market with less than 15% to the rest of the EC. In this sector, the productive units are much smaller and geographically much more evenly spread throughout the Community.

8.3.3. Purchasing Behavior of Japanese MNCs in the EC

Another interesting feature is the purchasing behavior of Japanese affiliates in the EC. Rather than giving insights about likely trade

---

[30] See also Chapter 4.

Table 3: Pattern of Sales by Japanese Affiliates in the EC (by Sector of Activity) (as of March 1991)

Sector	Total sales in billion Yen	Local	Europe[*]	Japan	US	Asia
Total manuf.	2917	57.6	37.9	1.22	1.4	0.2
Foodstuff	15	70.3	10.8	18.9	0.0	0.0
Textiles	29	55.0	45.0	0	0.0	0.0
Chemicals	181	46.8	44.6	0.3	8.3	0.0
Iron & steel	16	58.8	39.2	2.0	0.0	0.0
Non ferrous metals	7	48.7	38.4	3.1	7.3	0.0
General machinery	979	60.1	37.5	0.03	1.2	0.3
Electrical equipment	1040	61.5	32.4	2.3	0.7	0.2
Transport equipment	213	43.8	55.1	0.7	0.3	0.0
Precision machinery	39	75.5	14.4	2.5	5.1	1.3
Other	392	51.8	44.2	1.1	1.5	0.2

Source: MITI, *21st survey of overseas business activities of Japanese companies*, 1992.

[*] Europe refers to sales to all European countries except the country where the affiliate is located.

balance effects, purchasing behavior may constitute a good indicator of the extent to which foreign firms are integrated in the local industrial fabric and thus of the potential for inter-industry spillovers through the relationships with local parts suppliers and sub-contractors.

According to MITI data, purchases from Japan account for as much as 40% of the total purchases of Japanese affiliates and local sourcing (defined as purchases in the very country where the firm is located) amounts to 37% only. If purchases in the whole of the EC are added to purely local purchases, the share rises to 54%. Imports from the rest of the world are clearly negligible with less than 5% in all sectors, without a single exception.

Over time, there seems to be an increasing tendency for Japanese affiliates to source locally, as is apparent in Table 4.[31] The share of purely local purchases rose from 33% in 1986 to 37% five years later, while the share of regional purchases (including purchases in other EC countries) rose from 46% in 1986 to almost 55% in 1991. The

---

[31] According to Tyson (1992), such a phenomenon can be observed both in the US and in Europe.

Table 4: Evolution in the Pattern of Purchases of Japanese Affiliates in the EC (1986–1991)

	Total purchases bill. Yen	Local (%)	Europe (%)	Japan (%)	Other (%)
1986	651	33.1	13.0	51.2	2.7
1989	2065	35.1	17.9	41.9	5.1
1991	1599	37.1	17.5	40.3	5.1

Source: MITI, *21st survey of overseas business activities of Japanese companies*, 1992.

Note: Local refers to purchases in the country where the affiliate is located.

stronger increase in the latter proportion clearly indicates that there has been an intensification of intra-EC trade flows, as in the case of sales examined above although the trend may not be as obvious.

At the sectoral level, as can be seen in Table 5, the two sectors where Japanese investors are most active exhibit a significantly distinctive behavior. In the transport equipment sector, the share of local purchases is clearly below average (32%) and purchases in Japan are above average (59%). This is obviously due to large imports of parts and components from Japanese suppliers as local suppliers do not still master the necessary technology or are not yet able to satisfy the extremely high quality standards imposed by Japanese car producers.[32] The same holds true (although to a lesser extent) for the electrical equipment sector where purchases in Japan account for as much as 46% of total purchases. The snag is that these are the most important sectors within the EC. In general machinery by contrast, the share of local purchases is significantly higher than the average (with more than 47%).

As of 1991, according to the survey by the MITI, Japanese companies located in the EC with a local procurement ratio of more than 50% accounted for 76% in all manufacturing industries. Huge differences exist however across sectors, rendering these aggregate figures extremely misleading. In those sectors where the Japanese are the most active, namely in the electrical equipment sector, 55% only of the Japanese firms have a local procurement ratio of more than 50%, reflecting limited opportunities for inter-industry spillovers. In the transportation equipment sector by contrast all Japanese

---

[32] See Chapter 4.

Table 5:   Pattern of Purchases by Japanese Affiliates in the EC (by Sector of Activity; in Billions Yens and %)

Sector	Total purchases	Local	Europe	Japan	US	Asia
Total manuf.	1599	37.1	17.5	40.3	0.7	3.1
Foodstuff	11	99.9	0	0.1	0.0	0.0
Textiles	0.6	0.0	0	100	0.0	0.0
Chemicals	99	39.4	14.5	45.9	0.2	0.0
Iron & steel	15	1.9	98.1	0.0	0.0	0.0
Non ferrous metals	5	61.7	8.4	20.5	0.0	0.0
General machinery	300	47.6	7.9	39.2	0.1	1.8
Electric equipment	787	24.9	23.1	46.0	1.2	3.8
Transport equipment	157	32.0	8.3	59.1	0.1	0.5
Precision machinery	20	49.3	0.16	50.4	0.0	0.1
Other	200	69.7	15.3	7.3	0.4	7.2

Source: MITI, *21st survey of overseas business activities of Japanese companies*, 1992.

Note: Figures as of March 1991.

firms operating in the EC exhibit a local procurement ratio of more than 50%.

These results are corroborated by those reported in the latest JETRO survey.[33] According to this latter source, the percentage of Japanese affiliates established in Europe with a local content ratio of more than 50% is above 70% at the aggregate level, while it is lower in the electric appliance and electronic segment and the electronic component group (with about 57%).[34] The JETRO furthermore underlines the fact that Japanese affiliates have substantially increased their local content ratio since they started business in the EC. In early years of operations no more than 60% of all Japanese affiliates had a local content ratio of more than 50%. This testifies to definite efforts made by Japanese producers to increase the local content.[35]

The gradual integration into the local industrial fabric is also reflected in the increase in the proportion of Japanese affiliates employing local subcontractors. Altogether, this proportion rose from 23%

[33] The samples used in these two surveys are completely different; see the Appendix for further details.

[34] These two surveys cover different samples, yet the results obtained are rather close.

[35] JETRO (1992) and chapters on automobile and electronics.

Table 6: Employment of Local* Subcontractors over the Years

	Japanese manufacturers employing local subcontractors (%)	Japanese manufacturers not employing local subcontractors (%)	Number of answers
1984 survey	23.3	76.7	103
1987 survey	47.0	53.0	149
1988 survey	48.8	51.2	201
1989 survey	52.1	47.9	213
1990 survey	52.1	47.9	280
1991 survey	47.4	52.6	344

Source: JETRO (1992).

* This may also include Japanese suppliers established in the local market.

in 1984 to 52% in 1990. These figures should, however, be taken "with a pinch of salt" for two major reasons. First, again, because they are based on a survey, with all the usual shortcomings that this implies (limited number of answers, lack of reliability, bias due to the way questions are phrased, etc). Secondly, and more importantly, because the so-called local subcontractors may in fact be Japanese parts suppliers who moved abroad in the wake of Japanese final producers. If such is the case, the impact on the domestic economy is likely to be very different and much more limited. Some authors suggest that the EC is an economic entity more suitable for transplanting Japan's multilayered system of manufacturing than the US for instance, because wages and other labor-market conditions are regionally still extremely diverse and structurally heterogeneous so that a vertical division of labor through subcontracting may be more appropriately arranged and implemented.[36]

Recent trends indeed suggest that one outcome of policy for increasing local content is to foster inward investment by Japanese and US component suppliers.[37] Scant empirical evidence tends to prove that such a move by upstream firms already started in the EC. According to the 1992 JETRO survey, Japanese parts makers recently made inroads into the European scene. As of the end of January 1992, no less than 122 Japanese parts suppliers (73 electronic and electric appliances

[36] For further develoments on this issue, see Ozawa (1989).

[37] On this point, see Senker (1991).

Table 7:   Employment of Local Subcontractors in 1991

Industry	Employing (%)	Not employing (%)	Total
Processing and assembly	60.5	39.5	119
General machinery	58.1	41.9	31
Electronic & electric appliances	57.8	42.2	64
Transport equipment	75	25	12
Precision machinery	66.7	33.3	12
Parts & components	59.4	40.6	96
Chemicals	31.6	68.4	57
Raw materials	39.4	60.7	84
Other	25.0	75.0	32
Total	48.5	51.5	388

Source: JETRO (1992).

and components manufacturers and 49 transport equipment components makers) were present in the EC and EFTA, compared to 77
two years earlier and 111 one year earlier. Of the 721 Japanese firms
located in the EC, more than a hundred are used as subcontractors by
the remaining 600.

Despite an increasing resort to local suppliers and subcontractors,
European affiliates of Japanese firms still rely rather heavily on
Japanese suppliers. The persistently heavy reliance on Japan as a
source of parts and components is reflected in data about the local
content ratio of parts and materials of major products.[38] Table 8 shows
a decline in the parts and materials purchased in Japan from 54.5% to
33% in processing and assembly industries and from 45.6% to 31%
in parts and components from the time when business was started to
1990.

The establishment of R&D and design centers is also expected
to result in increased local sourcing. The increase in the number
of Japanese R&D centers located in the EC can be interpreted as
a further sign of a deepening integration of Japanese firms in the
European economy. Over the last couple of years, the number of such
centers rose quite substantially from 73 as of the end of January 1990

---

[38] Note: Local content ratio (%) is the ratio of the difference between the value of
shipments and the value of imports on a customs basis to the value of shipments.

Table 8: Local Content of Parts and Materials of Major Products (%)

	At start-up (333 items)				As of 1990 (354 items)			
	Within EC	Within EFTA	Japan	Other	Within EC	Within EFTA	Japan	Other
Processing & assembly	42.5	0.8	54.5	2.2	58.1	2.6	33.0	6.3
General machinery	60.4	0.2	38.6	0.8	70.6	5.1	23.0	1.3
Electronic & electric equipment	31.8	0.3	64.7	3.2	51.8	1.0	37.0	10.2
Transport equipment	55.7	0.5	43.8	0.0	65.6	1.7	31.7	1.0
Precision machinery	40.0	4.2	53.1	2.7	52.2	5.0	38.8	4.0
Parts & components	46.1	6.2	45.6	2.1	60.6	6.1	31.1	2.2
Electronic parts	38.8	3.4	54.1	3.7	55.7	3.1	37.5	3.7
Transport equipment parts	56.1	10.0	33.9	–	67.4	10.1	22.4	0.1
Raw materials	64.1	4.4	23.5	8.0	68.8	6.2	15.3	9.7
Chemicals	70.0	2.3	23.3	4.4	79.7	3.4	14.7	2.2
Other	43.0	0.1	52.4	4.5	69.9	0.2	23.4	6.5
Total	52.4	2.7	40.9	4.0	65.0	3.9	25.6	5.5

Source: JETRO (1991).

to 232 three years later. This, however, is not necessarily a source of spillovers onto the domestic economy as these centers are mainly addressed to product development for adaptation to local markets and tastes. (Micossi and Viesti (1991)).

At the aggregate level, there seems to be some potential for positive spillovers, through the intensification of intra-EC trade flows, through a rise in local sourcing and in the local-content ratio of final production. However, these conclusions need to be qualified and require a more detailed analysis of the impact of Japanese affiliates on individual countries and within these countries on specific regions. We now turn to examine the case of France from this perspective.

8.4.   THE FRENCH CASE

8.4.1.   Weight of Japanese Affiliates in the French Economy

The French economy is quite widely penetrated by foreign direct investors: As of January 1, 1991, about 24% of total industrial employment, 29% of total industrial sales, 28% of value-added, 33% of trading profit, 29% of investments and 32% of exports were due to foreign-owned firms.[39] All these percentages are higher than those obtained for most other EC countries (Germany and Italy in particular), as well as for the US and of course Japan, which is hardly penetrated by foreign direct investors. In Japan, for instance, no more than 1% of both manufacturing sales and employment are due to foreign-owned firms. The French situation is comparable to that observed in the UK.

In France, the rate of foreign penetration varies substantially across sectors. The most attractive sectors are hi-tech fast growing sectors which offer large profit opportunities. On the whole, foreign investors are found either in ailing sectors (where foreign investors have a technological leadership, such as the office equipment and electronic products industries) or in sectors where French firms are quite techno-logically advanced (such as the chemical industry). In the latter case, foreign investors are obviously interested in drawing on the French expertise.

The major source of foreign investment is the US, whose affiliates account for 34% of total sales by FOFs in France. The contribution of US-owned firms is only slightly smaller than that of all EC firms taken together, with a share of around 42% of total sales. The same picture emerges from other measures (investments, employment or value-added). Among EC firms, German affiliates rank first with about 15% of total sales, ahead of Britain with 10%.

Even though Japanese investors have been particularly active in France since the mid-1980s, their presence is still extremely modest as compared to other foreign interests. On the basis of Banque de France data, Japanese investors hold 3.1% of all foreign equity capital in the

---

[39] SESSI (1993).

Table 9: Foreign-owned Firms in the French Industry (as of 1.1.91)

	FOFs	French firms	All firms
Number of firms	2922	21382	24304
Employment (1000 workers)	773	2454	3227
%	23.9	76	100
Wages (millions FF)	110069	318082	428151
per worker (thousand FF)	142.3	129.6	132.6
Sales (millions FF)	824891	2048277	2873168
per worker (thousand FF)	1066.6	834.7	890.3
Value-added (millions FF)	266708	695164	961872
per worker (thousand FF)	344.8	283.3	298.0
Trading profit (millions FF)	90171	185587	275758
per worker (thousand FF)	116.6	75.6	85.4
Investments (millions FF)	44926	109750	154676
per worker (thousand FF)	58.0	44.7	47.9
Exports (millions FF)	257189	556315	813504
per worker (thousand FF)	332.5	226.7	252.0

Source: SESSI (1993).

country (compared to 20% for US investors, 16% for the UK and 9% for the Federal Republic of Germany).[40] The increase in Japanese involvement has been quite strong (+55%) compared to one year earlier. On the basis of balance of payments data, Japanese direct investments account for a mere 6% of total FDI in this country and about 1.5% of all Japanese direct investments abroad.[41]

As far as France is concerned, data on Japanese industrial activities on the French territory are certainly much better reflections of Japanese involvement in France than balance of payments statistics which do not include reinvested earnings. According to data from the DATAR (Délégation à l'aménagement du territoire et à l'action régionale), over the period extending from 1972 to 1992, some 158

---

[40] Figures as of the end of 1990, from the Bulletin trimestriel, Banque de France, Dec. 1992.

[41] Data from the Japanese Ministry of Finance.

Table 10:   Share of Major Foreign Investors in the French Industry (1986–91)

	Japan		US		Germany		EC	
	1986	1991	1986	1991	1986	1991	1986	1991
Number of firms	0.9	1.8	22.8	19.4	20.1	18.3	48.5	49.5
Employment	1.0	2.0	31.9	29.4	17.3	15.6	43.0	43.7
Sales	0.8	1.9	37.7	34.0	16.0	14.4	42.9	42.1
Investment	1.7	1.8	45.5	31.6	15.4	16.2	36.5	44.9
Value-added	0.6	1.6	39.6	36.3	15.4	14.4	40.6	40.5

Source: SESSI (1993).

Note: These are shares of total foreign involvement.

firms have been acquired or created from scratch by Japanese investors on the French territory. The progression has been particularly dramatic during the 1980s as 149 of these 158 firms have been acquired or created since 1980. As of January 1991, 0.5% of all manufacturing employment and 0.6% of total manufacturing sales were due to Japanese-owned affiliates. Compared to other foreign investors, Japan occupies a marginal position, with 1.9% of the sales by foreign-owned firms (34% for US-owned firms) and 2.0% of employment (30% for US affiliates).

Table 10 clearly shows an increase, even though still modest, in the weight of Japanese-owned firms over the period 1986-90. By contrast, the contribution of US-owned firms has been on the decline over the same period. Such is also the case with German firms, while the share of EC firms taken as a whole proves fairly constant.

Japanese investors are active in a limited number of industrial sectors in France. They are particularly involved in the office equipment sector (where they control 3.3% of total employment and almost 6% of foreign-controlled employment, as well as 4.9 of total sales) and in the rubber industry (with as much as 6.3% of total employment and 8.4% of total sales). Their weight is by contrast still marginal in the chemical industry (pharmaceutical as well as basic chemistry) which is yet quite heavily penetrated by other foreign investors (with a penetration index around 50% on average), and in the transport equipment sector, where they are known to be highly competitive.

In France, the preferred forms of Japanese direct investment are either joint ventures or M&A (99 out of 158 cases). Greenfield

Table 11:   Share of Japanese Capital in Selected Sectors as of January 1, 1991

Major industries penetrated by Japanese investment	Employment (%)	Sales (%)
Steel & non-ferrous metal	328 (0.7%)	332805 (0.4%)
Construction materials*	2777 (2.7%)	2457087 (2.9%)
Toilet preparations, etc	265(0.2%)	522934 (0.4%)
Pharmaceuticals	1288 (1.6%)	1745640 (1.7%)
Fabricated metal	366 (0.1%)	252261 (0.2%)
Office equipment	1860 (3.3%)	3816174 (4.9%)
Electronical products	1573 (0.7%)	1771962 (1.0%)
Transport equipment	1774 (0.5%)	1377913 (0.3%)
Clothing industry	396 (0.3%)	300248 (0.5%)
Rubber industry*	5254 (6.3%)	3808784 (8.4%)

* Figures as of January 1, 1990.

Source: SESSI (1993).

investments were more frequent in the electronic equipment sector as well as in the chemical sector. Beyond the short-term, as explained above, the form of investment is however almost immaterial in terms of employment or spillover effects.

The minor weight of Japanese FDI necessarily implies that its impact on the French economy will be all but extremely limited. This is certainly true at the national level but such is not necessarily the case at the regional level.

8.4.2.   Employment Effects

The number of jobs created in France by Japanese affiliates is ludicrously small if judged at the national level even though Japanese-owned firms are among the three most active foreign investors in this respect, with 13.5% of all the jobs created by FOFs in France during the 1980s, behind the US and Germany but ahead of Britain. The movement intensified in the late 1980s but dramatically slowed down in 1992: through greenfield investments or joint ventures and capital participations, Japanese industrialists created about 1200 jobs in 1989 almost 3100 in 1990, a little more than 1000 in 1991 and a mere 200

Table 12:   Number of Jobs Created in France as a Result of Creation/Extension of Industrial Sites (1981–90, by country of origin)

Country	Jobs (thousands)	%
United States	40.5	31.9
Japan	17.2	13.5
Germany	20.3	16.0
United Kingdom	11.4	9.0
Benelux	8.9	7.0
Nordic countries	6.6	5.2
Italy	7.4	5.8
Spain	2.6	2.0
Total	127.0	100

Source: DATAR.

in 1992.[42] As of June 1992, Japanese-owned firms employed some 25000 workers in their French facilities.

A major difficulty in the assessment of the impact of such job creations on the host-country is the accurate definition of the so-called counterfactual situation. As far as employment is concerned, there are basically two possibilities in the case of France: either Japanese invest in ailing industries (or lame duck firms, such as Dunlop which was acquired by Sumitomo), thus maintaining employment that would otherwise have been scrapped; or they invest in new hi-tech sectors in which they have the technological lead and that would not have developed otherwise (or at least not as fast and not to the same extent), thus fostering real job creations. On the whole, direct employment effects are likely to be positive in the case of Japanese investment in France.[43]

Even though these employment effects may appear negligible at the national level and even though they are unlikely to affect the national employment balance, at the local or regional level, the weight of the jobs created by Japanese-owned firms is necessarily perceived differently. Table 13 gives the number of firms and employees under Japanese control in the different regions of France.

---

[42] DATAR (1993).

[43] Possible indirect consequences for employment in supplying industries for instance are excluded from the discussion.

Table 13: Locational Distribution of Japanese Firms in France as of June 1992

Location	No. of firms	Number of employees	Date of establish't	Major companies & products
Alsace	12	2141	1984–92	Sony (CD players, VTRs), Honda (motorcycle engines)
Aquitaine	18	1725	1980–90	Sony (tapes)
Auvergne	4	1510	1983-89	Sumitomo (tires)
Bourgogne	6	1085	1985–91	JVC (VTRs), Toto (sanitary equipments)
Bretagne	8	1262	1983-91	Canon (photocopy machines, printers), Mitsubishi (car telephones)
Centre	11	1506	1983–91	Sumitomo (mattresses), Hitachi (computer disks)
Champagne-Ardenne	5	321	1985–89	Toto (sanitary equipments)
Franche-Comté	3	1435	1986–90	Seiko (watches)
Ile de France	29	1579	1970–92	Takeda (chemicals)
Languedoc-Roussillon	1	14	1991	Toshiba (vacuum contact breakers)
Limousin	2	280	1985–89	Toto (sanitary equipments)
Lorraine	10	1155	1983–91	JVC (CD players), Clarion (car stereos)
Midi-Pyrénées	1	31	1989	Fuji (film processing)
Nord Pas de Calais	5	1969	1972–91	Bridgestone (pneumatics)
Basse-Normandie	8	1061	1982–91	Akai (VTRs)
Haute-Normandie	6	1327	1978–91	Toshiba (photocopy machines)
Pays de la Loire	8	1645	1980–91	Toshiba (microwave ovens)
Picardie	7	2168	1976–90	Yamaha (motorcycles), Sumitomo (rubber)
Poitou-Charentes	2	50	1989–92	Suntory (wines)
Provence Alpes Côte d'Azur	4	133	1986–91	Nippon steel (thermoplastics)
Rhône Alpes	14	1641	1982–91	Koyo Seiko (steering boxes)

Source: DATAR (1992).

From the sheer point of view of regional development, such investments can only be welcomed. Employment objectives may, however, be at odds with the objectives of specific sectors.

A first striking feature is the existence of huge discrepancies across regions. Japanese investors tend to favor regions in the North and North-East (Picardie, Alsace, and Nord-Pas de Calais, with about 9% of all jobs each). This regional distribution is not terribly different from the pattern observed for other foreign investors, who also tend to concentrate their activities in the northern and north-eastern areas of the French territory. For these various regions, the likely job-creation effect is certainly an asset as it helps to vitalize the local industrial activity and this is why regional authorities may be induced to compete to obtain such investments.[44] Yet financial incentives do not appear to matter much for Japanese investors. Of the 3000 jobs that were created by them in 1990, less than a third were located in regions receiving grants or subsidies from the DATAR. Rather than such incentives, the "market" is the main determinant of location decisions together with the business environment.[45] Geography certainly also plays a role: the North-East of the French territory is clearly much more closely integrated with the rest of Europe than the rest of the country. Other foreign investors (in particular Germans) appear to be far more heavily influenced by financial incentives or allowances.

The major risk with such regional concentration is that it may lead to excessive imbalances within a given country and to strong regional disparities. In France, the risk may not be as high as in Spain for instance, because the degree of polarization is lower and economic activity slightly more evenly spread throughout the country,[46] but such a risk does exist.

8.4.3.   *The Economic Performances of Japanese Affiliates in France*

8.4.3.1.   Potential for technological spillovers

The present section tries to identify Japanese-owned firms' specificities as compared to other foreign-owned firms established in France

---

[44] See (Thomsen, Woolcock, 1993).

[45] See Chapters 2 and 7.

[46] The very strong concentration of FDI in Catalonia, which hosts more than 70% of all Japanese investments and about 45% of the manufacturing investments (compared to 14% in the Madrid area and 6% in Aragon), is the source of huge regional imbalances.

Table 14: Compared Performances of Foreign and Domestic Firms in the French Industry as of January 1, 1991

	Number of employees per firm	Sales per worker	Investment per worker	Value-added per worker
All firms	133	890	48	298
Domestic firms	115	835	45	283
FOFs	264	1067	58	345
US	402	1233	62	425
EC	233	1028	60	320
Germany	226	987	60	319
UK	242	1017	46	335
Japan	296	1012	52	275
Switzerland	198	921	50	317

Source: SESSI (1993).

as well as domestic firms in order to assess the likely potential for technological spillovers from Japanese investments.

On average, the staff is twice as large in FOFs than in domestic firms and from this point of view Japanese-owned firms make no exception. This is obviously due to the fact that foreign investors usually belong to large international groups while local firms are much more heterogeneous. Furthermore, at the aggregate level, Japanese firms, like other FOFs, have a higher level of sales per worker than domestic firms, as well as a higher level of investment per worker. This latter measure suggests that FOFs are mainly concentrated in capital-intensive sectors; this is confirmed by the higher ratio of investment to value-added observed in FOFs (17%) and to a larger extent in Japanese-owned firms (19%) as compared to domestic firms (16%). The apparent productivity of labor, as measured by the value-added per worker is found to be higher in FOFs than in domestic firms. In this respect, Japanese-owned firms stick out with a productivity of labor which is clearly below average and lower than that of domestic firms. As the level of wages is also slightly higher in FOFs than in domestic firms, the gross profitability of the former (as measured by the share of value-added devoted to the remuneration of capital) is likely to be lower in FOFs (in particular in Japanese-owned firms) than in domestic firms.

Such differences in aggregate behavioral patterns and in performances may be due to important differences in the industrial composition of foreign investments, as a result, a sectoral analysis is certainly warranted. Table 15 on the contrasted performances of FOFs and domestic firms in selected industries illustrates a number of interesting points.

Sales per worker are systematically larger in FOFs than in domestic firms, except in the transport equipment sector where the performances of French firms are definitely superior. In this sector, the performance of Japanese-owned firms is particularly poor (776000 FF compared to more than 1 million FF for the French firms). This sector is however an exception, in the sectors where the Japanese are expected to be competitive (office equipment, electronic equipment, rubber industry), sales per worker are higher in Japanese-owned firms than in the other FOFs, indicating a higher potential for positive spillovers on the domestic economy but also most probably a lower degree of integration.

More interestingly, the amount of value-added per worker, which measures the apparent productivity of labor[47] is often found to be lower for Japanese-owned firms than for the average FOFs. This indicator is quite low for Japanese-owned firms in sectors such as transport equipment, electronic equipment or office equipment, where they are alleged to have a technological comparative advantage. The only two cases in which Japanese producers perform better than other foreign competitors is the fabricated metals and the parachemical sectors. All this tends to prove that Japanese firms are still mainly assembly plants of a rather unsophisticated nature, and thus that they will induce very limited technological spillovers onto the rest of the economy. This may also be due to the fact that Japanese investors very often take over "lame duck" European companies that they haven't had time to shape up yet.

A crucial question is of course to determine whether such a low level of productivity of labor results from a deliberate strategy on the part of Japanese firms or whether this is simply due to the very young age of such productive units. Compared to the behavior of Japanese firms in other countries, the latter hypothesis is likely to be the right one,

---

[47] This measure does not reflect efficiency as capital endowment is not taken into account.

Table 15: Contribution of Foreign-owned Firms, Japanese Firms and Domestic Firms to the French Industry (as of 1.1.91) (in Thousand French Francs)

	Sales per worker	Investment per worker	Value-added per worker
Steel & non ferrous metals			
FOFs	1964	69	352
Japanese firms	1014	50	309
US firms	5425	26	314
French firms	1851	242	555
Fabricated metals			
FOFs	677	44	261
Japanese firms	689	45	305
US firms	753	64	284
French firms	590	32	247
Parachemical industry			
FOFs	1483	51	424
Japanese firms	1973	123	486
US firms	1431	50	438
French firms	1283	48	345
Chemicals[*]			
FOFs	1958	129	585
Japanese firms	1032	65	376
US firms	3093	140	858
French firms	1689	104	555
Pharmaceuticals			
FOFs	1413	53	451
Japanese firms	1355	30	314
US firms	1436	64	514
French firms	1282	38	358

Table 15: *Continued*

	Sales per worker	Investment per worker	Value-added per worker
Office equipment			
FOFs	1836	100	819
Japanese firms	2052	78	319
US firms	1945	115	926
French firms	794	42	339
Electronic equipment			
FOFs	944	41	288
Japanese firms	1126	57	237
US firms	942	38	306
French firms	761	35	320
Transport equipment			
FOFs	947	52	266
Japanese firms	776	25	205
US firms	1259	50	283
French firms	1288	81	302
Rubber industry[*]			
FOFs	660	35	258
Japanese firms	725	36	250
US firms	700	37	290
French firms	497	33	218

Source: SESSI (1992, 1993).

[*] values as of January 1, 1990.

but any conclusion on this point is bound to be tentative. In their analysis of Japanese affiliates in the US, Graham and Krugman (1991) observe that, in terms of productivity of labor, Japanese firms perform as well as the other FOFs and even better than British-owned firms located in the US for instance.

The amount of investment per worker may precisely shed some light on the ulterior motives of Japanese direct investors, since investment is by definition a forward-looking activity. The available data is only partly reassuring. In the office equipment industry, where the value-added per worker is extremely low for Japanese-owned firms, investment per worker is much higher than in domestic firms but lower than in other FOFs. In the electronic equipment industry this measure is higher than in both other FOFs and domestic firms. The same also holds true for the parachemical sector. The situation is however not that encouraging in the transport equipment sector. Japanese-owned firms are on the whole apparently more capital-intensive than other FOFs and domestic firms but are comparable to EC-owned firms. The situation is quite contrasted across sectors: Japanese affiliates are particularly capital-intensive in the office equipment and in the electronic sectors. Together with the previous observations, this suggests that the gross financial profitability of Japanese-owned firms is bound to be rather low.

8.4.3.2.   Are Japanese affiliates profitable?

Another critical issue is to determine the degree of efficiency of Japanese affiliates in France, since the likelihood for positive spillovers hinges partly on such an efficiency. The profitability of firms is one indicator of efficiency. Profitability of Japanese affiliates in France is found to be rather poor, as can be seen in Table 16 on foreign investors' performances in France as of the end of 1990. As compared to other foreign investors operating in France, Japanese firms are performing particularly badly with a profit to sales ratio of −0.4% (compared to 0.8% one year earlier), while EC firms obtain 2.4% and US investors about 3%. Spanish firms are the only ones to perform as badly as Japanese affiliates (with a negative profitability ratio of −1%).

The profitability ratio, defined as the ratio of profits to equity capital, is also found to be rather poor for Japanese-owned firms, around −2%, compared to almost 14% for US-owned firms or more than 6% on average for EC firms.

Such results are comparable to those obtained by Japanese affiliates in the UK in the early 1980s (see Dunning (1986)) or in the US (see Takaoka (1991)). The first hypothesis that comes to mind is that this low level of profitability may reflect a low level of value-added, a result that is partly corroborated by the indicators mentionned above. The level of profitability of Japanese-owned industrial firms may however be underestimated, as the available figures pertain to all types of FDI (both manufacturing and non-manufacturing). The heavy involvement of Japanese investors in the financial sector may partly explain

Table 16:   Foreign Investors' Performances in France (as of the end of 1990)

In million FF	Sales (1)	Profits (2)	Equity capital (3)	(2)/(1)	(2)/(3)
OECD	1202104	28011	385969	2.3 (2.9)	7.5 (10.0)
EC	629444	14973	240755	2.4 (2.9)	6.4 (8.2)
Netherlands	200983	4207	76480	2.1 (3.7)	5.8 (10.2)
United Kingdom	105976	4376	67266	4.1 (3.7)	6.8 (6.6)
Germany	168818	3593	39871	2.1 (2.6)	9.3 (10.2)
Belgium	82592	1428	24225	1.7 (1.5)	6.0 (5.2)
Italy	49842	1266	26209	2.5 (2.7)	5.0 (6.1)
Spain	9939	−96	3985	−1 (2.8)	−2.3 (4.9)
United States	348513	10433	82105	3.0 (3.2)	13.6 (15.9)
Canada	6802	−462	2556	−6.8 (1.1)	−14.9 (3.9)
Switzerland	135980	2923	34206	2.1 (2.7)	8.8 (12.3)
Japan	40361	−162	9426	−0.4 (0.8)	−1.7 (3.7)
Other	45442	−118	18472	−0.3 (1.8)	−0.6 (12.7)
Total	1247546	27893	404441	2.2 (3.0)	7.1 (10.1)

Source: Banque de France.

Note: Performances as of the end of 1989 are indicated between brackets.

the poor results since profitability in this sector is typically much lower than in both industrial and commercial activities. In 1990 the extremely poor result of Japanese-owned firms established in France was apparently due to the huge losses incurred by a large company involved in the service sector. (Banque de France, 1992).

A number of reasons may furthermore explain this a *priori* surprizing result. First Japanese companies gauge performance differently than their European counterparts do (Dunning, 1986). Their advance in the EC was not necessarily cost-advantageous on a short-term basis, because their primary objective was probably to defend their market shares against the background of trade frictions. These investments are part of a longer-term strategy, thus short-term profitability considerations may not be relevant or at least not paramount.

A further likely explanation is again related to the young age of these firms in the French industry. A number of these companies are yet to depreciate plants and facilities because the scale of their investment was quite large and not much time has elapsed since they set up their operations. Most Japanese affiliates have been present on the French market for less than 10 years, hence the most limited credence should be given to profitability data as an appropriate measure of efficiency. For Japanese firms established in the US, Takaoka (1991) observes that their level of profitability tends to depend on the period when they first advanced on the US market and to be higher the longer they have been operating.

8.4.4   Foreign Trade

A final point can be made on the trade impact of Japanese direct investment in France. As explained in the opening section of this chapter, it is extremely difficult to assess the impacts of FDI on the direction of trade flows. The trade behavior of Japanese affiliates in France may, however, shed light on the intentions of Japanese investors and thus help to determine whether they are harmful or innocent.

Overall, FOFs have a higher export ratio (32%) than domestic firms (28%). Japanese-owned firms make no exception in this respect: they are quite heavily export-oriented, since about 33% of their profits come from exports. This feature of FOFs is easily explained by the fact that they belong very often to large international outward-oriented companies. No definite conclusion can be derived from such an isolated observation, however.

Another interesting point is that there is no correlation between the degree of foreign penetration in a given sector and the trade balance of this sector. In 1990, the rubber industry, which was widely penetrated by Japanese capital, had a trade surplus (6 billion FF), while the office equipment sector (which is also widely penetrated by Japanese interests) had a trade deficit (23 billion FF).[48] Japanese investors may not be held responsible for possible sectoral trade imbalances, in one direction or the other.

Even though equivalent data are not available about imports of FOFs it is possible to get an approximate idea of their importing behavior through the analysis of the integration ratio. A rather low integration ratio in FOFs (defined as the ratio of value-added to sales) usually reflects a low level of value-added, thus indicating that FDI is likely to foster imports from the investing country (Vincent (1990)).

---

[48] Figures from the DREE (1991).

Table 17:   Integration Ratio of Various FOFs in France as of January 1, 1991 (Value-added to Sales Ratio)

Sector	Japanese	US	German	All FOFs	French
Steel & non ferrous metals	30	6	20	18	30
Parachemical industry	25	31	27	29	31
Pharmaceuticals	23	36	25	32	28
Fabricated metals	44	37	39	39	42
Office equipment	15	47	31	44	43
Industrial equipment	51	34	32	33	38
Clothing industry	29	44	33	29	36
Transport equipment	26	22	30	28	23
Electronical machinery	21	32	26	30	42
Rubber industry[*]	34	41	42	39	44
All industries	27	34	32	32	34

Source: SESSI (1992, 1993).

Note: [*] indicates that values are as of January 1, 1990.

FOFs are usually less integrated than domestic firms for the following reason. Foreign direct investment is thought to follow a standard pattern, in the wake of exports, it starts with commercial investments, followed by productive investments in downstream segments and eventually by investments in upstream segments. Before this final stage is reached, the propensity to import is obviously higher in FOFs than in domestic firms.

In France, FOFs have indeed a lower integration ratio than domestic firms and Japanese-owned firms are at the lower end of the scale, as can be seen in Table 17. The only exceptions are the pharmaceutical and the transport equipment sectors. The presumption is therefore that Japanese affiliates will tend to import quite heavily from Japan. This result corroborates those discussed above in the section on the impact of Japanese FDI on the EC.

The low integration ratio of Japanese-owned firms should not come as a surprise. Here again the young age of Japanese firms certainly provides an appropriate explanation. In those sectors where they are expected to be particularly competitive (office equipment, transport equipment, electronical products) Japanese firms have an extremely low integration ratio. This may be simply due to the fact that local producers are not yet technologically advanced enough to be able to supply parts and components of a sufficient quality. A comparison with other countries where Japanese firms have been present for a longer period of time shows that the domestic sourcing ratio tends to increase over time to reach a level comparable to that of other foreign-owned firms, which is typically slightly lower than that of indigenous competitors. In the US, Graham and Krugman (1991) among others observe that the import propensity tends to decline as FOFs (in particular Japanese-owned firms) mature but that a discrepancy continues to persist in the US between FOFs and domestic producers. A low integration ratio may also be the result of a globalization strategy based on a regional or international division of labor.

8.4.5   Concluding Remarks

Because first of their relatively marginal amount and second of their still extremely recent nature, Japanese direct investments can merely have a limited impact on the European economy as a whole and a fortiori on the French economy. The regional and local impacts of these investments are by contrast far from negligible, especially in terms of employment. Through the supply of capital, FDI may also ease the development of sectors under financial constraints. Moreover, Japanese direct investment certainly helps to fill important gaps in the European industrial fabric through the establishment of productive capacities in a number of sectors in which the European industry is not very competitive (this is particularly true for the electronic sector).

The analysis of the behavior of Japanese affiliates established in Europe leads to the following conclusions: first of all Japanese investors envisage the European market as one large market and not as a series of national markets; as a result, the wave of Japanese FDI has fostered the process of European integration through the intensification of intra-EC trade flows. Similarly, Japanese firms have been clearly more closely integrated into the local industrial fabric since the mid-1980s, as indicated by the gradual rise in the local-content ratio and in the use of local sub-contractors. Even if this integration is far from complete, positive spillovers (in terms of production and of management) are now much more likely to take place than in the past. The recent increase in the number of R&D centers in Europe also points in the same direction.

In France, Japanese affiliates are not yet fully integrated in the local fabric and this is probably why their performances are still relatively disappointing: this is illustrated among other things by the low level of value-added per worker, in particular as compared with other FOFs, and by their low level of profitability. But this situation is probably merely transitory.

It is certainly too early however to take a definite stand on the positive and negative impacts of Japanese investments on the European and the French economies. As a matter of fact, the experience with other foreign-owned firms established in France, as well as the observations of the performances of Japanese affiliates in other countries, such as the US or the UK, indicate that there are good reasons to be quite optimistic as to the emergence of possible positive spillovers from Japanese investments. Such a positive assessment is all the more justified since Japanese firms (although different from locally-owned firms) behave very much like other FOFs and do not particularly stick out as far as their motivations are concerned.

REFERENCES

Banque de France, *Bulletin trimestriel*, various issues.

Blomström, Magnus "Host Country Benefits of Foreign Investment", in Donald McFetridge (ed.), *Foreign Investment Technology and Economic Growth*, The University of Calgary Press, 1991.

Cantwell, John, "A Survey of Theories of International Production", in *The Nature of the Transnational Firm*, Christos N. Pitelis & Roger Sugden, Routledge, London, 1991.

Cantwell, John, *Technological Innovation and Multinational Corporations*, Basil Blackwell, London, 1989.

Caves, Richard, E., *Multinational Enterprise and Economic Analysis*, Cambridge University Press, 1982.

Caves, Richard, E., Drake, Tracey, A., "Changing Determinants of Japan's Foreign Investment in the United States", *mimeo*, Harvard Institute of Economic Research, Cambridge, May, 1990.

Commissariat général du Plan, *Investir en France, un espace attractif*, La Documentation française, Paris, 1992.

Dunning, John, H., *Multinational Enterprises and the Global Economy*, Addison-Wesley Publishing Company, 1993.

Dunning, John, H., *Japanese Participation in British Industry*, Routledge, London, 1986.

Glickman, Norman, J., and Woodward, Douglas, P., *The New Competitors: How Foreign Investors are Changing the US Economy*, Basic Books, New York, 1989.

Graham, Edward, M., Krugman, Paul, R., *Foreign Direct Investment in the United States*, Institute for International Economics, Washington, DC, 1991.

Jacquemot, Pierre, *La firme multinationale: une introduction économique*, Economica, Paris, 1990.

JETRO, *White Paper on Foreign Direct Investment 1992, The Role of Direct Investment in Filling the Gap between Capital Demand and Supply*, Summary, JETRO, 1992a

JETRO, *8th Survey of European Operations of Japanese Companies in the Manufacturing Sector*, JETRO, 1992b.

JETRO, *White Paper on Foreign Direct Investment, Direct Investment Promoting Restructuring of Economies Worldwide*, Summary, JETRO, 1991a.

JETRO, *Current Situation of Business Operations of Japanese. Manufacturing Enterprises in Europe*, The 7th Survey Report, JETRO, 1991b.

Julius, DeAnne, *Foreign Direct Investment: the Neglected Twin of Trade*, Occasional Papers, no. 33, Group of Thirty, Washington DC, 1991.

Kreinin, Mordechai, E., "How Closed is Japan's Market? Additional Evidence", *The World Economy*, vol. 11, no. 4, December, 1988.

Kudrle, Robert, T., "Good for the Gander? Foreign Direct Investment in the United States, *International organization*, 45.3, Summer, 1991.

Lipsey, Robert, E., *Foreign Direct Investment in the US: Changes over three Decades*, NBER/Working Paper, no. 4124, Cambridge, July, 1992.

Lipsey, Robert, E., "Foreign Direct Investment in the United States and US Trade", *The Annals of the American Academy of Political and Social Science*, Volume 516, July, 1991.

Micossi, Stefano, Viesti, Gianfranco, "Japanese direct manufacturing investment in Europe" in Winters, Alan, L., Venables, Anthony, J., *European integration: Trade and Industry*, Cambridge University Press, September, 1990.

Ministère de l'Industrie et de l'Amenagement du territoire, Direction générale de l'industrie, Service des Statistiques industrielles, *L'implantation étrangère dans l'industrie au 1 er janvier 1989*, no. 107, SESSI, 1989.

Ministère du Commerce extérieur et de l'industrie, *Activités des entreprises japonaises à l'étranger* (en japonais), 21st survey, May 1992.

Nicolaides, Phedon, "Foreign Direct Investment: its Causes, its Contribution and Some of its Consequences", *Business Strategy Review*, vol. 3, no. 2, Summer, 1992.

Ozawa, Terutomo, "Europe 1992 and Japanese Multinationals: Transplanting a Subcontracting System in the Expend Market", *mimeo*, Multinational Firms and European Integration, University of Geneva, 12–13, May, 1989.

Salvatore, Dominick, "Trade Protection and Foreign Direct Investment in the US", *The Annals of the American Academy of Political and Social Science*, Volume 516, July, 1991.

Senker, Jacqueline, "Information Technology and Japanese Investment in Europe, Implications for skills, employment and growth", *Futures*, October, 1991.

Stopford, John, M., Turner, Louis, *Britain and the Multinationals*, John Wiley & Sons, New York, 1985.

Strange, Roger, "The Economic Impact of Japanese Manufacturing Investment on UK Economy", *mimeo*, North West Centre for Japanese Studies, vol. 2, 7–9, June, 1992.

Takaoka, Hirobumi, "Present status and Impact of Japans's Investment in Manufacturing Industries in the United States", *EXIM Review*, vol. 11, no. 1, 1991.

Thomsen, Stephen, Nicolaides, Phedon, *The Evolution of Japanese Direct Investment in Europe*, Harvester Wheatsheaf, New York, 1991.

Tyson, Laura d'Andrea, *Who's Bashing Whom. Trade Conflict in High Technology Industries*, Institute for International Economics, Washington, 1993.

US Department of Commerce, *Foreign Direct Investment in the United States, Review and Analysis of Current Developments, A Report in Response to a Request by the US Congress*, US Development of Commerce, Economics and Statistics Administration, Office of the Chief Economist, August, 1991.

US Department of Commerce, *US Direct Investment Abroad. Operations of US Parent companies and their Foreign Affiliates, Preliminary 1988 Estimates*, US Department of Commerce, Bureau of Economic Analysis, July, 1990.

Vernon, Raymond, *Are Foreign-owned Subsidiaries good for the United States ?* Group of Thirty, Washington DC, 1992.

Vincent, Jean-Philippe, "L'évolution récente des flux d'investissement direct et son impact sur les comptes extérieurs", *Economie et prévision*, no. 94-95, 1990.

Yoshitomi, Masaru, *Japanese Direct Investment in Europe, Motives, Impact and Policy Implications,* The Royal Institute of International Affairs and Sumitomo-Life Research Institute, Avebury, 1991.

Conclusion

JAPANESE INVESTMENTS AND EUROPE

The impressive expansion of Japanese direct investment up to the beginning of the 1990s has to be considered in the general context of this period. Indeed, the 1980s have been a decade of globalization, in particular through the growth of direct investment flows from the industrialized countries in general. Japanese firms have been very active, but they were generally less internationalized than their American and European counterparts. Besides this catch up effect, the foreign investment boom can be explained by the specific macroeconomic conditions which Japan experienced during the 1980s. The change in these conditions in the early 1990s explains the dramatic reduction of foreign direct investment flows from Japan. As Japanese firms are still relatively little internationalized, there is scope for further expansion of investments abroad even though it is likely to be less rapid than during the 1980s.

Japanese investments in Europe have increased particularly rapidly during the second half of the 1980s. As a result, by the end of the decade, Europe had become the second host region for Japanese investment, behind the United States and before Asia.[1] However, the Japanese presence in Europe remains quite modest, especially as compared to intra-European and American investments. But Japanese investments in Europe are characterized by a strong sectoral concentration, in particular in the electronic and automobile sectors.

LESS EXOTIC JAPANESE FIRMS

The sectoral concentration of Japanese investments can be explained by the combination of the strong specialisation of Japanese manufacturing exports and of the protectionist reactions from the United States and Europe. The general analysis of the determinants of

---

[1] In 1993, Japanese firms have invested more heavily in Asia as part of their restructuring strategies.

Japanese investments and the sectoral chapters both show that the effects of trade barriers have been a fundamental factor in firms' decisions, especially in the electronic and automobile sectors. The successes of Japanese exports have triggered protectionist reactions which have threatened access to American and European markets and have thus constituted a strong motive for direct investment. The sectoral chapters have analyzed the different modes of entry which firms have chosen according to the precise market on which they compete. Besides, the study on chemicals shows that in a sector where European competitiveness is strong, Japanese investments are low and correspond to various motivations. Market access is one motivation, not because of protectionist measures, but because of the characteristics of products; some investments are rather determined by resource access, in particular to technology.

The book thus shows that the motivations of Japanese locations in Europe are quite classic: market access and ressource access. One of the immediate determinant of these investments, namely protectionist measures, is just as classic. Generally, Japanese firms are found to react to the different types of determinants of direct investments in the same way as other multinationals: they aim at making the most out of their competitive advantages. Japanese firms have specific competitive advantages, but, after all, multinational companies generally do have such advantages which they have built within their country of origin. Various studies have for example mentioned the role of research and marketing expenses as indicators of the competitive advantage of American multinationals. These indicators are much less relevant in the case of Japanese firms because the source of their competitive advantage rests essentially in the organization of production.

Japanese firms also take classic determinants into consideration in order to choose their modes of investment: risks, competencies or the types of activities of the foreign unit. In particular, these determinants enable to explain the choice of joint venture or cooperative agreements in certain cases, while Japanese firms tend to prefer to have full control over the units of production. Besides, as they gain international experience, Japanese firms tend to be less reluctant to acquire foreign companies.

ALL MULTINATIONALS CREATE TRANSPLANTS

Japanese subsidiaries in the United States and Europe have been called *transplants*. Americans have often given a pejorative meaning to the word which could lead to avoid it. But the notion of transplant is quite adequate for multinational companies, all of them.

In the 1960s, the European subsidiaries of American firms have been considered as transplants, that is to say as outsiders ... and subject to some hostile reactions. At the time they were accused to present the same characteristics as those of the Japanese subsidiaries in the 1980s (centralization of decision in the United States, alien resource management practices...). Beyond this historical parallel, all the firms which locate abroad import some specific practices which they have developed in their country of origin. The challenge for multinational organizations is actually to succeed in adapting these practices to foreign environments without endangering their own cohesion. Of course, this general matter constitutes a more serious problem when the firm has little experience of multinational operations and when the cultural distance (including management practices) between countries is important. It is thus quite logical that the transplantation of Japanese firms into Europe should still be quite limited. In this respect, one should stress the fact that Japanese presence in Europe has been increasing very rapidly during the 1980s. The process of adaptation is thus under way and further research will be necessary in order to evaluate its progression, its successes and failures.[2]

Japanese may help to win the Japanese challenge

There is yet another parallel to be drawn between Japanese investments in the 1980s and American investments in the 1960s: the challenge which they represent for Europe. The challenge is that of increased competition; through local subsidiaries, European firms are directly threatened by more efficient competitors. The introduction of the book underlined the fact that this challenge depends on two factors: the success to the transplantation of the Japanese production system in Europe and the success of European firms in learning this same system. Since the second half of the 1980s, both movements have been under way. By modifying certain elements, Japanese firms can adapt their production and management system to Europe, while some European companies succeed in using some of the Japanese methods.

---

[2]In this respect, the recession at the beginning of the 1990s, has shown that Japanese affiliates were still quite fragile, both in Europe and the United States.

The success of Japanese subsidiaries in Europe means increased competition for local firms but can also become an asset for host countries. Favorable spillovers can be direct or indirect. The transplantation of some technologies or other sources of competitive advantages has a direct impact on productivity. In some sectors, Japanese units can be sufficiently important to induce substantial progress in productivity and other performances at the national level. The British and Spanish automobile industries can be considered as such examples. In this perspective the Japanese model of foreign investment, which had been elaborated from the experience of investment in Asia during the 1960s, would regain some relevance. Indeed, Japanese firms transfer knowlegde into countries where labor cost is relatively low, so that their competitiviness increases. Japanese investments in production units in the British automobile sector have thus led to productivity and quality increases, which partly explain the renewed interest of carmakers in Great Britain as a production location.

Japanese locations also have an indirect impact on host countries. They generate spillovers by transfering knowledge to local firms, particularly in the fields of production management and product development. Intra-sectoral transfers are the most intense, either between competitors or between large firms and suppliers. Several chapters have examined the role which direct investments play in this process, but further analyses will be necessary to evaluate it thoroughly. It would be interesting to compare the different channels of transmission. More generally, it would be necessary to analyze the exact learning processes which both Japanese and European firms have used to adapt to the new situation. In this perspective, it seems that case studies of cooperative agreements between European and Japanese firms could be mostly interesting.

This book has insisted on technology and know-how transfers as a central feature in the effects of Japanese investments in Europe. Indeed the effects on trade balances or on employment seem quite limited, at least at the national level. It is quite difficult to evaluate knowledge transfers. Critics have often underlined the fact that Japanese companies invest in some fields in order to appropriate results from European or American research. This motivation does exist; it has been mentioned by the chapter on chemicals in particular. However, Japanese investments are also instrumental to transfers the other way round. The book has insisted on transfers in the field of management and organization, but there are also technology transfers.

Local adaptation and global organization

Japanese investments surged during the globalization decade; direct investments are actually part of this process of deepening internationalization. Besides, Japanese bright export successes have contributed to globalization by increasing the degree of world competition, as explained in the chapter on the automobile industry in particular.

Globalization has consequences for the evolution of FDI and the future organization of multinational companies. Foreign production units become both more necessary and more commonplace. In such a context, multinational companies have to organize differently. In particular, some of them build on their global scope to reinforce their competitiveness. The quite recent multinationalization of Japanese firms may constitute an asset in this respect. In Europe for example, they tend to rapidly design their organization at the regional rather than local level. There are indications that they indeed try to follow such a behavior, but in a number of cases, European markets remain too fragmented. The chapter dedicated to the organization of R&D activities by Japanese multinationals tends to show that they adopt a global perspective, especially for fundamental research. More generally, Japanese multinationals face the same type of strategic and organizational questions as their foreign competitors. This is the case in particular with respect to the interaction between globalization and regionalization trends.

General appendix

Foreign direct investment is defined by the IMF as an investment the purpose of which is to give a significant stake in the capital of a firm operating in a different country from the investor's. In such a definition, the investor's objective is to get some control over the operation and management of the firm.

As a result, FDI may take one of the following forms:

- greenfield investment by the foreign investor.

- acquisition of a minimum percentage of the capital of an existing foreign firm.[1]

- reinvested earnings of subsidiary located abroad.

- transaction between the parent-firm and the subsidiary (a loan or an increase in capital).

The purpose of this book is to examine both the flows of Japanese direct investment strictly speaking and the overseas activities of Japanese-owned subsidiaries. The sources we use are mainly Japanese, although Chapter 8 which focuses on Japanese direct investment in France makes quite an extensive use of French data.

1. Data from the Japanese Ministry of Finance (MoF).

These data pertain to all types of direct investment flows, they are based on notification of overseas investments.

Using these data is fraught with problems. First, FDI flows measure the share in overseas investments which is financed from Japan, a share which is not necessarily large.

Secondly, these data may be partly misleading as the country where the investment is made is not necessarily the country where the funds are used to increase manufacturing or sales capacity. For instance, Japanese firms' FDI to countries such as France or Germany often

---

[1] The threshold may vary from one country to the other. It is set at 10% in the US and the Netherlands and at 20% in France and in the United Kingdom.

flows through finance subsidiaries located in the Netherlands, a route which is preferred because of tax advantages.

Finally MoF data on cumulated investment flows are not corrected for inflation, leading to a possible overestimation of the most recent flows. By the same token inter-country comparisons may be biased as the countries which started investing recently are overestimated compared to more traditional investors.

2.   Data from the Japanese Ministry of International Trade and Industry (MITI).

These data are published in *Reports on the Foreign Activities of Japanese Firms* (in Japanese); they are based on a yearly survey conducted among Japanese multinational enterprises.

The major drawback of this source of information is that the survey is not mandatory and suffers from rather low response ratios. The response ratio also varies over time, urging caution in drawing conclusions concerning developments over time.

Another disadvantage of the surveys is that they use a rather broad industry classification. For instance, electronic components, consumer electronics, computers and industrial electronics are all grouped in the sector called "electrical machinery" while copiers are grouped together with the optical and clock industries in the sector "precision machinery".

3.   Data from the Japanese External Trade Organization (JETRO)

JETRO offices abroad (Europe, US) regularly carry out surveys among Japanese manufacturing subsidiaries. The point of such surveys is to identify the subsidiaries of Japanese firms located abroad. Surveys include questions about the motivations and the procurement and management practices of Japanese subsidiaries abroad.

The surveys generally suffer from a low response ratio, resulting in rather incomplete lists of manufacturing subsidiaries. In addition, the way questions are phrased may also lead to a number of biases in the answers.

4. Data from the Touyou Keizai

These data are collected by the consulting firm Touyou Keizai who publishes a yearly *Directory of Japanese Multinational Enterprises*. This is probably the most extensive data source of Japanese firms' investments abroad, even though information on employment for instance is lacking for a number of large firms.

There are three major causes for discrepancies between MITI and Touyou Keizai's data.

– The data based on Touyou Keizai provide an almost complete picture of manufacturing activities, while the response ratio of MITI's surveys hovers around 70–80 percent.

– The definition of the various industries varies from one source to the other.

– MITI's surveys include all foreign affiliates in which Japanese firms have a capital stake of more than 10%, while Touyou Keizai only includes affiliates with a capital stake of at least 40%.

5. Data from the French Service des Statistiques Industrielles (SESSI)

The "Service des Statistiques Industrielles" of the French Ministry of Industry publishes surveys of foreign firms' manufacturing activities in France with the title *"L'implantation étrangère dans l'industrie"*.

The data used in this publication are collected on the one hand by the Treasury and on the other by the Ministry of Industry.

The yearly survey is representative of all the manufacturing firms with more than 20 employees. The data include employment figures, sales, investments and value-added. They are classified by industry and by country of origin of the foreign-owned firm.

6. Data from the Délégation à l'Aménagement du Territoire et à l'Action Régionale (DATAR)

The French DATAR collects data on the activities of manufacturing foreign firms operating on the French territory. These data include mainly figures about the employment level in foreign subsidiaries established in France.

Index